SERIALS CATALOGING HANDBOOK

An Illustrative Guide to the Use of AACR2R and LC Rule Interpretations

Second Edition

by
Carol Liheng
Winnie S. Chan

While extensive effort has gone into ensuring the reliability of information appearing in this book, the publisher makes no warranty, express or implied, on the accuracy or reliability of the information, and does not assume and hereby disclaims any liability to any person for any loss or damage caused by errors or omissions in this publication.

Composition by the dotted i in Times using QuarkXpress 3.32 on a Macintosh 7600/32

Printed on 50-pound Finch Opaque, a pH-neutral stock, and bound in Roxite B cover stock by BookCrafters

The paper used in this publication meets the minimum requirements of American National Standard for Information Sciences—Permanence of Paper for Printed Library Materials, ANSI Z39.48-1992. ⊗

Library of Congress Cataloging-in-Publication Data

Liheng, Carol.
    Serials cataloging handbook : an illustrative guide to the use of AACR2R
  and LC rule interpretations / by Carol Liheng, Winnie S. Chan. — 2nd ed.
      p.   cm.
    Includes bibliographical references and index.
    ISBN 0-8389-0732-6 (alk. paper)
    1. Cataloging of serial publications—United States. 2. Anglo-
  American cataloguing rules. 3. Library of Congress rule interpretations.
  4. Descriptive cataloging—United States—Rules. I. Chan, Winnie S.
  II. Title.
  Z695.7.L56   1998
  025.3′432—dc21   98-2631

Printed in the United States of America.

02 01 00 99 98   5 4 3 2 1

Contents

Acknowledgments v
Introduction to the Second Edition vii

A. Source of Information 1
B. Title Proper 16
C. Parallel Titles and Parallel Statements of Responsibility 38
D. Other Title Information 67
E. Statement of Responsibility 83
F. Numeric and/or Alphabetic, Chronological, or Other Designation Area 100
G. Series Statement 125
H. Choice of Access Points 139
I. Changes of Persons or Bodies Responsible for a Work 170
J. Changes in Title Proper 182
K. Changes and Problems Considered in Other Areas 215
L. Related Works 240
M. Conference and Exhibition Publications 278
N. Added Entries 291
O. Uniform Title Headings and Uniform Titles 320
P. Microforms 348
Q. Nonprint Serials and Multiformat Accompanying Materials 356
R. Computer Files 381

Appendix A Display of Leader, 006 Field, and 008 Field as Appearing in OCLC, RLIN, DRA, and INNOPAC 429
Appendix B Cataloging Descriptive Areas and Tracings in $3'' \times 5''$ Image of a Bibliographic Record 435
Bibliography 437
Topical Index 439
Index to AACR2R Rules and LCRIs 445
Index to CONSER (CCM and CEG) 451
Index to Variable Data Fields 453

Acknowledgments

The authors would like to express their appreciation and gratitude to a number of people who have supported us throughout the entire process of research and writing of this work. We would like to thank Sharon Clark, Technical Services Division Chair and Head of Automated Services at the University of Illinois at Urbana-Champaign Library, for her encouragement and generous support in this research. Much appreciation is extended to all the coworkers of the Serials Cataloging unit in the Office of the Principal Cataloguer at the University Library for their patience and support during the past year.

The authors wish to acknowledge gratefully the assistance of Irene Shieh in the preparation of this edition. Her expertise and experience in cataloging have helped greatly in the writing of this work.

The authors are greatly indebted to Dr. Karen M. Dudas, Office of the Principal Cataloguer, for her assistance in preparing the manuscript. Her valuable advice and continuous encouragement have been a steady source of strength for the authors throughout the research project. Without her assistance and involvement this work could not have been completed.

The authors wish to acknowledge the Research and Publication Committee of the University of Illinois at Urbana-Champaign Library, which provided support for the completion of this research. The assistance of student assistants Florence Tang and Lila Fredenburg is also acknowledged.

Finally, a special note of acknowledgment goes to the family members of both authors for their unfailing encouragement throughout the years.

Introduction to the Second Edition

The first edition of this handbook was published in 1989. The handbook used a case method and problem-centered approach that focused on problem analysis and problem solving, as contrasted with mastery of a body of information. It included 178 serials cataloging examples in 17 sections. Since then several major developments in bibliographic standards and cataloging guidelines have made necessary an updated and expanded version of the first edition of the handbook to incorporate the developments since the publication of the *Anglo-American Cataloguing Rules,* second edition, 1988 revision (AACR2R). These developments include the cumulated LC Rule Interpretations (LCRI) as well as enhancements to the USMARC formats, the implementation of Format Integration in 1995 (phase I) and in 1996 (phase II), and the emergence of various types of electronic resources, for which access must be provided.

This second edition of the handbook has been thoroughly revised and covers all aspects of current serials cataloging practice, as did the previous edition. It retains the case method and problem-centered approach to discussion of situations encountered in serials cataloging. It consists of the same sections as the previous edition, updated, with new examples and discussion of the problem(s) represented in each example. Two new sections, Computer Files and Nonprint Serials and Multiformat Accompanying Materials, have been added. In all, the second edition contains 274 entries with 304 examples in 18 sections.

As in the first edition, a list of **Examples** following the section introduction provides users with a general overview of serials cataloging. Each example begins with the section number, consisting of a letter and a number, followed by a statement of **Problem Considered** and **Rule(s) Consulted.** Because the cataloging of a serial often involves several different problems, in addition to the single rule cited in the heading, some other related AACR2R rules and LCRIs may be listed as **Rule(s) Consulted.**

Although an illustration of the bibliographic record in catalog card format was given for each example in the first edition of this handbook, this edition dispenses with that practice, since current LCRIs tend to be strongly oriented toward bibliographic control in a machine-readable environment. Instead, as an aid to users who are mainly familiar with the terminology specific to the catalog card format, this edition contains Appendix B, which consists of a single image of a 3″ × 5″ catalog card, with area names and numbers indicated.

The **Tagged Data Record** for each example is based on OCLC/MARC coding. Each entry includes, in addition to the variable data fields, a display of the Leader, the fixed-length data elements (field 008), the physical description fixed field (field 007), if applicable, and the fixed-field data elements for additional material characteristics (field 006), if needed. As an easy guide to USMARC for users, an appendix (Appendix A,

Display of Leader, 006 Field, and 008 Field as Appearing in OCLC, RLIN, DRA, and INNOPAC) has been included.

The **Discussion** focuses on the part of the description that illustrates a particular rule or rules with an explanation of each rule consulted. Frequent references to particular AACR2R rules and LCRIs are given throughout the discussion. The LCRIs consulted in this handbook are decisions that were in force at the time of writing. Because LCRIs are ongoing and subject to change, readers should consult current issues of Cataloging Service Bulletin (CSB) for further interpretations.

Coding of the fixed-field elements and the variable data fields is also included in the discussion whenever necessary, using the guidelines contained in the second edition of *Bibliographic Formats and Standards*. Each cataloging area being discussed in the **Discussion** section is marked by an arrow in the **Tagged Data Record.** On the other hand, some examples are not accompanied by discussion of certain cataloging areas because the fields involved have been discussed in connection with other examples. An Index to the Variable Data Fields by MARC tag has been provided as a means of locating the main discussion for each field.

As with the first edition, a Topical Index has been included to provide users with quick access to each section where a particular topic is discussed. The Index to AACR2R Rules and LCRIs directs users to information on the practical application of each particular rule and LCRI.

We hope that the handbook will be of practical use to catalogers and will contribute to the production of serial bibliographic records that approach standardization and uniformity.

A. Source of Information

According to AACR2, 1988 revision (AACR2R), the bibliographic description of serial publications of all kinds and in all media is based on the first issue published or the first available issue. (For more discussion on the chief sources for microforms, nonprint serials, and computer files, see the introductions to the appropriate sections and also discussions of individual examples.) For a print serial, the chief source of information is the title page, if there is one. Title pages, however, are not generally found on periodicals and newsletters; they are most common on annual publications and less frequently published serials. If there is indeed no title page, use a title page substitute (12.0B1).

What differentiates a title page from a title page substitute is that a title page is a page that contains the title of the serial, usually (but not necessarily) along with the publisher and designation of the issue in a layout traditional for title pages. A title page does not contain text, a table of contents, or extensive editorial information. If there is no title page available, then a title page substitute should be chosen in the following order of preference: analytical title page (title page of an individual work in a series), cover, caption, masthead, editorial pages, colophon, other pages. A note should be included in the catalog record indicating what source was used as the title page substitute.

The prescribed sources of information for each area and corresponding MARC tag(s) used for descriptive cataloging of print serials are shown in the following table:

MARC Tag	Area	Prescribed Source
245	Title and statement of responsibility	Title page or title page substitute[†]
250	Edition area	Title page, title page substitute, or verso of title page, or any pages preceding the title page[†]
362	Numeric and/or alphabetic, chronological, or other designation	The whole publication[†]
260	Publication, distribution, etc.	The whole publication[†]
300	Physical description	The whole publication[†]
4xx	Series	The whole publication[†]
5xx	Notes	Any source
022	ISSN	Any source

[†]Enclose information in brackets if it is supplied by cataloger or taken from outside the prescribed source.

EXAMPLES

A1   Title proper appears in a single source within the item
A2   A single title proper appears in more than one source within the item
A3   More than one source of information appears in the item
A4   Chief source of information for cataloging a numbered series
A5   Use of source with stable title as title page substitute
A6   Colophon chosen as chief source of information
A7   Masthead chosen as chief source of information
A8   Chief source of information for reprint of a print serial

A1

PROBLEM CONSIDERED:

Title proper appears in a single source within the item (LCRI 12.0B1)

RULE(S) CONSULTED:

AACR2R: 12.7B3, 12.7B7b, 21.30E1

TAGGED DATA RECORD (based on OCLC #34375121)

LDR   *****cas_/22*****_a*4500

	00-05	06	07-14	15-17	18	19	20	21	22-28	29	30-32	33	34	35-37	38	39
008	960315	c	19969999	alu	f	r	l	p	-------	0	///	a	0	eng	-	d

022 0	1087-688X	
043	nm-----	
→ 245 00	Gulf of Mexico science.	
→ 260	Dauphin Island, AL : ≠b Dauphin Island Sea Lab, ≠c 1996-	
300	v. : ≠b ill. ; ≠c 26 cm.	
310	Semiannual	
362 0	Vol. 14, no. 1 (Mar. 1996)-	
500	Title from cover.	
650 0	Marine biology ≠z Mexico, Gulf of ≠x Periodicals.	
650 0	Oceanography ≠z Mexico, Gulf of ≠x Periodicals.	
650 0	Ocean engineering ≠z Mexico, Gulf of ≠x Periodicals.	
→ 710 2	Dauphin Island Sea Lab (Ala.)	
→ 780 00	≠t Northeast gulf science ≠x 0148-9836 ≠w (DLC)77644293 ≠w (OCoLC)3398258	

Cover

> *Gulf of Mexico*
> *Science*
> *An International Journal*   *Volume XIV No. 1*   *March, 1996*
>
> *Published by the Dauphin Island Sea Lab*
>   *Formerly Northeast Gulf Science*

Verso of cover

Department of Marine Sciences
University of South Alabama
Dauphin Island Sea Lab
PO Box 369-370
Dauphin Island, AL 36528

DISCUSSION

- When a title proper appears in a single source within an item, use this as the chief source for the item (LCRI 12.0B1). It happens quite often in serials that, as in this example, the cover is the only available source of title information. A note is needed on the source of the title proper whenever it is a source other than the chief source of information (i.e., title page) (12.7B3).
- An added entry is given for the corporate body as publisher, since it is prominently named (21.30E1).
- Because this title is a succeeding entry, formerly published under the title "Northeast Gulf Science," a note should be input citing the preceding entry (12.7B7b). Field 780 is used for this purpose. First indicator value "0" is used to generate a note on the bibliographic record. Second indicator value "0" generates the display constant "Continues:" for the note. The relationship between two or more serial titles may also be described in a Linking Entry Complexity Note, field 580. Whenever field 580 is used, the first indicator for linking field 780 should be set at "1" in order to suppress the display of a note derived from the linking field. For more details on the linking fields see section L, Related Works.

A2

PROBLEM CONSIDERED:

A single title proper appears in more than one source within the item (12.0B1)

RULE(S) CONSULTED:

AACR2R: 21.30E1
LCRI: 12.1E1

Winter 1960
Vol. 1, No. 1

**LOUISIANA
HISTORY**

The Journal of the
Louisiana Historical Association

Cover

LOUISIANA HISTORY

Published Quarterly by
Louisiana Historical Association
in cooperation with
Louisiana State University

Vol. 1, No. 1   Winter 1960

Caption

TAGGED DATA RECORD (based on OCLC #1782994)

LDR   *****cas_/22*****Ia*4500

00-05	06	07-14	15-17	18	19	20	21	22-28	29	30-32	33	34	35-37	38	39
741205	c	19609999	lau	q	r	l	p	-------	0	///	a	0	eng	-	d

008

043   n-us-la
→ 245 00 Louisiana history : ≠b the journal of the Louisiana Historical Association.
260   Lafayette, La. : ≠b The Association, ≠c 1960-
300   v. : ≠b ill. ; ≠c 24 cm.
310   Quarterly
362 0   Vol. 1, no. 1 (winter 1960)-
500   Title from cover.
550   Published in cooperation with Louisiana State University.
651   0 Louisiana ≠x History ≠x Periodicals.
→ 710 2   Louisiana Historical Association.

DISCUSSION

- When a single title proper appears in more than one source within an item, choose the chief source according to the preferred order of sources listed in 12.0B1. The chief source of information for a print serial is the title page if there is one. In this example the item lacks a title page; therefore, in keeping with the prescribed order of precedence, the cover is chosen as the title page substitute (12.0B1). Since the description is based on the cover, the statement "The Journal of the Louisiana Historical Association," which fits the conditions for inclusion as other title information, is transcribed in the title and statement of responsibility area (LCRI 12.1E1).

- Make an added entry for the corporate body responsible for the work, which, in this case, is the Louisiana Historical Association (21.30E1).

- Field 710 contains corporate names used as added entries. The first indicator is based on the type of corporate name. First indicator value "1" is used when the corporate body is a jurisdiction or a jurisdiction followed by a name. Value "2" is used when the corporate body is entered directly under its own name. The second indicator value is set to blank.

4

A3

PROBLEM CONSIDERED:

More than one source of information appears in the item (1.0H1c)

RULE(S) CONSULTED:

AACR2R: 12.0B1, 21.30J1

TAGGED DATA RECORD (based on OCLC #32207178)

LDR   *****cas_/22*****_a*4500

00-05	06	07-14	15-17	18	19	20	21	22-28	29	30-32	33	34	35-37	38	39
950327	c	19959999	enk	m	n		p	-------	0	///	a	0	eng	-	d

008

→ 245 00   Spectrochimica acta. ≠n Part A, ≠p Molecular and biomolecular spectroscopy.

→ 246 30   Molecular and biomolecular spectroscopy

→ 246 30   Molecular spectroscopy

→ 246 30   Biomolecular spectroscopy

→ 246 13   Spectrochimica acta. ≠n Part A, ≠p Molecular spectroscopy

→ 246 13   Spectrochimica acta. ≠n Part A, ≠p Biomolecular spectroscopy

260   Kidlington, Oxford, U.K. ; ≠a Tarrytown, NY : ≠b Pergamon, ≠c c1994-

300   v. : ≠b ill. ; ≠c 28 cm.

310   Monthly (plus additional issues in July and Nov.)

362 0   Vol. 51A, no. 1 (Jan. 1995)-

500   Title from cover.

650   0   Spectrum analysis ≠x Periodicals.

650   0   Molecular spectroscopy ≠x Periodicals.

650   0   Biomolecules ≠x Spectra ≠x Periodicals.

780 00   ≠t Spectrochimica acta. Part A, Molecular spectroscopy ≠x 0584-8539 ≠w (DLC)72002511 ≠w (OCoLC)1766328

Cover

SPECTROCHIMICA ACTA

PART A: MOLECULAR AND BIOMOLECULAR SPECTROSCOPY

January 1995,
Vol.51A, No.1

MOLECULAR
SPECTROSCOPY

BIOMOLECULAR
SPECTROSCOPY

SPECTROCHIMICA ACTA

PART A:

MOLECULAR SPECTROSCOPY

Title page

SPECTROCHIMICA ACTA

PART A:

BIOMOLECULAR SPECTROSCOPY

Added title page

DISCUSSION

- This item has more than one source of information: a cover title (consisting of common title, section number, and section title), a title page for part of the title, and an added title page for another part of the title. According to AACR2R, in dealing with an item with several sources, choose the title page as the chief source (12.0B1). However, in this example the title page does not carry the actual title for the publication, while the cover has the entire title. Therefore the cover is chosen as chief source over the title page (1.0H1c).

- Title added entries are made for all permutations related to the title proper, which includes in this example a common title, a section number, and a section title (21.30J1).

- Data elements in subfields ≠a, ≠n, and ≠p in field 245 are treated together as the title proper. The same is valid for variant titles in field 246. The first three 246 fields in this example are input with a second indicator value "0" for access to a portion of the title proper. The second indicator of the next two 246 fields generates a display constant "Other title:" with subfields ≠n and ≠p.

- For discussion with regard to a title proper consisting of a common title, section number, and section title, see section B, Title Proper.

A4

PROBLEM CONSIDERED:

Chief source of information for cataloging a numbered series (12.0B1)

RULE(S) CONSULTED:

AACR2R: 21.30J1, 12.7B3
LCRI: 12.0B1, 12.7B23

TAGGED DATA RECORD (based on OCLC #5158024)

LDR   *****cas_/22*****Ia*4500

00-05	06	07-14	15-17	18	19	20	21	22-28	29	30-32	33	34	35-37	38	39
790711	c	19739999	enk	u		u		m	-------	0	///	a	0	eng	-	d

008

130 00	Occasional paper (International Centre for Research in Accounting)
→ 245 00	Occasional paper / ≠c International Centre for Research in Accounting.
→ 246 14	ICRA occasional paper
260	Lancaster, Eng. : ≠b The Centre,
300	v. ; ≠c 30 cm.
362 1	Began in 1973.
→ 500	Description based on: No. 15, published in 1977; title from analytical title page.
650 0	Accounting.
710 2	International Centre for Research in Accounting.

ICRA OCCASIONAL PAPER   **No.15**

AN AUTOBIBLIOGRAPHY

Cover

by

Professor R. J. Chambers

**International Centre for Research in Accounting
University of Lancaster**

International Centre for Research in Accounting

Occasional Paper No. 15

AN AUTOBIBLIOGRAPHY

by

Professor R. J. Chambers

**Analytical
title page**

DISCUSSION

- The item in this example does not have a series title page. A series title page is an added title page bearing the series title proper and, usually, though not necessarily, other information about the series (CCM 3.2.1d). If the item lacks a series title page, the chief source for cataloging the series as a serial is the one source that appears first in the preferred order of sources listed in 12.0B1 (see also LCRI 12.0B1). Thus, in this example the analytical title page is chosen as the chief source. The title "Occasional paper" that appears on this page is taken as the title proper. The title "ICRA occasional paper" that appears on the cover is treated as a variant title, for which an added entry is made because it differs from the title proper (21.30J1).
- Field 246 is used for varying forms of the title. First indicator value "1" is used so that the varying form of the title prints as a note and as an added entry. The second indicator shows the type of title in field 246. In this case second indicator value "4" is used to generate a display constant "Cover title:" at the beginning of the note.
- Whenever a title page substitute is used as the chief source, such information is input in a separate 500 General Note (12.7B3) or combined with the field 500 "Description based on:" information (LCRI 12.7B23).

A5

PROBLEM CONSIDERED:

Use of source with stable title as title page substitute (12.0B1)

RULE(S) CONSULTED:

AACR2R: 21.30J1
LCRI: 12.0B1

Membership Directory

Society for American Baseball Research

SABR
July 1983

Cover

Directory
Society for American Baseball Research
SABR

1983

Caption

SABR

1984   **Directory**

Cover of a later issue

Directory
Society for American Baseball Research
SABR

1984

Caption of a later issue

TAGGED DATA RECORD (based on OCLC #11857182)

LDR   *****cas_/22*****Ia*4500

00-05	06	07-14	15-17	18	19	20	21	22-28	29	30-32	33	34	35-37	38	39
850328	d	19uu198u	nyu	a	r			--r----	1	///	a	0	eng	-	d

008 row above

110 2   Society for American Baseball Research.
→ 245 10   Directory / ≠c Society for American Baseball Research.
→ 246 14   Membership directory ≠f -1983
→ 246 14   SABR ... directory ≠f 1984-
   260   Cooperstown, N.Y. : ≠b The Society,
   300   v. ; ≠c 28 cm.
   310   Annual
   500   Description based on: 1983; title from caption.
   610 20   Society for American Baseball Research ≠x Directories.
   785 00   Society for American Baseball Research. ≠t Membership directory ≠w (DLC)sn88014192 ≠w (OCoLC)15501634

DISCUSSION

- The serial in this example does not have a title page. For that reason, the chief source of information (or the title page substitute) should be the cover, according to the preferred order of sources listed in rule 12.0B1. However, note that the titles which appear on the covers of the two issues shown in this example are different. Differences such as these might be considered to represent a title change, except for the fact that they are covered by a Library of Congress rule interpretation that provides an exception to the application of rule 12.0B1. This interpretation states that, in any instance where a title page is lacking and two or more issues are in hand and the title appearing in a less preferred source remains stable from issue to issue, the cataloger should use the source with the stable title (LCRI 12.0B1). In this particular example the exception is applied, since the caption title "Directory" apparently remains stable from issue to issue. Added entries are made for the variant cover titles (21.30J1).
- Field 110 is used for a corporate body heading used as main entry. First indicator value "1" is used when the corporate body is a place or a place followed by a name. Value "2" is used for all other corporate names. The second indicator is blank.
- Field 246 is input for the cover titles of the 1983 and the subsequent issues. First indicator value "1" is used to generate a title added entry and a note for the varying title. Second indicator value "4" is used to indicate that the entry is for a cover title.

A6

PROBLEM CONSIDERED:

Colophon chosen as chief source of information (12.0B1)

RULE(S) CONSULTED:

AACR2R: 1.1B1, 12.7B3, Appendix D (p. 616)
LCRI: 12.7B23

A6a Caption

*Bio*technology**CENTER**

**University of Illinois
at Urbana-Champaign**

Spring 1985

A6a Colophon area

Biotechnology Center Quarterly Bulletin is published quarterly by the
Biotechnology Center, University of Illinois at Urbana-Champaign,
...

Vol. 1, no. 1, Spring 1985.

A6a

TAGGED DATA RECORD (based on OCLC #19487521)

LDR   *****nas_/22*****Ia*4500

00-05	06	07-14	15-17	18	19	20	21	22-28	29	30-32	33	34	35-37	38	39
890403	c	19859999	ilu	q	r		p	------s	0	///	a	0	eng	-	d

008

→ 245 00   Biotechnology Center quarterly bulletin.

260   Urbana, Ill. : ≠b The Center, University of Illinois at Urbana-Champaign, ≠c 1985-

300   v. ; ≠c 28 cm.

310   Quarterly

362 0   Vol. 1, no. 1 (spring 1985)-

→ 500   Title from colophon.

610 20   University of Illinois at Urbana-Champaign. ≠b Biotechnology Center ≠x Periodicals.

650   0   Biochemistry ≠x Periodicals.

650   0   Biophysics ≠x Periodicals.

710 2   University of Illinois at Urbana-Champaign. ≠b Biotechnology Center.

A6b

TAGGED DATA RECORD (based on OCLC #31978007)

LDR   *****nas_/22*****Ia*4500

00-05	06	07-14	15-17	18	19	20	21	22-28	29	30-32	33	34	35-37	38	39
950213	c	19949999	ch	u	u		p	-------	0	///	e	0	chi	-	d

008

→ 245 00   Lo-yang wen hisen.

245 00   洛陽文獻.

260   T'ai-pei hsien Hsin-tien shih : ≠b Lo-yan wen hsien pien chi wei yüan hui, ≠c Min kuo 83 nien [1994]-

260   台北縣新店市 : ≠b 洛陽文獻編輯委員會, ≠c 民國 83 年 [1994]-

300   v. ; ≠c 21 cm.

362 0   Ti 1 ch'i (min kuo 83 nien yüan tan [Jan. 1, 1994])-

362 0   第 1 卷 (民國 83 年元旦 [Jan. 1, 1994])-

→ 500   Title from colophon.

651   0   Lo-yang shih (China) ≠x Periodicals.

710 2   Lo-yan wen hsien pien chi wei yüan hui.

710 2   洛陽文獻編輯委員會.

洛陽文獻
民國 83 年元旦 (1994) 出版
出版社
洛陽文獻編輯委員會

A6b Cover   **A6b Colophon**

DISCUSSION

- The colophon is defined as: "A statement at the end of an item giving information about one or more of the following: the title, author(s), publisher, printer, date of publication or printing" (AACR2R, p. 616, Appendix D). According to the general order of precedence in rule 12.0B1 for selecting a title page substitute as the chief source of information, the colophon is next to the last choice. Note, however, that the same rule specifies that for serials in oriental nonroman script, the colophon is the preferred source, as long as one of the other listed conditions is met.
- In example A6a the item does not have a title page. There is a caption, but this consists solely of the name of the responsible body, Biotechnology Center. The colophon area on the other hand contains full bibliographic information for the serial. For that reason the colophon is chosen over the caption as the chief source (1.1B1).
- Whenever a title page substitute is used as the chief source, such information is input in a separate 500 General Note (12.7B3) or combined with the field 500 "Description based on:" information (LCRI 12.7B23).

A7

PROBLEM CONSIDERED:
Masthead chosen as chief source of information (1.0H1c)

RULE(S) CONSULTED:
AACR2R: 21.30J1
LCRI: 12.0B1, 12.1B4

<table>
<tr><td>Caption</td></tr>
</table>

Caption	**HK dTc** **Business Alert**
	The latest developments in EU trade policy Issue No. 2 1996

Masthead area	Hong Kong Trade Development Council's Business Alert-EU is prepared exclusively for HKTDC's Research Department by Price Waterhouse.

Running title	**Business Alert - EU**

TAGGED DATA RECORD (based on OCLC #34705254)

LDR   *****nas_/22*****Ia*4500

	00-05	06	07-14	15-17	18	19	20	21	22-28	29	30-32	33	34	35-37	38	39
008	960510	c	19969999	hk	e	r		p	-------	0	///	a	0	eng	-	d

→ 245 00   Business alert. ≠p EU.
→ 246 30   EU
→ 246 13   Hong Kong Trade Development Council's business alert EU
→ 246 16   HKTDC business alert
→ 246 17   Business alert-EU
   260   Hong Kong : ≠b Hong Kong Trade Development Council,
   300   v. ; ≠c 30 cm.
   310   Biweekly
   362 1   Began publication in 1996.
   500   "The latest developments in EU trade policy."
→ 500   Description based on: Issue no. 2 (1996); title from masthead.
   550   Prepared for HKTDC's Research Dept. by Price Waterhouse.
   651 0   European Union countries ≠x Commerce ≠z China ≠z Hong Kong ≠x Periodicals.
   651 0   Hong Kong (China) ≠x Commerce ≠z European Union countries ≠x Periodicals.
   650 0   Foreign trade regulation ≠z European Union countries ≠x Periodicals.
   710 2   Hong Kong Trade Development Council.
   710 2   Price Waterhouse (Firm).

DISCUSSION

• This item has more than one source of cataloging information, with different forms of the title appearing in the caption, in the masthead area, and in the running title. A closer look at typography and layout, along with the knowledge that there is a related publication with the title "Business alert-US," reveals that the caption title seems to serve as the common title of a serial issued by the same publisher in a similar format. The title in the masthead area and in the running pages, on the other hand, seems to be the intended title for the publication, based on the fact that it gives an indication of a geographic coverage

"EU," which can serve as the section title of this publication. Furthermore, the running title takes the same form as the masthead title. In accordance with the AACR2R designated order of precedence, the caption should be chosen as the title page substitute. Nevertheless, the title in the masthead area appears to be the intended title (LCRI 12.0B1), and, therefore, in this case, the masthead area is chosen as the cataloging source (1.0H1c).

- Once it has been determined that the series "Business alert" is issued in different sections, treat "Business alert" as the comprehensive title and "EU" as the section title (LCRI 12.1B4). Title added entries are made to provide additional access to the publication (21.30J1).

- Field 245 subfield ≠a is input for the common title; subfield ≠p is used for the section title. Field 246 is used for variant forms of title. In this example, the variant forms include the caption title, the running title, and the variant form of title found in the masthead area.

A8

PROBLEM CONSIDERED:

Chief source of information for reprint of a print serial (LCRI 12.0B1)

RULE(S) CONSULTED:

AACR2R: 12.7B3, 12.7B23
LCRI: 25.5B, p.6

Title page
of the reprint

> ### "MARTIN FIERRO"
> **Periódico quincenal de
> arte y cítica libre**
>
> ### Revista
> ### Martín Fierro
> ### 1924-1927
> ### Edición
> ### Facsimilar
> *Estudio preliminar de Horacio Salas*

TAGGED DATA RECORD (based on OCLC #34666548)

LDR   *****cas_/22*****Ia*4500

	00-05	06	07-14	15-17	18	19	20	21	22-28	29	30-32	33	34	35-37	38	39
008	960502	d	19241927	ag	u	u		p	-r----u	0	///	b	0	spa	-	d

→ 130 0   Martín Fierro (Buenos Aires, Argentina : 1924)

→ 245 00   Martín Fierro.

→ 246 1   ≠i Reprint edition has title: ≠a Revista Martín Fierro

→ 260   Buenos Aires, Argentina : ≠b Fondo Nacional de las Artes, ≠c 1995.

300   1 v. : ≠b ill. ; ≠c 41 cm.

→ 362 0   Año 1, no. 1 (feb. 1924)-año 4, no. 44/45 (agosto/nov. 1927).

500   "Periódico quincenal de arte y cítica libre."

515   Año 1-año 3 called 2. época.

515   No numbers issued for Dec. 1924, Feb.-Apr. 1925, Jan.-Apr. 1926.

→ 580   Reprint, with an introduction by Horacio Salas. Originally published: Buenos Aires : [s.n.].

650 0   Arts ≠x Periodicals.

650 0   Arts ≠z Argentina ≠x Periodicals.

710 2   Fondo Nacional de las Artes (Argentina)

→ 775 1   ≠t Martín Fierro ≠w (DLC)38005054 ≠w (OCoLC)11634155

DISCUSSION

- In describing a reprint of a print serial, the earliest issue reproduced is used as the chief source for the first three areas of the description (LCRI 12.0B1). These areas are: title and statement of responsibility (field 245), edition statement (field 250), and material specific details (field 362). Information for these three areas may simply be transcribed from any place on the entire reprinted issue. Information that does not appear on the reprinted issue but that is known to appear on the original may be bracketed and included in the description.

- According to Library of Congress policy, a uniform title is needed only if the catalog record for the original title has one, and, in such a case, the uniform title should be identical to that used for the original. However, in libraries that choose not to follow this LC policy, the rule interpretation suggests that, if a uniform title is to be assigned, it should consist of the title (or uniform title) of the original, followed by a period and an appropriate term for the type of manifestation, e.g., Reprint, Microform, etc. (LCRI 25.5B, p. 6).

- Information in the imprint area (field 260), which includes the place of publication, publisher, and date of publication, is recorded for the reprint. Similarly, information in the physical description area should describe the reprint and not the original. If the reprinted issue appears in a series, that series is recorded in the series statement area. On the other hand, if the original appears in a series, this series statement must be included in a single note devoted to detailed information about the original (LCRI 12.0B1). Necessary information about the reprint may be given in other notes; however, notes on title sources (12.7B3) or those giving the issue on which the description is based (12.7B23) are not considered to be necessary.

The guidelines for cataloging a reprint of a regular-print serial are summarized as follows:

For the original:

130	Given as appropriate (see discussion above)
245	Title and statement of responsibility
250	Edition statement
362	Numeric and/or alphabetic, chronological, or other designation area
580	A note giving details of the original (frequency, place and name of publisher and series).

For the reprint:

260	Imprint
300	Physical description
4xx	Series

008 Fixed-field coding:

Character positions

06	(Type of date/publication status)	for the original
7–14	(Date1 and Date2)	for the original
15–17	(Country code)	for the reprint
18	(Frequency and Regularity)	for the reprint
23	(Form of item)	Code as "r"

Linking field for related work:

A field 775 (Other Edition Entry) should be used to link to any other editions of the serial that are available, such as other language editions, reprinted editions, or the original edition of a serial that has been reprinted. Because no other linking field is paired with field 775, all related records should carry field 775 when the information is readily available. The first indicator determines whether a note describing the other available edition will be printed. If a note is to be generated from the link, the first indicator is set to value "0." When a note has been input in field 580 or when no note is desired, the first indicator is set to value "1."

B. Title Proper

The title proper is the principal name of an item. A title proper may consist of a symbol, a sign, a generic term, a one-word title, or a long phrase. It may also consist of a corporate name alone or its initialism or acronym. The form of a title proper may also be complex, consisting of a common title, a section number, a section title, or a combination of these items, with the whole unit considered to be a single title proper.

The title proper should be transcribed exactly as it appears in the chief source of information unless it includes a variable number or a date. In certain cases the date or number may then be omitted or replaced by the mark of omission.

Some serials have an alternative title, which is the second part of a title proper connected to the first part by the word "or" or its equivalent in another language. The title proper and the alternative title together should be considered collectively as one single title proper.

Some serials have titles appearing in more than one language; however, only one should be coded as the title proper. Thus a parallel title is not considered to be a part of the title proper. Similarly, neither is any other title information considered to be part of the title proper.

EXAMPLES

B1	Title proper includes a symbol
B2	Title proper consists of a number
B3	Title proper consists of initials
B4	Mark of omission in title proper
B5	Corporate body is an integral part of the title proper
B6	Inclusion of a corporate name as part of the title proper
B7	Title proper consists of a corporate name alone, and the work is entered under title
B8	Title proper consists of a corporate name alone, and the work is entered under the name heading
B9	Title proper consists of common title and section title
B10	Title proper consists of common title, section number, and section title
B11	Title proper consists of common title and section title with subsection
B12	Single word in title proper intended to be used more than once
B13	Title proper of a serial alternating with sections in continuous enumeration
B14	Title proper consists of two journal titles
B15	Alternative title included in title proper
B16	Correction of title proper

B1

PROBLEM CONSIDERED:

Title proper includes a symbol (1.1B1)

RULE(S) CONSULTED:

AACR2R: 12.7B5, 21.30J1
LCRI: 1.0E, 12.7B9, 21.30J, p. 12

TAGGED DATA RECORD (based on OCLC #18474354)

LDR   *****cas_/22*****_a*4500

00-05	06	07-14	15-17	18	19	20	21	22-28	29	30-32	33	34	35-37	38	39
880912	c	19899999	nyu	m	n	l	p	-------	0	///	a	0	eng	-	d

008

022 0	1040-6042
→ 245 04	The C++ report.
→ 246 3	C plus plus report
→ 260	New York, N.Y. : ≠b JPAM, Inc., ≠c 1989-
300	v. : ≠b ill. ; ≠c 28 cm.
310	Monthly (Mar./Apr., July/Aug., and Nov./Dec. issues combined), ≠b <Mar./Apr. 1992->
321	Monthly (July/Aug. issue and Nov./Dec. issue combined), ≠b Jan. 1989-
362 0	Vol. 1, no. 1 (Jan. 1989)-
→ 500	"The international newsletter for C++ programmers," 1989- ; "The international authority on C++ development," <1993->
→ 500	Publisher varies: SIGS Publications, Inc., <Mar./Apr. 1992->
500	Title from caption.
515	Vol. for Mar./Apr. 1992 called also Premier magazine issue.
650 0	C++ (Computer program language) ≠x Periodicals.

Caption of first issue

> The
> **C++ REPORT**
> THE INTERNATIONAL NEWSLETTER FOR C++ PROGRAMMERS
>
> January 1989•Vol 1/No 1

Caption of a later issue

> The
> **C++ REPORT**
> THE INTERNATIONAL AUTHORITY ON C++ DEVELOPMENT
> A SIGS Publication
> January 1993•Vol 5/No 1

DISCUSSION

- In transcribing a symbol, transcribe it exactly as it is shown if it can be reproduced by the cataloging system you are using (1.1B1). The exceptions are as follows: replace ellipses ". . ." with a dash, and brackets "[ ]" with parentheses "( )." LCRI 1.0E details specific techniques for transcribing characters or symbols that cannot be reproduced by the facilities available. LCRI recommends use of a note as judged appropriate, to explain the presence of such character(s) and also recommends added entries to provide additional access.
- A title added entry is made, replacing symbols with the corresponding spelled-out words in the language of the title. In this case, "++" becomes "plus plus" (21.30J1; LCRI 21.30J, p. 12). Field 246 is input for access to the variant title. First indicator value "3" is used so that the varying form of title will print as an added entry but not as a note. Second indicator value blank is used, because the spelled-out form of the title in field 246 cannot be described by values "0–8."
- When a change in imprint (field 260) is considered important, give the change in a 500 General Note. In this example, a 500 note is used to describe a change in the name of the commercial publisher. If the change involves the name of a place used as the qualifier in a uniform title heading, the country code in field 008 positions 15–17 should also be changed to reflect the latest place of publication (LCRI 12.7B9).
- The current other title information, which differs from what appeared previously, may, at the discretion of the cataloger (12.7B5), be entered in a general note that includes the related date.

B2

PROBLEM CONSIDERED:

Title proper consists of a number (LCRI 21.30J, p. 11).

RULE(S) CONSULTED:

AACR2R: 21.30J1

Caption

> (1/1) **The Quarterly Journal of the**
> **Just Intonation Network**
> A Project of Other Music, Inc.
> Volume 1, Number 1 Winter 1985

TAGGED DATA RECORD (based on OCLC #11652544)

LDR   *****cas_/22*****_a*4500

00-05	06	07-14	15-17	18	19	20	21	22-28	29	30-32	33	34	35-37	38	39
850204	c	19859999	cau	q	r	1	p	-------	0	///	a	0	eng	-	d

008

→ 245 00   1/1 : ≠b the quarterly journal of the Just Intonation Network.
→ 246 3   One/one
   246 3   1 1
   246 3   One one
   260   San Francisco, CA : ≠b The Network, ≠c 1985-
   300   v. : ≠b ill. ; ≠c 28 cm.
   310   Quarterly
   362 0   Vol. 1, no. 1 (winter 1985)-
   500   Title from caption.
   650 0   Tuning ≠x Periodicals.
   710 2   Just Intonation Network (San Francisco, Calif.)

DISCUSSION

- Under the provision of rule 21.30J1, an added entry should be made for any version of the title that does not constitute a change in the title proper (the first five words). When a number occurs as one of the first five words filed in a title proper, it is reasonable to expect that someone might look for the title under the spelled-out version of the number, and, therefore a title added entry should be made containing the spelled-out form (LCRI 21.30J, p. 11). However, in the case of a mathematical expression or symbol (e.g.,1/10th), it would be unlikely that users would search under the spelled-out form, and, in such cases, no title added entry is needed. In spelling out numbers in English, follow the *Chicago Manual of Style.*

- In this example, the title proper is not a mathematical expression. Therefore, a field 246 derived added entry is made. The first indicator value is "3," because a note for the added entry is not needed; the second indicator value is a blank, because it is not necessary to generate a display constant describing the type of title recorded in the 246 field.

B3

PROBLEM CONSIDERED:

Title proper consists of initials (12.1B2)

RULE(S) CONSULTED:

AACR2R: 12.1E1, 21.30J1
LCRI: 21.30J, p. 9, p. 23

JACA
Journal of the Association
for
Communication Administration

No. 1 January 1993

Cover

TAGGED DATA RECORD (based on OCLC #28601760)

LDR   *****nas_/22*****_a*4500

00-05	06	07-14	15-17	18	19	20	21	22-28	29	30-32	33	34	35-37	38	39
930810	c	19939999	vau	t	x	1	p	-------	0	///	a	0	eng	-	d

008

022   0360-0939
→ 245 00   JACA : ≠b journal of the Association for Communication Administration.
→ 246 30   Journal of the Association for Communication Administration
   260   Annandale, VA : ≠b The Association, ≠c c1993-
   300   v. ; ≠c 26cm.
   310   Three nos. a year, ≠b 1994-
   321   4 nos. a year, ≠b 1993
   362 0   No. 1 (Jan. 1993)-
   500   Title from cover.
   650 0   Communications in education ≠x Periodicals.
   650 0   Communication ≠x Periodicals.
   650 0   School management and organization ≠x Periodicals.
   650 0   Theater ≠x Periodicals.
   710 2   Association for Communication Administration.
   780 00   ≠t ACA bulletin ≠x 0360-0939 ≠w (DLC)75646371 ≠w (OCoLC)2171786

DISCUSSION

- In this example the cover serves as the chief source of information. On the cover the title appears both in full and initialism form, with the initialism being the only form appearing elsewhere in the serial. According to rules 12.1B2 and 12.1E1, the initialism should be chosen as the title proper and the full title recorded as other title information. Once that choice has been made, make an added entry for the form of title not chosen as title proper (21.30J1; LCRI 21.30J, p. 23).
- Field 246 is used for recording a title that was not chosen as title proper and that appears as other title information. First indicator value "3" is used, specifying that an added entry for the variant title is to be derived from 246 and no note is needed. Second indicator value "0" is used when the entry is for a portion of the full title or for other title information that was rejected as title proper.
- Note that it is normally not necessary to make an added entry for other title information consisting of a phrase like "Journal of the Association for Communication Administration" unless, as in this example, it is a case of initialism versus full form of title. (See also example H8.)
- Also, when, as in this case, the initialism occurs in the title proper without spacing or separating punctuation, a title added entry with spacing or separating punctuation is normally not necessary; only when the opposite occurs and the initialism appears as one of the first five words in the title proper *with* spacing or separating punctuation is a title added entry without spacing or separating punctuation needed (LCRI 21.30J, p. 9).

B4

PROBLEM CONSIDERED:

Mark of omission in title proper (12.1B7)

RULE(S) CONSULTED:

LCRI: 12.1B7

TAGGED DATA RECORD (based on OCLC #31470767)

LDR   *****cas_/22*****_a*4500

00-05	06	07-14	15-17	18	19	20	21	22-28	29	30-32	33	34	35-37	38	39
941116	c	19949999	enk	a	r		p	-------	0	///	a	0	eng	-	d

008

→ 245 08   The ... Hali annual.
  260   London : ≠b Hali Publications, ≠c 1994-
  300   v. : ≠b col. ill. ; ≠c 32 cm.
  310   Annual
  362 0   No. 1 (1994)-
  500   Some vols. have also a distinctive title.
  650 0   Rugs ≠x Periodicals.
  650 0   Textile fabrics ≠x Periodicals.
  650 0   Rugs, Oriental ≠x Periodicals.
  650 0   Carpets ≠x Periodicals.
  650 0   Decorative arts ≠x Periodicals.

Title page

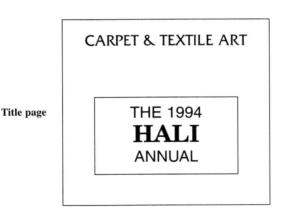

DISCUSSION

- A chronological date or numbering that occurs within a title proper can vary from issue to issue. Therefore, the cataloger should omit this information from the title proper and replace it by the mark of omission. However, according to rule 12.1B7, the mark of omission should not be used in place of a date or numbering that occurs at the beginning of the title proper. In such cases, the date should still be omitted, but no mark of omission should replace it. When the date or numbering occurs at the end of the title proper, use the mark of omission only when there is a linking word or phrase that links the date or numbering to the preceding part of the title proper (e.g., "Annual report for the year . . .") (LCRI 12.1B7).

- In this example the mark of omission is used in the title because the date is preceded by an article. Note that the second indicator value in field 245 is "8," which includes both the article and the mark of omission as filing characters.

B5

PROBLEM CONSIDERED:

Corporate body is an integral part of the title proper (1.1B2)

RULE(S) CONSULTED:

AACR2R: 1.1F3, 12.1F2, 21.29C, 21.30E1
LCRI: 21.30J, p. 9, p. 18

TAGGED DATA RECORD (based on OCLC #29290446)

LDR   *****cas_/22*****_a*4500

	00-05	06	07-14	15-17	18	19	20	21	22-28	29	30-32	33	34	35-37	38	39
→ 008	931109	c	19939999	fr	q	x		p	-------	0	///	b	0	fre	-	d

022	1243-8804 ≠y 0991-1367
→ 245 03	Le Bulletin de la S.H.M.C.
→ 246 17	Bulletin de la Société d'histoire moderne et contemporaine
→ 246 3	Bulletin de la SHMC
260	Paris : ≠b Société d'histoire moderne et contemporaine, ≠c 1993-
300	v. ; ≠c 24 cm.
310	Four no. a year
362 0	1993/1-2-
610 20	Société d'histoire moderne et contemporaine ≠x Periodicals
650 0	History, Modern ≠x Periodicals.
651 0	France ≠x History ≠x Periodicals.
710 2	Société d'histoire moderne et contemporaine.
730 0	Revue d'histoire moderne et contemporaine.
772 0	≠t Revue d'histoire moderne et contemporaine ≠w (DLC)a56002890 ≠w (OCoLC)1604668
780 00	≠t Bulletin de la Société d'histoire moderne ≠w (DLC)33001152 ≠w (OCoLC)2168685

Cover

> **Le BULLETIN**
> **de la S.H.M.C.**
>
> **1996/1-2**
>
> Supplément à la *Revue d'Histoire Moderne et Contemporaine,* tome 43
> SOCIETE D'HISTOIRE MODERNE ET CONTEMPORAINE

DISCUSSION

- When the name of a corporate body or a statement of responsibility is grammatically linked to the title proper, transcribe it as it appears (1.1B2). It is not necessary to make any further statement relating to that name in the statement of responsibility area. However, if the name of the responsible body also appears separately in the chief source of information as well as in the title proper, transcribe the name in the statement of responsibility area (12.1F2). Occasionally, such a name precedes the title proper in the chief source of information but at the same time, according to the language, layout, typography, etc., it is not an integral part of the title proper; in such cases, transpose it to the statement of responsibility area and do not make an "At head of title" note (1.1F3). An added entry is needed under the heading for the corporate body (21.30E1).
- There is a running title which spells out the initialism in the title proper. This is treated as a variant title and an added title entry is needed for the other form of title borne by the item (21.29C; LCRI 21.30J, p. 18). In this example, the added title entry for the running title is input in the title-derived 246 field. The first indicator is set to value "1" to generate a note; the second indicator is set to value "7" to generate the display constant, "Running title:" preceding the note.
- If a title contains separating punctuation between initials, make an added entry for the form without the separating punctuation (LCRI 21.30J p. 9). In this example, the second 246 field is input to record this variant form containing the initials without any separating punctuation. First indicator value "3" is used when a note in the bibliographic description for the title added entry is not necessary.

B6

PROBLEM CONSIDERED:

Inclusion of a corporate name as part of the title proper (12.1B3)

RULE(S) CONSULTED:

AACR2R: 1.1B2
LCRI: 12.1B1, 12.1B3; 21.30J, p. 13

Title page

> **1   World Bank Discussion Papers**
>
> **Public Enterprises
> in Sub-Saharan Africa**
>
> **John R. Nellis**
>
> **The World Bank
> Washington, D.C.
> 1986**

TAGGED DATA RECORD (based on OCLC #14155986)

LDR   *****cas_/22*****_a*4500

00-05	06	07-14	15-17	18	19	20	21	22-28	29	30-32	33	34	35-37	38	39
860828	c	19869999	dcu		x	0	m	-------	0	///	a	0	eng	-	d

008

022 0   0259-210X

043   d------

→ 245 00   World Bank discussion papers.

→ 246 30   Discussion papers

260   Washington, D.C. : ≠b The Bank, ≠c 1986-

300   v. ; ≠c 28 cm.

310   Irregular

362 0   1-

650   0   Economic development.

650   0   Economic development projects ≠z Developing countries.

710 2   World Bank.

DISCUSSION

- Whether to include a corporate body's name or an abbreviation of that name as part of the title proper is always a matter of debate. Ordinarily, the decision is based on the language, meaning, layout, typography, and appearance of the title in the chief source (1.1B2). In case of doubt, treat the name as part of the title proper only when it consistently appears as such on various sources of the item described, such as the cover, caption, masthead, colophon, editorial pages, etc. (12.1B3).
- The cataloger should apply the same approach in deciding whether a word, phrase, or other statement is part of the title proper (LCRI 12.1B3). However, do not include such statements as "formerly issued as . . . ," "incorporating . . . ," "continues . . . ," etc., as part of the title proper, even when such statements are present in various sources in the item and are grammatically linked to the title (LCRI 12.1B1).
- In this example, the name of the corporate body, "World Bank," is included in the title proper and an added entry is made for the portion of the title without the name of the corporate body, since the user might consider that form to be the title proper (LCRI 21.30J, p. 13).

B7

PROBLEM CONSIDERED:

Title proper consists of a corporate name alone, and the work is entered under title (1.1B3)

RULE(S) CONSULTED:

AACR2R: 21.1B2, 21.1C1c

LCRI: 25.5B, p. 7

TAGGED DATA RECORD (based on OCLC #33453484)

LDR   *****cas_/22*****_a*4500

00-05	06	07-14	15-17	18	19	20	21	22-28	29	30-32	33	34	35-37	38	39
951109	c	19959999	dcu	u	u	l	m	-------	0	///	a	0	eng	-	d

008

022 0	1088-6060
043	n-us--
→ 130 0	Cato Project on Social Security Privatization (Series)
→ 245 04	The Cato Project on Social Security Privatization.
246 30	Social security privatization
260	Washington, D. C. : ≠b Cato Institute, ≠c 1995-
300	v. : ≠b ill. ; ≠c 28 cm.
362 0	SSP no. 1-
500	Title from caption.
550	Issued by: Cato Project on Social Security Privatization.
650 0	Social security ≠z United States ≠x Periodicals.
650 0	Privatization ≠z United States ≠x Periodicals.
710 2	Cato Project on Social Security Privatization.
710 2	Cato Institute.

Caption

> # The Cato Project on Social Security Privatization
>
> **SSP No.1**
>
> Published by:
> Cato Institute
> Washington, D. C.

DISCUSSION

- Rule l.lB3 states: "If the title proper consists solely of the name of a person or body responsible for the item, give such a name as the title proper." Therefore, in this example, "Cato Project on Social Security Privatization" is treated as the title proper. Since the work does not meet the conditions for entry under corporate body (21.1B2), it is entered under title (21.1C1c).
- If the title of a serial entered under title consists solely of the name of a corporate body (or corporate name initials), create a uniform title heading that consists of the title proper qualified by the term "Series" in parentheses even if there is no conflict (LCRI 25.5B, p. 7). Note that when a corporate name is treated as title proper, that name as found on the item is used for formulating the uniform title heading—not the AACR2R form of heading for the body.
- Field 130 is used for a uniform title heading, i.e., for a uniform title that serves as the main entry heading. Do not confuse a uniform title heading with a uniform title; a uniform title is input in field 240 and can be used only on a record that has a 100, 110, or 111 field.

B8

PROBLEM CONSIDERED:

Title proper consists of a corporate name alone, and the work is entered under the name heading (1.1B3)

RULE(S) CONSULTED:

AACR2R: 1.1E6, 21.1B2d, 24.4B1

TAGGED DATA RECORD (based on OCLC #14404736)

LDR   *****cas_/22*****_a*4500

00-05	06	07-14	15-17	18	19	20	21	22-28	29	30-32	33	34	35-37	38	39
861016	d	19781988	nbu	g	r			-------	1	///	a	0	eng	-	d

008

043   n-usc--
→ 111 2   Joslyn Biennial (Exhibition)
→ 245 00   Joslyn Biennial : ≠b [catalog].
260   Omaha, Neb. : ≠b Joslyn Art Museum, ≠c 1978-1988.
300   6 v. : ≠b ill. ; ≠c 21 cm.
310   Biennial
362 0   15th (1978)-20th (1988).
611 20   Joslyn Biennial (Exhibition)
650 0   Art, American ≠z Middle West ≠x Exhibitions.
650 0   Art, Modern ≠y 20th century ≠z Middle West ≠x Exhibitions.
710 2   Joslyn Art Museum.
780 00   Joslyn Art Museum. ≠t Midwest biennial ≠w (DLC)72620667 ≠w (OCoLC)1783892

Title page

18TH JOSLYN BIENNIAL

Joslyn Art Museum Omaha Nebraska April 28 to June 24, 1984

DISCUSSION

- If the only term appearing on the chief source that could be treated as a title is the name of a person or body responsible for the item, treat such name as the title proper (1.1B3). In this example "Joslyn Biennial" is therefore given as the title proper. Because this work is the catalog of an exhibition, it seems appropriate to explain the nature of the publication by supplying the term "catalog" in brackets as other title information (1.1E6).

- Since this publication represents the collective activity of a named exhibition, it is entered under the heading for the exhibition (21.1B2d). According to rule 24.4B1, "if the name alone does not convey the idea of a corporate body, add a general designation in English." In this example the word "Exhibition" in parentheses is added to the name "Joslyn Biennial."
- Field 111 contains the name heading for the exhibition as main entry.
- In field 245 the first indicator regulates the generation of a title added entry. If no added entry is desired, first indicator value "0" is used; if a title added entry is desired, value "1" is used.

B9

PROBLEM CONSIDERED:

Title proper consists of common title and section title (1.1B9)

RULE(S) CONSULTED:

AACR2R: 12.0B1, 12.1B4, 12.1B6, 21.30J1
LCRI: 12.1B4

TAGGED DATA RECORD (based on OCLC #34382631)

LDR   *****nas_/22*****Ia*4500

00-05	06	07-14	15-17	18	19	20	21	22-28	29	30-32	33	34	35-37	38	39
960318	c	19969999	fr		x			------i	0	///	a	0	eng	-	d

008 (as above)

→ 245 00   Environmental performance reviews. ≠p United States.
→ 246 30   United States
   246 17   OECD environmental performance reviews
   260   Paris : ≠b Organisation for Economic Co-operation and Development ; ≠a [Washington, D. C. : ≠b OECD Publications and Information Centre, distributor], ≠c c1996-
   300   v. : ≠b col. ill. ; ≠c 23 cm.
   362 0   1996-
   650   0   Ecology ≠z United States.
   650   0   Environmental policy ≠z United States
   710 2   Organisation for Economic Co-operation and Development.

Title page

**ENVIRONMENTAL
PERFORMANCE
REVIEW**

UNITED STATES

ORGANISATION FOR ECONOMIC CO-OPERATION AND DEVELOPMENT

DISCUSSION

- When a common title that is common to many sections and a section title both appear in the same source within the item, record the common title first, followed by the section title (1.1B9). A section title usually represents a particular subject area within the scope of a comprehensive title, or it may be a supplement to the main serial.
- In applying rule 12.1B4 for serials with a common title and a section title, any source within the preliminaries (not necessarily the title page) containing both titles can be used as the chief source of information (LCRI 12.1B4). If there is no source containing both titles, choose the chief source according to normal rules of preference (12.0B1). Should the section title occur in the chief source without the common title, record only the section title as the title proper (12.1B6).
- In this example, the common title "Environmental performance reviews" and the section title "United States" make up the title proper. An added entry should be made for the section title, because it is an independent title (21.30J1).
- In field 245, subfield ≠p is input for the section title, subsection title, or subseries title, if needed. This subfield is repeatable only when it is used for coding sections and subsections or subseries, etc., as part of the title proper. It is not used in parallel section title, parallel subsection title, or parallel subseries title situations.

B10

PROBLEM CONSIDERED:

Title proper consists of common title, section number, and section title (12.1B5)

RULE(S) CONSULTED:

AACR2R: 12.0B1, 21.30J1

TAGGED DATA RECORD (based on OCLC #7193380)

LDR   *****cas_/22*****_a*4500

	00-05	06	07-14	15-17	18	19	20	21	22-28	29	30-32	33	34	35-37	38	39
008	810305	c	19809999	nyu	b	r	z	p	-------	0	///	a	0	eng	-	d

022 0   0143-8123

→ 245 00   Comments on modern biology. ≠n Part A, ≠p Comments on molecular and cellular biophysics.

→ 246 30   Comments on molecular and cellular biophysics

260   New York ; ≠a London : ≠b Gordon and Breach Science Publishers, ≠c c1980-

300   v. : ≠b ill. ; ≠c 22 cm.

310   Bimonthly

362 0   Vol. 1, no. 1 (Dec. 1980)-

500   Title from cover.

650   0   Molecular biology ≠x Periodicals.

650   0   Cytology ≠x Periodicals.

650   0   Biophysics ≠x Periodicals.

Cover

Comments
on
Molecular
and Cellular
Biophysics

A Journal of Critical Discussion of the Current Literature

Comments on Modern Biology:
Part A

Volume I
Number 1 (1980)   ISSN 0143-8123

DISCUSSION

- When a common title that is common to many sections, a section number, and a section title appear together within the item in the chief source of information, record the common title first, followed by the section number preceded by a full stop, and the section title preceded by a comma (12.1B5). In this example the cover is chosen as the chief source of information since the item does not have a title page (12.0B1). The common title (also considered to be the comprehensive title), "Comments on modern biology," the section number designated by "Part A," and the section title, "Comments on molecular and cellular biophysics," make up the title proper. An added entry should be made for the section title (21.30J1).

- In field 245, subfield ≠n is used for the section number and subfield ≠p is used for the section title and subsection title, if needed. Both subfields are repeatable if they are input as part of the title proper, but they are not repeated for the section number and section title as part of the parallel title.

B11

PROBLEM CONSIDERED:

Title proper consists of common title and section title with subsection (12.1B4)

TAGGED DATA RECORD (based on OCLC #34278890)

LDR   *****cas_/22*****_a*4500

00-05	06	07-14	15-17	18	19	20	21	22-28	29	30-32	33	34	35-37	38	39
960228	c	19959999	fi		x		m	-------	0	///		0	eng	-	d

008

022   ≠y 0355-0087
→ 245 00 Annales Academiae Scientiarum Fennicae. ≠p Mathematica. ≠p Dissertationes.
246 30 Mathematica. ≠p Dissertationes
246 30 Dissertationes
260   Helsinki : ≠b Suomalainen Tiedeakatemia, ≠c 1995-
300   v. ; ≠c 25 cm.
310   Irregular
362 0   101-
546   In English.
650 0 Mathematics.
710 2   Suomalainen Tiedeakatemia.
780 00 ≠t Annales Academiae Scientiarum Fennicae. Series A. I, Mathematica. Dissertationes ≠x 0355-0087 ≠w (DLC)sf86005002 ≠w (OCoLC)4175934

Title page

```
ANNALES
ACADEMLÆ SCIENTIARUM
FENNICÆ


MATHEMATICA

DISSERTATIONES

101


HELSINKI 1996
SUOMALAINEN TIEDEAKATEMIA
```

DISCUSSION

- In this example, the item has a section title that, in turn, has another subsection title. Both the section titles share a common title. In such cases, give the common title, "Annales Academiæ Scientiarum Fennicæ," which is the comprehensive title, followed by the main section, "Mathematica," preceded by a full stop and then by its subsection title, "Dissertationes," preceded also by a full stop (12.1B4).

- In field 245, subfield ≠p is input for the section title and subsection title, if needed. This subfield is repeatable when it is used for coding sections and subsections as part of the title proper.

B12

PROBLEM CONSIDERED:

Single word in title proper intended to be used more than once (1.1B5)

RULE(S) CONSULTED:

AACR2R: 1.1B8, 1.1D2, 21.30J1
LCRI: 21.30J, p. 24

TAGGED DATA RECORD (based on OCLC #35322347)

LDR   *****cas_/22*****_a*4500

00-05	06	07-14	15-17	18	19	20	21	22-28	29	30-32	33	34	35-37	38	39
960829	c	19969999	sz	f	r		p	-------	0	///	b	0	ger	-	d

008

022   1420-6846
041   gerfre ≠b engita
→ 245 00   Bulletin für angewandte Geologie = ≠b Bulletin pour la géologie appliquée = Bulletin for applied geology / ≠c Herausgeber, Schweizerische Vereinigung von Petroleum-Geologen und -Ingenieuren [und] Schweizerische Fachgruppe für Ingenieurgeologie.
→ 246 31   Bulletin pour la géologie appliquée
→ 246 31   Bulletin for applied geology
246 18   Bulletin VSP/ASP-SFIG-GSGI
260   Zürich : ≠b VSP, SFIG, ≠c 1996-
300   v. : ≠b ill. (some col.) ; ≠c 24 cm.
310   Semiannual
362 0   Vol. 1, Nr. 1 (Juni 1996)-
500   Title from cover.
546   Text in German and French; summaries in the other language and in English and Italian.
650 0   Engineering geology ≠x Periodicals.
650 0   Petroleum engineering ≠x Periodicals.
650 0   Petroleum ≠x Geology ≠x Periodicals.
710 2   Vereinigung Schweiz. Petroleum-Geologen und -Ingenieuren.
710 2   Schweizerische Fachgruppe für Ingenieurgeologie.
780 00   ≠t Bulletin der Vereinigung Schweiz. Petroleum-Geologen und -Ingenieure ≠x 0366-4848 ≠w (DLC)61033459 ≠w (OCoLC)7567863

Cover

BULLETIN

FÜR ANGEWANDTE GEOLOGIE
POUR LA GÉOLOGIE APPLIQUÉE
PER LA GEOLOGIA APPLICATA
FOR APPLIED GEOLOGY

Herausgeber / Editeurs / Editori / Editors

Schweizerische Vereinigung von Petroleum-Geologen und -Ingenieuren Association suisse des géologues et ingénieurs du pétrole Associazione svizzera del geologi e ingegneri del petrolio Swiss Association of Petroleum Geologists and Engineers	Schweizerische Fachgruppe für Ingenieurgeologie Groupement suisse de la géologie de l'ingenieur Gruppo svizzero della geologia dell'ingegnere Swiss Group for Engineering Geology

DISCUSSION

- In this example, the cover, which is the chief source of information, is set up with the word "Bulletin" functioning as part of the title in four different languages. Under the provisions of rule 1.1B5, the repeated word is transcribed without the use of brackets for the parallel titles.
- The German title is chosen as title proper because it is listed first in the chief source (1.1B8). In preparing a second-level description for items having parallel titles, give the first parallel title according to the sequence of the parallel titles on, or the layout of, the chief source; record any subsequent parallel title that is in English (1.1D2). In keeping with this, the two parallel titles recorded in this example are the French and English titles.
- Title added entries are needed for the English and French parallel titles (21.30J1; LCRI 21.30J, p. 24). Field 246 is input to provide access for title added entries. First indicator value "3" is used to suppress the display of a note but generate an added entry. Second indicator value "1" is used to indicate that access is for a parallel title.

B13

PROBLEM CONSIDERED:

Title proper of a serial alternating with sections in continuous enumeration (LCRI 12.0)

RULE(S) CONSULTED:

LCRI: 12.1B7; 21.30J, p. 20

PIMA'S NORTH AMERICAN **PAPERMAKER** January 1997	PIMA'S INTERNATIONAL **PAPERMAKER** February 1997
Cover	**Cover of another issue**

TAGGED DATA RECORD (based on OCLC #36353452)

00-05	06	07-14	15-17	18	19	20	21	22-28	29	30-32	33	34	35-37	38	39
008	800109	c	19979999	ilu	m	r	l	p	-------	0	///	a	0	eng	-	d

022 0	≠y 1046-4352

→ 245 00   PIMA's ... papermaker.

→ 246 1   ≠i Four issues a year have title: ≠a PIMA's international papermaker

→ 246 1   ≠i Four issues a year have title: ≠a PIMA's North American papermaker

246 30   Papermaker

260   Mount Prospect, IL : ≠b Paper Industry Management Association, ≠c 1997-

300   v. : ≠b ill. ; ≠c 28 cm.

310   Eight no. a year

362 0   Vol. 79, no. 1 (Jan. 1997)-

500   Title from cover.

515   Issue for Jan. 1997 called Jan. 1996 in the masthead in error.

515   Continues the numbering of: PIMA magazine.

580   Formed by the merger of: PIMA magazine, American papermaker, and: Canadian papermaker.

530   Issued also on microfilm by University Microfilms International.

650 0 Paper industry ≠x Periodicals.

650 0 Wood-pulp industry ≠x Periodicals.

710 2   Paper Industry Management Association.

780 14   ≠t PIMA magazine ≠x 1046-4352 ≠w (DLC)88654850 ≠w (OCoLC)17350292

780 14   ≠t American papermaker (Atlanta, Ga. : 1991) ≠x 1056-4772 ≠w (DLC)96643231 ≠w (OCoLC)23722397

780 14   ≠t Canadian papermaker ≠x 1191-887X ≠w (DLC)93658538 ≠w (OCoLC)26926275

DISCUSSION

- For a serial issued in parts, a cataloger may apply the criteria in LCRI 12.0 to judge whether the individual sections should be cataloged separately or whether the serial and its sections should be represented by a single cataloging record. In this example, eight issues are published yearly in two distinctive parts: Those devoted to regional focus carry the title "PIMA's North American papermaker," and those devoted to international focus carry the title "PIMA's international papermaker." In spite of the differences in title only one cataloging record is created, because these parts are numbered continuously and cannot be purchased separately (LCRI 12.0).

- Because the item carries two different titles, the wording that varies from issue to issue should be omitted from the title proper and replaced by the mark of omission (LCRI 12.1B7). Title added entries are needed for the actual titles that are being treated as the alternate forms of the title proper (LCRI 21.30J, p. 20).

- Two 246 fields are input, each with a subfield ≠i to provide information with regard to the publication pattern. First indicator value "1" is used to generate a note for display and provide access to the two alternate forms of the title proper.

B14

PROBLEM CONSIDERED:

Title proper consists of two journal titles (12.0B1)

RULE(S) CONSULTED:

AACR2R: 21.30J1, A.4C1

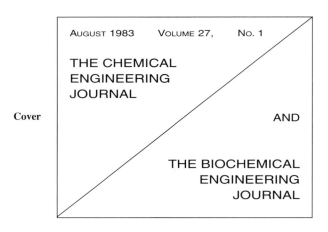

Cover

AUGUST 1983   VOLUME 27,   NO. 1

THE CHEMICAL
ENGINEERING
JOURNAL

AND

THE BIOCHEMICAL
ENGINEERING
JOURNAL

TAGGED DATA RECORD (based on OCLC #10112441)

LDR   *****cas_/22*****_a*4500

00-05	06	07-14	15-17	18	19	20	21	22-28	29	30-32	33	34	35-37	38	39
831109	d	19831996	sz	m	r	z	p	-------	0	///	a	0	eng	-	d

008

022   0923-0467 ≠y 0300-9467
041 0   engfreger
→ 245 04   The Chemical engineering journal and the biochemical engineering journal.
→ 246 30   Biochemical engineering journal
→ 246 13   Chemical engineering journal, the biochemical engineering journal
260   Lausanne : ≠b Elsevier Sequoia S.A., ≠c 1983-1996.
300   36 v. : ≠b ill. ; ≠c 28 cm.
310   Monthly, ≠b -1996
321   Bimonthly, ≠b Aug. 1983-
321   3 no. a year, ≠b <Nov. 1990-Nov. 1991>
362 0   Vol. 27, no. 1 (Aug. 1983)-v. 62, no. 3 (June 1996).
500   Title from cover.
546   English, French or German.
650   0   Chemical engineering ≠x Periodicals.
650   0   Biochemical engineering ≠x Periodicals.
780 00   ≠t Chemical engineering journal (Lausanne, Switzerland) ≠x 0300-9467 ≠w
           (DLC)76017923 ≠w (OCoLC)852029
785 00   ≠t Chemical engineering journal (Lausanne, Switzerland : 1996) ≠w
           (DLC)97647009 ≠w (OCoLC)35247001

DISCUSSION

- When two publications in closely related disciplines are issued under a consolidated cover, the joint publication may still keep the two entities distinct, as can be seen from the editorial page of this example. Because no title page exists, the cover is chosen as the chief source (12.0B1), and the title on the cover—"The Chemical engineering journal and the biochemical engineering journal"—becomes the title proper. Note that when one serial incorporates another serial, the first word of the incorporated title is not capitalized by the other rules of the language (A.4C1).
- Added entries are made for the second title and the combined titles as they appear on the editorial page (21.30J1).

B15

PROBLEM CONSIDERED:

Alternative title included in title proper (1.1B1)

RULE(S) CONSULTED:

AACR2R: Appendix D (p. 615)
LCRI: 21.30J, p. 13

Cover

The LADIES' Diary:

OR

WOMAN'S ALMANACK

FOR THE YEAR OF OUR LORD
1786

TAGGED DATA RECORD (based on OCLC #5536790)

LDR *****cas_/22*****Ia*4500

	00-05	06	07-14	15-17	18	19	20	21	22-28	29	30-32	33	34	35-37	38	39
008	791018	d	1uuu1uuu	enk	a	r			-------	0	///	a	0	eng	-	d

→ 245 04 The Ladies' diary, or, Woman's almanack.
→ 246 30 Ladies' diary
→ 246 30 Woman's almanack
  260 London : ≠b Printed for T. Carnan,
  300 v. ; ≠c 16 cm.
  500 "Containing new improvements in arts and sciences, and many entertaining particulars: designed for the use and diversion of the fair sex."
  500 Description based on: 1786; title from cover.
  650 0 Almanacs, English.

DISCUSSION

- As defined in AACR2R, an alternative title is: "The second part of a title proper that consists of two parts, each of which is a title; the parts are joined by the word 'or' or its equivalent in another language . . ." (AACR2R, p. 615, Appendix D). Therefore, an alternative title is part of the title proper. The word "or" or its equivalent in another language is preceded by a comma and a space and is followed by a comma. The first word of the alternative title is capitalized (1.1B1). An added entry is needed for the alternative title, and, in addition, one may also be needed for the first part of the title proper if the first part of the title proper consists of three words or less. This ensures that anyone searching an online system for either simple title will be able to access the record (LCRI 21.30J, p. 13). In this example, the first part of the title proper consists of only two words; therefore, an additional title added entry is made for "Ladies' diary."

- Field 245 contains the title statement, which consists of the title proper (subfield ≠a), remainder of title (subfield ≠b), and statement of responsibility (subfield ≠c). Since the alternative title is part of the title proper, it is included in subfield ≠a. First indicator value "0" is used because no title added entry is needed. Second indicator value "4" is used to indicate the number of characters to ignore in filing when the title begins with an article. To calculate the number of nonfiling characters, count the number of characters in the article along with spaces, punctuation, and diacritics that precede the first significant word.

- Two 246 fields are input for this record. One is for the first part of the title proper up to the word "or" and the other is for the part following the word "or." First indicator value "3" is used because a note displaying the title added entry is not needed. Second indicator value "0" is used because access is for a portion of the full title.

B16

PROBLEM CONSIDERED:

Correction of title proper (LCRI 12.0F)

RULE(S) CONSULTED:

AACR2R: 1.0F
LCRI: 21.30J, p. 23

SOCIAL DEVELOPMENT GUIDE MANNUAL

VOLUME 2, MAY, 1985

SUBJECT: WORKSHOP ON AGING REPORT AT GREEN HILLS HOTEL, NYERI
21st to 24th November, 1983

ORGANIZED BY:
KENYA NATIONAL COUNCIL OF SOCIAL SERVICE
AND FINANCED BY:
THE FORD FOUNDATION

Title page

TAGGED DATA RECORD (based on OCLC #20665877)

LDR   *****nas_/22*****_a*4500

00-05	06	07-14	15-17	18	19	20	21	22-28	29	30-32	33	34	35-37	38	39
891117	c	19859999	ke	u	u			------f	0	///	a	0	eng	-	d

008 (as above)

→ 245 00   Social development guide manual / ≠c organized by Kenya National Council of Social Service ; and financed by the Ford Foundation.

→ 246 0   ≠i Vol. 2 has title: ≠a Social development guide mannual

260   Nairobi, Kenya : ≠b The Council, ≠c 1985-

300   v. ; ≠c 30 cm.

362 1   Began publication in 1985.

500   Description based on: Vol. 2 (May 1985).

650 0   Social service ≠z Kenya.

650 0   Social work with the aged ≠z Kenya.

710 2   Kenya National Council of Social Service.

710 2   Ford Foundation.

DISCUSSION

- A special consideration is given to the transcription of incorrect titles proper for serials. According to LCRI 12.0F, do not transcribe inaccuracies as instructed in rule 1.0F. Instead, use the correct form as the title proper and make a note for the erroneous title, which should be treated as a variant title.

- In this example, there is evidence that the title proper in the piece being described has a misspelled word. Therefore, the correct form of the title proper is recorded in field 245, and the incorrect form of the title is recorded in field 246, with the source of the inaccuracy explicitly noted in subfield ≠i. In this record an added entry for the incorrect title has been judged not necessary, and, therefore, the first indicator in field 246 is coded value "0" so that no title added entry will be derived from the varying form of the title (LCRI 21.30J, p. 23).

C. Parallel Titles and Parallel Statements of Responsibility

According to AACR2R rule 1.1B8, "If the chief source of information bears titles in two or more languages or scripts, transcribe as the title proper the one in the language or script of the main written, spoken, or sung content of the item." If the language of the main portion of the item is not perfectly obvious or the text is equally divided between different languages, choose the first title given typographical prominence and treat the other titles as parallel titles.

If three or more titles in various languages appear on the chief source of information, record the first parallel title and any subsequent parallel title that is in English (1.1D2). Give each parallel title an access point. If parallel titles in other languages are from a source other than the chief source or from a later issue, give each title an access point with a note (e.g., Cover title in French: [French title]).

Parallel titles and parallel statements of responsibility may not always appear in a one-to-one relationship. In addition to a parallel title and a parallel statement of responsibility, there may appear on the item parallel other title information, a parallel publisher, parallel common title or parallel section title, parallel numeric system, parallel conference name, parallel supplement title, etc. In each case the cataloger must consult the provisions of the basic rule(s) applied to that particular area of description.

EXAMPLES

C1   Parallel title without corresponding parallel statement of responsibility
C2   Parallel title with corresponding parallel statement of responsibility
C3   Parallel statement of responsibility without corresponding parallel title
C4   Parallel title and parallel statement of responsibility under corporate name entry
C5   Added title page title and text in another language
C6   Title proper and parallel title with other title information corresponding to only one of them
C7   Parallel title with parallel other title information
C8   Parallel conference name and parallel title
C9   Parallel title with parallel numeric designation and parallel publisher
C10   More than one parallel publisher
C11   Parallel common title with parallel section number and section title
C12   Parallel common title with no parallel supplement title
C13   More than three parallel titles

C14   A change in order of title proper and parallel title
C15   A change in both title proper and parallel title
C16   Title in another language on later issues
C17   Parallel title lacking in a later issue
C18   Single word in title proper functioning also as a word in parallel title
C19   Choice of title proper in more than one language
C20   Parallel title varies

C1

PROBLEM CONSIDERED:

Parallel title without corresponding parallel statement of responsibility (1.1F10)

RULE(S) CONSULTED:

AACR2R: 1.1A1, 1.1D1, 1.1D2, 21.30J1
LCRI: 21.30J, p. 24

TAGGED DATA RECORD (based on OCLC #8771467)

LDR   *****cas_/22*****_a*4500

00-05	06	07-14	15-17	18	19	20	21	22-28	29	30-32	33	34	35-37	38	39
820914	d	19801986	gw	a	r			---lg--	0	///	b	0	eng	-	d

008

→ 041 0   engfreger
043   f------
→ 245 00   Jahrbuch für afrikanisches Recht = ≠b Annuaire de droit africain = Yearbook of African law / ≠c herausgegeben von Kurt Madlener im Auftrag der Gesellschaft für Afrikanisches Recht e. V.
→ 246 31   Annuaire de droit africain
→ 246 31   Yearbook of African law
260   Heidelberg : ≠b C.F. Müller Juristischer Verlag, ≠c 1981-1987.
300   6 v. ; ≠c 24 cm.
310   Annual
362 0   Bd. 1 (1980)-Bd. 6 (1985/86).
→ 546   English, French and German.
650   0   Law ≠z Africa.
700 1   Madlener, Kurt.
710 2   Gesellschaft für Afrikanisches Recht (Germany)

**Jahrbuch
für Afrikanisches Recht**
Annuaire de Droit Africain
Yearbook of African Law

**Band 1
(1980)**

**Herausgegeben von Kurt Madlener
im Auftrag der
Gesellschaft für Afrikanisches Recht e. V.**

**C.C. Müller Juristischer Verlag
Heidelberg**

Title page

DISCUSSION

- When recording parallel titles, transcribe the first parallel title and any subsequent parallel title given in English (1.1D2). When recording more than one parallel title, give the titles in order as they appear on the chief source (1.1D1). This item has three titles—one in German, one in French, and one in English. The German title is recorded as title proper; the French and English titles are recorded as parallel titles. Precede each parallel title with an equals (=) sign (1.1A1).
- When recording the statement of responsibility in only one language, give it at the end of all the parallel titles (1.1F10).
- Field 041 is used when more than one language is associated with the serial and when field 546 must also be input to include a note concerning the languages of the text. If there is no predominant language, as in this example, give the languages in alphabetic order.
- Title added entries are needed for the parallel titles (21.30J1; LCRI 21.30J, p. 24). Field 246 is input for parallel title added entries. First indicator value "3" is used to suppress the display of a note but generate an added entry. Second indicator value "1" is used to indicate that access is for a parallel title.

C2

PROBLEM CONSIDERED:
Parallel title with corresponding parallel statement of responsibility (1.1F10)

RULE(S) CONSULTED:
AACR2R: 1.1A1, 21.30J1

TAGGED DATA RECORD (based on OCLC #22226457)

00-05	06	07-14	15-17	18	19	20	21	22-28	29	30-32	33	34	35-37	38	39
008 900816	c	19899999	sa	u	u		p	-------	0	///	a	0	eng	-	d

→ 041 0   engafr
  043   f-sa---
  130 0   Newsletter (African Language Association of Southern Africa)
→ 245 00   Newsletter / ≠c African Language Association of Southern Africa =
           Nuusbrief / Afrikatale-Vereniging van Suider-Afrika.
→ 246 31   Nuusbrief
  260   Pretoria : ≠b ALASA, ≠c 1989-
  300   v. : ≠b ill. ; ≠c 21 cm.
  310   Irregular
  362 0   1989, no. 1-
  500   Title from cover.
→ 546   Chiefly in English; some text in Afrikaans.
  610 20   African Language Association of Southern Africa ≠x Periodicals.
  650 0   African languages ≠x Periodicals.
  650 0   Khoisan languages ≠x Periodicals.
  710 2   African Language Association of Southern Africa.
  780 00   ≠t Newsletter (African Language Association of Southern Africa. Khoisan
           Special Interest Group) ≠w (DLC)sn85021320 ≠w (OCoLC)12138413

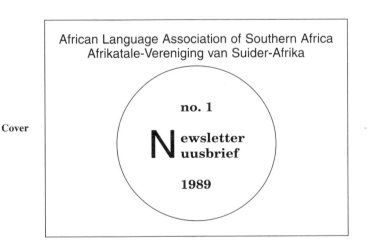

Cover

DISCUSSION

- In this example, a parallel title in Afrikaans with its corresponding parallel state-ment of responsibility appears on the item. In such a case, each statement of re-sponsibility should be transcribed along with its corresponding title proper in the title and statement of responsibility area (1.1F10). Precede each parallel title with an equals sign (1.1A1). An added entry is needed for the parallel title (21.30J1).
- A parallel title is normally input in subfield ≠b, with its statement of responsi-bility in subfield ≠c. However, in this example, subfield ≠b is not used for the parallel title. This is done because subfield ≠c has already been used for the

statement of responsibility transcribed preceding the parallel title, and a sub-field ≠c may not precede a subfield ≠b. Note also that the parallel statement of responsibility is not in a subfield ≠c, because subfield ≠c is not repeatable.

- Field 041 is used in addition to any language note given in field 546. First indicator value "0" indicates the work is not a translation. First indicator value "1" is used for an item that is a translation. Subfield ≠a is used for the language code of the text. These codes are assigned from the USMARC Code List for Languages, and the first language code in subfield ≠a should be the same as the language code in fixed field 008 character positions 35–37.

C3

PROBLEM CONSIDERED:

Parallel statement of responsibility without corresponding parallel title (1.1F11)

RULE(S) CONSULTED:

LCRI: 1.1F11

Cover	EUROPÄISCHES MEDIENINSTITUT THE EUROPEAN INSTITUTE FOR THE MEDIA INSTITUT EUROPÉEN DE LA COMMUNICATION **Overcoming language barriers in television:** **Dubbing and Subtitling for the European Audiences** **Georg-Michael Luyken** **Media Monograph No.13**

TAGGED DATA RECORD (based on OCLC #26252988)

	00-05	06	07-14	15-17	18	19	20	21	22-28	29	30-32	33	34	35-37	38	39
008	920724	c	19uu9999	enk		x		m	-------	0	///	a	0	eng	-	d

022	0267-4467
→ 043	e------
130 0	Media monograph (Manchester, England)
→ 245 00	Media monograph / ≠c The European Institute for the Media.
246 13	Media monographs series
260	Manchester : ≠b The Institute,
300	v. : ≠b ill. ; ≠c 21 cm.
310	Irregular
500	Each vol. has also a distinctive title.
500	Description based on: No. 13, published in 1991; title from cover.
650 0	Mass media.
650 0	Mass media ≠z Europe.
710 2	European Institute for the Media.

DISCUSSION

- If an item does not carry parallel titles but the statement of responsibility appears in more than one language, transcribe only the statement of responsibility in the language of the title proper (1.1F11). Do not transcribe any parallel statements of responsibility even though rule 1.1F11 does provide this option (LCRI 1.1F11).
- In this example, the statements of responsibility in German and French are not recorded. If there is no statement of responsibility corresponding to the language of the title proper, record the statement that appears first on the chief source.
- Field 043 is used when the assigned subject heading in field 6xx contains a geographic term or when the text of a work has a geographic orientation.

C4

PROBLEM CONSIDERED:

Parallel title and parallel statement of responsibility under corporate name entry (1.1F10)

RULE(S) CONSULTED:

AACR2R: 1.1A1, 1.1B8, 12.0B1, 21.1B2, 21.30J1, 24.18 type 1
LCRI: 21.30J, p. 24; 24.3A

TAGGED DATA RECORD (based on OCLC #28614189)

LDR   *****cas_/22*****Ma*4500

00-05	06	07-14	15-17	18	19	20	21	22-28	29	30-32	33	34	35-37	38	39
008	921021	d	198u198u	sa	a	r			------s	0	///	a	0	eng	-	d

041 0   engxho
043   f-sa---
→ 110 1   Ciskei (South Africa). ≠b Dept. of Finance.
→ 245 10   Intetho-nkqubo / ≠c Isebe Lezemali = Policy speech / Dept. of Finance.
→ 246 31   Policy speech
260   [Zwelitsha? : ≠b s. n.],
300   v. ; ≠c 15 x 21 cm.
310   Annual
500   Description based on: 1985 session; title from cover.
546   In English and Xhosa.
651   0   Ciskei (South Africa) ≠x Economic policy.
785 00   Ciskei (South Africa). Dept. of Finance and Economic Development. ≠t Policy speech by the Honourable Minister of Finance and Economic Development ≠w (OCoLC)28606592

```
                        ┌─────────────────────────────────┐
                        │                                 │
                        │       ISEBE LEZEMALI            │
                        │    DEPARTMENT OF FINANCE         │
                        │                                 │
                        │                                 │
                        │     INTETHO-NKQUBO              │
             Cover      │                                 │
                        │     POLICY SPEECH               │
                        │                                 │
                        │       1985 SESSION              │
                        │                                 │
                        │                                 │
                        └─────────────────────────────────┘
```

DISCUSSION

- Because this work is of an administrative nature and deals with the official policy statements of the corporate body itself, it is entered under the corporate name heading (21.1B2). The heading for the corporate body should be given in the form established in the LC authority record. If there is no authority record and the name appears on the item in more than one language, always choose the form in the official language of the corporate body (LCRI 24.3A). In this example, the corporate body, which is a government agency, is entered subordinately to the name of the government (24.18 type 1).

- According to rule 1.1B8, if the title appears in two or more languages, choose the one in the language of the written content of the item as the title proper and record the others as parallel titles. However, if the written content is also in two or more languages, with no language predominant, the title proper should be chosen according to the layout of the chief source of information. In this example, the Xhosa title is chosen as the title proper since no language is predominant in the content. A title added entry is needed for the English parallel title (21.30J1).

- This item has a parallel title and a parallel statement of responsibility. Each statement of responsibility is transcribed with its corresponding title proper (1.1F10), and an equals sign is used to separate the two sets (1.1A1). Because the place and publisher do not appear in the item being cataloged, that information is given in brackets (12.0B1).

- In field 245, subfield ≠b is not used for the parallel title because it cannot be used after subfield ≠c. Because subfield ≠c is not repeatable and it has already been used for the first statement of responsibility, it may not be used for the parallel statement of responsibility.

- In field 246, first indicator value "3" is used to suppress a note and to generate an added entry derived from the 245 field (LCRI 21.30J, p. 24). Second indicator value "1" is used to express the "nature" of the title (i.e., a parallel title).

- Field 041 is coded for the language of the content if the item contains more than one language or if the item is a translation. It is used in conjunction with fixed field 008 positions 35–37. (Whenever field 041 is used, the first language code in subfield ≠a should be the same as the code in field 008 positions 35–37.) In this example, field 041 is coded "engxho" for English and Xhosa in alphabetical order, because the text has no predominant language.

C5

PROBLEM CONSIDERED:

Added title page title and text in another language (1.1D4)

RULE(S) CONSULTED:

AACR2R: 12.7B2, 12.7B5, 21.1B2a

TAGGED DATA RECORD (based on OCLC #35302998)

LDR   *****cas_/22*****_a*4500

	00-05	06	07-14	15-17	18	19	20	21	22-28	29	30-32	33	34	35-37	38	39
008	960826	c	19989999	onc	a	r	4		------f	0	///	a	0	eng	-	d

022 0		1208-0470
041 0		engfre
043		n-cn---
110 1		Canada. ≠b Citizenship and Immigration Canada.
→ 245 10		Departmental outlook on program expenditures and priorities / ≠c Citizenship and Immigration Canada.
→ 246 15		Aperçu ministériel dépenses et priorités liées aux programmes
260		[Ottawa] : ≠b Citizenship and Immigration Canada, ≠c 1995-
300		v. ; ≠c 28 cm.
310		Annual
362 0		1995/96/1997/98-
→ 546		Text in English and French on inverted pages.
651 0		Canada ≠x Emigration and immigration ≠x Government policy.

Citizenship and Immigration
Canada

DEPARTMENTAL
OUTLOOK

on
Program
Expenditures
and
Priorities

1995-96 to 1997-98

Citoyenneté et Immigration
Canada

APERÇU
MINISTÉRIEL

Dépenses
et priorités
liées aux
programmes

1995-1996 à 1997-1998

Title page   Inverted title page

DISCUSSION

- In this example, the item is an administrative report of the government agency Citizenship and Immigration Canada. The catalog entry for this type of administrative publication is under the heading for the corporate body (21.1B2a).

- The text of this publication is in English and French on inverted pages, each with its own title page. If a title in another language appears outside the chief source of information, it should not be considered to be a parallel title and should therefore not be input in the title and statement of responsibility area (1.1D4). If it is determined that an access point is needed for such a title, the presence of the title may be recorded in a note, as in this example, where the French title appears in an "Added title page:" note (12.7B5), and a title added entry may then be input to provide access.
- The title added entry for the French title is input in field 246. First indicator value "1" is used to generate a note. Second indicator value "5" is used to display the constant "Added title page:" preceding the note.
- If the language(s) of a serial is(are) not apparent from the text of the title, input an explanatory note (12.7B2). In this example, such a language note is needed because the title proper is in English only, but the text is also in French.

C6

PROBLEM CONSIDERED:

Title proper and parallel title with other title information corresponding to only one of them (LCRI 1.1E5)

RULE(S) CONSULTED:
AACR2R: 1.1B8, 1.7B2

TAGGED DATA RECORD (based on OCLC #21878098)

LDR   *****cas_/22*****_a*4500

00-05	06	07-14	15-17	18	19	20	21	22-28	29	30-32	33	34	35-37	38	39
900618	c	19909999	ja	a	r		p	-------	0	///		0	eng	-	d

008

022	0915-0986
→ 041 0	engjpn
043	a-ja---
→ 245 00	Japan review : ≠b bulletin of the International Research Center for Japanese Studies = Nichibunken.
246 31	Nichibunken
260	Kyoto, Japan : ≠b The Center, ≠c 1990-
300	v. : ≠b ill. ; ≠c 26 cm.
310	Annual
362 0	No. 1 (1990)-
500	Title from cover.
→ 546	Chiefly in English; summaries and some text in Japanese.
580	Published also in Japanese.
651 0	Japan ≠x Civilization ≠x Periodicals.
710 2	Kokusai Nihon Bunka Kenkyū Sentā.
775 1	≠t Nichibunken ≠x 0915-0889 ≠w (DLC)91649004 ≠w (OCoLC)23098177

Cover

> NICHIBUNKEN
> # JAPAN REVIEW
>
> Bulletin of the International Research Center for Japanese Studies
> Number 1   1990

DISCUSSION

- In this example, the chief source of information, the cover, bears titles in two different languages. The English title is chosen as the title proper because the text is chiefly in English (1.1B8). The other title information, which appears only in English, is transcribed immediately following the English title to which it corresponds (LCRI 1.1E5).
- In field 245, subfield ≠b is not repeatable, and, therefore, because it already appears once following the title proper, it may not be used again for the parallel title.
- If more than one language is associated with the text, field 041 should be input. If the languages of the item are not apparent from the title data, give a Language Note (field 546), as appropriate (1.7B2).

C7

PROBLEM CONSIDERED:

Parallel title with parallel other title information (1.1E5).

RULE(S) CONSULTED:

AACR2R: 1.1B8
LCRI: 12.1E1

Caption

> # PLANTBESKERMINGSNUUS
> # PLANT PROTECTION NEWS
> _____
>
> BULLETIN VAN DIE NAVORSINGSINSTITUUT VIR PLANTBESKERMING
> BULLETIN OF THE PLANT PROTECTION RESEARCH INSTITUTE
>
> No. 1   September 1985
> No. 1   September 1985

TAGGED DATA RECORD (based on OCLC #14175860)

LDR   *****cas_/22*****_a*4500

00-05	06	07-14	15-17	18	19	20	21	22-28	29	30-32	33	34	35-37	38	39
860903	c	19859999	sa	q	r		p	------f	0	///	a	0	afr	-	d

008

022   1010-1640
041 0   afreng
043   f-sa----
→ 245 00   Plantbeskermingsnuus : ≠b bulletin van die Navorsingsinstituut vir
            Plantbeskerming = Plant protection news : bulletin of the Plant Protection
            Research Institute.
→ 246 31   Plant protection news
260   Pretoria : ≠b Departement van Landbou en Watervoorsiening, ≠c 1985-
300   v. : ≠b ill. ; ≠c 30 cm.
310   Quarterly
362 0   No. 1 (Sep. 1985)-
500   Title from caption.
546   Afrikaans and English.
650 0   Plants, Protection of ≠z South Africa ≠x Periodicals.
650 0   Plants ≠x Disease and pest resistance ≠x Periodicals.
650 0   Plants ≠x Wounds and injuries ≠x Periodicals.
710 2   Plant Protection Research Institute (South Africa)

DISCUSSION

- In serials cataloging, other title information can be transcribed in the title and statement of responsibility area only if it meets one of the three criteria given in LCRI 12.1E1. In this example, the other title information contains statements of responsibility in two languages, and it is necessary to transcribe both of them. One is transcribed following the title proper, and the other (parallel) one follows the parallel title (1.1E5).

- Note that, because the text of the publication in this example is in two languages, the Afrikaans title is chosen as the title proper, based on the layout of the chief source of information. Only when the text of the item is predominantly in one language may the title proper be chosen according to the language of the text (1.1B8).

- In field 245, subfield ≠b is not repeatable, and, therefore, it appears only once for the other title information following the title proper.

C8

PROBLEM CONSIDERED:
Parallel conference name and parallel title (21.1B2d)

RULE(S) CONSULTED:
AACR2R: 1.1B8, 1.1F10

TAGGED DATA RECORD (based on OCLC #34048709)

LDR   *****nas_/22*****Ia*4500

	00-05	06	07-14	15-17	18	19	20	21	22-28	29	30-32	33	34	35-37	38	39
008	960118	c	19uu9999	quc	a	r			-------	1	///	a	0	eng	-	d

041 0   eng ≠b fre

111 2   CACTS International Conference on Air Cushion Technology.

→ 245 00   Proceedings / ≠c CACTS Conference on Air Cushion Technology = Compte
             rendu / Conference de ... de la SCTCA sur la technologie du coussin d'air.

→ 246 31   Compte rendu

246 3   Proceedings ... CACTS Conference on Air Cushion Technology

260   Montreal, Quebec : ≠b The Conference,

300   v. : ≠b ill. ; ≠c 28 cm.

310   Annual

500   Description based on: 1994.

546   Introduction, abstracts and biographical notes also in French.

550   Sponsored by: Transportation Development Centre; and organized by:
        Canadian Air Cushion Technology.

650 0   Ground-cushion phenomenon ≠x Congresses.

650 0   Ground-effect machines ≠x Congresses.

710 2   Air Cushion Technology Society.

710 2   Transportation Development Centre (Canada)

780 00   Canadian Symposium on Air Cushion Technology. ≠t Air cushion technology
           ≠w (OCoLC)32476254

Title page

> Proceedings
> CACTS Conference on Air Cushion Technology
> 1994
>
> Compte rendu
> Conference de 1994 de la SCTCA sur la technologie du coussin d'air
>
> Sponsored by the Transportation Development Centre and
> Organized by the Canadia Air Cushion Technology.

DISCUSSION

- The conference in this example qualifies as a named conference, and it appears
  prominently in the item. Entry is therefore under the conference name (21.1B2d).
  The title for the item appears in both English and French, but only one of these
  can be used as the title proper. Since the text of this item is also in two languages, the English title is chosen as title proper, based on the layout of the
  chief source. Only when the text of the item is in a single language may the title proper be chosen according to the language of the text (1.1B8). The French
  parallel title and conference name are transcribed following the English title
  proper and statement of responsibility (1.1F10).

- Field 111 is used for a conference or meeting name. The first indicator is always set to value "2," since all conference headings are entered directly under
  their own name. The second indicator is always set to blank.

C9

PROBLEM CONSIDERED:

Parallel title with parallel numeric designation and parallel publisher (12.3B2)

RULE(S) CONSULTED:

AACR2R: 1.1F2, 1.4D2

TAGGED DATA RECORD (based on OCLC #31812548)

LDR   *****cas_/22*****_a*4500

00-05	06	07-14	15-17	18	19	20	21	22-28	29	30-32	33	34	35-37	38	39
950113	c	19949999	no	a	r			-------	0	///	b	0	eng	-	d

008

022	0803-6160
041 0	engnor
043	e-no---
→ 245 00	Norsk kunstårbok = ≠b Yearbook of Norwegian art.
246 31	Yearbook of Norwegian art
→ 260	Oslo, Norge : ≠b Universitetsforlaget, ≠c 1994-
300	v. : ≠b col. ill. ; ≠c 30 cm.
310	Annual
→ 362 0	Årg. 3 (1994)-
500	Title from cover.
546	English and Norwegian.
→ 550	Issued by: Kunstnernes informasjonskontor.
650 0	Art ≠z Norway ≠x Periodicals.
710 2	Kunstnernes informasjonskontor.
780 00	≠t Kunstårbok ≠w (DLC)95664054 ≠w (OCoLC)26037001

1994 **Norsk Kunstårbok** *Yearbook of Norwegian Art*	Norsk Kunstårbok 1994 Årgang 3 Yearbook of Norwegian Art 1994 Volume 3 Scandinavian University Press @Universitetsforlaget AS 1994 ISSN 0803-6160 ISBN 82-00-03946-3
Cover	Verso of cover

DISCUSSION

- In this example, the title appears in two languages on the cover, which serves as the chief source of information. The numeric designation, which also appears in two languages, but on the verso of the cover, is transcribed in field 362 in the language of the title proper (12.3B2).
- When transcribing the name of a publisher that appears in more than one language, use the form in the language of the title proper (1.4D2). The name of

the issuing body appears in a source other than the chief source, and it is given in an Issuing Body Note, field 550 (1.1F2).

C10

PROBLEM CONSIDERED:
More than one parallel publisher (1.4D2)

RULE(S) CONSULTED:
AACR2R: 21.30E1, 24.3A1, 24.4C3

<table>
<tr><td>Title page</td><td>

LATINOAMERICANISTAS EN EUROPA

1985

Registro bio-bibliográfico compilado por Jean Stroom

</td></tr>
</table>

<table>
<tr><td>Verso of title page</td><td>

A CEDLA Publication
Centrum voor Studie en Documentatie van Latijns Amerika
Centro de Estudios y Documentación Latinoamericanos
Centro de Estudio e Documentação Latino-Americanos
Centre for Latin American Research and Documentation

</td></tr>
</table>

TAGGED DATA RECORD (based on OCLC #14340193)

LDR   *****cas_/22*****_a*4500

00-05	06	07-14	15-17	18	19	20	21	22-28	29	30-32	33	34	35-37	38	39
861003	c	19739999	ne		x			---bhr-	0	///	b	0	spa	-	d

008 (as above)

```
         043      e------
→ 245 00          Latinoamericanistas en Europa.
→ 260             Amsterdam : ≠b Centro de Estudios y Documentación Latinoamericanos,
    300           v. ; ≠c 25 cm.
    310           Irregular
    362 1         Began with 1973 ed.
    500           Description based on: 1985.
    650  0        Latin Americanists ≠z Europe ≠x Bio-bibliography.
    650  0        Latin Americanists ≠z Europe ≠x Directories.
→ 710 2           Centrum voor Studie en Documentatie van Latijns Amerika (Amsterdam,
                  Netherlands)
    780 00        ≠t Directorio de latinoamericanistas europeos
```

DISCUSSION

- In this example, the title page, which is the chief source of information, has a title in Spanish only, without a parallel title. However, on the verso of the title page, the name of the publisher, which is also a responsible body, appears in more than one language. According to Library of Congress practice, do not input parallel publishers; always use the one that is in the language of the title proper (1.4D2). Therefore, in this example, the Spanish form of the publisher appears in the imprint area.

- An added entry should be made for the Center, which is the responsible body (21.30E1). Whenever the name of the corporate body appears in more than one language, use the form in the official language of the body (24.3A1). In this example, the official language of the corporate body is Dutch, and, therefore, the established form for the Center is in Dutch. The place name "Amsterdam, Netherlands" has been added to the name for the Center for better identification (24.4C3).

- Rule 24.3A1 gives further instructions on setting up corporate names in various situations involving multiple languages. In case of doubt, use the English, French, German, Spanish, or Russian form, in that order of preference. If these forms do not appear on the item, use the form in the language that comes first in English alphabetic order.

C11

PROBLEM CONSIDERED:

Parallel common title with parallel section number and section title (12.1D2)

RULE(S) CONSULTED:

AACR2R: 1.1B8, 12.1B5
LCRI: 21.30J, p. 24

Title page

> **PROVINCIAL STATISTICS**
> **PROVINSIALE STATISTIEKE**
> **1994**
> **PART / DEEL 10**
> **REPUBLIC OF SOUTH AFRICA / REPUBLIEK VAN SUID-AFRIKA**
>
> CSS REPORT
> SSD-VERSLAG
>
> Central Statistical Service   Sentrale Statistiekdiens
> Pretoria   Pretoria
> 1994   1994

TAGGED DATA RECORD (based on OCLC #32927659)

LDR   *****cas_/22*****_a*4500

00-05	06	07-14	15-17	18	19	20	21	22-28	29	30-32	33	34	35-37	38	39
950805	c	19949999	sa	a	r			--s---f	0	///	a	0	afr	-	d

008

041 0   afreng

043   f-sa---

→ 245 00   Provincial statistics. ≠n Part 10, ≠p Republic of South Africa = ≠b Provinsiale statistieke. Deel 10, Republiek van Suid-Afrika.

→ 246 31   Provinsiale statistieke. ≠n Deel 10, ≠p Republiek van Suid-Afrika

260   Pretoria : ≠b Central Statistical Service, ≠c 1994-

300   v. : ≠b ill., maps ; ≠c 21 x 30 cm.

310   Annual

362 0   1994-

490 1   CSS report = ≠a SSD-verslag

546   Afrikaans and English.

651   0   South Africa ≠x Statistics.

710 1   South Africa. ≠b Central Statistical Services.

830   0   Verslag (Series) (South Africa. Central Statistical Services)

DISCUSSION

- This item has a parallel common title, a parallel section number, and a parallel section title. Since the text appears in both English and Afrikaans, the criterion for choosing between the English and Afrikaans titles as title proper is based on the layout of the chief source (1.1B8). Thus, the English title, which appears first, is chosen as the title proper. It is followed by the section number, preceded by a period, and then by the section title, preceded by a comma (12.1B5). Record the full title proper, which consists of the common title, the section number, and the section title, followed by an equals sign and the parallel common title in Afrikaans, with its corresponding section number and section title (12.1D2).

- An added entry should be made for the Afrikaans common title and its corresponding section number and section title (LCRI 21.30J, p. 24). When judged to be needed for access, added entries for the section title and the parallel section title may also be made.

- In field 245, subfield ≠n is used for the section number. It is preceded by a period. Subfield ≠p is used for the section or supplement title. It is preceded by a period when the section or supplement follows the common title. It is preceded by a comma if it follows subfield ≠n (a section number or part designation). Subfield ≠n and subfield ≠p are not repeated for the section number and section title, respectively, as part of the parallel title.

C12

PROBLEM CONSIDERED:

Parallel common title with no parallel supplement title (12.1D2)

RULE(S) CONSULTED:

AACR2R: 1.1B8
LCRI: 12.7B5

TAGGED DATA RECORD (based on OCLC #13649849)

LDR   *****cas_/22*****_a*4500

	00-05	06	07-14	15-17	18	19	20	21	22-28	29	30-32	33	34	35-37	38	39
008	860252	c	19uu9999	gw	u	u			-------	0	///	a	0	eng	-	d

→ 245 00 International journal of rehabilitation research. ≠p Supplement = ≠b Internationale Zeitschrift für Rehabilitationsforschung = Revue internationale de recherches en réadaptation.

246 31 Internationale Zeitschrift für Rehabilitationsforschung

246 31 Revue internationale de recherches en réadaptation

260 Rheinstetten : ≠b Schindele,

300 v. ; ≠c 24-26 cm.

500 Description based on: No. 3 (1983); title from cover.

→ 500 No. 4- lack German and French title.

650 0 Rehabilitation.

710 2 Rehabilitation International.

Cover	Internationale Zeitschrift für Rehabilitationsforschung Revue internationale de recherches en réadaptation **INTERNATIONAL JOURNAL OF REHABILITATION RESEARCH** **Supplement No. 3 1983**

DISCUSSION

- In this example, there is more than one parallel common title, but there is only one corresponding section title in the chief source of the item described. Since the text is solely in English, the English title is chosen as the title proper, and it appears with its corresponding section title "Supplement" (1.1B8; 12.1D2).

- Although French and German parallel titles appear in the chief source of the item described, both of those titles are dropped in the chief source of the next issue. Therefore, a General Note must be added to inform the user that, beginning with a certain issue, the German and French titles are lacking (LCRI 12.7B5).

C13

PROBLEM CONSIDERED:

More than three parallel titles (1.1D2)

RULE(S) CONSULTED:

AACR2R: 1.1B8, 1.1D1
LCRI: 12.7B5, 21.2C; 21.30J, p. 24

<table>
<tr><td>

ES
eurostat

UDENRIGSHANDEL
Statistisk årbog
AUSSENHANDEL
Statistisches Jahrbuch
ĒΞΩTEPIKO EMΠOPIO
Στατιστικη επετηριδα
EXTERNAL TRADE
Statistical yearbook
COMMERCE EXTÉRIEUR
Annuaire statistique
COMMERCIO ESTERO
Annuario statistico
BUITENLANDSE HANDEL
Statistisch jaarboek
COMÉRCIO EXTERNO
Anuário estatístico

1985

</td><td>

ES
eurostat

COMERCIO EXTERIOR
Anuario estadístico
UDENRIGSHANDEL
Statistisk årbog
AUSSENHANDEL
Statistisches Jahrbuch
ĒΞΩTEPIKO EMΠOPIO
Στατιστικη επετηριδα
EXTERNAL TRADE
Statistical yearbook
COMMERCE EXTÉRIEUR
Annuaire statistique
COMMERCIO ESTERO
Annuario statistico
BUITENLANDSE HANDEL
Statistisch jaarboek
COMÉRCIO EXTERNO
Anuário estatístico

1987

Theme Thème   6
Foreign trade
Commerce extérieur
Series Série   A
Yearbooks
Annuaires

</td></tr>
<tr><td align="center">**Cover**</td><td align="center">**Cover of a later issue**</td></tr>
</table>

TAGGED DATA RECORD (based on OCLC #18276155)

LDR   *****cas_/22*****_a*4500

00-05	06	07-14	15-17	18	19	20	21	22-28	29	30-32	33	34	35-37	38	39
860422	d	19uu1991	lu	a	r			------i	0	///	b	0	eng	-	d

008

041 0   engfre ≠b dandutgergreita

043   e------

→ 245 00   Udenrigshandel. ≠p Statistisk årbog = ≠b Aussenhandel. Statistisches Jahrbuch = External trade. Statistical yearbook.

→ 246 31   Aussenhandel. ≠p Statistisches Jahrbuch

→ 246 31   External trade. ≠p Statistical yearbook

→ 246 1   ≠i Spanish title added 1987-1991: ≠a Comercio exterior. ≠p Anuario estadístico

260   Luxembourg : ≠b De Europæiske fællesskabers statistiske kontor,

300   v. : ≠b ill. ; ≠c 30 cm.

362 1   -1991.

→ 490 1   1986-1991: Theme 6, Foreign trade. Series A, Yearbooks = ≠a Thème 6, Commerce extérieur. Série A, Annuaires

500   Description based on: 1985; title from cover.

546   Text in English and French; titles and introductory material in Danish, Dutch, German, Greek, Italian, Portuguese, and Spanish.

580   Companion publication to: Månedlige bulletin over udenrigshandelen.

651 0   European Economic Community countries ≠x Commerce ≠x Statistics.

651 0   European Economic Community countries ≠x Commerce.

710 2   Statistical Office of the European Communities.

785 00   ≠t Udenrigshandelen ≠w (DLC)76649592 ≠w (OCoLC)3960601

787   ≠t Månedlige bulletin over udenrigshandelen ≠w (DLC)76649592 ≠w (OCoLC)3960601

→ 830 0   Theme 6—Foreign trade. ≠n Series A, ≠p Yearbooks.

DISCUSSION

- In this example, the cover is the chief source of information. The cataloging description was based on the 1985 issue, which listed the Dutch title first in the layout. The Dutch title is chosen as title proper because there is no one language predominant in the text (1.1B8). In preparing a second-level description for items having parallel titles, record the first parallel title according to the layout in the chief source (1.1D1). Record any subsequent parallel title that is in English. If there is no title in English, record as a second parallel title a title that is in French, German, Spanish, Latin, etc., in that order of preference (1.1D2). Therefore, in this example, where the item has more than three parallel titles, the two parallel titles to be recorded are those in German and English.

- Added entries for the parallel titles from the title and statement of responsibility area are recorded in field 246, with first indicator value "3" and second indicator value "1" (LCRI 21.30J, p. 24).

- In 1987, a Spanish title appeared at the head of the Dutch title on the cover. Note, however, that such a change in the lineup of multilanguage titles does not constitute a title change (LCRI 21.2C). Instead, a note on the addition of the Spanish title is recorded in field 246, subfield ≠i (LCRI 12.7B5, 21.30J, p.

24). The second indicator value is blank, since the source of the title added entry is not one of those represented by values "0–8."

- Because a series statement appeared on the later issues, give the chronological period during which the item was issued in the series (i.e., 1986–1991) at the beginning of the series statement in a 490 field with first indicator value "1." Record the AACR2R form of the series added entry in an 830 field. The series added entry in this item consists of a series ("Theme 6—Foreign trade") in subfield ≠a, a series designation ("Series A") in subfield ≠n, and a subseries ("Yearbooks") in subfield ≠p.

- The series statement in this example also contains a parallel title. Series parallel titles may be transcribed in 490 fields but should not be treated as series added entries (in 830 fields).

C14

PROBLEM CONSIDERED:

A change in order of title proper and parallel title (LCRI 12.7B5)

RULE(S) CONSULTED:

AACR2R: 1.1B8

TAGGED DATA RECORD (based on OCLC #10472085)

LDR   *****cas_/22*****_a*4500

00-05	06	07-14	15-17	18	19	20	21	22-28	29	30-32	33	34	35-37	38	39
840229	c	19839999	fr	f	r	z	p	-------	0	///	b	0	eng	-	d

008

022   0294-0442
041 0   engfre
043   e--k--- ≠a n-us---
→ 245 04 Les Cahiers de la nouvelle = ≠b Journal of the short story in English.
246 31   Journal of the short story in English
260   Angers : ≠b Presses de l'Université d'Angers, ≠c 1983-
300   v. ; ≠c 21-24 cm.
310   Semiannual
362 0   No. 1 (mars 1983)-
→ 500   Order of titles varies.
546   English or French.
550   Issued by: Université d'Angers, Centre d'études et de recherches sur la nouvelle en langue anglaise.
650 0   Short stories, American ≠x History and criticism ≠x Periodicals.
650 0   Short stories, English ≠x History and criticism ≠x Periodicals.
710 2   Université d'Angers. ≠b Centre d'études et de recherches sur la nouvelle en langue anglaise.

LES CAHIERS DE LA NOUVELLE *Journal of the Short Story in English* Nº 1 MARS 1983 PRESSES DE L'UNIVERSITÉ D'ANGERS	**JOURNAL OF THE SHORT STORY IN ENGLISH** *Les Cahiers de la Nouvelle* Nº 4 PRINTEMPS 1985 PRESSES DE L'UNIVERSITÉ D'ANGERS
Title page	**Title page of a later issue**

DISCUSSION

- The text of the item in this example is in English and French and neither language predominates over the other. Thus, the French title, "Les cahiers de la nouvelle," is chosen as the title proper of the serial based on the layout of the title page; the English title "Journal of the short story in English" is transcribed as the parallel title (1.1B8).
- It is common over time for parallel titles to be added or removed, or for them to appear in a different order on later issues. However, such changes do not warrant the creation of a new record; instead, notes should be input to explain the changes (LCRI 12.7B5). In this example, a change in the order of the two titles occurred in 1985, when the English title began to appear ahead of the French title. No new record was created, and the change in title order was simply acknowledged in a 500 General Note.

C15

PROBLEM CONSIDERED:

A change in both title proper and parallel title (21.2A1)

RULE(S) CONSULTED:

AACR2R: 12.7B7b

Title page

Information for Individuals & Organizations
Renseignements pour les particuliers et les organisations

1995

Tax Statistics on Individuals	Statistiques sur l'impôt des particuliers
1993 Tax Year	Année d'imposition 1993

TAGGED DATA RECORD (based on OCLC #34437798)

LDR   *****cas_/22*****_a*4500

00-05	06	07-14	15-17	18	19	20	21	22-28	29	30-32	33	34	35-37	38	39
008 960227	c	19959999	onc	a	r	4		--s---f	0	///	a	0	eng	-	d

022 0	1209-1103
041 0	engfre
043	n-cn---
→ 245 00	Tax statistics on individuals = ≠b Statistiques sur l'impôt des particuliers.
246 31	Statistiques sur l'impôt des particuliers
260	Ottawa : ≠b Revenue Canada, ≠c 1995-
300	v. ; ≠c 28 cm.
310	Annual
362 0	1995 ed.-
500	At head of title: Information for individuals & organizations. Renseignements pour les particuliers et les organisations.
515	Vols. for 1995- cover statistics for 1993-
515	Vol. for 1995 called also 50th ed.
546	Text in English and French.
550	Prepared by: Personal Taxation Statistics Section.
→ 580	Continues in part: Taxation statistics. Statistique fiscale.
650 0	Income tax ≠z Canada ≠x Statistics.
650 0	Tax returns ≠z Canada ≠x Statistics.
710 1	Canada. ≠b Revenue Canada.
710 1	Canada. ≠b Personal Taxation Statistics Section.
→ 780 11	≠t Taxation statistics ≠x 0700-1665 ≠w (DLC)76642766 ≠w (OCoLC)1552861

DISCUSSION

- When any word or words are added, changed, or deleted within the first five words of the title proper (within the first six words if the title begins with an initial article), consider the title to have changed (21.2A1). A separate record should be input with a linking note indicating that the new record continues an earlier title (12.7B7b). In this example, the first word of the title proper has changed, and the change is also reflected in the parallel title; therefore, a new record is created. Because the earlier title also carries a parallel title, it is useful to include a linking note that includes the parallel title.
- Field 780 is input for a linking note to the preceding entry. First indicator value "1" is used when there is a Linking Entry Complexity Note (field 580). When a note is to be generated from linking field 780, the first indicator is set to value "0."

C16

PROBLEM CONSIDERED:

Title in another language on later issues (LCRI 21.2C)

RULE(S) CONSULTED:

AACR2R: 21.30J1
LCRI: 12.7B5; 21.30J, p. 25

TAGGED DATA RECORD (based on OCLC #12229774)

LDR   *****cas_/22*****_a*4500

	00-05	06	07-14	15-17	18	19	20	21	22-28	29	30-32	33	34	35-37	38	39
008	850703	c	19uu9999	fr	b	x			-------	0	///	b	0	fre	-	d

→ 245 00   Cahiers bibliographiques de chimie organométallique.
→ 246 1   ≠i Vols. for <1985-> have title in English: ≠a Bibliographic notebooks for organometallic chemistry
  260   Rennes : ≠b Université de Rennes,
  300   v. ; ≠c 21 cm.
  310   Eight issues yearly
  500   Description based on: 1984, no. 1; title from cover.
  650   0 Organometallic compounds.
  710 2   Université de Rennes.

CAHIERS Bibliographiques de CHIMIE ORGANOMÉTALLIQUE 1984 No. 1	CAHIERS Bibliographiques de CHIMIE ORGANOMÉTALLIQUE Bibliographic NOTEBOOKS for ORGANOMETALLIC CHEMISTRY 1985 No. 1
Cover	**Cover of a later issue**

DISCUSSION

- In this example, the French title was the sole title on the first issue (i.e., 1984, no. 1) available for cataloging. In the following year, an English title was added to the chief source of information (i.e., the cover). According to LCRI 21.2C, whenever a parallel title is added or the order of titles has changed, do not consider the title proper to have changed, as long as the title proper of earlier issues continues to appear on the chief source of later issues. Therefore, no separate record should be created for this serial. However, information concerning the new addition may be recorded in a note (LCRI 12.7B5), and an added entry is needed for the English title in order to provide an access point for the user (21.30J1).

- Field 245 is input for the French title only, since it has been the title proper for many years. The first indicator is coded with value "0," since no added entry is needed. The second indicator value indicates the number of nonfiling characters. Because the title does not begin with an article, the number of nonfiling characters is zero.

- Field 246 is input to provide access for the English title. First indicator value "1" is used to generate an added entry and a note indicating the source of the title (the text is input in field 246, subfield ≠i) (LCRI 21.30J, p. 25). The second indicator value is blank, since the source of the title added entry is not one of those represented by values "0–8."

C17

PROBLEM CONSIDERED:

Parallel title lacking in a later issue (LCRI 12.7B5)

RULE(S) CONSULTED:

AACR2R: 1.1B8

TAGGED DATA RECORD (based on OCLC#2243542)

LDR   *****cas_/22*****_a*4500

00-05	06	07-14	15-17	18	19	20	21	22-28	29	30-32	33	34	35-37	38	39
760106	c	19749999	au		x	0	p	-------	0	///	a	0	eng	-	d

008

022   0378-2697

041 0   engfreger

→ 245 00 Plant systematics and evolution = ≠b Entwicklungsgeschichte und Systematik der Pflanzen.

→ 246 31 Entwicklungsgeschichte und Systematik der Pflanzen

260   Wien ; ≠a New York : ≠b Springer-Verlag, ≠c 1974-

300   v. : ≠b ill. ; ≠c 23-29 cm.

310   Irregular

362 0   Vol. 123, no. 1 (1974)-

500   Title from cover.

→ 500   Vols. for 1987- lack German title.

→ 546   Text in English, French or German, 1974-86; in English only, 1987-

650 0 Botany ≠x Morphology ≠x Periodicals.

650 0 Plants ≠x Evolution ≠x Periodicals.

770 0   ≠t Plant systematics and evolution. Supplementum ≠x 0172-6668 ≠w (DLC)sf91038000 ≠w (OCoLC)4148638

780 00 ≠t Österreichische botanische Zeitschrift ≠x 0029-8948 ≠w (OCoLC)7915698

PLANT SYSTEMATICS AND EVOLUTION

ENTWICKLUNGSGESCHICHTE
UND SYSTEMATIK DER PFLANZEN

Vol. 123 Number 1 1974
Continuatinzo of Osterreichische Botanische Zeitschrift

Springer-Verlag Wien New York

Cover

PLANT SYSTEMATICS AND EVOLUTION

Vol. 155 Number 1-4 1987

**Springer-Verlag
Wien New York**

Cover of a later issue

DISCUSSION

- This is the opposite of example C16. The serial began publication with both English and German titles appearing on the cover, which serves as the chief source of information. Because there is no predominant language, the English title "Plant systematics and evolution" is chosen as the title proper on the basis of the layout of the chief source, and the German title "Entwicklungsgeschichte und Systematik der Pflanzen" is treated as the parallel title (1.1B8). However, since 1987 the German title has been dropped from the cover and only papers written in English have been accepted for publication. In spite of this change on the chief source (the cover), no new catalog record is needed, because the original record was based on the chief source of the first piece. The fact that parallel titles have been removed from the chief source of issues of a serial is to be recorded in a note if this information is considered to be important (LCRI 12.7B5).

- In the 500 General Note, to avoid ambiguity, refer to the title by the name of the language rather than by the term "parallel title."

C18

PROBLEM CONSIDERED:

Single word in title proper functioning also as a word in parallel title (1.1B5)

RULE(S) CONSULTED:

AACR2R: 1.1B8
LCRI: 21.30J, p. 8

Cover

> **PARKS & RECREATION**
>
> **PARCS & LOISIRS**
>
> Premier Issue January/February - janvier/février 1996

Contents page

> **JANUARY/FEBRUARY - JANVIER/FÉVRIER 1996**
> **Contents**
> **table des matieres**
>
> PARKS & RECREATION CANADA
> is published six times annually.
> PARCS & LOISIRS CANADA
> est publié six fois l'an.

TAGGED DATA RECORD (based on OCLC #34336666)

LDR   *****cas_/22*****Ma*4500

00-05	06	07-14	15-17	18	19	20	21	22-28	29	30-32	33	34	35-37	38	39
960304	c	19969999	onc	b	r		p	-------	0	///	a	0	eng	-	d

008

041 0   engfre

→ 245 00   Parks & recreation Canada = ≠b Parcs & loisirs Canada.

→ 246 3   Parks and recreation Canada

→ 246 31   Parcs & loisirs Canada

260 0   Gloucester, Ont. : ≠b Canadian Parks/Recreation Association, ≠c 1996-

300   v. : ≠b ill. ; ≠c 28 cm.

310   Bimonthly

362 0   Jan./Feb. 1996-

500   Title from cover.

515   Issue for Jan./Feb. 1996 called also premier issue.

546   English and French.

650   0   Recreation ≠z Canada ≠x Periodicals.

650   0   Leisure ≠z Canada ≠x Periodicals.

710 2   Canadian Parks/Recreation Association.

780 00   ≠t Recreation Canada ≠x0031-2231 ≠w (DLC)ce76300295 ≠w (OCoLC)2130935

DISCUSSION

- In this example, the cover is the chief source of information. The English title is the title proper since the language of the publication is English (1.1B8). The French title is recorded as a parallel title.
- If a word or letter appears only once in the chief source but is meant to be read more than once, repeat it without the use of square brackets (1.1B5). In this example, "Canada" is such a word, and, therefore, it is repeatedly transcribed in the title and statement of responsibility area without being enclosed in brackets.
- If an ampersand or other symbol appears as one of the first five words of a title proper, make an added entry for the spelled-out form in the language of the title (LCRI 21.30J, p. 8). Field 246 is used in such situations. First indicator value "3" is used to suppress a note; the second indicator value is blank for an alternate form of title. Second indicator value "1" is used for a parallel title.

C19

PROBLEM CONSIDERED:

Choice of title proper in more than one language (1.1B8)

RULE(S) CONSULTED:

LCRI: 21.30J, p. 24

TAGGED DATA RECORD (based on OCLC #27047096)

LDR   *****cas_/22*****Ia*4500

00-05	06	07-14	15-17	18	19	20	21	22-28	29	30-32	33	34	35-37	38	39

→ 008 | 921201 | c | 19939999 | ilu | q | r | l | p | ------- | 0 | /// | a | 0 | eng | - | d |

```
       022 0   1066-7814
→ 041 0   engfre
→ 245 00   Canadian journal of applied physiology = ≠b Revue canadienne de
           physiologie appliquée.
→ 246 31   Revue canadienne de physiologie appliquée
       260 0   Champaign, IL: ≠b Human Kinetics Publishers, ≠c 1993-
       300     v. : ≠b ill. ; ≠c 23 cm.
       310     Quarterly
       362 0   Vol. 18, no. 1 (Mar. 1993)-
       500     Title from cover.
→ 546     Articles chiefly in English with some in French; summaries in both languages.
       550     Issued by: Canadian Society for Exercise Physiology.
       650  0   Exercise ≠x Physiological aspects ≠x Periodicals.
       650  0   Human physiology ≠x Periodicals.
       650  0   Sports ≠x Physiological aspects ≠x Periodicals.
       710 2   Canadian Society for Exercise Physiology.
       780 00   ≠t Canadian journal of sport sciences ≠x 0833-1235 ≠w (DLC)92662330 ≠w
                (OCoLC)15743331
```

Cover

Revue Canadienne de Physiologie Appliquée

Canadian Journal of Applied Physiology

Volume 18, numéro 1, Mars 1993   Volume 18, Number 1, March 1993

Canadian Journal of Applied Physiology / Revue Canadienne de Physiologie Appliquée / 18:1 1993

Spine title

Verso of cover

——————— **CJAP/RCPA** ———————

The Canadian Journal of Applied Physiology/Revue Canadienne de Physiologie Appliquée (ISSN 1066-7814) is published six times a year in . . .

DISCUSSION

- In this example, the cover, which serves as the chief source, has parallel titles in English and French. One might easily be inclined to choose the French title "Revue canadienne de physiologie appliquée," which appears first (on the left), as the title proper of the serial. However, if the text is predominantly in one language, the title in that language should be chosen as the title proper of the serial (1.1B8). Therefore, because the text of this serial is mainly in English, the English title "Canadian journal of applied physiology" should be transcribed as the title proper in spite of the layout on the cover. The French title is recorded as the parallel title (1.1B8). An added entry is provided for the parallel title from a 246 derived field (LCRI 21.30J, p. 24).

- Field 546 is a Language Note containing information concerning the languages of the text. It may be used in conjunction with the language information coded in field 041 if the item is multilingual or a translation, or has accompanying material, summaries, or tables of contents in another language. If field 041 is used, the first language code must be the same as the language code input in fixed field 008 positions 35–37, which is coded for the language of the title or the predominant language for a multilingual item.

C20

PROBLEM CONSIDERED:

Parallel title varies (LCRI 12.7B5)

RULE(S) CONSULTED:

AACR2R: 1.1B8
LCRI: 21.30J, p. 24, p. 25

Cover

Volume 12/Number 1	Volume 12/Numéro 1
Canadian Journal of Sport Sciences	**Journal canadien des sciences du sport**
March 1987	Mars 1987

Cover of a later issue

Volume 16 Number 1 March 1991

**Canadian Journal of
SPORT
SCIENCES**

**Revue Canadienne des
SCIENCES
du SPORT**

Volume 16 Numéro 1, Mars 1991

TAGGED DATA RECORD (based on OCLC #15743331)

LDR   *****cas_/22*****_a*4500

00-05	06	07-14	15-17	18	19	20	21	22-28	29	30-32	33	34	35-37	38	39
870528	d	19871992	ilu	q	r	l	p	-------	0	///	a	0	eng	-	d

008

022 0	0833-1235
041	engfre
→ 245 00	Canadian journal of sport sciences = ≠b Journal canadien des sciences du sport.
→ 246 31	Journal canadien des sciences du sport
→ 246 1	≠i Vols. for 1991-1992 have French title: ≠a Revue canadienne des sciences du sport
260	[Downsview, Ont.] : ≠b University of Toronto Press, Journal Dept., ≠c 1987-1992.
300	6 v. : ≠b ill. ; ≠c 28 cm.
310	Quarterly
362 0	Vol. 12, no. 1 (Mar. 1987)-v. 17, no. 4 (Dec. 1992).
500	Title from cover.
500	Published: Champaign, IL : Human Kinetics Publishers, 1991-1992.
500	Some issues include proceedings of annual meeting of Canadian Association of Sports Sciences.
→ 546	Articles chiefly in English with some in French; summaries in both languages.
550	Sponsored by: the Canadian Academy of Sports Medicine and other Canadian organizations.
650 0	Sports sciences ≠x Periodicals.
650 0	Sports ≠x Physiological aspects ≠x Periodicals.
710 2	Canadian Academy of Sports Medicine.
710 2	Canadian Association of Sports Sciences.
780 00	≠t Canadian journal of applied sport sciences ≠x 0700-3978 ≠w (DLC)cn77031335 ≠w (OCoLC)3264616
785 00	≠t Canadian journal of applied physiology ≠x 1066-7814 ≠w (DLC)93647799 ≠w (OCoLC)27047096

DISCUSSION

- Unlike changes to titles proper, changes affecting parallel titles do not constitute title changes, and, therefore, do not require the creation of new records (LCRI 12.7B5). Such changes are noted in the record, and, in most cases, title added entries for new parallel titles are made, as appropriate (LCRI 21.30J, p. 24).

- In this example, the English title "Canadian journal of sport sciences" is chosen as the title proper of the serial based on the language of the text (1.1B8). In 1991 the French parallel title changed from "Journal canadien des sciences du sport" to "Revue canadienne des sciences du sport." Although this change does not require the creation of a new record, it is nevertheless considered to be important; thus a note about the new parallel title is added to the bibliographic description (LCRI 12.7B5).

- Field 246 is input to provide access to the new parallel title. First indicator value "1" is used to generate an added entry, and a note indicating the source or type of the title text is input in field 246, subfield ≠i (LCRI 21.30J, p. 25). The second indicator value is blank.

D. Other Title Information

AACR2R defines other title information as: "a title borne by an item other than the title proper or parallel or series title(s); also any phrase appearing in conjunction with the title proper, etc., indicative of the character, contents, etc., of the item or the motives for, or occasion of, its production or publication. The term includes subtitles, avant-titres, etc., but does not include variations on the title proper (e.g., spine titles, sleeve titles, etc.)" (AACR2R p. 620, Appendix D).

The Library of Congress has decided in general to omit all other title information in the transcription of serial entries, although there are three exceptions to this (see LCRI guidelines below). The reason for this decision lies in the fact that other title information on many serials is lengthy, and there is always the possibility of changes in later issues. Therefore, a certain amount of recataloging can be avoided if this element is not recorded in the title area. (It may, however, be recorded in a note.)

LCRI 12.1E1 lists the following three situations when other title information should be included in a bibliographic record:

1. Record other title information when a statement of responsibility is an integral part of that other title information.
2. When a serial carries both the full form of a title and an acronym or initialism, record as other title information whichever form is not chosen as the title proper.
3. If necessary for explanatory purposes, other title information supplied by the cataloger may be included in a record.

In addition, other title information may be given whenever the cataloger determines that this information is useful to the description of the serial (LCRI 12.1E1). For example, titles other than the title proper (such as an alternative title without a connecting "or" or a title in the "At head of title" note) may be treated as other title information (CCM 6.3.3b).

EXAMPLES

D1   Other title information includes a statement of responsibility
D2   Full form of title proper as other title information
D3   Initialism of title proper as other title information
D4   Other title information supplied by cataloger for work entered under title
D5   More than one other title information
D6   Other title information in a note

D7	Common title and section title with other title information
D8	Parallel other title information
D9	A change in other title information
D10	Phrase at head of title as other title information
D11	Other title information as part of the title proper
D12	Alternative title without the preceding word "or" as other title information

D1

PROBLEM CONSIDERED:

Other title information includes a statement of responsibility (1.lE4)

RULE(S) CONSULTED:

AACR2R: 21.29B, 21.29C
LCRI: 12.1E1, 21.30J

TAGGED DATA RECORD (based on OCLC #32274806)

LDR   *****cas_/22*****_a*4500

00-05	06	07-14	15-17	18	19	20	21	22-28	29	30-32	33	34	35-37	38	39
950407	c	19959999	dcu	b	x	1	p	-------	0	///	a	0	eng	-	d

008

022 0	1084-4678 ≠y 0892-399X
→ 245 00	I-ways : ≠b digest of the Global Information Infrastructure Commission.
→ 246 3	I ways
260	Washington, D.C. : ≠b Transnational Data Reporting Service, ≠c 1995-
300	v. : ≠b ill. ; ≠c 28 cm.
310	Bimonthly
362 0	[Vol. 18, no. 1] (Jan./Feb. 1995)-
500	Title from cover.
515	First issue lacks vol. numbering and is called "Inaugural edition."
515	Some issues, published in combined form, have alternate designation; i.e., mid-year, year-end.
650 0	Data protection ≠x International cooperation ≠x Periodicals.
650 0	Computer networks ≠x International cooperation ≠x Periodicals.
650 0	Electronic data processing ≠x Government policy ≠x Periodicals.
650 0	Computers ≠x Access control ≠x International cooperation ≠x Periodicals.
→ 710 2	Global Information Infrastructure Commission.
710 2	Transnational Data Reporting Service.
780 00	≠t Transnational data and communications report ≠x 0892-399X ≠w (DLC)86647833 ≠w (OCoLC)13296400

```
┌─────────────────────────────────────────────────────────────┐
│                                      January/February 1995    │
│                                                               │
│  I-WAYS                                                       │
│  Digest of the Global Information Infrastructure Commission   │
│                                                               │
│  Inaugural Edition                                            │
│                                                               │
└─────────────────────────────────────────────────────────────┘
```

Cover of first issue

```
┌─────────────────────────────────────────────────────────────┐
│                            Vol. 18, no. 2 March/April 1995    │
│                                                               │
│  I-WAYS                                                       │
│  Digest of the Global Information Infrastructure Commission   │
│                                                               │
│                                                               │
└─────────────────────────────────────────────────────────────┘
```

Cover of second issue

DISCUSSION

- In serials cataloging, other title information can be transcribed in the title and statement of responsibility area only if it meets one of the three criteria described in LCRI 12.1E1. In this example, "Digest of . . ." is recorded as other title information in the title and statement of responsibility area, and not simply as a note, because it includes a statement of responsibility, which is one of the criteria required for transcription in that area (1.1E4). A title added entry should be made so that the other title information can be accessed (21.29C), and there should also be an added entry for the responsible body (21.29B).

- In this example, the first 246 field provides access to the title proper as two words, since hyphenated words often may be treated as two words in retrieval or filing, depending on the retrieval capability or filing rules used in local catalogs. First indicator value "3" is used so that the varying form of title will print as an added entry but not as a note. Second indicator value blank has been made valid since Format Integration for use in situations where none of the other indicators (as defined by value "0–8") apply. Usually it is used when field 246 contains a variant form of title that does not appear on the item, that is, a permutation related to the title proper (LCRI 21.30J).

D2

PROBLEM CONSIDERED:
Full form of title proper as other title information (LCRI 12.1E1)

RULE(S) CONSULTED:
AACR2R: 12.1B2
LCRI: 21.30J, p. 23, p. 24

Cover

TAGGED DATA RECORD (based on OCLC #8956099)

LDR   *****cas_/22*****_a*4500

00-05	06	07-14	15-17	18	19	20	21	22-28	29	30-32	33	34	35-37	38	39
821115	c	19819999	onc	t	r	4	p	-------	0	///	b	0	eng	-	d

008

022 0   0229-8651
043   engfre
→ 245 00   RSSI : ≠b recherches sémiotiques = RSSI : semiotic inquiry.
→ 246 30   Recherches sémiotiques
→ 246 30   Semiotic inquiry
260   Toronto : ≠b Association canadienne de sémiotique, ≠c 1981-
300   v. ; ≠c 23 cm.
310   Three no. a year, ≠b 1986-
321   Four no. a year, ≠b 1981-1985
362 0   Vol. 1, no. 1(1981)-
500   Title from cover.
500   Official publication of the Association.
530   Issued also on microfiche from:Toronto : Micromedia.
546   Text in English or French.
650   0   Semiotics ≠x Periodicals.
650   0   Signs and symbols ≠x Periodicals.
710 2   Canadian Semiotic Association.
776 1   ≠t RSSI ≠x 0229-8651
780 00   ≠t Canadian journal of research in semiotics ≠x 0316-7917 ≠w
           (DLC)78646129 ≠w (OCoLC)2248093

DISCUSSION

• In this example, the initialism of the serial, "RSSI," is chosen as title proper
  because it appears on the chief source and is the sole form that appears elsewhere in the item (12.1B2). The same initialism is also repeated as a parallel
  title because it is meant to be used in conjunction with the corresponding fuller
  form of title in English.

- Other title information can be transcribed in the title and statement of responsibility area of a serial record only if it meets one of the criteria described in LCRI 12.1E1. In this case, one of those criteria is met (i.e., the other title information contains the fuller form of the title, which was not chosen as title proper). Therefore, the first fuller form of the title, "Recherches sémiotiques," which is in French, is transcribed immediately after the title proper as its other title information; the second fuller form of the title, "Semiotic inquiry," which is in English, is transcribed as parallel other title information. Added entries are needed to provide access to each of the spelled-out forms of the initialism (LCRI 21.30J, p. 23, p. 24).
- Note that subfield ≠b in field 245 is not repeatable. Therefore, in this example subfield ≠b is used once for the French other title information; the rest of the 245 field (the parallel title and its parallel other title information) does not include subfield coding.
- Field 246 is used for a title added entry. There are two 246 fields in this example. In both cases the first indicator is set to "3" to suppress a note in the bibliographic record, and the second indicator value is set to "0" to indicate that the other title information is from a portion of the title in field 245.

D3

PROBLEM CONSIDERED:

Initialism of title proper as other title information (12.1B2)

RULE(S) CONSULTED:

AACR2R: 12.1E1
LCRI: 21.30J, p. 23

TAGGED DATA RECORD (based on OCLC #18792954)

LDR   *****nas_/22*****_a*4500

00-05	06	07-14	15-17	18	19	20	21	22-28	29	30-32	33	34	35-37	38	39
008	881122	c	19889999	ilu	m	x	1	p	-------	0	///	a	0	eng	-	d

022 0   1043-254X ≠y 0091-3979
→ 245 00 Journal of dental hygiene : ≠b JDH / ≠c American Dental Hygienists' Association.
→ 246 30 JDH
260   Chicago, Ill. : ≠b The Association, ≠c 1988-
300   v. : ≠b ill., ports ; ≠c 28 cm.
310   Ten no. a year
362 0   Vol. 62, no. 9 (Oct. 1988)-
500   Title from cover.
650 0   Dental hygiene ≠x Periodicals.
650 0   Dental hygienists ≠x Periodicals.
710 2   American Dental Hygienists' Association.
780 00 ≠t Dental hygiene ≠x 0091-3979 ≠w (DLC)7364254 ≠w (OCoLC)1785999

```
┌─────────────────────────────────────────────────────┐
│  American                              OCT 1988       │
│  Dental Hygienists'                                   │
│  Association                                          │
│                     JDH                               │
│              JOURNAL OF DENTAL HYGIENE                 │
│                                                       │
└─────────────────────────────────────────────────────┘
```
Cover

```
┌─────────────────────────────────────────────────────┐
│  ┌──────────────────┐            Oct. 1988            │
│  │                  │                                 │
│  │                  │              JDH                │
│  │  PUBLISHER       │      JOURNAL OF DENTAL HYGIENE   │
│  │  The Journal of Dental      Vol. 62, No. 9         │
│  │  Hygiene, ISSN 0091-                                │
│  │  3979, is published nine                            │
│  │  times a year by . . . │                           │
│  └──────────────────┘                                 │
└─────────────────────────────────────────────────────┘
```
Contents page

DISCUSSION

- Whenever both the full form of the title and an initialism appear in the chief source, routinely treat the full form of title as the title proper, unless the initialism appears as the only form presented in other locations in the item (12.1B2). In this example, the full form is chosen as title proper according to rule 12.1B2, because the initialism does not appear by itself in other locations in the item. In addition, the initialism should be treated as other title information because, even though the initialism is given prominence typographically, the serial title is consistently referred to by the full form, as shown in the masthead on the contents page.
- Whichever form is not chosen as title proper should be given as other title information (12.1E1). An added entry should be made for the title not chosen— in this case, the initialism—so it can be accessed (LCRI 21.30J, p. 23).

D4

PROBLEM CONSIDERED:

Other title information supplied by cataloger for work entered under title (1.1E6)

RULE(S) CONSULTED:

AACR2R: 1.1B3, 21.1B2
LCRI: 25.5B, p. 7

<table>
<tr><td></td></tr>
</table>

Title page

SOCIEDAD DE ESTUDIOS
HISTORICO-GENEALOGICOS
DE BUENOS AIRES

NO. 1

TAGGED DATA RECORD (based on OCLC #33232879)

LDR   *****nas_/22*****_a*4500

00-05	06	07-14	15-17	18	19	20	21	22-28	29	30-32	33	34	35-37	38	39
951003	c	19949999	ag	u	u		p	-------	0	///	b	0	spa	-	d

008

043   s-ag---
130 0   Sociedad de Estudios Histórico-Genealógicos de Buenos Aires (Series)
→ 245 00   Sociedad de Estudios Histórico-Genealógicos de Buenos Aires : ≠b [revista].
260   Buenos Aires : ≠b La Sociedad, ≠c 1994-
300   v. : ≠ b ill. ; ≠c 22 cm.
362 0   No. 1-
500   Title from cover.
651 0 Argentina ≠x Genealogy ≠x Periodicals.
650 0 Genealogy ≠x Periodicals.
710 2   Sociedad de Estudios Histórico-Genealógicos de Buenos Aires.

DISCUSSION

- In this example, the item, which is a publication emanating from a corporate body, does not fall into any of the types of work characterized in rule 21.1B2. Therefore, entry for this work must be under the title. Note, however, that, since nothing but the name of the issuing body appears on the chief source, that must serve as the title proper (1.1B3). But the fact that the title proper consists only of the name of a corporate body would seem to necessitate some sort of explanation to make the nature of the item clear to users (1.1E6). To accomplish this, a term in the language of the title proper, "revista," is added in brackets as other title information. No added entry is needed for other title information that is supplied by the cataloger (CCM 6.3.4).

- A uniform title heading is needed if the title proper of a serial is identical to the name of a corporate body, even though the entry form does not conflict with another series or serial title in the catalog. In such a case, the uniform title heading consists of the title qualified by the term "Series" (LCRI 25.5B, p. 7).

D5

PROBLEM CONSIDERED:

More than one other title information (12.1E1)

RULE(S) CONSULTED:

AACR2R: 12.1B2
LCRI: 12.1E1

Cover

INTERNATIONAL JOURNAL OF THE CLASSICAL TRADITION   IJCT

the official journal of the International Society for the Classical Tradition

Volume 1, no. 1   Summer 1994

TAGGED DATA RECORD (based on #29297230)

LDR   *****cas_/22*****_a*4500

	00-05	06	07-14	15-17	18	19	20	21	22-28	29	30-32	33	34	35-37	38	39
008	931110	c	19949999	nju	q	r	l	p	-------	0	///	b	0	eng	-	d

022 0	1073-0508
041 0	engfregeritaspa
→ 245 00	International journal of the classical tradition : ≠b IJCT : the official journal of the International Society for the Classical Tradition.
→ 246 30	IJCT
260	New Brunswick, N.J. : ≠b Transaction Periodicals Consortium, ≠c 1994-
300	v. ; ≠c 26 cm.
310	Quarterly
362 0	Vol. 1, no. 1 (summer 1994)-
500	Title from cover.
546	Articles in English, French, German, Italian and Spanish.
650 0	Literature, Comparative ≠x Classical and modern ≠x Periodicals.
650 0	Literature, Comparative ≠x Modern and classical ≠x Periodicals.
650 0	Civilization, Classical ≠x Periodicals.
710 2	International Society for the Classical Tradition.

DISCUSSION

- In this example, the cover, which serves as the chief source of information, contains two types of information that should be transcribed as other title information in the title and statement of responsibility area. In accordance with rule 12.1B2, whenever the full form of the title has been chosen as title proper, the initialism of the title should be treated as other title information (12.1E1). Therefore, the initialism "IJCT" appears in the record as other title information. The statement "the official journal of the International Society for the Classical Tradition" is also given as other title information because it has imbedded in it the statement of responsibility for the serial (LCRI 12.1E1).

- In field 245, subfield ≠b is not repeatable. Therefore, only one subfield ≠b appears in this field.

D6

PROBLEM CONSIDERED:

Other title information in a note (12.7B5)

RULE(S) CONSULTED:

AACR2R: 1.7A3
LCRI: 12.1E1

TAGGED DATA RECORD (based on OCLC #32246288)

LDR   *****cas_/22*****_a*4500

00-05	06	07-14	15-17	18	19	20	21	22-28	29	30-32	33	34	35-37	38	39
950403	c	19959999	ne	q	r		p	-------	0	///	a	0	eng	-	d

008

022 0	1022-0038
→ 245 00	Wireless networks.
260	Amsterdam : ≠b Baltzer Science Publishers, ≠c 1995-
300	v. : ≠b ill. ; ≠c 29 cm.
310	Quarterly
362 0	Vol. 1, no. 1 (Feb. 1995)-
500	Title from caption.
→ 500	"The journal of mobile communication, computation and information."
550	Sponsored by: ACM.
650 0	Wireless communication systems ≠x Periodicals.
650 0	Wide area networks (Computer networks) ≠x Periodicals.
650 0	Local area networks (Computer networks) ≠x Periodicals.
710 2	Association for Computing Machinery.

Caption

> ## Wireless networks
> The journal of mobile communication, computation and information.
>
> **Volume 1, no. 1   February 1995**

DISCUSSION

- The Library of Congress rule interpretation for AACR2R rule 12.1E1 lists three criteria under which other title information can be transcribed in the title and statement of responsibility area; generally, in all cases other than those three, other title information should not be transcribed in that area. It may, however, be quoted in a note if necessary (12.7B5 and 1.7A3). Bear in mind that this information may vary during the life span of the serial. By limiting the use of other title information in the title and statement of responsibility area, as prescribed in LCRI 12.1E1, and by exercising good judgment in making notes containing other title information, the need for recataloging serials for minor changes may be reduced.

- In this example, the phrase "The journal of mobile communication, computation and information" may not be transcribed in the title and statement of responsibility area, but it does give the subject coverage of the work. If the cataloger decides that this information is useful enough to be included in the bibliographic record, it should be given in a quoted note.

D7

PROBLEM CONSIDERED:

Common title and section title with other title information (LCRI 12.1E1)

RULE(S) CONSULTED:

AACR2R: 1.1B9, 12.1B5

TAGGED DATA RECORD (based on OCLC #32811341)

LDR   *****cas_/22*****_a*4500

00-05	06	07-14	15-17	18	19	20	21	22-28	29	30-32	33	34	35-37	38	39
950713	c	19969999	nyu	b	r	l	p	-------	0	///	a	0	eng	-	d

008

022 0   1083-4427

→ 245 00   IEEE transactions on systems, man, and cybernetics. ≠n Part A, ≠p Systems and humans : ≠b a publication of the IEEE Systems, Man, and Cybernetics Society.

246 30   Systems and humans

260   New York, NY : ≠b Institute of Electrical and Electronics Engineers, Inc., ≠c 1996-

300   v. : ≠b ill. ; ≠c 28 cm.

310   Bimonthly

362 0   Vol. 26, no. 1 (Jan. 1996)-

500   Title from cover.

650 0   Systems engineering ≠x Periodicals.

650 0   Man-machine systems ≠x Periodicals.

710 2   Institute of Electrical and Electronics Engineers.

710 2   IEEE Systems, Man, and Cybernetics Society.

780 01   ≠t IEEE transactions on systems, man, and cybernetics ≠x 0018-9472 ≠w (DLC)79640192 ≠w (OCoLC)1752562

<table>
<tr><td rowspan="5">Title page</td><td>

IEEE Transactions on
Systems, Man, and Cybernetics
Part A   Systems and Humans
A publication of the IEEE Systems, Man, and Cybernetics Society
Volume 26, No. 1   January 1996

</td></tr>
</table>

DISCUSSION

- When a common title that is common to many sections and a section title both appear on the item, record the common title first, followed by the section title preceded by a period (1.1B9). If a section title is preceded by a numeric or an alphabetic designation, record the common title, followed by the section designation and the section title. Separate the section designation and section title by a comma (12.1B5).

- If the other title information meets the criteria for transcription according to LCRI 12.1E1, it should be recorded at the end of the title proper. In this example, the other title information, "a publication of the IEEE Systems, Man, and Cybernetics Society," includes a statement of responsibility, one of the circumstances in which other title information should be transcribed. It is input immediately following the section title.

D8

PROBLEM CONSIDERED:

Parallel other title information (1.1E5)

RULE(S) CONSULTED:

LCRI: 1.1E5

TAGGED DATA RECORD (based on OCLC #8013180)

LDR   *****cas_/22*****_a*4500

00-05	06	07-14	15-17	18	19	20	21	22-28	29	30-32	33	34	35-37	38	39
008 811221	c	197u9999	cm	m	r		p	e-----f	0	///	a	0	eng	-	d

041 0   engfre
043   f-cm---
→ 245 00 Cameroon education today : ≠b the Ministry of National Education monthly journal = mensuel du Ministère de l'éducation nationale.
260   Yaoundé [Cameroon] : ≠b The Ministry,
300   v. : ≠b ill. ; ≠c 45 cm.
310   Monthly
500   Description based on: 1st year, no. 0004 (Dec. 1978); masthead title.
546   English and French.
650   0   Education ≠z Cameroon ≠x Periodicals.
710 1   Cameroon. ≠b Ministry of National Education.
780 00   ≠t Cameroon education to-day ≠w (DLC)81649335 ≠w (OCoLC)8012517

Masthead

> ## Cameroon
> ## Education
> ## Today
>
> Mensuel du Ministère de l'Éducation Nationale The Ministry of National Education Monthly Journal
>
> 1re Année   N° °0004 – Décembre 1978
> 1st Year   December

DISCUSSION

- If there are no parallel titles and if other title information is in more than one language, the cataloger is instructed to give the other title information that is in the language or script of the title proper or to give the other title information that appears first, if that is more appropriate (1.1E5). However, the cataloger may also generally apply the optional provision of this rule (LCRI 1.1E5), according to which the other title information in other languages may be given, with each parallel statement preceded by an equals sign.
- In this example, the title proper is in English only, but the other title information is in both English ("the Ministry of National Education Monthly Journal") and French ("Mensuel du Ministère de l'Éducation Nationale"). Applying rule 1.1E5 and its optional provision, the English other title information, which is in the language of the title proper even though it appears after its French counterpart, is given first and followed by an equals sign and the French other title information.
- In field 245, subfield ≠b is not repeatable. Therefore, it appears once, separating the first other title information from the title proper.

D9

PROBLEM CONSIDERED:

A change in other title information (12.7B5)

Caption

> # STRING NEWS
> ### A BULLETIN OF THE ILLINOIS STRING PLANNING CONFERENCE
> IN COOPERATION WITH THE AMERICAN STRING TEACHERS ASSOCIATION
>
> April   Number
> 1948   One

Caption of a later issue

STRING NEWS
IN THE INTEREST OF STRING EDUCATION IN THE STATE OF ILLINOIS
In cooperation with the American String Teachers Association and the MENC Committee on String Instruction

April   Number
1949   2

TAGGED DATA RECORD (based on OCLC #31149547)

LDR   *****nas_/22*****_a*4500

00-05	06	07-14	15-17	18	19	20	21	22-28	29	30-32	33	34	35-37	38	39
940921	u	1948uuuu	ilu			x		p	-------	0	///	a	0	eng	-	d

008

043   n-us-il
→ 245 00 String news : ≠b a bulletin of the Illinois String Planning Conference.
260   Urbana, Ill. : ≠b Published under the sponsorship of the Division of Extension, School of Music, University of Illinois, ≠c 1948-
300   v. : ≠b ill. ; ≠c 31 cm.
310   Irregular
362 0   No. 1 (Apr. 1948)-
500   Title from caption.
→ 500   Other title information varies.
550   Issued in cooperation with the American String Teachers Association, no. 1; with MENC Committee on String Instruction, no. 2-
650 0 String instrument music ≠x Instruction and study ≠x Periodicals.
650 0 String instrument music ≠z Illinois ≠x Periodicals.
711 2   Illinois String Planning Conference.
710 2   University of Illinois (Urbana-Champaign campus). ≠b Music Extension.
710 2   American String Teachers Association.
710 2   MENC Committee on String Instruction.

DISCUSSION

- In this example, the other title information "a bulletin of the Illinois String Planning Conference" changes to "in the interest of string education in the state of Illinois" on subsequent issues; but the title proper does not change and thus it is not necessary to create a separate record. However, because the original other title information appears in the cataloging record, which was based on the first issue, a note is needed to explain the change in the other title information on later issues (12.7B5).
- Use a 500 General Note stating that the other title information has varied.

D10

PROBLEM CONSIDERED:

Phrase at head of title as other title information (LCRI 12.1E1)

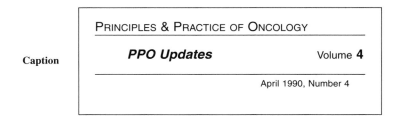

TAGGED DATA RECORD (based on OCLC #23672088)

LDR   *****cas_/22*****_a*4500

00-05	06	07-14	15-17	18	19	20	21	22-28	29	30-32	33	34	35-37	38	39
910501	c	19879999	pau	u	u		p	-------	0	///	a	0	eng	-	d

008   (per table above)

022   ≠y 0892-0567
→ 245 00 PPO updates : ≠b principles & practice of oncology.
→ 246 30 Principles & practice of oncology
   246 13 Principles and practice of oncology updates
   260   Philadelphia, PA : ≠b J.B. Lippincott,
   300   v. : ≠b ill. ; ≠c 28 cm.
   362 1   Began with v. 1, published in 1987.
   500   Description based on: Vol. 4, no. 4 (Apr. 1990); title from caption.
   580   Vols. for 1989- update: Cancer : principles & practice of oncology, 3rd ed. / edited by Vincent T. DeVita, Jr. and others.
   650 0   Oncology ≠x Periodicals.

DISCUSSION

- Sometimes a phrase appearing at the head of the title proper may be treated as other title information on the ground that such inclusion in the bibliographic description would make clear to users the scope of the publication (LCRI 12.1E1). Often application of this practice is seen in conjunction with titles consisting of initials or acronyms. Such is the case in this example, where the phrase "Principles & Practice of Oncology" appears at the head of the title proper "PPO updates." Instead of being cited in an "At head of title" note, this phrase, which relates to the scope covered by the serial, is noted more prominently as other title information in field 245 subfield ≠b.

D11

PROBLEM CONSIDERED:

Other title information as part of the title proper (LCRI 12.1B3)

RULE(S) CONSULTED:

LCRI: 12.1E1

TAGGED DATA RECORD (based on OCLC #18928332)

LDR   *****cas_/22*****Ia*4500

00-05	06	07-14	15-17	18	19	20	21	22-28	29	30-32	33	34	35-37	38	39
881220	c	19879999	dcu	u	u		p	------c	0	///	a	0	eng	-	d

008

043   n-us-dc
→ 245 00 M, the magazine of Metro.
→ 246 30 Magazine of Metro
    260   Washington, D.C. : ≠b Washington Metropolitan Area Transit Authority, ≠c 1987-
    300   v. : ≠b ill. ; ≠c 28 cm.
    362 0   No. 76 (June 1987)-
    500   Title from cover.
    650 0 Local transit ≠z Washington Metropolitan Area ≠x Periodicals.
    710 2   Washington Metropolitan Area Transit Authority.
    780 00 ≠t Metro memo ≠w (OCoLC)1645148

DISCUSSION

- It is sometimes difficult to decide whether a phrase should be treated as part of the title or as other title information. In this example, the phrase "the magazine of Metro" contains a form of the name of the responsible body and, therefore, meets one of the guidelines set forth in LCRI 12.1E1 for inclusion as other title information. Instead, however, the cataloger has decided to treat the phrase as part of the title proper. According to LCRI 12.1B3, if the word, phrase, or statement in question is consistently presented as part of the title in various locations on the item and/or if the serial is known by the title with the inclusion of such a word, phrase, or statement, then it should be treated as part of the title proper rather than as other title information. For that reason, in this example, the phrase "the magazine of Metro" is transcribed as part of the title proper.
- Because the phrase by itself may serve as a useful access point, it is input in field 246. Notice that the initial article is omitted from the phrase as it appears in the 246 field. The first indicator is set to "3" to suppress a note, and second indicator value "0" is used to indicate that the field contains a portion of the title proper.

D12

PROBLEM CONSIDERED:

Alternative title without the preceding word "or" as other title information (LCRI 12.1E1)

TAGGED DATA RECORD (based on OCLC #20066860)

LDR   *****cas_/22*****5a*4500

00-05	06	07-14	15-17	18	19	20	21	22-28	29	30-32	33	34	35-37	38	39
890725	c	19uu9999	dr	q	r		p	------i	0	///	a	0	eng	-	d

008 (preceding the table)

→ 245 00 INSTRAW news : ≠b women and development.
→ 246 30 Women and development
  260   Santo Domingo, Dominican Republic : ≠b United Nations International Research and Training Institute for the Advancement of Women,
  300   v. : ≠b ill. ; ≠c 27 cm.
  310   Quarterly
  500   Description based on: Vol. 1, no. 3 (Dec. 1984); title from cover.
  530   Issued also in French and Spanish.
610 20   International Research and Training Institute for the Advancement of Women ≠x Periodicals.
650 0   Women in development ≠x Periodicals.
710 2   International Research and Training Institute for the Advancement of Women.

Cover

INSTRAW News
Women and Development

Vol. 1, No. 3 December 1984

**International Research and Training Institute
for the Advancement of Women
United Nations**

DISCUSSION

- In most cases, an alternative title appears on the chief source preceded by the first title followed by the word "or" or its equivalent in another language. However, there are other cases that may also be thought of in terms of an alternative title in which two of these could stand alone as the title proper (CCM 6.3.3b). In such cases, the cataloger must use his or her judgment to choose which of the titles to treat as the title proper and which to treat as other title information (LCRI 12.1E1). In general, the most prominent title should be chosen as title proper.

E. Statement of Responsibility

A statement of responsibility relating to persons or corporate bodies that appear in the chief source of information should be recorded as it appears, regardless of whether the work is entered under a name heading or title main entry. However, an editor's name should not be recorded in this area (12.1F3). If an editor's name is considered to be of importance to users, it may be given in a note (12.7B6).

A statement relating to a responsible person or body appearing prominently in the chief source is the "statement of responsibility" for the item and should be transcribed in the form in which it appears (1.1F1). Usually, it appears at the head of the title. Occasionally, a phrase or name appears at the head of a title but is not considered to be the statement of responsibility; in such cases an "At head of title:" note may be used (LCRI 12.7B6). If the name of a responsible body appears at the foot of the title page, such positioning usually indicates that the body functions as a publisher, and the name should thus be transcribed in the publication, distribution, etc., area.

The statement of responsibility may also appear in an item in several other ways. For example, it may appear as part of the title proper (1.1B2), it may be imbedded in other title information (12.1E1), or it may appear in more than one language (1.1F10 and 1.1F11).

EXAMPLES

E1   Statement of responsibility appears after the title
E2   Statement of responsibility appears at head of the title for work entered under corporate name
E3   Corporate name appearing in the chief source is not transcribed in the title and statement of responsibility area
E4   Statement of responsibility as part of the title proper
E5   Personal statement of responsibility
E6   Statement of responsibility in a note
E7   Statement of responsibility in series statement
E8   Statement of responsibility imbedded in other title information
E9   Parallel title with statement of responsibility in one language only
E10   Parallel statement of responsibility with parallel title
E11   Statements of responsibility in more than one language with no corresponding parallel title
E12   Statement of responsibility for the title proper consisting of common title, section number, and section title

E1

PROBLEM CONSIDERED:

Statement of responsibility appears after the title (12.1F1)

RULE(S) CONSULTED:

AACR2R: 1.4D4, 21.1B2, 21.1C1, 21.30E1

TAGGED DATA RECORD (based on OCLC #10240545)

LDR   *****cas_/22*****_a*4500

00-05	06	07-14	15-17	18	19	20	21	22-28	29	30-32	33	34	35-37	38	39
008 831221	c	19829999	wiu	q	r		p	-------	0	///	a	0	eng	-	d

→ 245 00   AWV bulletin / ≠c Association for Women Veterinarians.
→ 260   Madison, Wis. : ≠b The Association,
   300   v. ; ≠c 22 cm.
   310   Quarterly
   362 1   Began in 1982.
   500   Description based on: Vol. 38, no. 1 (Jan. 1983); title from cover.
   650 0   Veterinary medicine ≠x Periodicals.
→ 710 2   Association for Women Veterinarians.
   780 00   ≠t AFWV bulletin ≠w (OCLC)7106977

Cover

> **VOL 38, NO. 1   JANUARY 1983**
>
> # AWV
>
> **BULLETIN**
>
> **ASSOCIATION FOR WOMEN VETERINARIANS**
>
> representing
>
> **Women Veterinarians of the Americas**

DISCUSSION

• This work emanates from a corporate body but does not fall into the categories given in rule 21.1B2; therefore, it is entered under title (21.1C1). Because the responsible body appears in the chief source in conjunction with the title, it is recorded in the statement of responsibility area following the title proper (12.1F1). An added entry for the corporate body is needed to provide access (21.30E1). Since the name of the publisher is the same as the one in the title and statement of responsibility area, it is given in the publication area in a shortened form (1.4D4).

- The statement of responsibility is input after the title proper and GMD (General Material Description) if there is one on the record, or other title information if other title information is recorded. It is coded in subfield ≠c of field 245 and preceded by a slash. Subfield ≠c is not repeatable.
- The added entry for the corporate body is entered in field 710. First indicator value "1" is used when the corporate body is a jurisdiction. Value "2" is used when the corporate body is entered directly under its own name. The second indicator is blank in this case, when it is not an analyzed added entry.

E2

PROBLEM CONSIDERED:

Statement of responsibility appears at head of the title for work entered under corporate name (12.1F1)

RULE(S) CONSULTED:

AACR2R: 1.1F3, 1.4D4, 21.1B2

TAGGED DATA RECORD (based on OCLC #20665697)

LDR   *****cas_/22*****Ia*4500

00-05	06	07-14	15-17	18	19	20	21	22-28	29	30-32	33	34	35-37	38	39
891117	c	19909999	iau	a	r			--r----	0	///	a	0	eng	-	d

008

043   n-us-ia
→ 110 2   Iowa Society of Certified Public Accountants.
→ 245 10   Membership & resource directory / ≠c Iowa Society of Certified Public Accountants.
246 3   Membership and resource directory
260   West Des Moines, Iowa : ≠b The Society, ≠c 1989-
300   v. ; ≠c 22 cm.
310   Annual
362 0   1989-90-
500   Title from cover.
610 20   Iowa Society of Certified Public Accountants ≠x Directories.
650 0   Accountants ≠z Iowa ≠x Directories.
780 00   Iowa Society of Certified Public Accountants. ≠t Directory of members ≠w (OCLC)11284087

Cover

DISCUSSION

- This work emanates from a corporate body, "Iowa Society of Certified Public Accountants," and, being a membership directory of the society, it meets the criteria given in rule 21.1B2 for entry under the heading for the corporate body.
- Because the name of the responsible body appears in the chief source, it should be recorded in the statement of responsibility area (12.1F1).
- If the statement of responsibility precedes the title, transpose it to the required position (1.1F3). Thus, in this example, the name of the responsible body is given in the title and statement of responsibility area at the end of the title proper. Again, as in example E1, when the name of the publisher is the same as the one in the title and statement of responsibility area, the full form is not repeated in the publication area (1.4D4).

E3

PROBLEM CONSIDERED:

Corporate name appearing in the chief source is not transcribed in the title and statement of responsibility area (1.1F15)

RULE(S) CONSULTED:
AACR2R: 12.0B1, 21.30E1

Cover

ASX PERSPECTIVE

A quarterly journal covering the securities markets
1st Quarter 1995

Australian Stock Exchange

TAGGED DATA RECORD (based on OCLC #33270710)

LDR   *****cas_/22*****_a*4500

	00-05	06	07-14	15-17	18	19	20	21	22-28	29	30-32	33	34	35-37	38	39
008	951011	c	19959999	at	q	r		p	-------	0	///	a	0	eng	-	d

022	1323-5877
043	u-at---
245 00	ASX perspective.
246 2	Australian Stock Exchange perspective
246 30	Perspective
→ 260	Sydney, N.S.W.? : ≠b Australian Stock Exchange Limited, ≠c [1994?-
300	v. ; ≠c 30 cm.
310	Quarterly
362 0	1st ; 1st quarter 1995-
500	Title from cover.
610 20	Australian Stock Exchange ≠x Periodicals.
650 0	Stock exchange ≠z Australia x≠ Periodicals.
→ 710 2	Australian Stock Exchange.

DISCUSSION

- The chief source of information for this printed serial is the cover (12.0B1). In this example, a responsible body is named at the foot of the page. Instead of being transcribed in the title and statement of responsibility area, the name of the corporate body is transcribed in the publication, distribution, etc., area, because such positioning usually indicates that the body functions as a publisher (1.1F15; CCM 10.2.1).
- Make an added entry under a prominently named publisher if its primary function is the issuance of the publication (21.30E1). In this example, the Australian Stock Exchange, not being an agency primarily in the business of publishing, is considered to be the issuing body for the publication. The added entry for an issuing body is input in field 710.

E4

PROBLEM CONSIDERED:

Statement of responsibility as part of the title proper (12.1F2)

RULE(S) CONSULTED:

AACR2R: 1.1B2, 1.1F13
LCRI: 25.5B

TAGGED DATA RECORD (based on OCLC #17316267)

LDR   *****cas_/22*****_a*4500

00-05	06	07-14	15-17	18	19	20	21	22-28	29	30-32	33	34	35-37	38	39
880107	c	19879999	dcu	q	r	l	p	-------	0	///	a	0	eng	-	d

008

022 0   1046-9508 ≠y 0010-0935
→ 130 0   CUPA journal (Washington, D.C. : 1987)
→ 245 00   CUPA journal / ≠c College and University Personnel Association.
260   Washington, DC : ≠b The Association, ≠c 1987-
300   v. : ≠b ill.; ≠c 28 cm.
310   Quarterly
362 0   Vol. 38, no. 1 (Oct. 1987)-
500   Title from cover.
650 0   Universities and colleges ≠x Employees ≠x Periodicals.
650 0   College personnel management ≠x Periodicals.
710 2   College and University Personnel Association.
780 00   ≠t Journal of the College & University Personnel Association ≠x 0010-0935
         ≠w (DLC)sc80000251 ≠w (OCoLC)5180503

Cover

CUPA
JOURNAL

COLLEGE AND UNIVERSITY PERSONNEL ASSOCIATION

Fall 1987 Vol. 38, No. 1

DISCUSSION

- If a statement of responsibility is included in the title proper, do not give a further statement of responsibility unless such a statement appears separately in the chief source (12.1F2). In this example, the initials of the organization "CUPA" form an integral part of the title proper (1.1B2). Since there is also a separate statement of responsibility on the chief source, the Association's name is transcribed both in the title and in the statement of responsibility area (1.1F13).

- A uniform title heading, field 130, has been included in the tagged record in order to distinguish the serial being cataloged from another serial under the same name in the catalog (LCRI 25.5B). Uniform titles are created only for serials being cataloged; they are not added to the records for serials cataloged earlier. Generally, the place of publication is the choice of qualifying term in a uniform title; but in this case both place and date of publication are used as the most appropriate terms to distinguish the serial being cataloged from a previously cataloged serial with the same title.

E5

PROBLEM CONSIDERED:

Personal statement of responsibility (LCRI 21.1A2)

RULE(S) CONSULTED:

AACR2R: 12.1F1, 12.2B2, 21.1A1
LCRI: 12.1F3

<table>
<tr><td>

The
Book Collector's
HANDBOOK
OF VALUES
BY
VAN ALLEN BRADLEY

G. P. Putnam's Sons
New York

</td><td>

The Book Collector's
HANDBOOK
OF VALUES
by
VAN ALLEN BRADLEY

1982-1983 edition

G. P. Putnam's Sons
New York

</td></tr>
<tr><td style="text-align:center">**Title page**</td><td style="text-align:center">**Title page of a later edition**</td></tr>
</table>

TAGGED DATA RECORD (based on OCLC #8334152)

LDR   *****cas_/22*****Ia*4500

00-05	06	07-14	15-17	18	19	20	21	22-28	29	30-32	33	34	35-37	38	39
820414	c	19729999	nyu	u		u		--b----	0	///	a	0	eng	-	d

008

043		e-uk--- ≠a n-us---
→ 100	1	Bradley, Van Allen, ≠d 1913-
→ 245	14	The book collector's handbook of values / ≠c by Van Allen Bradley.
246	30	Handbook of values
260		New York : ≠b Putnam, ≠c 1972-
300		v. ; ≠c 24 cm.
→ 362	0	[1st ed.] (1972)-
520		An alphabetical, author-title listing of selected rare books published since 1800.
650	0	Rare books ≠x Handbooks, manuals, etc.
650	0	Rare books ≠x Bibliography.
651	0	Great Britain ≠x Imprints ≠x Bibliography.
651	0	United States ≠x Imprints ≠x Bibliography.

DISCUSSION

- In serial cataloging very few works can be entered under the personal author. For a serial to be entered under personal author, the cataloger must first ascertain that the work meets the general condition for personal authorship stated in rule 21.1A1: "A personal author is the person chiefly responsible for the creation of the intellectual or artistic content of a work." Second, it must be determined that the person in question is so closely involved with the work that the serial is unlikely to continue with a different person (LCRI 21.1A2). In addition, the Library of Congress advises that catalogers "should always lean toward not entering a serial under the heading for a person" (LCRI 21.1A2). Consequently, fewer serials are being cataloged under personal author.

- This example is typical of the type of serial that may be entered under a personal name. Because the personal name appears on the title page, it is transcribed in the title and statement of responsibility area as it is (12.1F1). Be sure to distinguish between cases like this and those in which there is a statement identifying a personal *editor*. The latter may not be recorded as a statement of responsibility; if such information is considered important and if it is necessary to record it, it may only be given in a note (LCRI 12.1F3).
- If an edition statement includes some type of numerical or chronological designation, it should not be given in the edition statement area (field 250). Rather, as in this example, it should be given in the numeric and/or alphabetic, chronological, or other designation area (12.2B2).
- Field 100 contains personal names used as main entries. Because the use of personal name main entries is greatly restricted in serial cataloging, this field is infrequently used. First indicator value "1" is used for a single surname. The second indicator is blank.

E6

PROBLEM CONSIDERED:
Statement of responsibility in a note (1.1F2)

RULE(S) CONSULTED:
AACR2R: 1.1F1, 1.4D3, 12.7B6

Title page	**ADVANCES IN TEST ANXIETY RESEARCH** VOLUME 1 PUBLISHED FOR THE INTERNATIONAL SOCIETY FOR TEST ANXIETY RESEARCH **STAR** 1982

TAGGED DATA RECORD (based on OCLC #9135225)

LDR   *****cas_/22*****_a*4500

00-05	06	07-14	15-17	18	19	20	21	22-28	29	30-32	33	34	35-37	38	39
830117	c	19829999	ne	u	u		p	-------	0	///	a	0	eng	-	d

008

022	0923-019x
→ 245 00	Advances in test anxiety research.
246 30	Test anxiety research
260	Lisse : ≠b Swets and Zeitlinger ; ≠a Hillsdale, NJ : ≠b L. Erlbaum Associates, ≠c 1982-
300	v. : ≠b ill. ; ≠c 25 cm.
362 0	Vol. 1 (1982)-
→ 550	Published for the International Society for Test Anxiety Research (STAR), 1982-
650 0	Test anxiety ≠x Research ≠x Periodicals.
→ 710 2	International Society for Test Anxiety Research.

DISCUSSION

- It is often the case in serial cataloging that the name of a responsible body is not actually transcribed in the title and statement of responsibility area. This example represents one such case. According to rule 1.1F1, statements of responsibility that appear prominently in the chief source may be transcribed in that area. However, statements of responsibility with prefatory words, such as "Published for . . . ," "Issued by . . . ," "Published under the auspices of . . . ," "Prepared under the direction of . . . ," etc., usually are not recorded in the title and statement of responsibility area even when they appear in the chief source, because statements of this type normally do not appear in conjunction with the title. Such statements not only are lengthy, but often may change in later issues. However, they may be given in the Issuing Body Note (field 550) or in the publication, distribution, etc., area if the statements are grammatically linked to the publisher statement (1.1F2; 1.4D3).
- In this example, the statement "Published for the International Society for Test Anxiety Research (STAR)" is not linked grammatically to the publisher statement and, therefore, is given separately in a note (12.7B6).
- Field 550 is used for issuing bodies notes. Field 550 includes information on earlier or later issuing bodies, changes in the names of responsible bodies when the change or addition does not constitute a title change, or names of corporate bodies for which added entries are desired.

E7

PROBLEM CONSIDERED:

Statement of responsibility in series statement (LCRI 1.6E1)

RULE(S) CONSULTED:

AACR2R: 1.1F1, 1.6B1
LCRI: 21.30L

TAGGED DATA RECORD (based on OCLC #21264378)

LDR   *****cas_/22*****_a*4500

00-05	06	07-14	15-17	18	19	20	21	22-28	29	30-32	33	34	35-37	38	39
900326	c	19909999	nyu		x	l		-------	0	///	a	0	eng	-	d

008

022 0	1067-3016
043	f-bs---
→245 00	Doing business in Botswana.
246 18	Botswana
260	[New York] : ≠b Price Waterhouse World Firm Ltd., ≠c 1990-
300	v. ; ≠c 23 cm.
310	Irregular
362 0	90/3-
→490 1	Information guide / Price Waterhouse
500	Title from cover.
525	Supplements accompany some issues.
650 0	Business law ≠z Botswana.
650 0	Investments, Foreign ≠x Law and legislation ≠z Botswana.
650 0	Taxation ≠x Law and legislation ≠z Botswana.
650 0	Labor laws and legislation ≠z Botswana.
710 2	Price Waterhouse (Firm). ≠b World Firm.
→830 0	Information guide (Price Waterhouse (Firm))

Information Guide

Doing business in
Botswana

Price Waterhouse

90/3

This guide is published by Price Waterhouse World Firm Limited, a nonpracticing limited liability company.

1990 Price Waterhouse
Printed in U.S.A.
3/90

Cover   **Verso of the cover**

DISCUSSION

- The serial in this example is issued as part of a series. The title proper of the series is transcribed in the series statement area (1.6B1). A series statement of responsibility that does not appear in conjunction with the series title needs to be recorded only for the purpose of providing better identification of the series (LCRI 1.6E1). Such information is useful especially for generic series titles, such as the one in this example. Therefore "Price Waterhouse" is transcribed as the series statement of responsibility following the series title (as instructed in rule 1.1F1), preceded by space, slash, space.

- A series added entry is usually needed whenever a series statement appears in the record. However, if a series added entry is not considered to be useful, the cataloger may optionally omit the series statement. In many cases, the series added entry may be derived directly from the series statement; that is, the form in the series statement is exactly the same as the series title on the series authority record, and we say that the series is "traced the same" (LCRI 21.30L). However, in this example, the series added entry cannot be traced the same because the title is such that it requires a uniform title series added entry. In this case, the created uniform title consists of the series title "Information guide" plus a corporate name "Price Waterhouse," which, itself qualified by the word "Firm," serves as the qualifier.
- Field 490 is used for a series statement that is not traced or is traced in a different form. First indicator value "0" is used when no tracing is desired. Note that value "0" is seldom used in series cataloging. Value "1" is used when the series is traced differently, and an 800–830 field must also be input to provide the appropriate series added entry. Field 830 is used for a uniform title series added entry. The first indicator is blank. The second indicator shows the number of characters to be ignored in filing when the title begins with an article. Omit all initial articles from uniform titles.

E8

PROBLEM CONSIDERED:

Statement of responsibility imbedded in other title information (1.1E4)

RULE(S) CONSULTED:

LCRI: 12.1E1

TAGGED DATA RECORD (based on OCLC #34689205)

LDR   *****cas_/22*****_a*4500

00-05	06	07-14	15-17	18	19	20	21	22-28	29	30-32	33	34	35-37	38	39
960507	c	19969999	enk	m	r		p	-------	0	///	a	0	eng	-	d

008

022   1361-2042

→ 245 00   Mathematics today : ≠b bulletin of the Institute of Mathematics and Its Applications.

260   Southend-on-Sea, Essex : ≠b The Institute, ≠c 1996-

300   v. ; ≠c 30 cm

310   Monthly

362 0   Vol. 32, nos. 1/2 (Jan./Feb. 1996)-

500   Title from cover.

525   Some numbers accompanied by supplements.

650   0   Mathematics ≠x Periodicals.

710 2   Institute of Mathematics and Its Applications.

→ 780 00   ≠t Bulletin (Institute of Mathematics and Its Applications) ≠x 0950-5628 ≠w (DLC)sn87008400 ≠w (OCoLC)4093455

MATHEMATICS TODAY

BULLETIN OF THE INSTITUTE OF MATHEMATICS AND ITS APPLICATIONS

Cover

Volume 32, nos. 1/2   January/February 1996

DISCUSSION

- "Mathematics today" is the title proper for this item, and "Bulletin of the In-stitute of Mathematics and Its Applications," which appears also in the chief source of information and contains the statement of responsibility as an inte-gral part, is transcribed as the other title information (1.1E4; LCRI 12.1E1). In this case, a title added entry is not made for other title information that con-tains a statement of responsibility (see CCM 6.3.4). For cases where an added entry is necessary for other title information, see examples in section D.
- In field 245, subfield ≠b is used for other title information.
- Field 780 is used for a link to a preceding title. The linking entry must be the cataloging entry for the related serial. Thus, whenever linking to a related record, always link to the uniform title if the related work is entered under a uniform title. In this example, the linking entry is a uniform title: "Bulletin (In-stitute of Mathematics and Its Applications)."

E9

PROBLEM CONSIDERED:

Parallel title with statement of responsibility in one language only (1.1F10)

RULE(S) CONSULTED:

AACR2R: 12.7B2

Biotechnologie, Agronomie Société et Environnement

B A
S E

Biotechnology, Agronomy Society and Environment

Cover

CRA   gembloux
Gembloux   faculté universitaire
                             des sciences agronomiques

TAGGED DATA RECORD (based on OCLC #36626809)

LDR   *****cas_/22*****Ia*4500

00-05	06	07-14	15-17	18	19	20	21	22-28	29	30-32	33	34	35-37	38	39
970325	c	19979999	be	q	r		p	-------	0	///	b	0	fre	-	d

→ 008

022   1370-6233

→ 041 0   freeng

→ 245 00   Biotechnologie, agronomie, société et environnement = ≠b Biotechnology, agronomy, society and environment : BASE / ≠c CRA, Gembloux [et] Gembloux, Faculté universitaire des sciences agronomiques.

246 30   BASE

246 31   Biotechnology, agronomy, society and environment

260   Gembloux (Belgique) : ≠b Bibliothèque de la Faculté, ≠c 1997-

300   v. : ≠b ill. ; ≠c 28 cm

310   Quarterly

362 0   Vol. 1, no. 1 (1997)-

500   Title from cover.

→ 546   French or English; summaries in both languages.

650 0   Agricultural biotechnology ≠x Periodicals.

650 0   Agriculture ≠x Environmental aspects ≠x Periodicals.

650 0   Agriculture ≠x Periodicals.

710 2   Centre de recherches agronomique, Gembloux.

710 2   Faculté universitaire des sciences agronomiques de Gembloux.

780 00   ≠t Bulletin des recherches agronomiques de Gembloux ≠x 0435-2033 ≠w (DLC)sn79002365 ≠w (OCoLC)2715408

DISCUSSION

- If an item has parallel titles, but the statement of responsibility appears in only one language, the statement of responsibility is given after the parallel titles (1.1F10). In this example, the item has a parallel title in English. The statement of responsibility, which is in French only, is transcribed immediately following the parallel title. Note that the names of the responsible bodies are linked with a connecting word in French, the same language of the statement of responsibility.

- A Language Note, field 546, is used to make note on the languages of the item if they are not apparent from the rest of the description (12.7B2). However, if there is more than one language in the text, the language information must be given in field 041, which in turn is coded in conjunction with fixed field 008, positions 35–37. In this example, French is the predominant language and is mentioned first in field 546, even though there are summaries in both English and French. This language predominancy is reflected in fixed field 008, positions 35–37, and in the first code of field 041.

E10

PROBLEM CONSIDERED:

Parallel statement of responsibility with parallel title (1.1F10)

RULE(S) CONSULTED:

AACR2R: 1.1A1

LCRI: 25.5B, p. 2

TAGGED DATA RECORD (based on OCLC #30065137)

LDR   *****cas_/22*****_a*4500

00-05	06	07-14	15-17	18	19	20	21	22-28	29	30-32	33	34	35-37	38	39
940401	c	19919999	nyu	g	r			------i	0	///	a	0	eng	-	d

008

022   0082-8459

041 0   engfre

→ 130 0   Statistical yearbook (United Nations. Statistical Division)

→ 245 00   Statistical yearbook / ≠c Department of Economic and Social Information and Policy Analysis, Statistical Division = Annuaire statistique / Département de l'information économique et sociale et de l'analyse des politiques, Division de statistique.

246 31   Annuaire statistique

260   New York : ≠b United Nations, ≠c 1993-

300   v. ; ≠c 30 cm.

310   Biennial

362 0   38th issue (1990/91)-

530   Issued also on CD-ROM with the same title.

546   English and French

580   Updated by: Monthly bulletin of statistics (United Nations. Statistical Division).

650 0   Statistics.

710 2   United Nations. ≠b Statistical Division.

775 1   ≠t Statistical yearbook (United Nations. Statistical Division) ≠w (DLC)95660575 ≠w (OCoLC)30064530

→ 780 00   United Nations. Statistical Office. ≠t Statistical yearbook ≠w (DLC)50002746 ≠w (OCoLC)1768086

787 1   ≠t Monthly bulletin of statistics (United Nations. Statistical Division) ≠w (DLC)95641265 ≠w (OCoLC)30339106

Title page

Department of Economic and Social Information and Policy Analysis Statistical Division

Statistical Yearbook

Thirty-eighth issue

1990-91

Data available as of 31 March 1993

Département de l'information économique et sociale et de l'analyse des politiques Division de statistique

Annuaire statistique

Trente et huitième édition

DISCUSSION

- The item in this example has a parallel title with a corresponding parallel statement of responsibility. In such a case, each statement of responsibility should be recorded after the title proper to which it relates (1.1F10). An equals sign is used to separate each pairing of parallel title and statement of responsibility (1.1A1).
- A uniform title heading is needed for this item to distinguish the serial from others with the same title. It uses as the qualifying term the heading for the corporate body by which the work was issued, because the title proper of the

serial is indicative of the nature of the work (LCRI 25.5B, p. 2). (Note that the responsible body is transcribed in field 245 exactly as it appears in the chief source, while the corporate body qualifier in the uniform title heading is formulated according to the AACR2R form of entry for the heading.)

E11

PROBLEM CONSIDERED:

Statements of responsibility in more than one language with no corresponding parallel title (LCRI 1.1F11)

RULE(S) CONSULTED:

AACR2R: 1.1F1, 1.1F11, 12.7B7b, 21.1B2a

TAGGED DATA RECORD (based on OCLC #35564478)

LDR   *****cas_/22*****_a*4500

00-05	06	07-14	15-17	18	19	20	21	22-28	29	30-32	33	34	35-37	38	39
008	960916	c	19969999	sa	a	r			------f	0	///	a	0	eng	-	d

043   f-sa---
→ 110 1   South Africa. ≠b Commission on Restitution of Land Rights.
→ 245 00   Annual report / ≠c Commission on Restitution of Land Rights.
260   [Cape Town?] : ≠b The Commission, ≠c 1996-
300   v. : ≠b col. Ill. ; ≠c 30 cm.
310   Annual
362 0   1st (1996)-
500   Title from cover.
610 10   South Africa. ≠b Commission on Restitution of Land Rights.
650   0   Land titles ≠z South Africa.
650   0   Land tenure ≠z South Africa.
→ 780 00   South Africa. Commission on Land Allocation. ≠t Annual report ≠w (DLC)96644002 ≠w (OCoLC)34909448

Cover

FIRST
ANNUAL
REPORT
1996

COMMISSION ON RESTITUTION OF LAND RIGHTS
KOMMISSIE OP HERSTEL VAN GRONDREGTE

DISCUSSION

- The work in this example emanates from a corporate body, the South African Commission on Restitution of Land Rights, and deals with the corporate body itself; therefore, the main entry is under the corporate body (21.1B2a). Since the name of the corporate body appears prominently on the cover, which serves as the chief source of information, it is recorded in the statement of responsibility area (1.1F1).

- On the same source the name of the corporate body also appears in Africaans. When the statement of responsibility appears in more than one language, but there is no parallel title to which the parallel statement relates, transcribe the one in the language of the title proper (1.1F11). The optional provision of this rule, however, is not recommended (LCRI 1.1F11). Thus, the Africaans name of the corporate body "Kommissie op herstel van grondregte" is ignored.

- The preceding title of this serial is given in a linking note (12.7B7b). Field 780 (Linking Entry Field for Preceding Title) is used for such purposes. Notice that the entry in field 780 includes a main entry under the former name of the corporate body because linking entry fields are given in accordance with AACR2R choice of entry and form. For more information on linking fields see section L.

E12

PROBLEM CONSIDERED:

Statement of responsibility for title proper consisting of common title, section number, and section title (12.1F4)

RULE(S) CONSULTED:

AACR2R: 1.4D4, 21.30E1

Cover

```
UNIVERSITE DE OUAGADOUGOU


              ANNALES

              VOLUME 1
                1988

              Série A:
     Sciences Humaines et Sociales
```

TAGGED DATA RECORD (based on OCLC #20688181)

LDR   *****cas_/22*****_a*4500

	00-05	06	07-14	15-17	18	19	20	21	22-28	29	30-32	33	34	35-37	38	39
008	891122	u	1988uuuu	uv	a	r			-------	0	///	b	0	fre	-	d

	043	f-uv---
→	245 00	Annales. ≠n Série A, ≠p Sciences humaines et sociales / ≠c Université de Ouagadougou.
	246 30	Sciences humaines et sociales
→	260	Ouagadougou : ≠b L'Université, ≠c 1988-
	300	v. ; ≠c 29 cm.
	310	Annual
	362 0	Vol. 1 (1988)-
	500	Title from cover.
	650 0	Social sciences.
	651 0	Burkina Faso ≠x Social conditions.
→	710 2	Université de Ouagadougou.

DISCUSSION

- For serials with a title proper consisting of a common title, a section number, and a section title, transcribe the statement of responsibility at the end of the title proper (12.1F4). In this example, the serial has the common title "Annales," the section designation "Série A," and the section title "Sciences humaines et sociales." Thus, the statement of responsibility "Université de Ouagadougou" is transposed to its required position at the end of the title proper.

- Because the corporate body in the statement of responsibility is also the publisher, the name of that body may be shortened in the publication, distribution, etc., area (1.4D4). Thus, the shortened form "L'Université" in French is used in the publishing statement.

- The statement of responsibility is input in field 245, subfield ≠c, immediately following the title proper and before the other title information if such is present. In this example, since subfields ≠n and ≠p are part of the title proper, the statement of responsibility, subfield ≠c, follows subfield ≠p in field 245.

- An added entry is made under the heading for the corporate body "Université de Ouagadougou" because it is the prominently named body responsible for the work (21.30E1).

- Field 710 is used for the added entry for a corporate body. First indicator value "2" is used for a heading entered directly under the name of the body. The second indicator is blank.

F. Numeric and/or Alphabetic, Chronological, or Other Designation Area

A serial must bear a numeric and/or chronological designation. This area of description records the designation of the first and/or last issue of a serial. If the first and/or last issue is in hand, the designation is recorded in a formatted 362 field with first indicator value "0." Such information will appear in the body of the cataloging record immediately after the title and statement of responsibility area or edition statement, if one is present. If the beginning or ending designation of the serial is supplied from sources other than the issues in hand, the information is coded in an unformatted 362 field with first indicator value "1." Such information will be displayed in the note area. Whenever the first issue is not in hand, the designation of the first issue available is given in a 500 General Note preceded by the words "Description based on:".

The prescribed source of information for the numeric and/or alphabetic, chronological, or other designation area is the entire publication (12.0B1.) The preferred form of designation is the one that can best identify the issue. Following are the basic guidelines outlined in rules 12.3D1 and 12.7B8, and LCRIs 12.3, 12.3B1, 12.3C1, 12.3C4, 12.3E, and 12.3G for recording numbering and/or chronological designations:

1. A number or date that is used alone as a designation must sufficiently identify each issue.

Chief source (weekly):	Vol. 1, no. 1, January 10, 1990
362 field:	Vol. 1, no. 1 (Jan. 10, 1990)-

Chief source (1st issue):	Vol. 83, no. 1573, October 1983
(2nd issue):	Vol. 83, no. 1574, November 1983
362 field:	No. 1573 (Oct. 1983)-
515 field:	Issues for Oct. 1983- called also v. 83-
	(Volume number does not have internal number repeated each year)

Chief source:	1995 conference held April 4–6, 1995
362 field:	1995-

2. If a serial carries both a number and a date, even if they do not appear in the same source, record both as the designation. If the elements of the numeric designation do not appear on the same source, the cataloger must decide whether to piece them together or to omit part of the numbering. If in doubt, do not piece them together.

Chief source:	May 1983
Contents page:	Vol. 1, no. 1
362 field:	Vol. 1, no. 1 (May 1983)-

3. If a publication clearly intended to be a serial does not carry a date or number, or if there is no prominently stated date or number which can serve as a designation, record the designation from an informal source, such as the preface or introduction.

Chief source (copyright date):	c1996
Preface:	This report covers 1995
362 field:	1995-

4. If such words as "First issue" or "Premier issue," or other words with similar meaning, appear on the first issue, replace the statement with numbering in brackets when such continues to appear on subsequent issues.

Chief source (1st issue):	Inaugural issue, January 1995
(2nd issue):	Vol. 1, no. 2, February 1995
362 field:	[Vol. 1, no. 1] (Jan. 1995)-
515 field:	Issue for Jan. 1995 called Inaugural issue.

5. If a date serves as the volume number, with internal numbering repeated each year, record the number following the date.

Chief source:	1/1984
362 field:	1984/1-

Chief source:	84-1, January 1984
362 field:	84-1 (Jan. 1984)-

Chief source:	No. 1, 1981
362 field:	1981, no. 1-

6. If a serial has more than one alternative system of designation, and each system serves to identify the issue, record a second or third system with the first system in field 362. Choose as the first system the one that uses the form of volume number and internal number. Always record the chronological designation, if it is available, with the first numeric system. If the alternative numbering system does not identify the item but appears prominently enough on the publication for one to assume that the serial may be asked for by that system, record the information in a note (field 515).

Chief source (1st issue):	Vol. 1, no. 1, January 1995
	"New Series" designation appears on the item.
Chief source (2nd issue):	Vol. 1, no. 2, February 1995
	"New Series" designation appears on the item.
362 field:	Vol. 1, no. 1 (Jan. 1995)-
515 field:	Issues for 1995- called also new series.

7. When the numbering system starts over again and the new numbering system does not carry a designation such as "new series," "second series," or similar wording, create a separate record, even though the title remains the same.

First designation system
Chief source (1st issue):   Vol. 1, no. 1, April 1982
                (last issue):   Vol. 10, no. 12, December 1991

Second designation system
Chief source (1st issue):   Vol. 1, no. 1, January 1992

Earlier record (for first designation system)
362 field: Vol. 1, no. 1 (Apr. 1982)-v. 10, no. 12 (Dec. 1991).

Later record (for second designation system)
362 field: Vol. 1, no. 1 (Jan. 1992)-

8. When the numbering system starts over again and the new numbering system carries a designation such as "new series," "second series," or similar wording, *do not* create a separate record.

   362 field: Vol. 1, no. 1 (fall 1977)-v. 9, no. 1 (fall 1985) ; new ser., v. 1, no. 1 (1986)-

9. When the numbering system starts over again and the new numbering system has a different designation term, or changes from a chronological to a numeric designation or vice versa, *do not* create a separate record. Add a Numbering Peculiarity Note (field 515), as appropriate.

   362 field: Bd. 1 (1984)-Bd. 10 (1993) ; v. 1 (1994)-

   362 field: Issue 1 (June 27, 1968)-issue 182 (Dec. 1975) ; v. 9 (Jan. 16, 1976)-

   515 field: Issues for 1968-75 lack vol. numbering, but constitute v. 1-8.

EXAMPLES

F1   Numeric and alphabetic designation do not appear in the same source
F2   Numeric and/or alphabetic designation appears in two or more languages
F3   Date serves as the volume number
F4   More than one system of designation
F5   Volume designation on first issue is dropped on subsequent issues
F6   Volume designation added on subsequent issues; no designation on first issue
F7   Vol. 0, no. 0 issued prior to vol. 1, no. 1
F8   Vol. 1, no. 1 preceded by an issue
F9   Successive designation begins over again with the same numbering system without a "new series" designation (Create a separate record)
F10   Successive designation begins with a different numbering system without a "new series" designation (Do not create a separate record)
F11   Successive designation begins with a "new series" designation (Do not create a separate record)
F12   "New series" as additional numbering designation
F13   Volume designation is not sufficient to identify the issue
F14   Successive designations given in the Numbering Peculiarities Note

F15   Section volume number shares sequence with the overall numbering system
F16   Numbering Peculiarities Note
F17   Recording of the duration of publication

F1

PROBLEM CONSIDERED:

Numeric and alphabetic designation do not appear in the same source (LCRI 12.3)

RULE(S) CONSULTED:

AACR2R: 1.4F6

BISON Brookfield Zoo **BISON Brookfield Zoo** Volume 3 Number 1	Contents Brookfield Zoo Bison is published twice each year by the Chicago Zoological Society, Brookfield, Illinois 60513 ©1988 Chicago Zoological Society
Cover	**Contents page**

TAGGED DATA RECORD (based on OCLC #27315686)

LDR   *****cas_/22*****Ia*4500

	00-05	06	07-14	15-17	18	19	20	21	22-28	29	30-32	33	34	35-37	38	39
008	930125	c	19889999	ilu	f	r		p	-------	0	///	a	0	eng	-	d

022   8756-3479
→ 245 00   Bison, Brookfield Zoo.
246 30   Bison
→ 260   Brookfield, Ill. : ≠b Chicago Zoological Society, ≠c c1988-
300   v. : ≠b ill. (some col.) ; ≠c 28 cm.
310   Semiannual
→ 362 0   Vol. 3, no. 1 (1988)-
500   Title from cover.
650 0   Zoology ≠x Periodicals.
650 0   Wildlife conservation ≠x Periodicals.
650 0   Zoo animals ≠x Periodicals.
710 2   Brookfield Zoo (Ill.)
710 2   Chicago Zoological Society (Ill.)
780 00   ≠t Brookfield Zoo Bison ≠w (OCoLC)11540694

DISCUSSION

- In this example, the title continues an earlier work, "Brookfield Zoo Bison," which lasted only for two volumes. The publication has the numeric designation on its cover and a copyright date on the contents page. In forming the designation for field 362, use the numeric and chronological designations if both are available, even though they do not appear on the same source (LCRI 12.3). In this example, the volume number and the date, which is the copyright date, are pieced together. The copyright date is recorded in field 260, subfield ≠c, since no date of publication appears in the item (1.4F6).
- When the first issue is available, give the numeric and/or chronological designation in a formatted field 362 with first indicator value "0." Without the first issue in hand, give the numeric and/or chronological designation information, if available, in an unformatted field 362 (first indicator "1"), which displays as a note in the bibliographic record.

F2

PROBLEM CONSIDERED:

Numeric and/or alphabetic designation appears in two or more languages (12.3B2)

TAGGED DATA RECORD (based on OCLC #21264897)

LDR   *****cas_/22*****_a*4500

00-05	06	07-14	15-17	18	19	20	21	22-28	29	30-32	33	34	35-37	38	39
900326	c	19909999	sz	b	x		p	-------	0	///	a	0	ger	-	d

008 (as above)

022	1018-7987
041 0	gerengfre
043	e-sz---
→ 245 00	Schweizerische Zeitschrift für Wirtschaftsrecht = ≠b Revue suisse de droit des affaires = Swiss review of business law.
246 31	Revue suisse de droit des affaires
246 31	Swiss review of business law
246 17	SZW
246 17	RSDA
260	Zürich : ≠b Schulthess Polygraphischer Verlag, ≠c 1990-
300	v. ; ≠c 30 cm.
310	Six issues yearly
→ 362 0	62. Jahrg., 1-
500	Title from cover.
546	Text in German or French; some in English.
650 0	Corporation law ≠z Switzerland ≠x Periodicals.
650 0	Commercial law ≠z Switzerland ≠x Periodicals.
650 0	Corporation law ≠x Periodicals.
650 0	Commercial law ≠x Periodicals.
780 00	≠t Schweizerische Aktiengesellschaft ≠x 1018-6263

Cover

> **Schweizerische Zeitschrift für Wirtschaftsrecht**
> **Revue suisse de droit des affaires**
> **Swiss Review of Business Law**
>
>
> **SZW 1**   **62 Jahrgang / 62ᵉ année 1990**

DISCUSSION

- When the numeric or alphabetic designation appears in two or more languages, always record the one that is in the language of the title proper (12.3B2). In this example, the title proper is in German, with two parallel titles (French and English), and the numeric designation on the chief source is in German and French. According to the rule, the designation in German is chosen for transcription in the numeric and/or alphabetic, chronological, or other designation area.

F3

PROBLEM CONSIDERED:

Date serves as the volume number (LCRI 12.3C1)

RULE(S) CONSULTED:

AACR2R: 12.0B1
LCRI: 12.3C4

Cover

> **affärer & forskning**   1/93
> **Tidskrifft från Svenska handelshögskolan**

Verso of cover

> affärer
> &
> forskning
>
> Nr. 1
> maj 1993

TAGGED DATA RECORD (based on OCLC #34491380)

LDR   *****cas_/22*****Ma*4500

00-05	06	07-14	15-17	18	19	20	21	22-28	29	30-32	33	34	35-37	38	39
960315	c	19939999	fi	f	r		p	-------	0	///	a	0	swe	-	d

008

022   0787-7072
043   e-fi----
245 00 Affärer & forskning : ≠b tidskrifft från Svenska handelshögskolan.
→ 260   Helsingfors : ≠b Svenska handelshögskolan, ≠c 1993-
300   v. : ≠b ill. (some col) ; ≠c 30 cm.
310   Two no. a year
→ 362 0 93/1 (maj 1993)-
500   Title from cover.
650 0 Business education ≠z Finland ≠x Periodicals.
710 2   Svenska handelshögskolan.

DISCUSSION

- The whole publication serves as the chief source of information for transcribing the numeric/chronological designation (12.0B1). If a serial carries only a chronological designation, the elements of chronology may be pieced together from different sources when such is necessary to identify the serial (LCRI 12.3C4).
- When a date, or portion of the date, serves as the volume number preceded or followed by a number that repeats each year, treat the designation as a numeric designation; record the number following the date, e.g., 93/1 (LCRI 12.3C4). In this example, the chronological date preceded by internal numbering (i.e., 1/93) is transcribed as 93/1. Record a separate chronological designation, e.g., "maj 1993" in this example, only when such information appears on the publication (LCRI 12.3C1).
- Field 362 is used for the numeric and/or alphabetic, chronological, or other designation associated with the serial. First indicator value "0" is used for formatted style, that is, when the cataloger has the first and/or last piece in hand. First indicator value "1" is used for unformatted style, that is, when the cataloger does not have the first or last piece in hand but the duration of publication is known, and that information is input in note form. The second indicator is blank.
- In field 260, subfield ≠c is input only when the cataloger has the first or last issue in hand. However, no date should be input in this subfield even when the duration of publication is known and the information is given in field 362 (in note form).

F4

PROBLEM CONSIDERED:

More than one system of designation (LCRI 12.3E)

RULE(S) CONSULTED:

AACR2R: 12.3A1
LCRI: 12.3

JOURNAL OF
THE INTERNATIONAL ASSOCIATION
FOR SHELL AND SPATIAL STRUCTURES

Cover

Vol. 37 (1996) n. 1
April n. 120

TAGGED DATA RECORD (based on OCLC #35038970)

LDR   *****cas_/22*****_a*4500

00-05	06	07-14	15-17	18	19	20	21	22-28	29	30-32	33	34	35-37	38	39
960708	c	19969999	sp	t	r		p	-------	0	///	a	0	eng	-	d

008

022   ≠y 0304-3622
245 00   Journal of the International Association for Shell and Spatial Structures.
246 13   Journal of the IASS
260   Madrid : ≠b International Association for Shell and Spatial Structures, ≠c 1996-
300   v. : ≠b ill. ; ≠c 28 cm.
310   Three times a year
→ 362 0   Vol. 37, no. 1 (Apr. 1996)- = n. 120-
500   Title from cover.
650 0   Space frame structures ≠x Periodicals.
650 0   Roofs, Shell ≠x Periodicals.
710 2   International Association for Shell and Spatial Structures.
780 00   ≠t Bulletin of the International Association for Shell and Spatial Structures
≠x 0304-3622 ≠w (DLC)79646501 ≠w (OCoLC)2262488

DISCUSSION

- Whenever a serial has more than one system of designation, normally record as the first system the one that uses the volume and internal number (LCRI 12.3E). Record a second or third system preceded by an equals sign (12.3A1).
- Although in this example the second designation system is recorded in field 362, there are two situations in which the second or third designation system would be given in a Numbering Peculiarities Note, field 515, rather than in field 362. These situations are those in which the first issue is not in hand or the second or third designation system does not identify the issue (LCRI 12.3).

F5

PROBLEM CONSIDERED:

Volume designation on first issue is dropped on subsequent issues (LCRI 12.3G)

RULE(S) CONSULTED:

AACR2R: 12.3F1, 12.7B8

Vol. 1, No. 1 Spring 1991 THE **BEIRUT** REVIEW A Journal on Lebanon and the Middle East	**No. 3 Spring 1992** THE **BEIRUT** REVIEW A Journal on Lebanon and the Middle East
Cover	**Cover of a later issue**

TAGGED DATA RECORD (based on OCLC #27214684)

LDR   *****cas_/22*****_a*4500

00-05	06	07-14	15-17	18	19	20	21	22-28	29	30-32	33	34	35-37	38	39
008 930108	d	19911994	le	f	r		p	-------	0	///	a	0	eng	-	d

022   1019-0732
043   a-le----- ≠a aw-----
245 04 The Beirut review : ≠b a journal on Lebanon and the Middle East.
260   Beirut : ≠b Lebanese Center for Policy Studies, ≠c [1991-1995?]
300   8 v. ; ≠c 23 cm.
310   Semiannual
→ 362 0 Vol. 1, no. 1 (spring 1991)-no. 8 (fall 1994).
500   Title from cover.
→ 515   Vol. numbering dropped beginning with no. 3.
651 0 Lebanon ≠x Politics and government ≠y 1975- ≠x Periodicals.
651 0 Middle East ≠x Politics and government ≠y 1979- ≠x Periodicals.
710 2   Markaz al-Lubnānī lil-Dirāsāt.

DISCUSSION

- When a change occurs in numbering designation that does not require the creation of a new cataloging record, that change is described in a Numbering Peculiarities Note, field 515 (12.7B8). In this example, the volume numbering is transcribed as it appears on the first issue. With the third issue, however, the volume designation is dropped and the numbering changes to a whole numbering system. Because this change is not considered to be the adoption of a new designation system (LCRI 12.3G), this information is given in field 515.

Field 515 may also contain notes on irregularities or peculiarities in publishing patterns, such as items not published, suspension of publication, etc. In addition, it may be used for notes concerning report year coverage.

- For a completed serial, the numbering designation of the last issue, if available, is transcribed as it appears on the item (12.3F1).

F6

PROBLEM CONSIDERED:

Volume designation added on subsequent issues; no designation on first issue (12.3D1)

RULE(S) CONSULTED:

AACR2R: 12.7B8

CJ INTERNATIONAL
Winter 1985

CJ INTERNATIONAL
Volume 1, Number 2

Caption   Caption of a later issue

TAGGED DATA RECORD (based on OCLC #11777838)

LDR   *****cas_/22*****_a*4500

00-05	06	07-14	15-17	18	19	20	21	22-28	29	30-32	33	34	35-37	38	39
850308	c	19859999	ilu	b	x	1	p	-------	0	///	a	0	eng	-	d

008

022 0   0882-0244 ≠y 0882-0252
245 00   CJ international.
260   Chicago, Ill. : ≠b Center for Research in Law and Justice, ≠c 1985-
300   v. : ≠b ill. ; ≠c 28 cm.
310   Bimonthly
→ 362 0 [Vol. 1, no. 1] (winter 1985)-
500   Title from caption.
→ 515   Issue for winter 1985 lacks numbering. Numbering began with v. 1, no. 2 (spring 1985).
580   Has companion publications: C.J. the Americas; and: CJ Europe.
650 0   Criminal justice, Administration of ≠x Periodicals.
650 0   Crime ≠x Periodicals.
710 2   University of Illinois at Chicago. ≠b Center for Research in Law and Justice.
787 1   ≠t C.J. the Americas ≠x 0896-9922 ≠w (DLC)sn88000061 ≠w (OCoLC)17363629
787 1   ≠t CJ Europe ≠x 1059-2423 ≠w (DLC)93660056 ≠w (OCoLC)24516294

DISCUSSION

- This example is the opposite of example F5. When only the first issue of a serial lacks numeric or alphabetic designation, or there is evidence that subsequent issues consistently carry a numbering system, the numbering designation may be supplied in brackets for the first issue in the 362 field (12.3D1). In the serial under discussion here, the volume and number designation begins with the second issue (v. 1, no. 2, spring 1985) and consistently appears in the subsequent issues. Thus, this information is input in a 515 Numbering Peculiarities Note, and "Vol. 1, no. 1" enclosed in brackets appears in the 362 field (12.7B8).

F7

PROBLEM CONSIDERED:

Vol. 0, no. 0 issued prior to vol. 1, no. 1 (LCRI 12.0B1)

RULE(S) CONSULTED:

AACR2R: 12.7B8

	RIVISTA TRIMESTRALE DI LETTERATURA
Cover	**ARSENALE**
	NUMERO ZERO OTTOBRE-DICEMBRE 1984

	RIVISTA TRIMESTRALE DI LETTERATURA
Cover of a subsequent issue	**ARSENALE**
	NUMERO UNO GENNAIO-MARZO 1985

TAGGED DATA RECORD (based on OCLC #13313338)

LDR   *****cas_/22*****_a*4500

00-05	06	07-14	15-17	18	19	20	21	22-28	29	30-32	33	34	35-37	38	39
008															
860319	d	19841987	it	q	r		p	-------	0	///	a	0	ita	-	d

245 00 Arsenale.

260   Roma : ≠b Arsenale, ≠c 1984-1987.

300   12 v. : ≠b ill. ; ≠c 24 cm.

310   Quarterly

→ 362 0 N. 0 (ott.-dic. 1984)-n. 11/12 (luglio-dic. 1987).

500   Title from cover.

650 0   Italian literature ≠y 20th century ≠x Periodicals.

DISCUSSION

- See example F8.

F8

PROBLEM CONSIDERED:

Vol. 1, no. 1 preceded by an issue (LCRI 12.0B1)

RULE(S) CONSULTED:

AACR2R: 12.7B8

Caption

$\mathcal{NE}$
$\mathcal{HGS}$ **NEXUS**

THE BIMONTHLY NEWSLETTER OF
THE NEW ENGLAND HISTORIC GENEALOGICAL SOCIETY

| Vol. VI, No. 5 | October 1989 |

TAGGED DATA RECORD (based on OCLC #10864963)

LDR   *****cas_/22*****Ia*4500

00-05	06	07-14	15-17	18	19	20	21	22-28	29	30-32	33	34	35-37	38	39
008 840620	d	19841994	mau	b	r	l	p	-------	0	///	a	0	eng	-	d

022 0   0747-9891
043   n-usn--
245 00   NEHGS nexus.
246 2   New England Historic Genealogical Society nexus
246 30   Nexus
246 17   NEHGS ≠f Apr. 1984-
260   Boston, Mass. : ≠b New England Historic Genealogical Society, ≠c 1984-1994.
300   11 v. : ≠b ill. ; ≠c 28 cm.
310   Bimonthly
→ 362 0 Vol. 1, #1 (Feb. 1984)-v. 11, nos. 3 & 4 (June-Sept. 1994).
500   Title from caption.
→ 515   Vol. 1, #1 called also preliminary issue and preceded by another preliminary
         issue, published in Dec. 1983.
610 20   New England Historic Genealogical Society ≠x Periodicals.
651 0   New England ≠x Genealogy ≠x Periodicals.
710 2   New England Historic Genealogical Society.
785 00   ≠t Nexus (New England Historic Genealogical Society)

DISCUSSION

- The basis for the description in serial cataloging is the first issue of the serial.
  In determining which issue is first, according to LCRI 12.0B1, the first issue
  is the one with the lowest or earliest designation. For serials that do not carry

numeric or alphabetic designations, the first issue is the one with the earliest chronological designation.

- A preliminary issue of the serial in example F8 was published in December 1983. Because this issue was clearly an introductory issue and also did not carry any numbering, it is not treated as the first issue (LCRI 12.0B1). The first true issue appeared in February 1984 and was numbered "vol. 1, #1." (Note that this issue was also called "preliminary issue.") The description of the serial is therefore based on this issue, and "Vol. 1, #1 (Feb. 1984)-" is entered in field 362. A 515 note is input to indicate that the first issue of the serial was called also "preliminary issue" and was preceded by another preliminary issue published in December 1983 (12.7B8).
- Note that not all preliminary issues or issues numbered zero should be treated as first issues. The cataloger must consider each case individually and distinguish between true first issues and cases where issue number zero is merely a pilot, trial, or sample issue. In example F7, an issue called "no. 0" precedes issue "no. 1," but the cataloger has judged that clear evidence exists that the issue was not merely a sample or introductory issue; therefore, issue no. 0 in this example is treated as the first issue (LCRI 12.0B1) and used as the basis of the cataloging description.

F9

PROBLEM CONSIDERED:

Successive designation begins over again with the same numbering system without a "new series" designation (Create a separate record) (LCRI 12.3G)

RULE(S) CONSULTED:
AACR2R: 12.3G1
LCRI: 25.5B

Cover

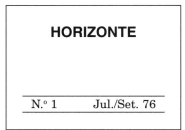

Title page of an earlier issue

Contents page of the earlier issue

TAGGED DATA RECORD (based on OCLC #20316171)

LDR   *****cas_/22*****_a*4500

00-05	06	07-14	15-17	18	19	20	21	22-28	29	30-32	33	34	35-37	38	39
890908	c	19879999	bl	q	r		p	-------	0	///	a	0	por	-	d

008

130 0   Horizonte (João Pessoa, Paraíba, Brazil : 1987)

245 00   Horizonte : ≠b revista trimestral da Universidade Federal da Paraíba.

260   [João Pessoa, Paraíba] : ≠b UFPb/Editora Universitária, ≠c 1987-

300   v. : ≠b ill. ; ≠c 28 cm.

310   Quarterly

→ 362 0   Ano 01, no. 01 (jan./mar. 1987)-

500   Title from cover.

710 2   Universidade Federal da Paraíba

780 00   ≠t Horizonte ≠w (DLC)79645057 ≠w (OCoLC)4871959

DISCUSSION

- When the title proper of a serial remains the same but the numbering system starts over and the publisher does not link the old and new systems with a designation such as "new series" or "second series," create a separate record for the title with the new system if the new system adopts the pattern of the earlier numbering system (LCRI 12.3G). In other words, do not apply rule 12.3G1.

- In this example, the numbering repeats the old numbering scheme (i.e., ano 01, no. 01) in January 1987 without a designation such as "new series." Thus, a separate record is created for the new publication. A uniform title is input for the new serial record to distinguish it from the earlier one with the same title (LCRI 25.5B).

F10

PROBLEM CONSIDERED:

Successive designation begins with a different numbering system without a "new series" designation (Do not create a separate record) (12.3G1)

RULE(S) CONSULTED:

AACR2R: 12.3E1, 12.7B8
LCRI: 12.3G

LOCUS

The Newspaper
of the
Science Fiction Field

Issue 182
December 17, 1975

Caption

LOCUS

The Newspaper
of the
Science Fiction Field

Issue 183
Volume 9 no. 1   January 16, 1976

Caption of a later issue

TAGGED DATA RECORD (based on OCLC #2255782)

LDR   *****cas_/22*****_a*4500

00-05	06	07-14	15-17	18	19	20	21	22-28	29	30-32	33	34	35-37	38	39
008	760620	c	19689999	cau	m	r	l	p	-------	0	///	a	0	eng	-	d

022 0	0047-4959
130 0	Locus (Cambridge, Mass.)
245 00	Locus.
260	Cambridge, Mass. : ≠b C. Brown, ≠c 1968-
300	v. : ≠b ill. ; ≠c 28 cm.
310	Monthly, ≠b <Dec. 1977->
321	Fifteen times a year, ≠b <Dec. 17, 1975->
321	Biweekly, ≠b June 27, 1968-
→ 362 0	1 (June 27, 1968)-issue 182 (Dec. 17, 1975) ; v. 9, no. 1 (Jan. 16, 1976)- =Issue 183-
500	Title from caption.
500	Published: Oakland, Calif. : Locus Publications, <Dec. 1991->
515	First issue preceded by two trial issues, no. 1-2.
→ 515	Issues for 1968-75 lack vol. numbering, but constitute v. 1-8.
530	Available on microfiche and microfilm from UMI.
580	Data from the "books received" section in issues for Jan.-Dec. 1986- are compiled in: Science fiction, fantasy & horror, 1986-
650 0	Science fiction ≠x Periodicals.
775 0	≠t Locus ≠w (DLC)78648218 ≠w (OCoLC)4386151
787 1	≠t Science fiction, fantasy & horror ≠x 0898-4077 ≠w (DLC)88645572 ≠w (OCoLC)16845495

DISCUSSION

- In this example, the title proper of the serial remains the same and the chronological designation system remains consecutive. However, in addition to the consecutive numbering, issues published since 1976 carry a new numbering system consisting of volume and internal number, which starts with volume 9. Because this system is consecutive (earlier issues account for 8 volumes), a separate record should not be created (LCRI 12.3G). In such a case, record the designation of the first and last issues under the old system, followed by a semicolon and the first issue of the designation under the new system (12.3G1).

- After the adoption of the volume and internal numbering system, the consecutive "whole" numbering becomes a second numbering designation. Therefore, "Issue 183" is input as an alternative numbering system, preceded by an equals sign (12.3E1).

- A Numbering Peculiarities Note, field 515, is added to explain that issue 1 to issue 182 do not have volume numbering, and thus to account for the fact that the new numbering begins with v. 9 (12.7B8).

114

F11

PROBLEM CONSIDERED:

Successive designation begins with a "new series" designation (Do not create a separate record (LCRI 12.3G)

RULE(S) CONSULTED:

AACR2R: 12.3G1

ACTA ZOOLOGICA MEXICANA

Publicacion del Museo de Historía Natural de la Cuidad de México

Vol. 8, No. 1-2   Mayo 15 de 1966

Caption

ACTA ZOOLOGICA MEXICANA

NUEVA SERIE

NÚMERO 1
Abril de 1984

Instituto de Ecología México, D.F.

Cover of a later issue

TAGGED DATA RECORD (based on OCLC #1461038)

LDR   *****cas_/22*****_a*4500
022 0   0065-1737 ≠y 0185-5476

	00-05	06	07-14	15-17	18	19	20	21	22-28	29	30-32	33	34	35-37	38	39
008	750720	c	19559999	me		x	z		-------	0	///	a	0	spa	-	d

043   n-mx---
245 00   Acta zoologica mexicana.
260   México, D.F. : ≠b [s.n.], ≠c 1955-
300   v. : ≠b ill. ; ≠c 24 cm.
310   Irregular
→ 362 0 Vol. 1 (jul. 15 de 1955)-v. 10, no. 4 (dic. 15 de 1971) ; nueva ser., no. 1 (abr. de 1984)-
515   Publication suspended 1972-1983.
550   Issued by: Museo de Historía Natural de la Cuidad de México, 1966-71; Instituto de Ecología, 1984-
500   Title from caption.
650 0   Zoology ≠x Periodicals.
650 0   Zoology ≠z Mexico ≠x Periodicals.
710 2   Museo de Historía Natural de la Cuidad de México.
710 2   Instituto de Ecología (Mexico).

DISCUSSION

- When the title proper of a serial remains the same but the numbering system starts over (e.g., a designation such as "Vol. 1" is used again), and, at the same time, a linking statement such as "new series" also appears on the item, do not consider a new serial to have begun. No separate record should be made in such a case (LCRI 12.3G). In this example, the successive designations for the serial are given in accordance with rule 12.3G1, with the designations of the first and last issues under the old system followed by space, semicolon, space and "new series" followed by the designation of the first issue under the new system.

F12

PROBLEM CONSIDERED:

"New series" as additional numbering designation (LCRI 12.3G)

RULE(S) CONSULTED:

AACR2R: 12.1B4

Title page

SIGNO **3** Marzo-Mayo 1957 **LA PAZ**

Title page of
a later issue

SIGNO **CVADERNOS BOLIVIANOS DE CVLTVRA** **11** Marzo, 1984 NUEVA EPOCA **LA PAZ**

TAGGED DATA RECORD (based on OCLC #2267699)

LDR   *****cas_/22*****_a*4500

00-05	06	07-14	15-17	18	19	20	21	22-28	29	30-32	33	34	35-37	38	39
760620	c	19659999	bo		x		p	-------	0	///	b	0	spa	-	d

008

022	0258-2112
043	s-bo---
130 0	Signo (La Paz, Bolivia)
245 00	Signo.
260	La Paz : ≠b Signo,
300	v. ; ≠c 24 cm.
310	Irregular
→ 362 1	Began with 1 (oct./nov. 1956).
500	Description based on: 3 (marzo-mayo 1957).
515	Publication suspended 1969-1983; resumed with no. 11 (marzo 1984).
→ 515	No. 11- also called nueva época.
555	No. 1-10 (1956-1968) 1 v.
651 0	Bolivia ≠x Intellectual life ≠x Periodicals.
651 0	Bolivia ≠x Periodicals.

DISCUSSION

- When the title proper of a serial remains the same and the numerical designation system remains consecutive but a new designation, such as "new series" or some similar wording, appears in addition to the consecutive numbering designation, do not make a separate record (LCRI 12.3G). Nor should the "new series" designation be treated as a section title (12.1B4). Instead, add to the existing record a note explaining the additional numbering designation. Thus, in this example, the information concerning the designation "nueva época" appears in a note, "No. 11- also called nueva época."

F13

PROBLEM CONSIDERED:

Volume designation is not sufficient to identify the issue (LCRI 12.3)

RULE(S) CONSULTED:

LCRI: 12.0A, 12.5B2

TAGGED DATA RECORD (based on OCLC #20557634)

LDR   *****cas_/22*****_a*4500

00-05	06	07-14	15-17	18	19	20	21	22-28	29	30-32	33	34	35-37	38	39
891027	c	19899999	enk	m	r	z	p	-------	0	///	a	0	eng	-	d

008

022   0959-8332 ≠y 0266-3244 ≠y 0959-8330
245 00   Electronics world + wireless world.
246 3   Electronics world plus wireless world
246 30   Wireless world
260   Sutton, Surrey : ≠b Reed Business Pub., ≠c 1989-
300   v. : ≠b ill. ; ≠c 30 cm.
310   Monthly
→ 362 0   Vol. 95, no. 1644 (Oct. 1989)-
500   Title from cover.
650   0   Radio ≠x Periodicals.
650   0   Television ≠x Periodicals.
650   0   Computers ≠x Periodicals.
650   0   Electronics ≠x Periodicals.
780 00   ≠t Electronics & wireless world ≠x 0266-3244 ≠w (DLC)85647145 ≠w (OCoLC)10026434

Cover

**ELECTRONICS
WORLD**
\+ WIRELESS WORLD

OCTOBER 1989

Spine | ELECTRONICS WORLD+WIRELESS WORLD   October 1989   Vol. 95 No. 1644

DISCUSSION

- A publication must carry some kind of numbering system in order to be considered a serial (LCRI 12.0A), and the numeric or chronological designation, when used alone, must identify the individual issues of the serial (LCRI 12.3). In this example, each issue carries no internal number but does carry a consecutive number. Note that the volume number alone is not enough to identify the issue. In such cases, both the volume and the number are recorded as the numeric designation, that is, "Vol. 95, no. 1644" in this example. This publication is monthly, and therefore the month and year are both transcribed as the chronological designation.

F14

PROBLEM CONSIDERED:
Successive designations given in the Numbering Peculiarities Note (LCRI 12.3G)

RULE(S) CONSULTED:
AACR2R: 12.3G1, 12.7B8

Caption

Composer/USA

BULLETIN OF THE NATIONAL ASSOCIATION OF COMPOSERS, U.S.A.

fall 1982

Caption of
a later issue

Composer/USA

BULLETIN OF THE NATIONAL ASSOCIATION OF COMPOSERS, U.S.A.

Series 4, Volume 1, Number 1   Summer 1994

TAGGED DATA RECORD (based on OCLC #11454462)

LDR   *****cas_/22*****Ia*4500

00-05	06	07-14	15-17	18	19	20	21	22-28	29	30-32	33	34	35-37	38	39
841205	c	19uu9999	cau	q	r		p	-------	0	///	a	0	eng	-	d

008

245 00   Composer USA : ≠b bulletin of the National Association of Composers, U.S.A.

260   Woodland Hills, Calif. : ≠b The Association,

300   v. ; ≠c 28 cm.

310   Quarterly

→ 515   Issues for <fall 1984>-spring/summer 1989 called <ser. 2, v. 1, no. 2>-v. 4, no. 3; issues for winter 1989-90-spring 1994 called ser. 3, v. 1, no. 1-v. 5, no. 2; issues for summer 1994- called ser. 4, v. 1, no. 1- .

500   Description based on: fall 1982; title from caption.

650 0   Composers ≠z United States ≠x Periodicals.

650 0   Music ≠x Periodicals.

710 2   National Association of Composers, U.S.A.

DISCUSSION

- When the title proper of a serial remains the same but later issues carry a new sequence of numbering, such as "series 2," "series III," etc., the serial should be cataloged as one title even if the numbering starts over in the different system (LCRI 12.3G).

- Once it has been decided that only one serial is involved, the successive designations should be given in the record in accordance with rule 12.3G1. That is, give the designation of the first and last issues under the old system followed by the designation of the new system. This information should be recorded in a 362 field, if the cataloger has the first issue of the serial in hand. However, when the first issue is not available, as was the case in this example, the new sequence of numbering should be given in a Numbering Peculiarities Note, field 515 (12.7B8).

F15

PROBLEM CONSIDERED:

Section volume number shares sequence with the overall numbering system (LCRI 12.0)

RULE(S) CONSULTED:

AACR2R: 12.7B8, 21.30J1

TAGGED DATA RECORD (OCLC #5855268)

LDR   *****cas_/22*****_a*4500

	00-05	06	07-14	15-17	18	19	20	21	22-28	29	30-32	33	34	35-37	38	39
008	800109	c	19809999	nyu	m	x	1	p	-------	0	///	a	0	eng	-	d

022 0	0196-4763 ≠y 2234-1677	
→ 245 00	Cytometry.	
→ 246 1	≠i Vols. for 1994- have a topical section, issued four times a year, under title: ≠a Communications in clinical cytometry	
→ 246 3	Cytometry. ≠p Communications in clinical cytometry	
260	New York : ≠b Wiley-Liss, ≠c 1980-	
300	v. : ≠b ill. ; ≠c 28 cm.	
310	Monthly, ≠b 1994-	
321	Eight no. a year, ≠b 1990-1993	
321	Bimonthly, ≠b 1980-1989	
362 0	Vol. 1, no. 1 (July 1980)-	
→ 515	Issues of the topical section numbered continuously with other issues but run parallel to the overall Cytometry publication scheme.	
550	Journal of the Society for Analytical Cytology, 1980-1989, Journal of the International Society for Analytical Cytology, 1990- (Topical section: official publication of the Society and the Clinical Cytometry Society, 1994-)	
650 0	Flow cytometry ≠x Diagnostic use ≠x Periodicals.	
710 2	Society for Analytical Cytology (U.S.)	
710 2	International Society for Analytical Cytology.	
710 2	Clinical Cytometry Society.	
770 0	≠t Cytometry. Supplement ≠x 0146-7386 ≠w (DLC)sc88034086 ≠w (OCoLC)16310808	

Cover

VOLUME 22, NUMBER 1   MARCH 15, 1995

THE JOURNAL OF THE INTERNATIONAL SOCIETY FOR ANALYTICAL CYTOLOGY

Cytometry

**Communications
in Clinical Cytometry**

WILEY-LISS
ISSN 0196-4763

Verso of cover

Publication Schedule for 1995

1995	Cytometry	Clinical Cytometry Section
Jan	19.1	
Feb	19:2	
Mar	19:3	22:1
Apr	19:4	
May	20:1	
Jun	20:2	22:2
Jul	20:3	
Aug	20:4	
Sep	21:1	22:3
Oct	21:2	
Nov	21:3	
Dec	21:4	22:4
4 Vols.	3 Vols.	1 Vol.
19-22	19-21	22
16 issues	12 issues	4 issues

DISCUSSION

- The serial in this example changes its publication pattern in 1994 with the introduction of a new topical section "Communications in clinical cytometry." Note, however, that the topical section is numbered in the same sequence with the regular issues, and it can only be purchased in conjunction with the main serial. For these reasons the section does not warrant its own catalog record (LCRI 12.0). Instead, notes about the section should be included on the record for the main serial (12.7B8), and an added title entry should be made for the section title (21.30J1). There should be a second title added entry to provide access to the common title and section title in combination (21.30J1).
- The Numbering Peculiarities Note, field 515, is input to explain how the section is related to the whole numbering scheme.
- Two 246 fields are input. One is used to provide access to the section title, "Communications in clinical cytometry," with a subfield ≠i giving the source of the title. The other, for the common title and section title combination, includes a subfield ≠p containing the section title.

F16

PROBLEM CONSIDERED:

Numbering Peculiarities Note (12.7B8)

RULE(S) CONSULTED:

AACR2R: 12.3C1
LCRI: 12.7B

Information for Individuals & Organizations
Renseignements pour les particuliers et les organisations

1995

Title page

| **Tax Statistics on Individuals** | **Statistiques sur l'impôt des particuliers** |

1993 Tax Year   Année d'imposition 1993

TAGGED DATA RECORD (based on OCLC #34437798)

LDR   *****cas_/22*****_a*4500

00-05	06	07-14	15-17	18	19	20	21	22-28	29	30-32	33	34	35-37	38	39
960227	c	19959999	onc	a	r	4		--s---f	0	///	a	0	eng	-	d

008

022 0	1209-1103
041 0	engfre
043	n-cn---
245 00	Tax statistics on individuals = ≠b Statistiques sur l'impôt des particuliers.
246 31	Statistiques sur l'impôt des particuliers
260	Ottawa : ≠b Revenue Canada, ≠c 1995-
300	v. ; ≠c 28 cm.
362 0	1995 ed.-
500	At head of title: Information for individuals & organizations. Renseignements pour les particuliers et les organisations
→ 515	Vols. for 1995- cover statistics for 1993-
→ 515	Vol. for 1995 called also 50th ed.
546	Text in English and French.
550	Prepared by: Personal Taxation Statistics Section.
580	Continues in part: Taxation statistics. Statistique fiscale.
650 0	Income tax ≠z Canada ≠x Statistics.
650 0	Tax returns ≠z Canada ≠x Statistics.
710 1	Canada. ≠b Revenue Canada.
710 1	Canada. ≠b Personal Taxation Statistics Section.
780 11	≠t Taxation statistics ≠x 0700-1665 ≠w (DLC)76642766 ≠w (OCoLC)1552861

DISCUSSION

- If an item has a chronological designation, and the date on the title page, which is the chief source of information, differs from that of the report year, record the date in the chief source as it appears (12.3C1) and express the report year coverage in a Numbering Peculiarities Note, field 515 (12.7B8).
- In this example, the first Numbering Peculiarities Note clarifies the coverage year of the report, since it differs from the chronological designation. Other examples of possible report year coverage notes are "Report year ends June

30," "Report year covers fiscal year," or "Includes the outlook for the following year."

- The second Numbering Peculiarities Note in this record gives irregularities in the numbering pattern. Other examples of numbering irregularities or peculiarities in numbering or publishing patterns are "Some numbers are combined issues," and "Issues for 1995 lack numbering, but constitute v. 45."
- When giving dates in a Numbering Peculiarities Note, prefer the chronological designations if both numeric and chronological designations are present (LCRI 12.7B). Numeric and chronological designations may be condensed. For example, use 1995/96 for a report year covering July 1, 1995, through June 30, 1996.

F17

PROBLEM CONSIDERED:

Recording of the duration of publication (LCRI 12.7B8)

RULE(S) CONSULTED:

AACR2R: 12.3F1
LCRI: 12.5B2

Cover

TAGGED DATA RECORD (based on OCLC #2258045)

LDR   *****cas_/22*****Ia*4500

	00-05	06	07-14	15-17	18	19	20	21	22-28	29	30-32	33	34	35-37	38	39
008	760620	d	19571962	txu	q	r		p	-------	0	///	a	0	eng	-	d

245 00   Background on world politics.
260   Waco, Tex. : ≠b Background on World Politics, ≠c 1957?-1962.
300   5 v. ; ≠c 22-28 cm.
310   Quarterly
→ 362 1   Began in 1957; ceased with v. 5, no. 4 (winter 1962).
500   Description based on: Vol. 4, no. 1 (spring 1960); title from cover.
650 0   World politics ≠y 1955-1965 ≠x Periodicals.
785 00   ≠t Background ≠x 0361-5448 ≠w (DLC)88651781 ≠w (OCoLC)6976443

DISCUSSION

- When the beginning and ending dates of publication are available, give in the publication, distribution, etc., area the designation of the first issue followed by the designation of the last issue (12.3F1). If such information is available but the issues involved are not in hand, give this information in a note (LCRI 12.7B8). In this example, the duration of publication is known but the issues are not available, and the information for the beginning issue and the last issue is combined into one statement in one unformatted 362 field with first indicator value "1" in a note, "Began in 1957; ceased with v. 5, no. 4 (winter 1962)."
- For a completed serial, give extent of item information according to the number of bibliographic units, regardless of whether the volumes were issued in parts or in combined form (LCRI 12.5B2).
- Fixed field 008 character positions 6, 7–14 and field 260 subfield ≠c may be coded to reflect the duration of the publication. In this example, position 6 in field 008 is coded as "d" for ceased publication, positions 7–10 (DATE1) as "1957" and positions 11–14 (DATE2) as "1962." In field 260 subfield ≠c, the date of publication for the last issue is input, while the beginning date of publication is estimated.

G. Series Statement

A series, according to the definition in Appendix D of AACR2R, is "a group of separate items related to one another by the fact that each item bears, in addition to its own title proper, a collective title applying to the group as a whole. The individual items may or may not be numbered" (p. 622). Although in most cases the individual items in a series are monographs, it should be noted that serials may also be issued in series. A serial, like a monograph, may be issued within a single series or within multiple series. Because serials continue over time, some issues may be within a series, while later issues are not.

A subseries is a series within a main series. A subseries may or may not be dependent on a main series. The main series may also be numbered or unnumbered. To determine whether a series should be established under a main series and subseries together or under the subseries alone as the title proper, apply AACR2R 12.1B4–12.1B6 and LCRI 1.6H.

The chief source for a series is the series title page or the analytical title page (a title page that includes the series title and the analyzable title) when there is no series title page. If the series does not appear in either place, the series statement may be transcribed from anywhere in the item. If the series consists of a main series and subseries, both titles must appear on the same source in order to be recorded together in the series statement (LCRI 1.6A2).

The series statement may be taken from anywhere in the item being cataloged, and it should always be transcribed in the series statement area exactly as it appears on the item. It is important to note that for this reason a series statement itself is not an access point; it is only a part of the bibliographic description. Rather, it is the series added entry, which must be in AACR2R choice and form of entry, that serves as the access point. (Note, however, that if the series statement as it appears on the item is identical to the AACR2R form of entry, the series can be traced the same, providing an access point without an actual series added entry in the bibliographic record.)

EXAMPLES

G1   Parallel series title
G2   Initialism or full form of the corporate body as series
G3   Variant forms of the series title
G4   Unnumbered series in series statement
G5   Main series or subseries as a serial
G6   Series designation and subseries as a serial

G7   Main series and series designation in series statement
G8   A known span of issues of a serial carries the same series number
G9   A span of issues of a serial carries distinct numbers of a series

G1

PROBLEM CONSIDERED:

Parallel series title (LCRI 1.6B)

RULE(S) CONSULTED:

AACR2R: 1.1F10, 1.6C1
LCRI: 21.30L

TAGGED DATA RECORD (based on OCLC #33373489)

LDR   *****cas_/22*****_a*4500

00-05	06	07-14	15-17	18	19	20	21	22-28	29	30-32	33	34	35-37	38	39
951026	c	19959999	onc	q	r			------f	0	///	a	0	eng	-	d

008

022   1201-6772
041 0   engfre
043   n-cn---
→ 245 00 National economic and financial accounts. ≠p Quarterly estimates / ≠c Statistics Canada, National Accounts and Environment Division = Comptes économiques et financiers nationaux. Estimations trimestrielles / Statistique Canada, Division des comptes nationaux et de l'environment.
246 31   Comptes économiques et financiers nationaux. Estimations trimestrielles
260   Ottawa : ≠b Statistics Canada, ≠c 1995-
300   v. : ≠b ill. ; ≠c 28 cm.
310   Quarterly
362 0   Vol. 43, no. 1 (1st quarter 1995)-
→ 490 1   System of national accounts = ≠a Système de comptabilité nationale
515   Numbering continues that of National income and expenditure accounts.
546   English and French.
580   Merger of: National income and expenditure accounts, and: Financial flow accounts.
650 0   National income ≠z Canada ≠x Accounting.
710 2   Statistics Canada. ≠b National Accounts and Environment Division.
780 14   ≠t National income and expenditure accounts ≠x 0318-708X ≠w (DLC)74647432 ≠w (OCoLC)1795875
780 14   ≠t Financial flow accounts (Preliminary) ≠x 0380-0938 ≠w (DLC)86648087 ≠w (OCoLC)2443648
→ 830 0 System of national accounts

```
┌─────────────────────────────────────────────────────────────┐
│                                                               │
│   System of National Accounts    Système de comptabilité nationale │
│                                                               │
│   National                       Comptes                      │
│   Economic                       économiques                  │
│   and Financial                  et financiers                │
│   Accounts                       nationaux                    │
│                                                               │
│   Quarterly Estimates            Estimations trimestrielles   │
│   First Quarter 1995             Premier trimestre 1995        │
│                                                               │
│   Statistics Canada              Statistique Canada           │
│   National Accounts and          Division des comptes nationaux et │
│   Environment Division           de l'environnement           │
│                                                               │
└─────────────────────────────────────────────────────────────┘
```

Title page

DISCUSSION

- This item has a parallel title and a corresponding parallel statement of responsibility. The statement of responsibility is given after each title proper and parallel title to which it relates (1.1F10). The series for this item also appears in two languages. The English language series title is chosen as the title proper for the series statement because it corresponds to the language of the title proper of the item being cataloged (LCRI 1.6B). The series parallel title is also recorded in the series statement area, since it appears with the series title (1.6C1).
- An added entry for the series is needed to provide access (LCRI 21.30L). Field 440 is used when the series statement is in the authority form. However, if an additional element, such as a parallel title, a statement of responsibility, or other title information appears along with the title, the series statement should be entered in field 490 and the series should be traced in an 8xx field. In this example, the series statement includes, in addition to the series title, a French parallel title, and therefore it is input in field 490.
- Field 490 is used for a series title not traced or traced differently. First indicator value "0" is used for a series not traced, and first indicator value "1" is used for a series traced differently. The second indicator is undefined.
- Whenever first indicator value "1" is used for field 490, an 800–830 field must also be input to provide the appropriate series added entry. In this case, field 830 is input for the series added entry. The first indicator for field 830 is undefined, and the second indicator is "0–9" for the number of nonfiling characters. Initial articles are omitted from field 830 according to Library of Congress policy; therefore, the second indicator is always set to value "0."

G2

PROBLEM CONSIDERED:

Initialism or full form of the corporate body as series (LCRI 25.5B, p. 7)

RULE(S) CONSULTED:

LCRI: 21.30L

PVP-VOL. 252

PLANT SYSTEMS/COMPONENTS AGING MANAGEMENT—1993

Title page

presented at
THE 1993 PRESSURE VESSELS AND PIPING
CONFERENCE
DENVER, COLORADO
JULY 25-29, 1993

TAGGED DATA RECORD (based on OCLC #33180957)

LDR   *****cas_/22*****_a*4500

00-05	06	07-14	15-17	18	19	20	21	22-28	29	30-32	33	34	35-37	38	39
950921	c	19939999	nyu	u		u		-------	1	///	a	0	eng	-	d

008

245 00   Plant systems/components aging management.

246 3   Plant systems components aging management.

260   New York, N.Y. : ≠b American Society of Mechanical Engineers,

300   v. : ≠b ill. ; ≠c 28 cm.

362 1   Began with issue for 1993?

→ 490 1   PVP

500   Vols. for 1993-1994 presented at the … Pressure Vessels and Piping
          Conference; 1995- presented at the Joint ASME/JSME Pressure Vessels and
          Piping Conference.

→ 550   Sponsored by: the Pressure Vessels and Piping Division, ASME.

650 0   Nuclear power plants ≠x Equipment and supplies ≠x Maintainability ≠x
          Congresses.

650 0   Pressure vessels ≠x Maintainability ≠x Congresses.

650 0   Service life (Engineering) ≠x Congresses.

711 2   Pressure Vessels and Piping Conference.

711 2   Joint ASME/JSME Pressure Vessels and Piping Conference.

710 2   American Society of Mechanical Engineers. ≠b Pressure Vessels and Piping
          Division.

→ 830 0 PVP (Series).

DISCUSSION

- In this example, the corporate body, the Pressure Vessels and Piping Division of the American Society of Mechanical Engineers, has been the sponsor of a series of conferences. The publications of those conferences, of which this item is a part, are issued in a series known solely by the Division's initials, PVP. Thus, when cataloging this item, the cataloger has treated the name "PVP" as a series and transcribed it as it appears on the piece. A series added entry is needed (LCRI 21.30L).

- A series added entry must consist of the authority form of the series. If the title of the series as it appears on the piece consists solely of the name or initials of a corporate body, according to LCRI 25.5B, p. 7, a uniform title should be created by adding to the series title the qualifying term "Series" in parentheses. This heading may then be used for a series added entry. Thus, in this example, the series added entry consists of "PVP," the initials of the Division, plus "Series" as the qualifier.

- In this example, field 490 is used for a series statement appearing on the item that is different from the authority series record. First indicator value "1" is used if the series is to be traced differently. Field 830 is used for the series title in authority form, which in this case is a uniform title.

G3

PROBLEM CONSIDERED:
Variant forms of the series title (1.6B1)

RULE(S) CONSULTED:
AACR2R: 12.6B1
LCRI: 21.30L

MATERIALS RESEARCH SOCIETY SYMPOSIUM PROCEEDINGS VOLUME 224

Title page

Rapid Thermal and Integrated Processing

Symposium held April 30-May 3, 1991, Anaheim, California, U.S.A.

TAGGED DATA RECORD (based on OCLC #31276602)

LDR   *****cas_/22*****_a*4500

00-05	06	07-14	15-17	18	19	20	21	22-28	29	30-32	33	34	35-37	38	39
941013	c	19919999	pau	u	u			-------	1	///		0	eng	-	d

008

245 00	Rapid thermal and integrated processing.
260	Pittsburgh, Pa. : ≠b Materials Research Society, ≠c c1991-
300	v. : ≠b ill. ; ≠c 24 cm.
362 0	[1] (1991)-
→ 490 1	Materials Research Society symposium proceedings, ≠x 0272-9172
650 0	Semiconductors ≠x Heat treatment ≠x Congresses.
650 0	Semiconductor doping ≠x Congresses.
650 0	Vapor-plating ≠x Congresses.
650 0	Rapid thermal processing ≠x Congresses.
710 2	Materials Research Society.
→ 830 0	Materials Research Society symposia proceedings.

DISCUSSION

- In this example, the title page is the chief source for the serial. Although the item lacks a title page for the series, the series title appears in the chief source for the serial as "Materials Research Society symposium proceedings," and this form is transcribed as the title proper of the series (1.6B1). The series number "224," which appears on the item, is not included in the series statement, because to do so would indicate that every item in the serial will carry the series number "224" (12.6B1). In fact, in this example every item in the serial will have a different series number.

- If variant forms of the title of the series appear from issue to issue (as in this example), and if the authority record for a particular series title has not yet been established, the cataloger must establish the series title based on the chief source of the first issue or the first available issue (1.6B1).

- In dealing with a series title, the cataloger has to decide whether it would be useful to patrons to be able to access that particular title—that is, whether the series title should be traced. In general, if series information is not considered to be useful enough to require tracing, it is normally not recorded in the series area of the cataloging record. If the series is to be traced, it should be transcribed in the series statement area. It may then either be traced exactly as it appears in the series statement (i.e., a series added entry will be derived from the series statement) or it may be traced in a form that differs from the transcription in the series statement area (i.e., a series added entry in an established form will be input (LCRI 21.30L)). In this example, the series is traced differently because the series authority record has already been established in a different form; thus, the series added entry is given according to that form as "Materials Research Society symposia proceedings."

- Field 490 is used for a series statement that is not traced or is traced in a different form. First indicator "0" is used when no tracing is desired. In general, this indicator is seldom used; there is little reason to record a series that is not important or useful enough to deserve access. First indicator value "1" is used when the series is to be traced differently, and an 8xx field must also be input to provide the appropriate series added entry. In this example, field 830 is input for the series added entry in its authority form, i.e., the form found in the LC series authority record.

G4

PROBLEM CONSIDERED:

Unnumbered series in series statement (LCRI 12.1B4b)

RULE(S) CONSULTED:

LCRI: 12.1B4, 12.1B4a

TAGGED DATA RECORD (based on OCLC #27200335)

LDR   *****cas_/22*****Ia*4500

00-05	06	07-14	15-17	18	19	20	21	22-28	29	30-32	33	34	35-37	38	39
930106	c	19939999	nyu	a	r			-------	0	///	a	0	eng	-	d

008

043   e------

→ 245 00   Fodor's ... affordable Europe.

246 30   Affordable Europe

260   New York, N.Y. : ≠b Fodor's Travel Publications, Inc.,

300   v. : ≠b ill. ; ≠c 22 cm.

310   Annual

362   Began in 1993.

→ 440   0   Fodor's affordables

500   Description based on: 3rd ed. ('96).

651   0   Europe ≠x Guidebooks.

Title page

> **<u>Fodor's affordables</u>**
>
> **FODOR'S 96**
> **AFFORDABLE**
> **EUROPE**

DISCUSSION

- In this example, two titles—"Fodor's affordables" and "Fodor's . . . affordable Europe"—appear in the chief source in the item. When only one numbering designation is involved, it is often difficult to determine whether to treat both titles as a combination of common title and section title, or to treat the more comprehensive title as an unnumbered series. One way, mentioned in LCRI 12.1B4, to arrive at a decision is a close examination of how other records with the same common title are treated in the catalog. The same rule interpretation also provides guidelines for distinguishing a common title from an unnumbered series. In order to enter a work under common title and section title as the title proper, two conditions must be met: First, both titles must be present in the same source; and second, the section title should be a dependent title or have some indication of subject dependency upon the more general title (LCRI 12.1B4a). The two titles in this example do not meet the second condition, even though the first condition is met, and, therefore, LCRI 12.1B4b is to be applied; the more comprehensive title, "Fodor's affordables," is treated as a series, and the more specific title, "Fodor's . . . affordable Europe," is used as the title proper of the serial.
- Field 440 is used for a series statement in tracing form. The first indicator is blank. The second indicator shows the number of characters to be ignored in filing.

G5

PROBLEM CONSIDERED:

Main series or subseries as a serial (LCRI 12.1B4b)

RULE(S) CONSULTED:

LCRI: 12.6B1

G5a-b
Caption

No. 172-A/April 22, 1997

Financial
Accounting Series

Status Report

No. 287

Financial Accounting Standards Board

G5a

TAGGED DATA RECORD (based on OCLC #12828403)

LDR   *****cas_/22*****_a*4500

	00-05	06	07-14	15-17	18	19	20	21	22-28	29	30-32	33	34	35-37	38	39
008	851121	c	19859999	ctu		x	1		-------	0	///		0	eng	-	d

022 0	0885-9051
→ 245 00	Financial accounting series.
260	Stamford, CT : ≠b Financial Accounting Standards Board, ≠c 1985-
300	v. ; ≠c 23 cm.
310	Irregular
362 0	No. 001 (June 12, 1985)-
500	Title from caption.
→ 580	Has numerous subseries.
650 0	Accounting.
650 0	Accounting ≠x Standards ≠z United States.
710 2	Financial Accounting Standards Board.
→ 762 1	≠x 0885-9116 ≠w (DLC)sc90034047 ≠w (OCoLC)2630137
→ 762 1	≠x 0886-4535 ≠w (DLC)sc90034052 ≠w (OCoLC)5918022
→ 762 1	≠x 0149-8452 ≠w (DLC)sc77001040 ≠w (OCoLC)1370503
→ 762 1	≠x 0276-1378 ≠w (DLC)sc79000319 ≠w (OCoLC)4530800
→ 762 1	≠x 0746-7486 ≠w (DLC)sf78000479 ≠w (OCoLC)1781699

G5b

TAGGED DATA RECORD (based on OCLC #1370503)

LDR   *****cas_/22*****_a*4500

00-05	06	07-14	15-17	18	19	20	21	22-28	29	30-32	33	34	35-37	38	39
750603	c	19739999	ctu	m	x	1		-------	0	///		0	eng	-	d

008

022 0	0149-8452
043	n-us---
110 2	Financial Accounting Standards Board.
→ 245 10	Status report / ≠c Financial Accounting Standards Board.
260	Stamford, CT : ≠b The Board ≠c 1973-
300	v. ; ≠c 28 cm.
310	Monthly (with extra editions as developments warrant)
362 0	No. 1 (1973)-
→ 490 1	June 12, 1985- : Financial accounting series
500	Title from caption.
580	Issues for 1984- include as occasional feature: FASB viewpoints, previously published separately.
650 0	Accounting ≠x Standards ≠z United States ≠x Periodicals.
610 20	Financial Accounting Standards Board ≠x Periodicals.
730 0	FASB viewpoints.
→ 760 1	≠x 0885-9051 ≠w (OCoLC)12828403
770 0	≠t Highlights of financial reporting issues ≠x 0884-7428 ≠w (DLC)sc84001188 ≠w (OCoLC)7373429
770 0	≠t Highlights of financial reporting issues
785 15	≠t FASB viewpoints ≠w (DLC)sn81002460 ≠w (OCoLC)5424715

DISCUSSION

- If an item carries two separate titles, with one for the main series and the other for the subseries, and each of them has its own numbering designation system, there are two possible approaches from which the cataloger may choose. One approach is to catalog the main series as the title proper of the serial and make reference to the individual subseries titles, as in example G5a. The other approach, which is generally preferred, is to catalog the subseries as the title proper of the serial and the main series as the title proper of the series, as illustrated in example G5b (LCRI 12.1B4b).

- In example G5a, the main series of the item is "Financial accounting series." The five subseries are described in general terms in a 580 note, "Has numerous subseries."

- In a different approach, example G5b shows a record taking the subseries "Status report" as the title proper of the serial and treating the more comprehensive title "Financial accounting series" as the series (i.e., in the series statement).

- Field 490 is used for a series statement if the series is not in tracing form. In example G5b, the series statement itself is identical to the established authority form, but, because there is an element (in this case the chronological date of the issues contained in the series) preceding the series title (LCRI 12.6B1), it must be input in field 490 rather than field 440 (see discussion for examples G8 and G9).

• Field 760 is used for the entry of the main series on a catalog record for a subseries. Field 762 is used for the entry of the subseries on the catalog record for the main series. For either field first indicator value "0" is defined to generate a note with "Subseries of:" or "Has subseries:", respectively. As of July 1986, these two fields are mandatory for use by ISSN centers only. When updating existing records, LC will delete all subfields except ≠x and ≠w (as illustrated in the examples) and remove linking fields entirely, if these two subfields are not present.

G6

PROBLEM CONSIDERED:

Series designation and subseries as a serial (LCRI 1.6B)

RULE(S) CONSULTED:

AACR2R: 12.1B6

The Institute for Comparative Research in Human Culture **Instituttet for sammenlignende kulturforskning** **Serie B: Skrifter** **LXI** 1979	**Gård, Skatt or Matrikkel** **Andreas Holmsen** The Institute for Comparative Research in Human Culture Universitetsforlage Oslo 1979
Series title page	**Analytical title page**

TAGGED DATA RECORD (based on OCLC #1589486)

LDR   *****cas_/22*****Ia*4500

	00-05	06	07-14	15-17	18	19	20	21	22-28	29	30-32	33	34	35-37	38	39
008	750901	c	19259999	no		x		m	-------	0	///	b	0	nor	-	d

022   0332-6217
041 0   norengfregerswe
→ 245 00 Serie B--Skrifter / ≠c Instituttet for sammenlignende kulturforskning.
260   Oslo : ≠b H. Aschehoug, ≠c 1925-
300   v. : ≠b ill. ; ≠c 20-23 cm.
310   Irregular
362 0   1 (1925)-
500   Each vol. has also a distinctive title.
546   Chiefly in Norwegian; some in English, French, German or Swedish.
650 0   Ethnology.
710 2   Instituttet for sammenlignende kulturforskning.

DISCUSSION

- In this example, the chief source of information is the series title page. The title proper consists of the designation of a subseries and a series title without a main series title. In such a case, treat the grouping as the title proper (12.1B6). Such a grouping (that is, a designation plus a subseries title in the absence of a main series title) may also appear in series statements and in established series authority records (LCRI 1.6B). LC/NACO practice is to use two adjacent hyphens (or a long dash) in place of a comma-space to connect the two parts (i.e., the designation of the subseries series and subseries title) in order to make clear that the entire grouping is to be considered as the title proper. For example, the series authority record for the monographic volumes in this series would be "Serie B--Skrifter." (See also example H20.)
- In field 245 the entire grouping is included in subfield ≠a. It should not be further coded in subfield ≠n (which is used for section number/series designation) or subfield ≠p (which is used for the section/subseries title).

G7

PROBLEM CONSIDERED:
Main series and series designation in series statement (LCRI 1.6H)

RULE(S) CONSULTED:
AACR2R: 1.6H2, 12.1B5, 12.6B1

Title page

PACIFIC LINGUISTICS
Series A-78

PAPERS IN AUSTRONESIAN LINGUISTICS NO. 1

Title page
of a later issue

PACIFIC LINGUISTICS
Series A-84

PAPERS IN AUSTRONESIAN LINGUISTICS NO. 3

TAGGED DATA RECORD (based on OCLC #26970735)

LDR *****cas_/22*****_a*4500

	00-05	06	07-14	15-17	18	19	20	21	22-28	29	30-32	33	34	35-37	38	39
008	921113	c	19919999	at		x		p	-------	0	///		0	eng	-	d

043 n-io---
→ 245 00 Papers in Austronesian linguistics.
260 Canberra, A.C.T. : ≠b Dept. of Linguistics, Research School of Pacific Studies, Australian National University, ≠c c1991-
300 v. : ≠b ill. ; ≠c 25 cm.
310 Irregular
362 0 No. 1-
→ 440 0 Pacific linguistics. ≠n Series A
550 Issued by: Linguistic Circle of Canberra.
650 0 Austronesian languages ≠x Periodicals.
710 2 Australian National University. ≠b Research School of Pacific Studies. ≠b Dept. of Linguistics.
710 2 Linguistic Circle of Canberra.

DISCUSSION

- In this example, the series consists of a main series "Pacific linguistics" and a series designation "Series A." Because both appear in the chief source, they are recorded together in the series statement (12.1B5). Note that the subseries has only the designation "Series A" without a subseries title (see 1.6H2).
- The subseries is analyzable (LCRI 1.6H). The analytical title may be a monograph or a serial. In this example, the analytical title is a serial titled "Papers in Austronesian linguistics."
- Because each issue of the serial is separately numbered within the series, the series number "78" is omitted from the series statement (12.6B1).

G8

PROBLEM CONSIDERED:

A known span of issues of a serial carries the same series number (LCRI 12.6B1)

RULE(S) CONSULTED:

LCRI: 1.6J

TAGGED DATA RECORD (based on OCLC #3234170)

LDR *****cas_/22*****_a*4500

	00-05	06	07-14	15-17	18	19	20	21	22-28	29	30-32	33	34	35-37	38	39
008	770901	c	19589999	mdu	a	r	1		---s--f	0	///		0	eng	-	d

022 0147-7153
043 n-us---
245 00 Disability days, United States

260	Hyattsville, Md. : ≠b U.S. Dept. of Health and Human Services, Public Health Service, National Center for Health Statistics ; ≠a Washington, D.C. : ≠b For sale by the Supt. of Docs., U.S. G.P.O.,
300	v. : ≠b ill. ; ≠c 26 cm.
310	Annual
362 1	Began with 1957/58.
→ 490 1	1957/58-1959/60: Health statistics. Ser. B (RA11.B15475)
→ 490 1	1957/58-1959/60: Public Health Service publication ; ≠v no. 584-B
→ 490 1	1961/62-<1971>: Public Health Service publication ; ≠v no. 1000, ser. 10
→ 490 1	1961/62- :Vital and health statistics. Series 10, Data from the National Health Survey
→ 490 1	<1972-1977>: DHEW publication ; ≠v (HRA)
→ 490 1	<1978-> : DHHS publication ; ≠v (PHS)
550	Vols. for 1957/58- issued by U.S. Dept. of Health, Education and Welfare, Public Health Service, Health Resources Administration, National Center for Health Statistics.
650 0	Diseases ≠z United States ≠x Periodicals.
650 0	Medical care ≠x Utilization ≠z United States ≠x Statistics.
650 0	Health surveys ≠z United States.
710 2	National Center for Health Statistics (U.S.)
→ 830 0	Health statistics from the U.S. National Health Survey. ≠n Ser. B.
→ 830 0	Public Health Service publication ; ≠v no. 584-B.
→ 830 0	Public Health Service publication ; ≠v no. 1000, ser. 10.
→ 830 0	Vital and health statistics. ≠n Series 10, ≠p Data from the National Health Survey.
→ 830 0	DHEW publication ; ≠v no. (HRA)
→ 830 0	DHHS publication ; ≠v no. (PHS)

DISCUSSION

- See example G9.

G9

PROBLEM CONSIDERED:

A span of issues of a serial carries distinct numbers of a series (LCRI 12.6B1)

RULE(S) CONSULTED:

AACR2R: 12.6B1
LCRI: 1.6J

Cover	**The Conference Board** Report Number 985 **Human Resources Outlook 1992**

TAGGED DATA RECORD (based on OCLC #15149142)

LDR   *****cas_/22*****_a*4500

	00-05	06	07-14	15-17	18	19	20	21	22-28	29	30-32	33	34	35-37	38	39
008	870204	c	19879999	nyu	a	r	l		-------	0	///	a	0	eng	a	d

043		n-us---
→ 245	00	Human resources outlook / ≠c the Conference Board.
260		New York, N.Y. : ≠b The Board, ≠c c1986-
300		v. : ≠b ill. ; ≠c 28 cm.
310		Annual
362	0	1987-
→ 490	1	1987-1990: Research bulletin
→ 490	1	1991- : Report
500		Title from caption.
650	0	Industrial relations ≠z United States ≠x Periodicals.
650	0	Collective bargaining ≠z United States ≠x Periodicals.
650	0	Wages ≠z United States ≠x Periodicals.
710	2	Conference Board.
780	00	≠t Labor outlook ≠x 0196-3910 ≠w (DLC)79644808 ≠w (OCoLC)15785765
→ 830	0	Research bulletin (Conference Board)
→ 830	0	Conference Board report.

DISCUSSION

- If a single issue of a serial or some issues of a serial are published within one numbered series and others are published in another series, precede the series title in the series statement with the numbering of the issues contained in the series, followed by a colon-space (LCRI 1.6J). Record the number of the series in the series statement and in the series tracing, if it is a single issue or the series numbering is in a sequence, or if part of the series numbering remains the same (LCRI 12.6B1), or else omit the series number altogether (12.6B1).

- In example G8, the item has been issued as part of six different series in succession. In four of those series the item retains a constant series designation (e.g., 584-B; no. 1000, ser. 10; (HRA); (PHS)) for a span of issues. As a result, the series statements, input in individual 490 fields, are transcribed in a format that includes the dates of the span and the constant series number (LCRI 1.6J). The other two series do not retain the same numbering for the item being cataloged, and, as a result, the series statements, which also appear in 490 fields, are transcribed without series numbering. Due to the inclusion of dates and other elements in the series statements, an 830 field must also be input for each to provide access to the proper form of the series entries.

- Subfield ≠v is used in field 490 as well as in field 830 when a single issue of the series or a limited number of issues of the serial occur in a span of consecutive numbers of a series (LCRI 12.6B1). When part of the series numbering remains the same, it may also be included in subfield ≠v.

- The serial in example G9 was issued in the "Conference Board research bulletin" during the period 1987–1990 and has been issued in the "Conference Board report" since 1991. All issues that appear in the two series are numbered separately within their respective series. In keeping with rule 12.6B1 and LCRI 1.6J, the two series statements are therefore input in field 490 without series numbering.

H. Choice of Access Points

AACR2R drastically limits the use of the corporate main entry for serial publications. The only rule that deals specifically with the entry of items under corporate names is 21.1B2. According to this rule, if a work emanates from a corporate body and its content falls into one of the five categories given in the rule, the work should be entered under the heading for the corporate body. If a work emanates from a corporate body, but its content does not fall into any of the five categories, that work should be entered under title. As a result, most serials cataloged under AACR2R rule(s) are entered under title main entry, including a great number of serials with nondistinctive titles. To distinguish between individual serials that share the same nondistinctive title, the uniform title heading has been developed. The uniform title heading consists of the title proper plus a qualifying term in parentheses (see section O on Uniform Title Headings and Uniform Titles).

Because the application of rule 21.1B2 is based on the content of the item being described, the cataloger is urged to be especially cautious in applying and interpreting this rule. Careful application will lead to greater uniformity in the choice between entry under corporate body or entry under title. In addition to and apart from this, the cataloger will also encounter various complex problems concerning choice of entry when it has already been determined that entry should be made under title (e.g., whether a corporate body should be a part of the title proper, whether an initialism or a full form of title should be chosen, plus numerous other questions involving the choice of title proper).

EXAMPLES

H1	Choice of title proper with terms related to incorporation as part of the title proper
H2	Choice of title proper with terms related to incorporation not as part of the title proper
H3	Choice of stable title in a less preferred source as title proper
H4	Choice of corporate body's name as part of the title proper
H5	Choice of corporate body's name in possessive case as part of the title proper
H6	Choice of conference name as title proper
H7	Choice of full form of title as title proper
H8	Choice of acronym/initialism of title as title proper
H9	Choice of a phrase as part of the title proper
H10	Choice of title proper according to the language of the text
H11	Determination of title proper from an ambiguous chief source
H12	Work emanating from a corporate body entered under corporate body (its membership)

H13   Work emanating from a corporate body entered under corporate body (its resources)

H14   Work with report-like title not emanating from a corporate body

H15   Work entered under a personal name

H16   Work entered under the heading for a subordinate body

H17   Work entered under common title and section title

H18   Work entered under common title, section number, and section title

H19   Work entered under section title

H20   Work entered under series designation and subseries as title proper

H1

PROBLEM CONSIDERED:

Choice of title proper with terms related to incorporation as part of the title proper (LCRI 12.1B1)

RULE(S) CONSULTED:

AACR2R: 12.7B7d, A.4C1
LCRI: 12.1B3, 12.1E1

No. 1 pp. 1-200
ISSN 0001-7884 January/February 1996   Volume 82

ACUSTICA united with **acta acustica**

The Journal of the European Acoustics Association (EEIG)

ACUSTICA

**Masthead area
from back cover**

ACUSTICA united with **acta acustica**

The Journal of the European Acoustics Association (EEIG)

ACUSTICA

TAGGED DATA RECORD (based on OCLC #35093501)

LDR   *****cas_/22*****_a*4500

008

00-05	06	07-14	15-17	18	19	20	21	22-28	29	30-32	33	34	35-37	38	39
960716	c	19969999	gw	b	r		p	-------	0	///	a	0	eng	-	d

→ 006

00	01-02	03	04	05	06-12	13-14	15-17
i	nn	n	-	f	-------	s-	---

(sound disc)

022	≠y 0001-7884
041 0	engfreger ≠f eng
→ 245 00	Acustica united with acta acustica : ≠b the journal of the European Acoustics Association (EEIG).
→ 246 30	Acustica
→ 246 30	Acta acustica
246 17	Acustica, acta acustica
260	Stuttgart : ≠b S. Hirzel Verlag, ≠c c1996-
300	v. : ≠b ill ; ≠c 30 cm.
310	Bimonthly
362 0	Vol. 82, no. 1 (Jan./Feb. 1996)-
500	Title from cover.
525	Some issues accompanied by supplements.
→ 525	One issue annually accompanied by a sound disc (digital, stereo ; 4 3/4 in.) with sounds that illustrate articles.
546	Articles in English, French, and German; summaries and tables of contents in English only.
→ 580	Merger of: Acustica, and: Acta acustica, adopting the numbering of the former.
650 0	Sound ≠x Periodicals.
650 0	Acoustical engineering ≠x Periodicals.
650 0	Vibration ≠x Periodicals.
710 2	European Acoustics Association.
→ 780 14	≠t Acustica ≠x 0001-7884 ≠w (DLC)58031694 ≠w (OCoLC)1461065
→ 780 14	≠t Acta acustica ≠x 1022-4793 ≠w (OCoLC)31794258

DISCUSSION

- Among the various possible titles appearing on the cover of the serial in this example, "Acustica united with acta acustica" has been chosen as the title proper. The choice is based on the fact that this is the title that appears not only on the serial's cover, but also on the verso of the cover, contents page, editorial page, and back cover. Note that LCRI 12.1B1 says statements mentioning an earlier title, title absorbed, etc., should not be included as part of the title proper, even when consistently so present elsewhere in the serial. At first glance this would seem to rule out "Acustica united with acta acustica" as title proper. Note, however, that in this example, the phrase "united with acta acustica" is considered to be *part of* the title proper (LCRI 12.1B3).
- In transcribing the title proper with an incorporated title, do not capitalize the first word of the incorporated title (A.4C1).

- The phrase "The journal of the European Acoustics Association (EEIG)" is transcribed as other title information in field 245, subfield ≠b, because it fulfills the first condition in LCRI 12.1E1—that is, it includes a statement of responsibility and the statement is an integral part of the other title information (see also CCM 6.3.3a1).
- Because some users might consider either "Acustica" or "acta acustica" to be the title, both are given added title entries using field 246 with second indicator "0" for portion of title.
- The titles of the serials that were merged are given in a Linking Entry Complexity Note (12.7B7d) using field 580. This note contains the information that the resulting serial adopts the numbering of the former merged serial "Acustica." Two corresponding 780 fields are used for the preceding titles "Acustica" and "Acta acustica." First indicator value "1" is used here since a field 580, Linking Entry Complexity Note, is already present and there is thus no need for a note to be generated from the 780 field. Second indicator value "4" is used to generate the display constant "Merger of: . . . and: . . . ."
- Field 525 is used to describe supplements or special issues that are neither cataloged in separate records nor recorded in a linking entry field 770. In this case, it indicates that one issue of the journal is accompanied by a sound disc. Under format integration, a 006 field is used to describe the accompanying sound disc's physical characteristics, which cannot be coded in field 008. Character position 00 (Form of Material) is coded "i" for Non-Musical Sound Recording, and the remaining positions 01–17 follow field 008 positions 18–34 configuration for Music.

H2

PROBLEM CONSIDERED:

Choice of title proper with terms related to incorporation not as part of the title proper (LCRI 12.1B1)

TAGGED DATA RECORD (based on OCLC #1461155)

LDR   *****cas_/22*****_a*4500

00-05	06	07-14	15-17	18	19	20	21	22-28	29	30-32	33	34	35-37	38	39
750720	c	19639999	enk		x	z		-------	0	///	a	0	eng	-	d

008

022	0065-2296
→ 245 00	Advances in botanical research.
→ 246 1	≠i Issues for 1995- called: ≠a Advances in botanical research incorporating advances in plant pathology
260	London : ≠b Academic Press, ≠c c1963-
300	v. : ≠b ill (some col.) ; ≠c 24 cm.
310	Irregular
362 0	Vol. 1-
650 0	Botany.
650 0	Botany ≠x Research.
→ 780 05	≠t Advances in plant pathology ≠g 1995 ≠x 0736-4539 ≠w (DLC)83642797 ≠w (OCoLC)8861704

```
┌─────────────────────────────────────────────────────┐
│                                                       │
│                      Advances in                      │
│               BOTANICAL RESEARCH                      │
│                     incorporating                     │
│              Advances in Plant Pathology              │
│                                                       │
│                     VOLUME 21                         │
│                                                       │
│                        1995                           │
│                                                       │
└─────────────────────────────────────────────────────┘
```

Title page (label to the left of the box)

DISCUSSION

- Serials constantly merge with or absorb other titles. When this happens, it is common for the title to include a statement that mentions an earlier title, a title absorbed, etc. In this example, beginning with volume 21, the journal "Advances in botanical research" has incorporated "Advances in plant pathology." Although the phrase "incorporating Advances in plant pathology" appears on the chief source, and in the preface the publisher states that the two serials have been brought together under the title "Advances in botanical research incorporating Advances in plant pathology," the cataloger should not treat the phrase relating to incorporation as part of the title proper, since, according to LCRI 12.1B1, such statements generally should not be included as part of the title proper. Another reason is the layout of the title page. The phrase relating to incorporation is set in a much smaller font underneath the title proper "Advances in botanical research," and the phrase itself is not grammatically linked to the title proper (see also CCM 6.17d).

- It is reasonable to expect that some users may try to access the serial using the entire title, including the terms related to incorporation. This variant title should therefore be given as an added entry. Use field 246 with first indicator value "1" to generate both a note and a title added entry from the field; the second indicator is blank, since the source of the title recorded in this field cannot be adequately described by any of the values "0–8."

- The absorbed title "Advances in plant pathology" should be recorded in linking entry field 780. First indicator value "0" is used to generate a note; second indicator value "5" indicates that the title in hand has absorbed the preceding entry, with the display constant "Absorbed:".

H3

PROBLEM CONSIDERED:

Choice of stable title in a less preferred source as title proper (12.0B1)

RULE(S) CONSULTED:

LCRI: 12.0B1

```
┌─────────────────────────────────┐
│                                 │
│                                 │
│   Key Business Directory        │
│        INDIA                    │
│                                 │
│                                 │
└─────────────────────────────────┘
          Cover of first ed.
```

```
┌────────────────────────────────┐
│                                │
│   Key Business                 │
│   Directory of                 │
│   INDIA                        │
│                                │
└────────────────────────────────┘
          On spine of first ed.
```

```
┌─────────────────────────────────┐
│                                 │
│   KEY                           │
│   BUSINESS                      │
│   DIRECTORY                     │
│   OF INDIA                      │
│                                 │
│   1993/94 Edition               │
│                                 │
└─────────────────────────────────┘
    Title page of subsequent ed.
```

```
┌─────────────────────────────────┐
│                                 │
│   KEY                           │
│   BUSINESS                      │
│   DIRECTORY                     │
│   OF INDIA                      │
│                                 │
│   1994/95 Edition               │
│                                 │
└─────────────────────────────────┘
    Title page of subsequent ed.
```

TAGGED DATA RECORD (based on OCLC #35041036)

LDR   *****cas_/22*****_a*4500

	00-05	06	07-14	15-17	18	19	20	21	22-28	29	30-32	33	34	35-37	38	39
008	960708	c	19929999	ii	a	r			--r----	0	///	a	0	eng	-	d

043   a-ii---
→ 245 00 Key business directory of India.
  246 17 Dun's KBD India
  246 1   ≠i Title varies slightly: ≠a Key business directory, India
  260   Singapore : ≠b Dun & Bradstreet (Singapore), ≠c 1992-
  300   v. ; ≠c 30 cm.
  310   Annual
  362 0   1st ed. [(1992)]-
  440 0 Dun's KBD
→ 500   Title from spine.
  500   Published: Dun & Bradstreet (India), 1995-
  650 0 Corporations ≠z India ≠x Directories.
  650 0 Business enterprises ≠z India ≠x Directories.
  651 0 India ≠x Commerce ≠x Directories.
  710 2   Dun & Bradstreet (Singapore)
  710 2   Dun & Bradstreet (India)

DISCUSSION

- Although AACR2R 12.0B1 stipulates that the chief source of information for printed serials is the title page or the title page substitute of the first issue or first available issue, the LC Rule Interpretations provide some exceptions to this rule, allowing the choice of a stable title in a less preferred source as title proper if an item lacks a title page.

- In cataloging this serial, the cataloger applies the second exception in LCRI 12.0B1: Two or more issues of the serial are in hand, and it is clear that the title "Key business directory of India" is more stable from issue to issue than the title "Key business directory, India," which appears on the cover of the first issue. Another consideration is the difference in title between the first issue and subsequent issues. Note that beginning with the 1993/94 edition, the word "of" has been added to the title. This would constitute a title change, necessitating two separate records. To avoid this, the cataloger has applied the exception in LCRI, and the more stable title "Key business directory of India," which appears on a less preferred source (i.e., the spine) rather than the preferred source (i.e., the cover), is chosen as the title proper (see also CCM 3.2.2g).

H4

PROBLEM CONSIDERED:

Choice of corporate body's name as part of the title proper (12.1B3)

RULE(S) CONSULTED:

AACR2R: 12.1F2, 21.1B3, 21.29C, 21.30E1

Cover

> **Illinois Natural History Survey Biological**
> Notes 131
>
>
> April 1988

TAGGED DATA RECORD (based on OCLC #24586379)

LDR   *****cas_/22*****_a*4500

00-05	06	07-14	15-17	18	19	20	21	22-28	29	30-32	33	34	35-37	38	39
911018	c	19889999	ilu		x	1		--b---s	0	///	a	0	eng	-	d

008

022   1076-4712 ≠y 0073-490X
043   n-us-il
→ 245 00 Illinois Natural History Survey biological notes.
→ 246 30 Biological notes
260   Champaign, Ill. : ≠b The Survey, ≠c 1988-
300   v. : ≠b ill. ; ≠c 28 cm.
310   Irregular
362 0   131-
500   Title from cover.
650 0 Biology ≠z Illinois ≠x Periodicals ≠x Bibliography.
→ 710 1   Illinois. ≠b Natural History Survey Division.
780 00 ≠t Biological notes ≠x 0073-490X ≠w (DLC)42025021 ≠w (OCoLC)1278014

DISCUSSION

- According to AACR2R 12.1B3, "In case of doubt about whether a corporate body's name or an abbreviation of that name is part of the title proper, treat the name as such only if it is consistently so presented in various locations in the serial . . . ." The title "Illinois Natural History Survey biological notes" appears on the cover of this item as well as in various other locations. Hence, the corporate body "Illinois Natural History Survey" in this case is treated as part of the title proper rather than being transcribed in the statement of responsibility area.

- Because the corporate body is already treated as part of the title proper and does not appear separately in the chief source of information, a further statement of responsibility is not given (12.1F2).

- Additional title access in the form of a variant title is provided in field 246. First indicator value "3" indicates that no note but a title added entry is to be generated. Second indicator value "0" indicates that the title given in field 246 is for a portion of the title for which access is desired—in this case, the portion of the title without the name of the corporate body.

- Because the corporate body "Illinois Natural History Survey Division" is not selected as the main entry (21.1B3), it is given as an added entry (21.30E1). AACR2R 21.29C also states that an added entry should be made under the heading for a person or a corporate body or for a title if some catalog users might suppose that the record for an item would be found under that heading or title.

H5

PROBLEM CONSIDERED:

Choice of corporate body's name in possessive case as part of the title proper (1.1B2)

RULE(S) CONSULTED:

AACR2R: 12.1B7, 12.1F2
LCRI: 12.1B7

ASEE's 1994-95 Directory of

Engineering
Graduate Studies &
Research

American Society for Engineering Education

Title page

Directory of Engineering Graduate Studies & Research

American Society for
Engineering Education   **93**

Title page of an earlier issue

TAGGED DATA RECORD (based on OCLC #32401683)

LDR   *****cas_/22*****_a*4500

00-05	06	07-14	15-17	18	19	20	21	22-28	29	30-32	33	34	35-37	38	39
008															
950501	c	19959999	dcu	a	r			--r----	0	///	a	0	eng	-	d

022   ≠y 1057-5286
043   n-us--- ≠a n-cn---
→ 245 00   ASEE's … directory of engineering graduate studies & research.
246 30   Directory of engineering graduate studies & research
246 30   Engineering graduate studies & research
260   Washington, D.C. : ≠b American Society for Engineering Education, ≠c 1994-
300   v. ; ≠c 28 cm.
310   Annual
362 0   1994-95-
650 0   Engineering ≠x Study and teaching (Graduate) ≠z United States ≠x Directories.
650 0   Engineering ≠x Study and teaching (Graduate) ≠z Canada ≠x Directories
710 2   American Society for Engineering Education.
→ 780 00   ≠t Directory of engineering graduate studies & research ≠x 1067-9022 ≠w (DLC)93641947 ≠w (OCoLC)26934603

DISCUSSION

- This example presents an interesting case in which the corporate body's name appears in the possessive case on the chief source. As a result, the cataloger must decide whether this name is to be treated as part of the title proper. According to AACR2R 1.1B2, if the name is an integral part of the title proper (i.e., linked by the use of an apostrophe or a grammatical case ending), the name should be transcribed as part of the title proper. In this example, the name "ASEE's" is grammatically linked to the title and should be regarded as an integral part of the title (see also CCM 6.1.5).

- Since the date occurring as part of the title proper varies from issue to issue, this date is replaced by the mark of omission (12.1B7) in transcription of the title proper. For use of the mark of omission at the end of the title, see LCRI 12.1B7.

- A statement of responsibility is not given because it is already embedded, in abbreviated form, as part of the title proper, and such a statement does not appear separately in the chief source (12.1F2).

- Field 780 is used for citing a preceding entry. First indicator value "0" will generate a note on the bibliographic record. The second indicator describes the relationship of the serial being cataloged and the preceding entry. Value "0" generates a note with the introductory phrase "Continues:" followed by the preceding entry "Directory of engineering graduate studies & research."

H6

PROBLEM CONSIDERED:

Choice of conference name as title proper (1.1B3)

RULE(S) CONSULTED:

AACR2R: 1.1E6, 12.1B7, 21.1B2d, 21.30J1b
LCRI: 12.1B7

Title page

```
INSTITUTE FOR SPACE
AND NUCLEAR POWER STUDIES

10TH SYMPOSIUM ON SPACE NUCLEAR
POWER AND PROPULSION

January 10-14, 1993

AMERICAN INSTITUTE OF PHYSICS    NEW YORK
```

Title page of
1994 symposium

```
PROCEEDINGS
OF THE 11TH SYMPOSIUM
ON SPACE NUCLEAR POWER
AND PROPULSION

January 9-13, 1994

AMERICAN INSTITUTE OF PHYSICS    NEW YORK
```

Title page of
1995 symposium

```
INSTITUTE FOR SPACE AND
NUCLEAR POWER STUDIES

12TH SYMPOSIUM ON SPACE NUCLEAR
POWER AND PROPULSION

January 8-12, 1995

AMERICAN INSTITUTE OF PHYSICS    NEW YORK
```

TAGGED DATA RECORD (based on OCLC #28058911)

LDR   *****cas_/22*****_a*4500

00-05	06	07-14	15-17	18	19	20	21	22-28	29	30-32	33	34	35-37	38	39
930507	c	19939999	nyu	a	r			-------	1	///	a	0	eng	-	d

008

→ 111 2   Symposium on Space Nuclear Power and Propulsion.

→ 245 10   Symposium on Space Nuclear Power and Propulsion : ≠b [proceedings].

→ 246 1   ≠i Some issues have title: ≠a Proceedings of the ... Symposium on Space Nuclear Power and Propulsion

→ 246 18   Space nuclear power and propulsion

260   New York : ≠b American Institute of Physics, ≠c 1993-

300   v. : ≠b ill. ; ≠c 29 cm.

310   Annual

362 0   10th (1993)-

440   0   AIP conference proceedings

515   Issued in 3 pts.

550   Sponsored by: Institute for Space and Nuclear Power Studies, Chemical and Nuclear Engineering Department, University of New Mexico, 1993; in cooperation and co-sponsorship with numerous other scientific and governmental bodies.

650   0   Space vehicles ≠x Nuclear power plants ≠x Congresses.

650   0   Space vehicles ≠x Propulsion systems ≠x Congresses.

710 2   American Institute of Physics.

710 2   University of New Mexico. ≠b Institute for Space and Nuclear Power Studies.

780 00 Symposium on Space Nuclear Power Systems. ≠t Proceedings of the ... Symposium on Space Nuclear Power Systems ≠w (DLC)96644748 ≠w (OCoLC)21653438

DISCUSSION

- It is very common in conference publications to find in the chief source only the name of the conference, without any title proper. In such a case, the name of the conference should be treated as the title proper (1.1B3; see also CCM 6.1.8). "Symposium on Space Nuclear Power and Propulsion" is the name of the conference, in this example. Since no title proper appears on the title page, the name of the conference is treated as the title proper. Note that the numbering of the conference, which occurs at the beginning of the title, is omitted when the conference name is transcribed as the title proper (12.1B7).

- Other title information may be supplied by the cataloger if it seems necessary to make the nature of the item clear to users. In this example, "Proceedings" is added in brackets as other title information (1.1E6; see also CCM 3.3.2). No added entry, however, is needed for other title information composed by the cataloger (21.30J1b).

- Because this conference carries its own name and the conference name appears in the chief source, the work is entered under the name of the conference (21.1B2d).

- Because no title proper appears on the proceedings for either the 10th or the 12th symposium, the name of the conference is treated as the title proper. However, the 11th symposium has the title "Proceedings of the 11th Symposium on Space Nuclear Power and Propulsion." This is treated as a fluctuating title that does not constitute a title change. However, it is necessary to provide access using field 246 for the title not selected to be the title proper (CCM 7.2.4b). First indicator value "1" is used to generate both a note and a title added entry; second indicator value blank indicates that the title is one that is not specified by one of the other second indicator values. Note that the numbering of the symposium, which occurs in the middle of the title, is omitted and replaced by the mark of omission (LCRI 12.1B7).

- An additional 246 field is given to provide variant title access for the spine title "Space nuclear power and propulsion." Second indicator value "8" is associated with the display constant "Spine title:".

H7

PROBLEM CONSIDERED:

Choice of full form of title as title proper (12.1B2)

RULE(S) CONSULTED:

AACR2R: 1.1E4, 1.1E6, 12.1E1
LCRI: 12.1E1; 21.30J, p. 23

TAGGED DATA RECORD (based on OCLC #15814360)

LDR   *****cas_/22*****_a*4500

00-05	06	07-14	15-17	18	19	20	21	22-28	29	30-32	33	34	35-37	38	39
870605	c	19889999	nyu	b	n	l	p	-------	0	///	a	0	eng	-	d

008

022 0	0894-1777
→ 245 00	Experimental thermal and fluid science : ≠b ETF science.
→ 246 30	ETF science
246 13	ETFS
260	New York, N.Y. : ≠b Elsevier, ≠c 1988-
300	v. : ≠b ill. ; ≠c 28 cm.
310	8 no. a year, ≠b 1993-
321	Quarterly, ≠b 1988-1989
321	Bimonthly, ≠b 1990-1992
362 0	Vol. 1, no. 1 (Jan. 1988)-
→ 500	"International journal of experimental heat transfer, thermodynamics, and fluid mechanics."
650 0	Heat ≠x Transmission ≠x Periodicals.
650 0	Fluid dynamics ≠x Periodicals.

> **ETF**
> **SCIENCE**
>
> **Experimental**
> **Thermal and**
> **Fluid Science**
>
> International Journal
> of Experimental
> Heat Transfer,
> Thermodynamics,
> and Fluid Mechanics
>
> VOLUME 1, NUMBER 1, JANUARY 1988

Title page

DISCUSSION

- It is very common for journal covers or title pages to bear an acronym or initialism in addition to the spelled out or full form of the title. According to AACR2R 12.1B2, the full form should be chosen as the title proper, unless the acronym or initialism is the only form of title presented in other locations in the serial. In this example, both the full form and the initialism appear on the chief source of information. The full form, in addition to appearing on the title page, also appears on the cover, spine, and title page verso, and is referred to by the publisher, whereas the initialism is found only on the title page. Although the typography and layout on the chief source of information seem to indicate that the initialism and the full form of the title are equally important, the full form is chosen as the title proper because it fulfills the above condition stated in AACR2R (see also CCM 6.1.4d).
- Whichever form is not chosen as the title proper should then be given as other title information (12.1E1). An added entry is also made for the title not chosen, "ETF Science," to provide access (LCRI 21.30J, p. 23).
- The phrase "International journal of experimental heat transfer . . ." is given as a quoted note in field 500. This is transcribed according to LCRI 12.1E1, which states that other title information should not generally be given for serials, unless it meets one of the three circumstances stated and related to AACR2R 1.1E4, 12.1E1, and 1.1E6. Since the presence of the phrase here does not meet any of the stated circumstances, the cataloger has transcribed it in a quoted note rather than in field 245, subfield ≠b, as other title information.

H8

PROBLEM CONSIDERED:

Choice of acronym/initialism of title as title proper (12.1B1)

RULE(S) CONSULTED:

AACR2R: 12.1E1, Appendix D (p. 620)
LCRI: 1.1E, 12.1E1

EER
Energy Efficiency Research

A publication for sharing information on new technology developments in energy conservation

Title page

TAGGED DATA RECORD (based on OCLC #2805352)

LDR   *****cas_/22*****_a*4500

00-05	06	07-14	15-17	18	19	20	21	22-28	29	30-32	33	34	35-37	38	39
770315	c	19uu9999	dcu	u	u	l	p	------f	0	///	a	0	eng	-	d

008

022   0276-0304

043   n-us---

→ 245 00   EER : ≠b Energy efficiency research.

→ 246 30   Energy efficiency research

260   [Washington, D.C. : ≠b U.S. Energy Research and Development Administration, Office of Conservation],

300   v. : ≠b ill ; ≠c 27 cm.

→ 500   "A publication for sharing information on new technology developments in energy conservation."

710 1   United States. ≠b Energy Research and Development Administration. ≠b Office of Conservation.

DISCUSSION

- Similar to the preceding example, this serial has both the initialism and full form of the title appearing in the chief source. However, the abbreviated form of the title, "EER," is chosen as title proper because not only is it present in locations other than the chief source, but also it is the only form of title present in these other locations (12.1B1), that is, on the cover and as the running title in this case. Since the abbreviated form is taken as title proper, the full form "Energy efficiency research" (i.e., the one not chosen as the title proper) should be transcribed as other title information (12.1E1; see also CCM 6.1.4d).

- The other title information "Energy efficiency research" is given access through an added entry using field 246 (CCM 6.3.4a). First indicator "3" is used so that the title will print as an added entry but not as a note. Second indicator "0" is used to indicate that the added entry is taken from field 245, subfield ≠b.

- The cataloger has rejected the phrase "A publication for sharing information on new technology developments in energy conservation" as other title information and has given it as a quoted note because this phrase does not meet the criteria of "other title information" as defined by AACR2R (p. 620, Appendix D). CCM 6.3.3a2 is very helpful with respect to how AACR2R's definition is to be interpreted. The phrase "A publication for . . ." here does not add any further to the understanding of the title proper, which already defines the subject coverage of the serial. Although this is subject to the cataloger's judgment, CCM gives clear guidelines on choosing to record various types of other title information.

H9

PROBLEM CONSIDERED:

Choice of a phrase as part of the title proper (12.1B3)

RULE(S) CONSULTED:

AACR2R: 1.1B1, 12.1B2
LCRI: 12.1B3

<table>
<tr>
<td>

JOURNAL OF
ELECTRONIC TESTING:
Theory and Applications

(JETTA)

Volume 1
1990

Title page

</td>
<td>

JOURNAL OF
ELECTRONIC TESTING:
Theory and Applications

(JETTA)

Back cover

</td>
</tr>
</table>

TAGGED DATA RECORD (based on OCLC #22270507)

LDR   *****cas_/22*****_a*4500

00-05	06	07-14	15-17	18	19	20	21	22-28	29	30-32	33	34	35-37	38	39
900824	c	19909999	mau	b	r	z	p	-------	0	///	a	0	eng	-	d

008

022	0923-8174
→ 245 00	Journal of electronic testing, theory and applications : ≠b JETTA.
→ 246 30	JETTA
260	Boston, U.S.A. : ≠b Kluwer Academic Publishers, ≠c 1990-
300	v. : ≠b ill ; ≠c 26 cm.
310	Bimonthly, ≠b <Apr. 1995->
321	Four no. a year
362 0	Vol. 1, no. 1 (Feb. 1990)-
650 0	Electronic apparatus and appliances ≠x Testing ≠x Periodicals.

DISCUSSION

- In this example, the title "Journal of electronic testing" is followed by a colon and the phrase "theory and applications." In deciding whether this phrase is part of the title proper, the rule regarding the inclusion of a corporate body's name as part of the title proper should be applied (LCRI 12.1B3). This phrase not only appears on the title page, but also is present along with "Journal of electronic testing" on the masthead on the back cover. Therefore, it should be treated as part of the title proper (12.1B3). The colon has been changed to a comma according to AACR2R 1.1B1 (see also CCM 6.1.3d).
- The presence of the initialism "JETTA" should also be taken into consideration. Clearly this initialism includes the first letters of the words in the phrase

"Journal of electronic testing," as well as the first letters from the phrase "theory and applications." This indicates that the entire phrase "Journal of electronic testing, theory and applications" is considered to be a unit and therefore should be transcribed as the title proper (LCRI 12.1B3).

• Because both the full form of the title proper and an initialism appear on the chief source, and the full form is transcribed as the title proper, the initialism is treated as other title information and an added entry is made for it in field 246 (12.1B2; see also CCM 7.2.1f).

H10

PROBLEM CONSIDERED:

Choice of title proper according to the language of the text (1.1B8)

TAGGED DATA RECORD (based on OCLC #11276063)

LDR   *****cas_/22*****_a*4500

00-05	06	07-14	15-17	18	19	20	21	22-28	29	30-32	33	34	35-37	38	39
841017	c	19849999	ch	q	r			---b---	0	///	a	0	eng	-	d

008

022	0256-9655
041 0	engfregerjpn
043	a-ch---
→ 245 00	Current contents of foreign periodicals in Chinese studies = ≠b Wai wen ch'i k'an Han hsüeh lun p'ing hui mu.
→ 246 31	Wai wen ch'i k'an Han hsüeh lun p'ing hui mu
260	T'ai-pei shih : ≠b Han hsüeh yen chiu chung hsin,
300	v. ; ≠c 25 cm.
310	Quarterly
362 1	Began with ti 1 chüan ti 1 ch'i (Chung-hua min kuo 73 nien 2 yüeh [i.e. Feb. 1984]).
500	Description based on: Ti 12 chüan ti 1 ch'i (Chung-hua min kuo 84 nien 2 yüeh [i.e. Feb. 1995]); title from cover.
515	Issues for ti 12 chüan ti 1 ch'i- called also tsung hao ti 45 hao-
546	English, French, German or Japanese.
651 0	China ≠x Periodicals ≠x Bibliography.
651 0	China ≠x Bibliography.
710 2	Han hsüeh yen chiu chung hsin (China)

154

ISSN 0256 9655

Title page

外文期刊漢學論評彙目

Current Contents
of Foreign Periodicals in Chinese Studies

第十二卷第一期（總號第45號）   中華民國八十四年二月出版

漢學研究中心編印

DISCUSSION

- According to rule 1.1B8, if the title appears in two or more languages, choose the one in the language of the written content of the item as the title proper and record the others as parallel titles. In this example, the Chinese title appears as the first title, followed by the English title, with numeric designations and publisher in Chinese only. However, since the text of the item is primarily in English and there is no Chinese language in the text, the English title is chosen as the title proper. It is followed by the parallel Chinese title in its romanized form (see also CCM 6.1.4c and 6.4). According to LC practice, the Chinese title is romanized in Wade-Giles.
- The Chinese title in its romanized form is given as an added entry to provide access for the parallel title (see also CCM 7.2.1e). The field 246 second indicator specifies the type of title recorded. Value "1" here indicates that the title given in field 246 is a parallel title.
- Because the content of this serial is primarily in English, character positions 35–37 for Language in field 008 are coded "eng" rather than "chi." Field 546 is used to include a note concerning languages of the text, with a corresponding field 041 to record the language codes of the text. These codes are assigned from the OCLC MARC code list, and the first language code in field 041 subfield ≠a should be the same as the code in the fixed field.

H11

PROBLEM CONSIDERED:

Determination of title proper from an ambiguous chief source (21.0B1)

RULE(S) CONSULTED:

AACR2R: A.23
LCRI: 12.7B6; 21.30J, p. 21

```
                              IAgrE Journal
           Cover              Landwards


                           Volume 51 No. 1  Spring 1996
```

TAGGED DATA RECORD (based on OCLC #34626646)

LDR   *****cas_/22*****_a*4500

00-05	06	07-14	15-17	18	19	20	21	22-28	29	30-32	33	34	35-37	38	39
960425	c	19969999	enk	q	r			p	-------	0	///	a	0	eng	-	d

008

022   1363-8300 ≠y 0308-3732
043   e-uk---
→ 245 00   Landwards.
→ 246 1   ≠i At head of title: ≠a IAgrE journal
246 3   Institution of Agricultural Engineers journal
260   Bedford : ≠b Institution of Agricultural Engineers, ≠c 1996-
300   v. : ≠b ill ; ≠c 30 cm.
310   Quarterly
362 0   Vol. 51, no. 1 (spring 1996)-
500   Title from cover.
500   Journal for professional engineers in agriculture, forestry, environment and
        amenity.
650 0   Agricultural engineering ≠x Periodicals.
650 0   Agricultural engineering ≠z Great Britain ≠x Periodicals.
710 2   Institution of Agricultural Engineers.
780 00   ≠t Agricultural engineer ≠x 0308-5732 ≠w (DLC)sn85010511 ≠w
        (OCoLC)3506458

DISCUSSION

- When the information appearing in the chief source or chief source substitute
  is ambiguous or insufficient, use information appearing in the contents of the
  item (such as introduction, contents, text) or even outside the item to determine access points (21.0B1). Both "IAgrE journal" and "Landwards" appear
  on the chief source of this journal. It is difficult to determine which of these
  two should be treated as the title proper. However, by applying rule 21.0B1,
  the one-word title "Landwards" is chosen as the title proper, since this title appears also in the contents page and editorial.
- "IAgrE journal" does not appear in other locations in the journal, so it is not
  treated as part of the title proper; nor is it other title information, because it
  appears at the head of the title and is not an integral part of the title. According
  to LCRI 12.7B6, a phrase or name that is not a statement of responsibility appearing at the head of the title should be given in an "At head of title" note.
- It is reasonable to assume that this serial may be known as "IAgrE journal."
  An added entry for this title should be made using field 246 (LCRI 21.30J, p.
  21). Since the source of this varying title is not adequately represented by second indicator values "4–8," the words "At head of title" may be explicitly

recorded in subfield ≠i preceding the title. Another 246 field is also made to provide additional access to the full form of the "At head of title" data.
- When transcribing the chronological designation in field 362, do not capitalize the name of a season (A.23).

H12

PROBLEM CONSIDERED:

Work emanating from a corporate body entered under corporate body (its membership) (21.1B2a)

RULE(S) CONSULTED:

LCRI: 21.1B2; 21.30J, p. 8

TAGGED DATA RECORD (based on OCLC #23199401)

LDR   *****cas_/22*****_a*4500

00-05	06	07-14	15-17	18	19	20	21	22-28	29	30-32	33	34	35-37	38	39
910307	c	19uu9999	cau	u	u			--r----	0	///	a	0	eng	-	d

008 (row above)

→ 110 2   Society for Computer Simulation.
→ 245 10   SCS membership directory / ≠c the Society for Computer Simulation.
→ 246 3   Society for Computer Simulation membership directory
  260   San Diego, Calif. : ≠b The Society,
  300   v. : ≠b maps ; ≠c 23 cm.
  500   Description based on: 1991; title from cover.
  610 20   Society for Computer Simulation ≠x Membership ≠x Directories.
  650 0   Computer simulation ≠x Periodicals.
  650 0   Simulation methods ≠x Periodicals.

Cover

> 1991
> SCS Membership Directory
>
> [SCS]   The Society for
>   Computer Simulation

DISCUSSION

- The serial cataloger is regularly confronted with the question of whether a serial should be entered under corporate body or title. The most relevant rule in AACR2R is 21.1B2, which defines conditions under which entry can be made under a corporate body (see also LCRI 21.1B2; CCM 4.1.5). The first decision the cataloger has to make is whether the work "emanates" from the corporate body involved. In this example, the corporate body "Society for Computer Simulation" has issued the work, and the content of the work is about the corporate body. This fulfills the first necessary condition for the work to be entered under corporate body as main entry (see also CCM 4.3).

- The second question to ask is whether the work falls into one or more of the categories listed in AACR2R 21.1B2. Since the work here is the membership directory of the Society for Computer Simulation, it clearly falls under Category A of 21.1B2 (see also CCM 4.4.1).
- Because the name of the corporate body appears in abbreviated form in the title and some users may assume that the form was spelled out in the source, a 246-derived title added entry using the spelled-out form should be made (LCRI 21.30J, p. 8; see also CCM 7.2.3a). First indicator value "3" means that there will be no note but a title added entry will be generated from the field. Second indicator value blank is used for titles not handled by the other values (for example, titles not on the piece or, as in this case, the spelled-out form).

H13

PROBLEM CONSIDERED:

Work emanating from a corporate body entered under corporate body (its resources) (21.1B2a)

RULE(S) CONSULTED:

AACR2R: 12.1F2
LCRI: 21.1B2

<table>
<tr><td rowspan="3">Cover</td><td>*Association for Supervision and*
Curriculum Development</td></tr>
<tr><td>Curriculum Materials
1974</td></tr>
</table>

TAGGED DATA RECORD (based on OCLC #6524215)

LDR   *****cas_/22*****_a*4500

00-05	06	07-14	15-17	18	19	20	21	22-28	29	30-32	33	34	35-37	38	39
800717	d	19uu198u	dcu	a	r			-------	0	///	a	0	eng	-	d

008 is the tag for the fixed field row above.

→ 110 2   Association for Supervision and Curriculum Development.
→ 245 10   Curriculum materials / ≠c Association for Supervision and Curriculum Development.
260   [Washington, D.C.] : ≠b The Association,
300   v. : ≠b ill. ; ≠c 22 cm.
310   Annual
500   Includes the ASCD exhibit of curriculum materials at the ... annual conference and also catalogs the materials received by the Curriculum Materials Committee for the ... ASCD annual conference.
500   Description based on: 1974; title from cover.
650 0   Education ≠x Curricula ≠x Bibliography.
785 00   ≠t Curriculum materials digest ≠w (DLC)sn90012603 ≠w (OCoLC)12036071

DISCUSSION

- Here is another example of a serial entered under corporate body, in a case fairly similar to that of H12. Again, the first decision to be made by the cataloger is whether the work "emanates" from the corporate body. Since the "Association for Supervision and Curriculum Development" issues this work as well as publishes it, it fulfills the first condition under LCRI 21.1B2 (see also CCM 4.3).
- This work contains curriculum materials as well as a catalog of the materials held by the Association. Its content clearly falls under Category A of 21.1B2, i.e., "those of an administrative nature dealing with the corporate body itself . . . or its resources (e.g., catalogues, inventories)" (see also CCM 4.4.1). With these two conditions fulfilled, the work is accordingly entered under corporate body.
- The corporate name "Association for Supervision and Curriculum Development" is also transcribed as the statement of responsibility in field 245 subfield ≠c since it appears in the chief source of information (12.1F2).

H14

PROBLEM CONSIDERED:

Work with report-like title not emanating from a corporate body (21.1B2)

RULE(S) CONSULTED:

AACR2R: 25.5B1
LCRI: 25.5B4

Cover & title page

Multiculturalism and Citizenship Canada
Multiculturalisme et Citoyennete Canada

**Operation of
The Canadian
Multiculturalism Act**

**ANNUAL
REPORT
1988/89**

Inverted title page

Multiculturalism and Citizenship Canada
Multiculturalisme et Citoyennete Canada

**L'application de la
Loi sur le
multiculturalisme canadien**

**RAPPORT
ANNUEL
1988-1989**

TAGGED DATA RECORD (based on OCLC #22418906)

LDR   *****cas_/22*****_a*4500

00-05	06	07-14	15-17	18	19	20	21	22-28	29	30-32	33	34	35-37	38	39
900921	d	19891992	onc	a	r	4		-------	0	///	a	0	eng	-	d

008

022 0   0848-418X
041 0   engfre
043   n-cn---
→ 130 0   Annual report (Canada. Multiculturalism and Citizenship Canada)
→ 245 00   Annual report
→ 246 15   Rapport annuel
246 1   ≠i At head of title: ≠a Operation of the Canadian Multiculturalism Act
260   Ottawa : ≠b Multiculturalism and Citizenship Canada, ≠c 1989-1992.
300   4 v. ; ≠c 28 cm.
310   Annual
362 0   1988/89-1991/92.
515   Report year ends Mar. 31.
546   Text in English and French with French text on inverted pages.
610 10   Canada. ≠b Canadian Multiculturalism Act.
650 0   Race discrimination ≠x Law and legislation ≠z Canada.
650 0   Civil rights ≠z Canada.
651 0   Canada ≠x Race relations.
650 0   Multiculturalism ≠z Canada.
710 1   Canada. ≠b Multiculturalism and Citizenship Canada.
785 00   ≠t Annual report on the operation of the Canadian Multiculturalism Act ≠x
         1200-2569 ≠w (OCoLC)32309975

DISCUSSION

- This is an annual report issued and published by the corporate body "Multiculturalism and Citizenship Canada." However, the work does not deal with the corporate body itself. AACR2R 21.1B2 states that for a work to be entered under a corporate body heading, the work must emanate from the corporate body and must fall into one or more of the listed categories. Since this work does not fulfill the conditions in 21.1B2, it should not be entered under the corporate body. Thus, the work is entered under the title "Annual report."

- Because the title "Annual report" is a generic title, a uniform title heading is established to distinguish it from other works with the same title (25.5B1). In accordance with LCRI 25.5B4, the name of the corporate body responsible for the work is used as the qualifier.

- The French title "Rapport annuel," which appears on the inverted title page, should be given as a title added entry using field 246. First indicator value "1" generates a note from the field; second indicator value "5" indicates that the title is an added title page title, and will generate the display constant "Added title page title:".

H15

PROBLEM CONSIDERED:

Work entered under a personal name (21.1A1)

RULE(S) CONSULTED:

LCRI: 21.1A2

Title page

> **The Computer Glossary**
> **The Complete Illustrated Desk Reference**
> Fourth Edition
>
> **Alan Freedman**
>
> amacom
> American Management Association

Title page of
a later edition
in hand

> **The Computer Glossary**
> **The Complete Illustrated Desk Reference**
> Fifth Edition
>
> **Alan Freedman**
>
> amacom
> American Management Association

TAGGED DATA RECORD (based on OCLC #28873383)

LDR   *****cas_/22*****_a*4500

00-05	06	07-14	15-17	18	19	20	21	22-28	29	30-32	33	34	35-37	38	39
930922	c	19899999	nyu	g	r			--d----	0	///	a	0	eng	-	d

008

→ 100 1   Freedman, Alan, ≠d 1942-
→ 245 14   The computer glossary / ≠c Alan Freedman.
260   New York : ≠b AMACOM, ≠c c1989-
300   v. : ≠b ill ; ≠c 26 cm.
310   Biennial
362 0   4th ed.-
500   "The complete illustrated desk reference."
580   Continues: His Computer glossary for everyone. 3rd ed. Published in 1983.
650 0   Computers ≠x Dictionaries.
650 0   Electronic data processing ≠x Dictionaries.
780 10   Freedman, Alan, ≠d 1942- ≠t Computer glossary for everyone ≠w
           (OCoLC)9257490

DISCUSSION

- Very few serials may be entered under personal author, because, according to AACR2R 21.1A1 and LCRI 21.1A2, to be chosen as the main entry the person must be chiefly responsible for every issue of the serial. In this example, Alan Freedman is given as the author of the item. He is not the editor or compiler but the author, solely responsible for the contents of the publication, as stipulated in LCRI 21.1A2.
- Also, when making the decision whether to enter a serial under a personal name, the cataloger should consider all issues in hand, if not the entire run, since the person chosen as main entry should continue to be closely associated with the serial. In the example here, Alan Freedman is the only person associated with the serial throughout its many editions (at least up to the sixth edition when this serial was cataloged). Thus his name is chosen as the main entry for this publication (see also CCM 4.6 and 6.5.5).

H16

PROBLEM CONSIDERED:

Work entered under the heading for a subordinate body (21.1B4a)

RULE(S) CONSULTED:

AACR2R: 24.13A type 6
LCRI: 12.1B7, 24.13 type 6

TAGGED DATA RECORD (based on OCLC #16828111)

LDR   *****cas_/22*****_a*4500

00-05	06	07-14	15-17	18	19	20	21	22-28	29	30-32	33	34	35-37	38	39
871008	c	19869999	mau	a	r	1		---bc--	0	///	a	0	eng	-	d

008

022 0   0898-7300
043   n-us-ny
→ 110 2   Museum of Modern Art (New York, N.Y.). ≠b Library.
→ 245 10   Annual bibliography of modern art / ≠c the Museum of Modern Art Library, New York.
246 30   Bibliography of modern art
260   Boston, Mass. : ≠b G.K. Hall, ≠c 1987-
300   v. ; ≠c 28 cm.
310   Annual
362 0   1986-
500   "This listing of the acquisitions of the museum library is compiled from RLIN records of both new and older publications acquired by purchase, gift, or exchange …"--Introd.
650   0   Arts, Modern ≠y 19th century ≠x Bibliography ≠x Catalogs.
650   0   Arts, Modern ≠y 20th century ≠x Bibliography ≠x Catalogs.
610 20   Museum of Modern Art (New York, N.Y.). ≠b Library ≠x Catalogs.

> ### Annual Bibliography of Modern Art, 1986
>
> The Museum of Modern Art Library, New York
>
> G.K. Hall & Co., Boston, Massachusetts
> 1987

Title page

DISCUSSION

- In serials cataloging, a perennial question for the cataloger on choice of entry is whether or not a given work can be entered under a corporate body. If it may be so entered, then the cataloger must sometimes decide under which body entry should be made. Often this involves a choice between a parent body and its subordinate unit whose names both appear on the chief source. In such cases, AACR2R 21.1B4a states that if the responsibility of the named subordinate unit is stated prominently, the work should be entered under the heading for the subordinate unit.
- In this example, the name of the subordinate unit (the Library of the Museum of Modern Art) appears on the title page and is therefore clearly considered to be of prominent responsibility. The work is a listing of the Library's acquisitions compiled and cataloged by the Library (subordinate unit), not the Museum (parent body). Entry should therefore be made under the heading for the Library (see also CCM 4.5). The heading "Museum of Modern Art (New York, N.Y.). Library" is established according to 24.13A type 6 (see also LCRI 24.13 type 6). Since the name "Museum of Modern Art Library" includes the entire name of the higher body "Museum of Modern Art," its subordinate body "Library" is entered as a subheading.
- A date occurs at the end of the title proper, but, in accordance with LCRI 12.1B7, this is not transcribed as part of the title proper. In this case, no mark of omission is needed.

H17

PROBLEM CONSIDERED:
Work entered under common title and section title (1.1B9)

RULE(S) CONSULTED:
AACR2R: 12.1B4, 12.1B6
LCRI: 12.1B4; 21.30J, p. 13

```
                    isbn     Boletín
                             Bibliográfico
                             Bimestral
                             Septiembre - Octubre
                             Noviembre - Diciembre
        Cover                1994

                             CAMARA
                             ARGENTINA
                             DEL LIBRO
```

TAGGED DATA RECORD (based on OCLC #30652186)

LDR   *****cas_/22*****_a*4500

00-05	06	07-14	15-17	18	19	20	21	22-28	29	30-32	33	34	35-37	38	39
008	940623	c	19939999	ag	b	r			--b----	0	///	b	0	spa	-	d

022   0327-9189
043   s-ag---
→ 245 00   Boletín bibliográfico bimestral. ≠p ISBN.
→ 246 30   ISBN
260   Buenos Aires : ≠b Cámara Argentina del Libro, ≠c [1993-
300   v. ; ≠c 28 cm.
310   Bimonthly
362 0   Año 1, no. 1 (enero-feb. 1993)-
500   Title from cover.
651 0 Argentina ≠x Imprints.
650 0 International Standard Book Numbers ≠z Argentina.
710 2   Cámara Argentina del Libro.

DISCUSSION

- When a common title that is common to many sections and a section title both appear within the item on the same source and the two parts of the titles are not grammatically linked, record the common title first, followed by the section title preceded by a period (1.1B9). A section title usually represents a particular subject area within the scope of a comprehensive title, or it may be a supplement to the main serial (LCRI 12.1B4; see also CCM 6.2.1). Note that for serials with both a common title and a section title, any source within the preliminaries (not necessarily the title page) containing both titles should be preferred as the chief source of information (12.1B4). If there is no source containing both titles, apply 12.1B6 and give the section title as the title proper and the common title as a series (see also CCM 6.2.3).

- In this example, the common title is "Boletín bibliográfico bimestral." "ISBN" is one of the many sections that have been issued under this common title. Since both the common title and the section title are present on the chief source, and they are not grammatically linked to each other, "Boletín bibliográfico bimestral" is transcribed as the common title in field 245 subfield ≠a and "ISBN" as the section title in subfield ≠p.

- Because the section title is an independent title in itself, an added entry is always made for it to provide additional access to the serial (LCRI 21.30J, p. 13). Use field 246 with first indicator value "3" so that no note but a title added entry can be generated from the field; use second indicator value "0" to show that this is a portion of a title (see also CCM 7.2.1c).

H18

PROBLEM CONSIDERED:

Work entered under common title, section number, and section title (12.1B5)

RULE(S) CONSULTED:

AACR2R: 12.7B17

TAGGED DATA RECORD (based on OCLC #9921721)

LDR   *****cas_/22*****_a*4500

00-05	06	07-14	15-17	18	19	20	21	22-28	29	30-32	33	34	35-37	38	39
008	830919	d	19841993	dcu	m	r	1	p	-------	0	///	a	0	eng	-	d

	022 0	0740-3232
→	245 00	Journal of the Optical Society of America. ≠n A, ≠p Optics and image science.
→	246 30	Optics and image science
	246 13	JOSA A
	260	Washington, D.C. : ≠b The Society, ≠c 1984-1993.
	300	10 v. : ≠b ill. ; ≠c 29 cm.
	310	Monthly
	362 0	Vol. 1, no. 1 (Jan. 1984)-v. 10, no. 7 (July 1993).
	500	Title from cover.
	515	Vols. for Jan. 1984- called also ser. 2.
	530	Issued also in microform.
→	555	Cumulative index for all OSA journals issued separately with title: Optics index.
	580	Continues in part: Journal of the Optical Society of America (1930).
	650 0	Optics ≠x Periodicals.
	650 0	Imaging systems ≠x Periodicals.
	710 2	Optical Society of America.
	780 11	≠t Journal of the Optical Society of America (1930) ≠x 0030-3941 ≠w (OCoLC) 1334208 ≠w (DLC)24004175
	785 00	≠t Journal of Optical Society of America. A, Optics, image science, and vision ≠x 1084-7529 ≠w (DLC)95657088 ≠w (OCoLC)9130751
→	787 1	≠t Optics index ≠w (DLC)86641353 ≠w (OCoLC)9130751

Cover

ISSN: 0740-3232

Journal of the
Optical Society
of America A

OPTICS and
IMAGE SCIENCE

Volume 1, Number 1   January 1984

DISCUSSION

- If a common title and section title appear on the same source and the section title is given a section number, the section number should be treated as part of the title proper. Give the common title first, followed by the section number, then the section title (12.1B5; see also CCM 6.2.2).
- In this example, the section title "Optics and image science" has a section number, which is an alphabetical designation "A." Thus, the title proper should consist first of the common title "Journal of the Optical Society of America" in subfield ≠a, a full stop, followed by the section designation "A" in subfield ≠n, a comma, and the section title "Optics and image science" in subfield ≠p.
- A note is made to indicate the presence of cumulative indexes issued separately (12.7B17). Field 555 first indicator blank enables the generation of a display constant "Indexes:".
- The separately issued index "Optics index" is given access via a corresponding 787 field, Nonspecific Relationship Entry—that is, the related record does not fit into any of the cases defined in linking fields 760–785.

H19

PROBLEM CONSIDERED:
Work entered under section title (12.1B6)

RULE(S) CONSULTED:
AACR2R: 12.7B7j
LCRI: 21.28B

Caption

THE PHYSICAL EDUCATION ASSOCIATION
of Great Britain and Northern Ireland

RESEARCH SUPPLEMENT
NO. 1 - JULY 1987

TAGGED DATA RECORD (based on OCLC #18265724)

LDR   *****cas_/22*****_a*4500

	00-05	06	07-14	15-17	18	19	20	21	22-28	29	30-32	33	34	35-37	38	39
008	880725	c	19879999	enk	u	u		p	-------	0	///	a	0	eng	-	d

130 0   Research supplement (Physical Education Association of Great Britain and
          Northern Ireland)
→ 245 00   Research supplement / ≠c the Physical Education Association of Great
          Britain and Northern Ireland.
→ 246 13   British journal of physical education research supplement
260   London : ≠b The Association, ≠c 1987-
300   v. : ≠b ill. ; ≠c 30 cm.
362 0   No.1 (July 1987)-
500   Title from caption.
→ 580   Issued as a supplement to: British journal of physical education, published in 1983.
650 0   Physical education and training ≠x Periodicals.
710 2   Physical Education Association of Great Britain and Northern Ireland.
→ 730 0   British journal of physical education (1983)
→ 772 1   ≠t British journal of physical education (1983) ≠x 0144-3569 ≠w
          (DLC)sn85012202 ≠w (OCoLC)10166683

DISCUSSION

- In this example, the title of the supplement "Research supplement" appears in the chief source, but the title of the main serial "British journal of physical education" does not appear there. So the supplement title alone is transcribed as the title proper (12.1B6; see also CCM 6.2.3).
- A variant title added entry is provided through field 246, since this "Research supplement" is probably also known to users in its full form as "British journal of physical education research supplement," which appears in the introduction. First indicator value "1" indicates that a note and a title added entry are generated from the field. Second indicator value "3" indicates that the title given is an "other title" that appears on the piece.
- In the case of a supplement title treated as the title proper, also give the title of the main serial in a note (12.7B7j). Field 580 is a Linking Entry Complexity Note used to express a complex relationship between the item "Research supplement" described in this record and the main serial "British journal of physical education."
- Field 772 is a linking field for the main serial or the parent record entry when the item in hand is a supplement or special issue that is cataloged as a separate record. First indicator value "1" indicates that no note is to be generated from the field. Second indicator value is blank.
- A field 730 added entry is still needed for the related serial, because linking fields such as 772 provide machine links to related records but do not take the place of added entries (LCRI 21.28B). Field 730 is used for related titles that are established in cataloging entry form. The first indicator shows the number of nonfiling characters and is always set to value "0," according to Library of Congress practice. The second indicator is blank, since the added entry is not for an analytic.

H20

PROBLEM CONSIDERED:

Work entered under series designation and subseries as title proper (LCRI 1.6B)

RULE(S) CONSULTED:

AACR2R: 1.1B5, 1.1D2, 12.1B6

Title page

> European University Institute
>
> **Series C:**
>
> Political and Social Sciences
> Sciences politiques et sociales
> Politik- und Sozialwissenschaften
> Scienze politiche e sociali
>
> **1**
>
> **1984**

TAGGED DATA RECORD (based on OCLC #14761226)

LDR   *****cas_/22*****Ia*4500

00-05	06	07-14	15-17	18	19	20	21	22-28	29	30-32	33	34	35-37	38	39
008 861118	c	19849999	gw	u	u		m	-------	0	///	a	0	eng	-	d

→ 245 00   Series C--Political and social sciences = ≠b Series C--Sciences politiques et sociales.

→ 246 31   Series C--Sciences politiques et sociales

246 30   Political and social sciences

260   Berlin : ≠b W. de Gruyter, ≠c 1984-

300   v. ; ≠c 24 cm.

362 0   1-

→ 500   Series has parallel titles in French, German, and Italian.

550   Issued by: European University Institute.

710 2   European University Institute.

DISCUSSION

- The title proper of the monographic series publication in this example consists only of a series designation "Series C" and a subseries "Political and social sciences," without a main series. According to 12.1B6, the title of the section should be treated as the title proper if the title of a section or supplement is presented in the chief source of information without the title that is common to all sections (or the title of the main serial). In cases when the title proper is composed of a designation plus title, Library of Congress practice is to use a dash (two adjacent hyphens) in place of a comma-space to connect the two parts (i.e., a designation of a subseries and the subseries title) to make it clear that the entire grouping is the title proper (LCRI 1.6B). Therefore, the title proper of this publication should be transcribed as "Series C--Political and social sciences," and *not* "Series C, Political and social sciences." In field 245, the entire grouping is input in subfield ≠a and should not be divided into subfield ≠a plus subfield ≠p.

- Note that this publication also has parallel subseries titles. The designation of the subseries "Series C" appears only once, but the design of the chief source of information makes it clear that it is intended to be read more than once. In this case, the series designation is repeated when transcribing the parallel title, as in field 245 subfield ≠b (1.1B5).
- The next issue to be addressed is the transcription of parallel titles. This publication has parallel titles in French, German, and Italian. According to rule 1.1D2, in a second-level description the first parallel title is transcribed, and, therefore, only the French title is transcribed here.

I. Changes of Persons or Bodies Responsible for a Work

Serials catalogers are constantly having to deal with the various changes that are so characteristic of serial publications. Many of these changes can be addressed in the note area of a catalog record. However, other changes involving the title or main entry, fitting the criteria described in rule 21.2 and rule 21.3, call for the creation of a new record. This section focuses on changes in personal or corporate main entries for serials, while section J deals with changes in the title proper.

The name of the responsible body may change, or there can be a change in the person or corporate body responsible for the publication. Rule 21.3B1 lists two cases when such a change necessitates the creation of a separate record, even though the title of the item remains the same and the numbering system continues. The first is when the work is entered under the corporate body from which it emanates (i.e, when rule 21.1B2 applies), and the heading for that body changes. The second is when the person or corporate heading whose name is used as the main entry is no longer responsible for the publication of the serial. LCRI 21.3B adds two other conditions that also necessitate the creation of a new record: when the change is in a corporate body that is used as the qualifier in a uniform title heading; and when the change involves certain other types of qualifiers in the uniform title heading. The latter case is further explained in section O on Uniform Title Headings and Uniform Titles.

A change in the responsible corporate body or its name does not necessitate a separate record when the work is entered under a title main entry. Because AACR2R has limited the use of corporate name main entry, most serial publications are entered under title, with an added entry, when necessary, for the responsible corporate body. The number of separate records that would otherwise have resulted from changes in corporate bodies are thus greatly reduced.

EXAMPLES

I1   Work entered under a corporate name heading and the corporate name changes

I2   Work entered under title and the name of the responsible body changes

I3   Work entered under a subordinate name heading and the subordinate name changes

I4   Work entered under the name of a conference and the conference name changes

I5   Work entered under title and the name of the corporate body imbedded in the title proper changes

I6   Work entered under title and the corporate body imbedded in other title information changes

I7   Work entered under a corporate body and the corporate body imbedded in the title is dropped

I8   Work entered under uniform title heading and the name of the corporate body used as qualifier in the uniform title heading changes

I1

PROBLEM CONSIDERED:

Work entered under a corporate name heading and the corporate name changes (21.3B1)

RULE(S) CONSULTED:

AACR2R: 12.1F1, 12.7B7b, 21.1B2, 21.1B2a
LCRI: 21.30J, p. 7

Cover

> **1995
> Metropolitan
> Toronto
> Reference
> Library**
>
> **Annual
> Report**

TAGGED DATA RECORD (based on OCLC #35323245)

LDR   *****cas_/22*****_a*4500

00-05	06	07-14	15-17	18	19	20	21	22-28	29	30-32	33	34	35-37	38	39
960829	c	19959999	onc	a	r			------1	0	///	a	0	eng	-	d

008

043   n-cn-on
→ 110 2   Metropolitan Toronto Reference Library.
→ 245 00 Annual report / ≠c Metropolitan Toronto Reference Library.
  246 17 Metropolitan Toronto Library Board annual report
  260   Toronto, Ont. : ≠b The Library, ≠c 1996-
  300   v. : ≠b ill. ; ≠c 27 cm.
  310   Annual
  362 0   27th (1995)-
  500   Title from cover.
  610 20 Metropolitan Toronto Reference Library.
→ 780 00 Metropolitan Toronto Library Board. ≠t Annual report ≠w (DLC)73612935
          ≠w (OCoLC)2239463

DISCUSSION

- The majority of serial publications cataloged according to AACR2R will be entered under title. However, those publications dealing exclusively with the affairs of a responsible corporate body will be entered under the heading for that body (21.1B2). This example involves an annual report of an administrative nature dealing with the responsible corporate body itself, so that entry is accordingly made under the corporate name (21.1B2a). Because the statement of responsibility appears in the chief source of information, it is transcribed in the title and statement of responsibility area (12.1FI).
- Whenever the name of a corporate body under which a serial is entered changes, even though the title proper remains the same, a separate record should be made (21.3B1). In this example, the corporate body emanating the work changed from "Metropolitan Toronto Library Board" to "Metropolitan Toronto Reference Library," making a separate record (i.e., a succeeding record) under the new name necessary. The related preceding entry is given in a note (12.7B7b).
- According to Library of Congress practice, a title added entry is not made when the serial title is entered under a corporate body main entry and the title proper consists of no more than the English words "Annual report" (LCRI 21.30J, p. 7). Thus, the first indicator of field 245 is set to value "0," so that no title added entry is generated.
- A corporate body main entry is input in field 110. First indicator value "1" is used when the corporate body is entered under a place.
- Field 780 is used to provide a link to the preceding entry. The first indicator is set to value "0" in order to generate a note from the link. The second indicator describes the relationship between the serial being cataloged and the preceding entry. Second indicator value "0" generates a note beginning with the display text "Continues:".

I2

PROBLEM CONSIDERED:

Work entered under title and the name of the responsible body changes (21.29F)

RULE(S) CONSULTED:

AACR2R: 12.7B6, 21.29B, 24.1C1

JEWISH EDUCATION VOLUME 49 NUMBER 1 SPRING 1981	JEWISH EDUCATION Published by the NATIONAL COUNCIL FOR JEWISH EDUCATION
Cover	**Verso of cover**

```
JEWISH
EDUCATION



VOLUME 49    NUMBER 2    SUMMER 1981
```

Cover of a later issue

```
JEWISH EDUCATION


Published by the

COUNCIL FOR
JEWISH EDUCATION
```

Verso of cover of the later issue

TAGGED DATA RECORD (based on OCLC #1754277)

LDR   *****cas_/22*****Ia*4500

00-05	06	07-14	15-17	18	19	20	21	22-28	29	30-32	33	34	35-37	38	39
751101	d	19291993	nyu	t	r	l	p	---bo--	0	///	a	0	eng	-	d

008

| 022 0 | 0021-6429 |

| 043 | n-us--- |

→ 245 00   Jewish education.

260   New York : ≠b National Council for Jewish Education, ≠c 1929-1993.

300   60 v. ; ≠c 25 cm.

310   3 nos. a year, ≠b 1990-93

321   Quarterly, ≠b 1929-89

362 0   Vol. 1, no. 1 (Jan. 1929)-v. 60, no. 2 (summer 1993).

515   Vol. 60, no. 1 and 2 also called 60th anniversary issue part 1 and 2.

→ 550   Issued by: National Council for Jewish Education, 1929-spring 1981; Council for Jewish Education, summer 1981-1993.

550   Published with the assistance of the American Association for Jewish Education, -1981; of the Jewish Education Service of North America, 1982-93.

650 0   Jews ≠x Education ≠x Periodicals.

650 0   Jews ≠x Education ≠z United States ≠x Periodicals.

→ 710 2   National Council for Jewish Education.

710 2   American Association for Jewish Education.

710 2   Jewish Education Service of North America.

→ 710 2   Council for Jewish Education.

785 00   ≠t Journal of Jewish education ≠w (DLC)sn94040511 ≠w (OCoLC)30901914

DISCUSSION

- If the title proper under which a serial is entered remains the same, but the name of the corporate body responsible for the serial changes (as in this example, where the name of the corporate body responsible for the serial changes from "National Council for Jewish Education" to "Council for Jewish Education"), do not make a new record for the serial. Instead, record the change in an Issuing Body Note and give information on old and new names or former and current issuing bodies (21.29F). The note should also include relevant chronological information, if such is available, following the corporate name or body it applies to, and separated from that body by a comma and a space (12.7B6). Establish a new heading for the corporate body (24.1C1) and make added entries to provide access to the record under the old and new names for the corporate body (21.29B).

- Field 550 is used for notes referring to issuing bodies.
- Field 710 is used for corporate body added entries. First indicator value "2" is used for a corporate body's name cited in direct order. The second indicator is blank.

I3

PROBLEM CONSIDERED:

Work entered under a subordinate name heading and the subordinate name changes (21.3B1)

RULE(S) CONSULTED:

AACR2R: 12.7B6, 21.1B4

Title page	**NEW SOUTH WALES** **Department of Water Resources** **Annual Report** **1987/88** . . . doing more with water

Cover of an earlier issue	**Water Resources Commission** **Annual Report 1982-83**

TAGGED DATA RECORD (based on OCLC #20161176)

LDR   *****cas_/22*****_a*4500

	00-05	06	07-14		15-17	18	19	20	21	22-28	29	30-32	33	34	35-37	38	39
008	890811	c	198u9999		at	a	r			------s	0	///	a	0	eng	-	

022   1032-9706 ≠y 0155-9834
043   u-at-ne
→ 110 1   New South Wales. ≠b Dept. of Water Resources.
→ 245 00   Annual report / ≠c Department of Water Resources.
260   Parramatta, NSW : ≠b The Dept.,
300   v. : ≠b ill. (some col.) ; ≠c 25 cm.
310   Annual
500   Description based on: 1987/88.
515   Report year ends June 30.
650   0   Water-supply ≠z Australia ≠z New South Wales ≠x Management.
610 10   New South Wales. ≠b Dept. of Water Resources.
780 00   New South Wales. Water Resources Commission. ≠t Annual report ≠x
0155-9834 ≠w (DLC)81641169 ≠w (OCoLC)7383137

DISCUSSION

- Rule 21.1B4 gives two provisions for works entered under the heading of a corporate body where the responsible body is a subordinate unit of the parent body:

    Enter a work under the heading for the subordinate body if that body is named prominently in the chief source of information;

    Enter the work under the parent body if only the parent body appears in the chief source, even though the name of the subordinate body may appear in other locations.

- In the first case, when the name of the subordinate body changes, a separate record should be created (21.3B1). In the second case, where the parent body is the main entry, any changes in the name of the subordinate body do not necessitate creation of a new record; instead, such changes should be described in a note (12.7B6).

- Thus, in this example, the main entry is under the name of the subordinate body, which appears prominently in the chief source. When the name "Water Resources Commission" changed to "Dept. of Water Resources," a separate record was created under the heading for the new name, even though the title proper remained "Annual report" (21.3B1).

I4

PROBLEM CONSIDERED:

Work entered under the name of a conference and the conference name changes (21.3B1a)

RULE(S) CONSULTED:

AACR2R: 21.1B1, 21.1B2d, 24.7A1

CHROMOSOMES TODAY

VOLUME 6

Title page

Proceedings of the Sixth International
Chromosome Conference held in
Helsinki, Finland, August 29-31, 1977

TAGGED DATA RECORD (based on OCLC #3533134)

LDR *****cas_/22*****Ia4500

00-05	06	07-14	15-17	18	19	20	21	22-28	29	30-32	33	34	35-37	38	39
780105	c	19779999	enk	u			u		-------	1	///	a	0	eng	-	d

008

022 0 0069-3944

→ 111 2 International Chromosome Conference.

→ 245 10 Chromosomes today : ≠b Proceedings of the ... International Chromosome Conference.

246 30 Proceedings of the ... International Chromosome Conference

260 Amsterdam ; ≠a New York : ≠b Elsevier/North Holland Biomedical Press., ≠c 1977-

300 v. : ≠b ill. ; ≠c 25 cm.

362 0 Vol. 6 (1977)-

500 Published : London : Allen & Unwin, 1981-1987; Unwin Hyman, 1990-

650 0 Chromosomes ≠x Congresses.

780 00 Leiden Chromosome Conference. ≠t Chromosomes today ≠x 0069-3944 ≠w (DLC)sn84043186 ≠w (OCoLC)11522891

DISCUSSION

- According to AACR2R, for cataloging purposes, named conferences should be treated as corporate bodies (21.1B1). Accordingly, conference publications are entered under the heading for a named conference if the named conference appears prominently in the item (21.1B2d).
- When the conference is ongoing and its name heading is thus representative of a series of conferences, the conference number, date, and place should not be added to the heading, even if all the meetings are held in the same place. In addition, omit from the name of a conference words that denote its frequency or year of convocation, etc. (24.7A1).
- Whenever there is a change in the name of the conference under which a serial is entered, a separate entry should be made, even though the title proper remains the same (21.3B1a). In this example, the conference name "Leiden Chromosome Conference" changed to "International Chromosome Conference"; therefore, a separate record was made for the succeeding entry under the named conference heading.

I5

PROBLEM CONSIDERED:

Work entered under title and the name of the corporate body imbedded in the title proper changes (LCRI 21.2A)

RULE(S) CONSULTED:

AACR2R: 21.2A1b

TAGGED DATA RECORD (based on OCLC #36235039)

LDR   *****cas_/22*****Ia*4500

00-05	06	07-14	15-17	18	19	20	21	22-28	29	30-32	33	34	35-37	38	39
008	970121	c	19939999	quc	q	r	4	p	-------	0	///	a	0	eng	-	d

022 0	1196-9679
→ 245 04	The Journal of the Canadian Rheumatology Association.
260	Pointe Claire, Quebec. : ≠b STA Communications, ≠c 1993-
300	v. : ≠b ill. ; ≠c 28 cm.
310	Quarterly
362 0	Vol. 2, no. 4 (Dec. 1993)-
500	Title from cover.
550	Published for the Canadian Rheumatology Association.
650 0	Rheumatism ≠x Periodicals.
710 2	Canadian Rheumatology Association.
775 0	≠t Journal de la Société canadienne de rhumatologie ≠x 1196-9687 ≠w (OCoLC)36235041
→ 780 00	≠t Journal of the Canadian Rheumatism Association ≠x 1196-9660 ≠w (OCoLC)36235040

DISCUSSION

- In this example, the corporate body whose name is imbedded in the title proper of the serial was originally called "Canadian Rheumatism Association." In late 1993, the association changed its name to "Canadian Rheumatology Association." When there is a change in the name of a body that is part of the title proper, and as a result the body takes a new form of heading, this constitutes a title change (LCRI 21.2A).
- Note that this specific condition overrules the provisions in rule 21.2A1b concerning additions, deletions, or changes after the first five significant words in the title proper and all the conditions stated in LCRI 21.2A for determining whether a serial title has changed.

I6

PROBLEM CONSIDERED:

Work entered under title and the corporate body imbedded in other title information changes (12.1E1)

RULE(S) CONSULTED:

AACR2R: 12.7B5, 21.30A1

TAGGED DATA RECORD (based on OCLC #2673707)

LDR   *****cas_/22*****Ia*4500

00-05	06	07-14	15-17	18	19	20	21	22-28	29	30-32	33	34	35-37	38	39
770112	d	19731991	nyu		x	l	p	-------	0	///	a	0	eng	-	d

008

022 0   0090-7405

043   n-us---

→ 245 04   The Socialist republic : ≠b publication of the League for Socialist Reconstruction.

260   New York : ≠b The League, ≠c 1973-1991.

300   22 v. : ≠b ill. ; ≠c 28 cm.

310   Irregular

362 0   Vol. 1, no. 1 (Jan.-Feb. 1973)-v. 10, no. 1 (spring 1984) ; no. 25 (summer 1984)-no. 35 (winter/spring 1991).

500   Title from caption.

→ 550   Publication of the Industrial Union Party, 1981-1991.

650 0   Socialism ≠z United States ≠x Periodicals.

710 2   League for Socialist Reconstruction (U.S.)

→ 710 2   Industrial Union Party (U.S.)

780 00   ≠t Socialist reconstruction ≠w (DLC)sn90018075 ≠w (OCoLC)21577417

785 00   ≠t People for a new system ≠x 1082-8745 ≠w (DLC)95651283 ≠w (OCoLC)27052182

Caption

THE *SOCIALIST REPUBLIC*

Publication of The League for Socialist Reconstruction

vol. 5, no. 1   spring 1978

Caption of a later issue

THE *SOCIALIST REPUBLIC*

Publication of the Industrial Union Party

no. 35 winter/spring 1991

DISCUSSION

- In serials cataloging, if the name of the corporate body responsible for a serial is imbedded in other title information that appears in the chief source of information, that other title information should be transcribed as it appears (12.1E1).

- If the work is entered under title and the name of the corporate body imbedded in the other title information changes, or the responsible corporate body imbedded in the other title information changes, this change does not necessitate a title change, as long as the title proper remains the same. In this example, the other title information "Publication of the League for Socialist Reconstruction" changes to "Publication of the Industrial Union Party" in 1981. Because the work is entered under title and the title proper remains the same, it is not necessary to create a separate record. However, the change in other title information should be recorded in a note. In this example, the other title information "Publication of the Industrial Union Party" is recorded in the Issuing Body Note, field 550 (12.7B5). The note should also include the date when responsibility changed; this date is set off from the rest of the note by a comma. The added entry for a new responsible body or for the new name of the responsible body (as in this example) can also be justified by this note (21.30A1).

I7

PROBLEM CONSIDERED:

Work entered under a corporate body and the corporate body imbedded in the title is dropped (21.2A1c)

TAGGED DATA RECORD (based on OCLC #32753442)

LDR   *****cas_/22*****_a*4500

00-05	06	07-14	15-17	18	19	20	21	22-28	29	30-32	33	34	35-37	38	39
950703	d	19901993	nz	a	r			------f	0	///	a	0	eng	-	d

008 as above

043   u-nz---
→ 110 2   New Zealand. ≠b Earthquake and War Damage Commission.
→ 245 10 Annual report of the Earthquake and War Damage Commission, EQC, for the year ended 31 Mar. ...
→ 246 1   ≠i Vol. for 1991 has title: ≠a Annual report
260   [Wellington, New Zealand] : ≠b The Commission, ≠c 1990-1993.
300   4 v. ; ≠c 30 cm.
310   Annual
362 0   1989-90-1992-1993.
500   Title varies slightly.
515   Report for 1992/1993 ends 30 June.
650 0   Insurance, Earthquake ≠z New Zealand.
650 0   Insurance ≠z New Zealand ≠x War risks.
610 20   New Zealand. ≠b Earthquake and War Damage Commission.
780 00   New Zealand. Earthquake and War Damage Commission. ≠t Report of the Earthquake and War Damage Commission established under the Earthquake and War Damage Act, 1944, for the year ended 31st Mar. ≠w (DLC)95658563 ≠w (OCoLC)32714868
785 00   New Zealand. Earthquake Commission. ≠t Annual report ≠w (DLC)95658565 ≠w (OCoLC)32753854

DISCUSSION

- The item in this example is entered under the heading for a corporate body, and the name of that body is imbedded in the title proper: "Annual report of the Earthquake and War Damage Commission, EQC, for the year ended 31 Mar. . . ." When the name of the body is dropped from the 1991 issue, the title proper simply reads "Annual report." If the only difference in the title proper is the deletion or addition of the name of an issuing body, do not consider the title proper to have changed (21.2A1c); in such cases, the change in title is simply mentioned in a note and no separate record should be made. (See also example J11.)

- Field 246 is used for a variant form of the title proper. In this case, subfield ≠i is used to indicate the 1991 issue has a variant title, i.e., the one without the name of the corporate body at the end.

I8

PROBLEM CONSIDERED:

Work entered under uniform title heading and the name of the corporate body used as qualifier in the uniform title heading changes (LCRI 21.3B)

RULE(S) CONSULTED:

LCRI: 25.5B, p. 1, p. 2

TAGGED DATA RECORD (based on OCLC #26630226)

LDR   *****cas_/22*****_a*4500

00-05	06	07-14	15-17	18	19	20	21	22-28	29	30-32	33	34	35-37	38	39
008	920918	c	19919999	at		x		m	------s	0	///	a	0	eng	-	d

022	1035-9826
043	u-at-qn
→ 130 0	Technical paper (Queensland Forest Service)
→ 245 00	Technical paper / ≠c Queensland Forest Service.
260	Brisbane? : ≠b The Service, ≠c 1991-
300	v. : ≠b ill. ; ≠c 26-30 cm.
310	Irregular
362 0	No. 48-
500	Title from cover.
650 0	Forests and forestry ≠z Australia ≠z Queensland.
710 2	Queensland Forest Service.
→ 780 00	≠t Technical paper (Queensland. Dept. of Forestry) ≠x 0155-9664 ≠w (DLC)sc88036033 ≠w (OCoLC)2255874

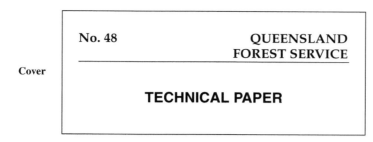

DISCUSSION

- The work in this example is entered under a uniform title heading, since the title proper is nondistinctive. The uniform title heading consists of the title proper and a parenthetical qualifier, which is the heading for the corporate body responsible for the work (LCRI 25.5B, p. 2).
- When the name of a corporate body is used as the qualifier in a uniform title heading and the established name of the body changes or responsibility changes to another body, a separate record should be made (LCRI 21.3B). In this example, "Queensland. Dept. of Forestry" changed to "Queensland Forest Service." Even though the title proper remains the same, a separate record must be made with a uniform title heading using the new form of name as qualifier. If the place of publication had been used as the qualifying term in the uniform title heading, a change in that element would normally not necessitate a separate record.
- When making linking notes or references to records entered under a uniform title heading, always refer to the uniform title and not to the title proper (LCRI 25.5B, p. 1).

J.   Changes in Title Proper

AACR2R 21.2C1 says, "If the title proper of a serial changes, make a separate main entry for each title." What constitutes a change of title proper? Although many changes are obvious, others are less clear. Rule 21.2A1 gives the basic condition for a change of title proper—when any word is added, deleted, or changed, or if the order of the first five words (six words, if the title begins with an article) is changed—and, along with LCRI 21.2A, lists other situations where a change in title proper should not be treated as a title change. The following summarizes the situations where a new catalog entry should not be created:

1. Do not consider the title proper to have changed if any of the following occur *within* the first five (or six, if an initial article is included) words of the title proper:

    Arabic numeral(s) vs. roman numeral(s)
    Abbreviated words vs. full form of words
    Hyphenated words vs. unhyphenated words
    Initialisms and letters with or without separating punctuation
    Numbers or dates vs. spelled-out forms
    One spelling vs. another spelling
    One-word compounds vs. Two-word compounds, whether hyphenated or not
    Signs and symbols vs. spelled-out forms
    Singular forms vs. plural forms
    The word added, changed, or deleted is an article, preposition, or conjunction

    Or,

    The name or different forms of the name of the *same* issuing body or an element of its hierarchy is added to the end of the title proper or deleted from the end of the title proper.

2. Do not consider the title proper to have changed if any of the following occur *beyond* the first five (or six, if an initial article is included) words of the title proper:

    Any word or words are added, changed, or deleted
    The order of the words is changed

Generally, an added entry may be given for a variant title, or a general note such as "Title varies slightly" may be included in the bibliographic record. However, if the change affects the scope and coverage of the item, or the change requires a new heading for a corporate body included in the title, consider the title proper to have changed.

3. Do not consider the title proper to have changed if the serial title fluctuates:

> The title switches back to a former title but it seems clear that the publisher did not intend to change the title.
> Alternate issues are published with a different title.
> The title changes according to the language of the text.
> Most issues carry one title, but a few randomly spaced issues have another.

4. For serials with parallel titles, do not consider the title proper to have changed if changes occur in the order of serial titles:

> The order of titles changes in the layout of the chief source (e.g., the parallel title in an earlier issue appears first in the chief source of later issues).
> A parallel title is added in the chief source of later issues.
> A parallel title is dropped from the chief source of later issues.

Once it has been determined that the situation does not involve any of the preceding situations, one may consider a title proper to have changed if words have been added, changed, or deleted within the first five words of the title proper or if there is any change in the order of the first five words (within the first six words if the title proper begins with an initial article).

Note that when the serial is not entered under title, rule 21.3B1 and LCRI 21.3B give certain guidelines for making a new entry for the serial, even when the title proper remains the same (e.g., under corporate entry, see section I; under conference entry, see section M; and under uniform title heading, see section O).

EXAMPLES

J1	Change within first five words of title proper necessitating a separate record
J2	Change within first five words of title proper not necessitating a separate record
J3	Change beyond first five words of title proper necessitating a separate record
J4	Change beyond first five words of title proper not necessitating a separate record
J5	Change in title proper for a work entered under a corporate name heading
J6	"Annual report" changes to "Biennial report"
J7	Abbreviated form of words in title proper vs. full form not necessitating a separate record
J8	Acronym or initialism of words in title proper vs. full form necessitating a separate record
J9	Change in name of corporate body imbedded in title proper
J10	Corporate name imbedded in title proper has a different form
J11	The name of the same issuing body is added or deleted at the end of the title proper
J12	Corporate name added or deleted from the beginning of the title proper
J13	Change in the order of words of the title proper
J14	Change in the order of title proper and parallel title not necessitating a separate record
J15	Title proper fluctuates
J16	Title proper changes from one language to another
J17	Section title remains the same and common title changes

J18   Common title remains the same and section title changes or is dropped
J19   Parallel title dropped not necessitating a separate record
J20   Alternating section titles in a single record

J1

PROBLEM CONSIDERED:

Change within first five words of title proper necessitating a separate record (21.2A1)

RULE(S) CONSULTED:

AACR2R: 12.7B7b

TAGGED DATA RECORD (based on OCLC #18158727)

LDR   *****cas_/22*****Ia*4500

00-05	06	07-14	15-17	18	19	20	21	22-28	29	30-32	33	34	35-37	38	39
008	880701	c	19869999	mx	a	r			--s---f	0	///	b	0	spa	-	d

→ 245 00   Anuario estadístico del Estado de Tabasco.
260   México, D.F. : ≠b Instituto Nacional de Estadística, Geografía e Informática ; ≠a [Tabasco] : ≠b Gobierno del Estado de Tabasco, ≠c 1987-
300   v. : ≠b maps ; ≠c 28 cm.
310   Annual
362 0   1986-
515   Vols. for 1986-<1987> issued in more than 1 v.
651 0   Tabasco (Mexico : State) ≠x Statistics.
710 2   Instituto Nacional de Estadística, Geografía e Informática (Mexico)
710 1   Tabasco (Mexico : State)
→ 780 00   ≠t Anuario estadístico de Tabasco ≠w (DLC)87654631 ≠w (OCoLC)12986581

Title page

**Anuario
Estadístico
del Estado de
Tabasco**

1986

INSTITUTO NACIONAL DE ESTADISTICA
GEOGRAFIA E INFORMATICA

Gobierno del Estado de
Tabasco

DISCUSSION

- AACR2R 21.2A1 states that if any word within the first five words of the title proper (within the first six words if the title begins with an initial article), other than an article, preposition, or conjunction, is changed, added, or deleted, consider the title proper to have changed and make a separate record for the serial under its new title. In this example, "Anuario estadístico de Tabasco" changed to "Anuario estadístico del Estado de Tabasco," necessitating a separate record under the new title.
- Whenever the title proper has changed, the related preceding entry is given in a note (12.7B7b). A linking note for the preceding entry is input in field 780. The first indicator is set to value "0" in order to generate a note from the link. The second indicator describes the relationship between the serial being cataloged and the preceding entry. Second indicator value "0" generates the display constant "Continues:".

J2

PROBLEM CONSIDERED:

Change within first five words of title proper not necessitating a separate record (21.2A1)

RULE(S) CONSULTED:

AACR2R: 12.7B4

TAGGED DATA RECORD (based on OCLC #9023666)

LDR   *****cas_/22*****_a*4500

	00-05	06	07-14	15-17	18	19	20	21	22-28	29	30-32	33	34	35-37	38	39
008	821206	c	19uu9999	mou	a	r			--r----	0	///	a	0	eng	-	d

→ 245 00   Directory of internship and residencies matching program for . . . / ≠c prepared by the American Association of Veterinary Clinicians.

246 13   Veterinary internship and residency matching program

246 13   VIRMP directory

→ 246 1   ≠i Vols. for <1995-96-> have title: ≠a Directory of internships and residencies … matching program

260   St. Louis, Mo. : ≠b Ralston Purina Company,

300   v. : ≠c 28 cm.

310   Annual

500   Description based on: 1984-85; title from cover.

525   Updated by occasional supplements between editions.

650 0   Veterinary medicine ≠x Study and teaching ≠z United States ≠x Directories.

650 0   Veterinary colleges ≠z United States ≠x Directories.

710 2   American Association of Veterinary Clinicians.

710 2   Ralston Purina Company.

DIRECTORY OF INTERNSHIP AND RESIDENCIES MATCHING PROGRAM for 1984-1985 *Prepared by the American Association of Veterinary Clinicians*	DIRECTORY OF INTERNSHIPS AND RESIDENCIES 1995-1996 MATCHING PROGRAM *Prepared by the American Association of Veterinary Clinicians*
Cover	**Cover of a later issue**

DISCUSSION

- According to rule 21.2A1, a change involving singular versus plural forms of the same word in a title is not considered to be a change of title proper; therefore, in this example, the use of the plural form "internships" in the title of the 1995–96 edition does not necessitate creation of a new record.
- Give in a note a variant title that is not considered to constitute a change in title proper, and provide access to that form in an added entry (12.7B4). The added title entry is input in field 246. The first indicator value "1" generates a note for the variant title preceded by the text specified in subfield ≠i. The second indicator value is blank whenever subfield ≠i is used.

J3

PROBLEM CONSIDERED:

Change beyond first five words of title proper necessitating a separate record (21.2A1)

RULE(S) CONSULTED:

AACR2R: 12.7B7b

DIRECTORY OF BOOK PUBLISHERS AND WHOLESALERS *1989* *The* BOOKSELLERS ASSOCIATION *of Great Britain & Ireland*	Directory of Book Publishers and Wholesalers with their terms and agents for overseas publishers *1982* *The* BOOKSELLERS ASSOCIATION *of Great Britain & Ireland*
Title page	**Title page of an earlier issue**

TAGGED DATA RECORD (based on OCLC #19891273)

LDR   *****cas_/22*****Ia*4500

	00-05	06	07-14	15-17	18	19	20	21	22-28	29	30-32	33	34	35-37	38	39
008	890618	d	198u199u	enk	a	r			--r----	0	///	a	0	eng	-	d

043   e-uk--- ≠a e-ie---

→ 245 00   Directory of book publishers and wholesalers / ≠c The Booksellers Association of Great Britain and Ireland.

260   London : ≠b The Association,

300   v. ; ≠c 24 cm.

500   Description based on: 18th ed. (1989)

650 0   Book industries and trade ≠z Great Britain ≠x Directories.

650 0   Book industries and trade ≠z Ireland ≠x Directories.

650 0   Booksellers and bookselling ≠z Great Britain ≠x Directories.

650 0   Booksellers and bookselling ≠z Ireland ≠x Directories.

650 0   Publishers and publishing ≠z Great Britain ≠x Directories.

650 0   Publishers and publishing ≠z Ireland ≠x Directories.

710 2   Booksellers Association of Great Britain and Ireland.

→ 780 00   ≠t Directory of book publishers and wholesalers with their terms, and agents for overseas publishers ≠w (DLC)sc84001917 ≠w (OCoLC)9136978

→ 785 00   ≠t Directory of book publishers, distributors, and wholesalers ≠w (DLC)95644699 ≠w (OCoLC)28308367

DISCUSSION

- According to 21.2A1, if any word within the first five words of the title proper (within the first six words if the title begins with an initial article), other than an article, preposition, or conjunction, is changed, added, or deleted, consider the title proper to have changed. However, if the change occurs beyond the first five words of the title proper (or after the first six words if the title begins with an initial article), consider the title proper to have changed only if the change affects the *scope and coverage of the work's content* (see also CCM 16.2.1).

- In this example, "Directory of book publishers, distributors, and wholesalers with their terms and agents for overseas publishers" changed to "Directory of book publishers and wholesalers." Although this change occurs beyond the first five words in the title, it is still considered to be a title change, because the scope of the work has been affected, i.e., the changed title no longer covers terms of wholesalers and agents for overseas publishers. A separate record is therefore created for the new title.

- The directory later changes from "Directory of book publishers and wholesalers" to "Directory of book publishers, distributors and wholesalers." Again, this is considered to be a title change, because the change has occurred within the first five words of the title.

- Whenever the title proper has changed, the related preceding or succeeding entries are given in a note (12.7B7b). In this case, links are made for the preceding and succeeding titles in fields 780 and 785 respectively, and the appropriate notes are generated from these.

J4

PROBLEM CONSIDERED:

Change beyond first five words of title proper not necessitating a separate record (21.2A1)

RULE(S) CONSULTED:

AACR2R: 12.7B4, 21.30J1
LCRI: 21.2A

TAGGED DATA RECORD (based on OCLC #23885471)

LDR   *****cas_/22*****Ia*4500

00-05	06	07-14	15-17	18	19	20	21	22-28	29	30-32	33	34	35-37	38	39
910605	c	19uu9999	dcu	a	r			--s---f	0	///	a	0	eng	-	d

008

043   n-us---

→ 245 00   Chart book, composition of the U.S. merchandise trade deficit.

246 30   Chart book

246 3   Chartbook

→ 246 1   ≠i Some issues have title: ≠a Chart book, composition of US merchandise trade

260   Washington, D.C. : ≠b U.S. International Trade Commission,

300   v. : ≠b ill. ; ≠c 28 cm.

310   Annual

→ 500   Description based on: 1982-1986 (published Feb. 1987); title from cover.

→ 515   Each issue covers preceding 5 years.

530   Distributed to depository libraries in microfiche.

580   Special ed. of: International economic review.

651 0   United States ≠x Commerce ≠x Statistics.

710 2   United States International Trade Commission.

730 0   International economic review (Washington, D.C.)

776 1   ≠t Chart book, composition of the U.S. merchandise trade deficit ≠d Supt. of Docs., U.S. G.P.O. ≠w (DLC)sn93027351 ≠w (OCoLC)27325996

787 1   ≠t International economic review (Washington, D.C.) ≠x 0895-7185 ≠w (DLC)sn87042030 ≠w (OCoLC)15181193

Chart book Composition of the U.S. Merchandise Trade Deficit **1982-86** Washington, DC U.S. International Trade Commission February 1987

Cover

Chart book Composition of US Merchandise Trade **1985-89** Washington, DC U.S. International Trade Commission February 1990

Cover of a later issue

DISCUSSION

- In this example, the title proper changes from "Chart book, composition of the U.S. merchandise trade deficit" to "Chart book, composition of US merchandise trade." The change has occurred at the fifth and sixth words of the title, where an article has been dropped and the punctuation removed from the abbreviation "U.S.". The last word "deficit" has also been dropped from the title. Because none of these changes alters the meaning of the title proper or affects the scope or coverage of the work, the change does not necessitate a separate record (21.2A1; LCRI 21.2A).

- As the title proper is considered *not* to have changed, a field 500 general note, such as "Title varies slightly," may be added to the existing record (12.7B4). If the variation in title is considered important, an added entry for the variant title should also be made to provide access for users (21.30J1). Use field 246 to input the varying form of title. First indicator value "1" generates a note for the variant title preceded by the text specified in subfield ≠i "Some issues have title:". Second indicator value blank is always used whenever subfield ≠i is used.

- Note that in the "description based on" note in field 500, the issue designation is the coverage date "1982–1986." As a result, items are marked by the date of coverage "1982–1986" and not by the publication date "1987." This peculiarity is noted in field 515, which is used for notes on irregularities or peculiarities in numbering, such as multiple numbering systems, combined issues or volumes, numbering lacking, numbering dropped, numbering added, numbering that does not begin with volume 1, items issued in parts, etc. It may also contain notes on irregularities or peculiarities in publishing patterns, such as items not published, suspension of publication, etc. In addition, field 515 may be used for notes on report year coverage, as in this case.

J5

PROBLEM CONSIDERED:

Change in title proper for a work entered under a corporate name heading (21.2A1)

RULE(S) CONSULTED:
AACR2R: 12.7B7b, 21.1B2a

THE ASSOCIATION FOR ASIAN STUDIES MEMBERSHIP DIRECTORY 1977	THE ASSOCIATION FOR ASIAN STUDIES MEMBERSHIP ROSTER 1964
Title page	Title page of an earlier issue

TAGGED DATA RECORD (based on OCLC #4917202)

LDR   *****cas_/22*****Ia*4500

00-05	06	07-14	15-17	18	19	20	21	22-28	29	30-32	33	34	35-37	38	39
790502	c	19uu9999	miu	a	r	l		--r----	0	///	a	0	eng	-	d

008

022	1071-6742
043	n-us---
→ 110 2	Association for Asian Studies.
→ 245 10	Membership directory / ≠c Association for Asian Studies, Inc.
260	Ann Arbor : ≠b The Association,
300	v. ; ≠c 28 cm.
310	Annual, ≠b <1992->
500	Description based on: 1977.
515	Vols. for 1994- issued in two parts: Part I, Names, addresses, telephone, fax, electronic numbers; Part II, Members by primary discipline, area of interest, state/postal code/country, programs/centers.
610 20	Association for Asian Studies ≠x Directories.
650 0	Orientalists ≠z United States ≠x Directories.
650 0	Orientalists ≠x Directories.
→ 780 00	Association for Asian Studies. ≠t Membership roster ≠w (OCoLC)31333033

DISCUSSION

- The work in this example emanates from a corporate body and deals with the corporate body itself; thus, it falls under rule 21.1B2a and is entered under the corporate body heading. The title of the work changes from "Membership roster" to "Membership directory." Since the change takes place within the first five important (i.e., not an article, preposition, or conjunction) words of the title proper, a separate record is required for the new title, even though the corporate name remains the same (21.2A1).

- Whenever the title proper has changed, the related preceding entry is given in a note (12.7B7b). A linking entry for the preceding title is input in field 780. The first indicator is set to value "0" in order to generate a note from the link. The second indicator describes the relationship between the serial being cataloged and the preceding entry. Second indicator value "0" generates the display constant "Continues:". Since the preceding entry is also entered under a corporate body main entry, subfield ≠a (Main Entry Heading) should be used, followed by the title "Membership roster" in subfield ≠t.

J6

PROBLEM CONSIDERED:

"Annual report" changes to "Biennial report" (21.2A1)

RULE(S) CONSULTED:

AACR2R: 21.1B2a

TAGGED DATA RECORD (based on OCLC #33601932)

LDR   *****cas_/22*****Ia*4500

00-05	06	07-14	15-17	18	19	20	21	22-28	29	30-32	33	34	35-37	38	39

008 | 951120 | c | 19929999 | ilu | g | r | | | ------s | 0 | /// | a | 0 | eng | - | d |

043	n-us-il
→ 110 1	Illinois. ≠b Dept. of Nuclear Safety.
→ 245 10	Biennial report / ≠c Illinois Department of Nuclear Safety.
260	Springfield, Ill. : ≠b The Dept., ≠c [1993-
300	v. : ≠b ill. ; ≠c 28 cm.
310	Biennial
362 0	1991-92-
500	Title from cover.
650 0	Radiation ≠z Illinois ≠x Safety measures.
650 0	Radioactive waste disposal ≠z Illinois ≠x Safety measures.
650 0	Radioactive substances ≠z Illinois ≠x Transportation ≠x Safety measures.
650 0	Radiography, Medical ≠z Illinois ≠x Safety measures.
650 0	Nuclear power plants ≠z Illinois ≠x Safety measures.
→ 780 00	Illinois. Dept. of Nuclear Safety. ≠t Annual report ≠w (DLC)85641966 ≠w (OCoLC)10994102

Title page

> **Illinois Department of**
> **Nuclear Safety**
>
>
>   **1991-92**
>   **Biennial**
>   **Report**

DISCUSSION

- Similar to J5, this example emanates from a corporate body and deals with the internal workings of the corporate body itself. Therefore, in accordance with rule 21.1B2a, main entry is under the corporate body heading.
- Beginning with the 1991–92 issue, the frequency of the work changed from annual to biennial and this change was reflected in the title, which at that point changed from "Annual report" to "Biennial report." This change necessitates a new record for the new title—not because of the change of frequency, but because the change from "Annual report" to "Biennial report" constitutes a change within the first five important words of the title (21.2A1).

J7

PROBLEM CONSIDERED:

Abbreviated form of words in title proper vs. full form not necessitating a separate record (21.2A1a)

RULE(S) CONSULTED:

AACR2R: 12.7B4

TAGGED DATA RECORD (based on OCLC #20836879)

LDR   *****cas_/22*****Ia*4500

00-05	06	07-14	15-17	18	19	20	21	22-28	29	30-32	33	34	35-37	38	39
900102	u	19uuuuuu	mdu		x		m	------s	0	///	a	0	eng	-	d

008

043	n-us-md

→ 245 00 Misc. publication.
→ 246 1   ≠i Some issues have title: ≠a Miscellaneous publication
→ 246 1   ≠i Some issues have title: ≠a Misc. pub.
   260   College Park, Md. : ≠b Extension Service, University of Maryland,
   300   v. : ≠b ill. ; ≠c 28 cm.
   310   Irregular
   500   Each issue has a distinctive title.
   515   Some issues are also in revised editions.
   500   Description based on: no. 120; title from cover.
   650 0 Agriculture ≠z Maryland.
   650 0 Agricultural extension work ≠z Maryland.
   710 2   University of Maryland, College Park. ≠b Extension Service.

DISCUSSION

- The publication in this example has abbreviated words in its title proper. The abbreviated words appear in their full form, however, in some issues of the serial and they also appear in a different abbreviated form "Misc. pub." in some other issues of the serial. According to 21.2A1a, if the change in title proper is in the representation of a word or words, such as abbreviated words or symbol versus spelled out form, as in this case, then it should not be considered a title change.
- Field 246 is used to make an added entry for the varying form of title. First indicator value "1" generates a note and an added entry for the variant title preceded by the text specified in subfield ≠i "Some issues have title:". In this case, a 246 field is input for each of the variant titles "Miscellaneous publication" and "Misc. pub." (12.7B4).

J8

PROBLEM CONSIDERED:

Acronym or initialism of words in title proper vs. full form necessitating a separate record (21.2A1a)

RULE(S) CONSULTED:

LCRI: 21.2A

TAGGED DATA RECORD (based on OCLC #23150430)

LDR   *****cas_/22*****Ia*4500

	00-05	06	07-14	15-17	18	19	20	21	22-28	29	30-32	33	34	35-37	38	39
008	910225	c	19899999	nyu	q	x	l	p	-------	0	///	a	0	eng	-	d

022	1057-896X ≠y 0162-8453	
→ 245 00	JCT.	
246 13	Journal of curriculum theorizing	
260	Rochester, N.Y. : ≠b Corporation for Curriculum Research, ≠c 1991?-	
300	v. : ≠b ill. ; ≠c 21 cm.	
310	Four no. per vol.	
362 0	9, issue 1 (spring 1989)-	
500	Title from cover.	
500	"An interdisciplinary journal of curriculum studies."	
515	Issue for spring 1989- called also issue 9:1-	
650 0	Curriculum planning ≠x Periodicals.	
→ 780 00	≠t Journal of curriculum theorizing ≠x 0162-8453 ≠w (DLC)79640288 ≠w (OCoLC)4240858	

JCT

AN INTERDISCIPLINARY JOURNAL OF CURRICULUM STUDIES 9:1

Cover

The
Journal
of
Curriculum Theorizing

Vol. 1, No. 1 winter 1979

Cover of an earlier issue

DISCUSSION

- In this example, the title proper "Journal of curriculum theorizing" changed in 1989 to the corresponding initialism "JCT." According to 21.2A1a, a title proper is not considered to have changed if the change involves abbreviated words or symbols versus their spelled-out forms. However, neither that rule nor LCRI 21.2A makes any provisions for cases like this where the change involves acronyms or initialisms versus their spelled-out forms. Consequently, the change to the initialism "JCT" must be treated as a title change, and a separate record must be made (see also CCM 16.2.3).

J9

PROBLEM CONSIDERED:

Change in name of corporate body imbedded in title proper (LCRI 21.2A)

RULE(S) CONSULTED:

AACR2R: 12.7B17

TAGGED DATA RECORD (based on OCLC #1332171)

LDR   *****cas_/22*****Ia*4500

00-05	06	07-14	15-17	18	19	20	21	22-28	29	30-32	33	34	35-37	38	39
750514	d	19381987	lau		x	l	m	------s	0	///	a	0	eng	-	d

008

022	0097-0425
→ 245 00	Occasional papers of the Museum of Zoology.
260	University, La. : ≠b Louisiana State University Press, ≠c [1938-1987].
300	63 v. : ≠b ill. ; ≠c 23 cm.
310	Irregular
362 0	No. 1 (4 May, 1938)-no. 63 (13 July 1987).
500	Title from caption
500	Place of publication varies: Baton Rouge, La., no. 9-63.
550	Issued by the Museum under Louisiana State University and Agricultural and Mechanical College, no. 1-29; under Louisiana State University (Baton Rouge, La.), no. 30-63.
→ 555	No. 1 (May 4, 1938)-no. 20 (Dec. 30, 1944) in no. 20.
650 0	Zoology.
710 2	Louisiana State University and Agricultural and Mechanical College. ≠b Museum of Zoology.
710 2	Louisiana State University (Baton Rouge, La.). ≠b Museum of Zoology.
→ 785 00	≠t Occasional papers of the Museum of Natural Science ≠x 1050-4842 ≠w (DLC)90649819 ≠w (OCoLC)20663722

Caption

NUMBER 1   4 MAY 1938

OCCASIONAL PAPERS OF THE
MUSEUM OF ZOOLOGY

LOUISIANA STATE UNIVERSITY

DISCUSSION

• When the title proper of a serial includes the name of a corporate body, there is great opportunity for variations to occur. It is quite common for the name of the corporate body to change, for a different form of the corporate name to be used in the title (see J10), or for the name of the corporate body to be deleted from or added to the title (see J11). All these changes can affect the cataloging decision.

- In this example, the name of the corporate body imbedded in the title proper changed, so the journal title went from "Occasional papers of the Museum of Zoology" to "Occasional papers of the Museum of Natural Science." According to LCRI 21.2A, when there is a change in the name of a body that is part of the title proper and that change requires the creation of a new heading for the body, it is necessary to consider the title proper to have changed. In this case, the heading for the body imbedded in the title proper changed from "Museum of Zoology" to "Museum of Natural Science," necessitating a separate record. Note that this specific condition takes precedence over all the other conditions (such as Arabic numeral(s) vs. roman numeral(s); hyphenated words vs. un-hyphenated words, etc.) stated in LCRI 21.2A for title changes of serials.

- Field 555 is used for a Cumulative Index or Finding Aids Note. For serials, this field contains a statement of volumes and/or dates covered by cumulative indexes of an item and a statement of the location of these indexes. When the first indicator is blank, the display constant "Indexes:" is generated, and no display constant is generated when the indicator is set to value "8." Make notes on the presence of cumulative indexes and also on separately published indexes (12.7B17).

J10

PROBLEM CONSIDERED:

Corporate name imbedded in title proper has a different form (LCRI 21.2A)

RULE(S) CONSULTED:

AACR2R: 21.2A1, 21.30G1, 21.30J1

1956 Volume 3 Number 1

Journal

of the Association for Computing Machinery

January 1996 • Volume 43 • Number 1

Journal

OF THE ACM

Title page   Title page from 1996 onward

TAGGED DATA RECORD (based on OCLC #1514518)

LDR   *****cas_/22*****Ia*4500

00-05	06	07-14		15-17	18	19	20	21	22-28	29	30-32	33	34	35-37	38	39
750806	c	19549999	nyu	b	r	l	p	-------	0	///	a	0	eng	-	d		

008

| Row mapping |

008   750806 | c | 19549999 | nyu | b | r | l | p | ------- | 0 | /// | a | 0 | eng | - | d

022   0004-5411

→ 245 00   Journal of the Association for Computing Machinery.

→ 246 1   ≠i Vols. for 1996- have title: ≠a Journal of the ACM

   260   New York, N.Y. : ≠b The Association,

   300   v. : ≠b ill. ; ≠c 25 cm.

   310   Bimonthly, ≠b July 1993-

   321   Quarterly, ≠b -Apr. 1993

   362 1   Began in Jan. 1954.

   500   Description based on: Vol. 3 (1956)

→ 525   Vols. 1-4 include as a supplement a reprint of the Digital computer newsletter, v. 6-9 (1954-57).

   530   Issued also on microfilm by Waverly Press and on microfiche by Johnson Associates.

   555 8   Author index: Vols. 1 (1954)-10 (1963) in v. 10.

   650 0 Computers ≠x Periodicals.

   710 2   Association for Computing Machinery.

→ 770 1   ≠t Digital computer newsletter ≠g 1954-57 ≠w (OCoLC)2110413

DISCUSSION

- This example also involves a change in the name of a corporate body imbedded in the title proper of a serial. Here the corporate name "Association for Computing Machinery" imbedded in the title proper has changed to the initialism "ACM" in issues for 1996 on. Although this change occurred within the first five important words of the title (21.2A1), it does not require a separate record. According to LCRI 21.2A, the title proper is not considered to have changed if the name of an issuing body at the end of the title changes from one form to another. Had this change happened in the beginning or in the middle of the title, rule 21.2A1 would apply—i.e., treat an acronym or initialism versus full form as a title change, but not an abbreviated form versus full form (see also CCM 16.2.3).
- Because a separate record is not necessary, an added entry may be made under the variant title "Journal of the ACM" to provide access for users (21.30J1). Use field 246 to input the varying form of title. First indicator value "1" generates a note for the variant title preceded by the text specified in subfield ≠i "Vols. for 1996- have title:". Second indicator value blank is always used whenever subfield ≠i is present.
- Some volumes of this journal include a reprint of the "Digital computer newsletter" as a supplement. This should be recorded in a supplement note using field 525. This field contains a note that describes any supplements or special issues that are not separately cataloged.
- A linking note using field 770, Supplement/Special Issue Entry, should be made to provide access to the related work "Digital computer newsletter" (21.30G1). First indicator value "1" is used so that a note will not be gener-

ated from the field, since a note for display is already recorded in field 525 (Supplement Note). Subfield ≠g (Relationship Information) contains such information as dates and volume numbers indicating the specific piece(s) involved in the relationship with the target item. In this case, the related item "Digital computer newsletter" is issued as a supplement to the target item "Journal of the Association for Computing Machinery" only during the years 1954–57. This data is accordingly input in subfield ≠g.

J11

PROBLEM CONSIDERED:

The name of the same issuing body is added or deleted at the end of the title proper (21.2A1c)

RULE(S) CONSULTED:
AACR2R: 21.30J1
LCRI: 21.30J, p. 25

TAGGED DATA RECORD (based on OCLC #3885393)

LDR   *****cas_/22*****Ia*4500

00-05	06	07-14	15-17	18	19	20	21	22-28	29	30-32	33	34	35-37	38	39
780511	d	19771993	scu	a	r			--s---s	0	///	a	0	eng	-	d

008

043   n-us-sc
→ 110 1   South Carolina. ≠b Dept. of Highways and Public Transportation.
→ 245 10   Annual report of the South Carolina Department of Highways and Public Transportation to the General Assembly.
→ 246 1   ≠i Vols. for 1988-89- have title: ≠a Annual report
260   Columbia, S.C. : ≠b The Dept., ≠c 1977-1993.
300   v. : ≠b ill. ; ≠c 23 cm.
362 0   1976/77-
362 1   Ceased in 1993?
500   Report year ends June 30.
580   Split into: South Carolina. Dept. of Transportation. Annual report; South Carolina. Dept. of Public Safety. Annual report; and: South Carolina. Dept. of Revenue and Taxation. Annual report.
610 10   South Carolina. ≠b Dept. of Highways and Public Transportation.
650 0   Roads ≠z South Carolina.
650 0   Transportation and state ≠z South Carolina.
→ 785 16 South Carolina. Dept. of Transportation. ≠t Annual report ≠w (DLC)96646524 ≠w (OCoLC)34460855
→ 785 16 South Carolina. Dept. of Public Safety. ≠t Annual report ≠w (DLC)96646519 ≠w (OCoLC)34460877
→ 785 16 South Carolina. Dept. of Revenue and Taxation. ≠t Annual report ≠w (DLC)96646515 ≠w (OCoLC)32001589

Annual Report of the South Carolina Department of Highways and Public Transportation to the General Assembly **1976/77**	**SOUTH CAROLINA DEPARTMENT OF HIGHWAYS AND PUBLIC TRANSPORTATION** **ANNUAL REPORT 1988-1989**
Title page of first issue	Title page of a later issue

DISCUSSION

- This example involves a change in title proper that includes the name of a corporate body. The work "Annual report of the South Carolina Department of Highways and Public Transportation to the General Assembly" changed to simply "Annual report" from 1988–89 on. The name of the issuing body "South Carolina Department of Highways and Public Transportation" has been deleted from the end of the title proper. However, this does not constitute a title change, since, according to 21.2A1c, the addition or deletion of the name of the issuing body at the end of the title is *not* considered a title change, regardless of whether the change occurs within or beyond the first five important words of the title.

- Note, however, that when this work later ceases publication and splits into three different works under different corporate bodies, separate records under the different corporate body headings are needed, in accordance with successive entry cataloging.

- Because a separate record is not necessary, an added entry may be made under the variant title "Annual report" to provide access for users (21.30J1). Use field 246 to input the varying form of title. First indicator value "1" generates a note for the variant title preceded by the text specified in subfield ≠i "Vols. for 1988-89- have title:". Second indicator value blank is always used whenever subfield ≠i is used (see examples in LCRI 21.30J, p. 25).

J12

PROBLEM CONSIDERED:

Corporate name added or deleted from the beginning of the title proper (21.2A1c)

RULE(S) CONSULTED:

AACR2R: 12.1B3

TAGGED DATA RECORD (based on OCLC #943680)

LDR   *****cas_/22*****Ia*4500

00-05	06	07-14	15-17	18	19	20	21	22-28	29	30-32	33	34	35-37	38	39
740711	d	19711984	nyu	q	r	l		---ib--	0	///	a	0	eng	-	d

008 (as above)

022 0	0048-5810
→ 245 00	Foreign language index.
→ 246 13	Public Affairs Information Service foreign language index
260	New York : ≠b Public Affairs Information Service,
300	14 v. ; ≠c 27 cm.
310	Quarterly, the 4th issue being the annual cumulation, ≠b 1972-1984
362 0	Vol. 1 (1968/71)-v. 14 (1984).
500	"Covers materials in French, German, Italian, Portuguese and Spanish."
650 0	Economics ≠x Indexes.
650 0	Economics ≠x Periodicals ≠x Indexes.
650 0	Economics ≠x Bibliography.
650 0	Social science ≠x Indexes.
650 0	Social science ≠x Periodicals ≠x Indexes.
650 0	Social science ≠x Bibliography.
710 2	Public Affairs Information Service.
→ 785 00	≠t PAIS foreign language index ≠x 0896-792X ≠w (DLC)86642861 ≠w (OCoLC)13323845

PUBLIC AFFAIRS
INFORMATION
SERVICE

**FOREIGN LANGUAGE
INDEX**
VOLUME 14
1984

NEW YORK
PUBLIC AFFAIRS INFORMATION SERVICE, INC.
1984

Title page

**PAIS
FOREIGN LANGUAGE
INDEX**
1985
VOLUME 15

NEW YORK
PUBLIC AFFAIRS INFORMATION SERVICE, INC.
1985

Title page of a later volume

DISCUSSION

- The serial publication in this example is entitled "Foreign language index" from volume 1 through volume 14. From volume 15 on, the name of the issuing body (initialism form) "PAIS" has been added to the beginning of the title proper to form "PAIS foreign language index." According to 21.2A1c, a title proper is not considered to have changed if the only change is the addition or deletion of the name of the issuing body at the *end of the title*. However, in this case, the name of the issuing body has been added to the *beginning* of the title proper, therefore necessitating a separate record under the new title "PAIS foreign language index," as recorded in field 785 for succeeding entry.
- Note that in this record, a variant title added entry using field 246 is entered for the title "Public Affairs Information Service foreign language index." The name of the issuing body "Public Affairs Information Service" is not treated as part of the title proper, since it does not appear as such in other locations in the serial (12.1B3). In the chief source it appears only in the "At head of title" position and is neither grammatically nor typographically linked to the title proper "Foreign language index."

J13

PROBLEM CONSIDERED:

Change in the order of words of the title proper (21.2A1)

RULE(S) CONSULTED:

AACR2R: 12.7B7b

DIRECTORY OF NONPUBLIC SCHOOLS AND ADMINISTRATORS	DIRECTORY OF NEW YORK STATE NONPUBLIC SCHOOLS AND ADMINISTRATORS
NEW YORK STATE 1993-94	**NEW YORK STATE 1976-77**
Cover	Cover of preceding title

TAGGED DATA RECORD (based on OCLC #3927846)

LDR   *****cas_/22*****_a*4500

00-05	06	07-14	15-17	18	19	20	21	22-28	29	30-32	33	34	35-37	38	39
780525	c	19789999	nyu	a	r			--r---s	0	///	a	0	eng	-	d

008

043   n-us-ny
→ 245 00 Directory of nonpublic schools and administrators, New York State.
260   Albany, N.Y. : ≠b University of the State of New York, State Education Dept.,
         Information Center on Education, ≠c 1978-
300   v. ; ≠c 28 cm.
310   Annual
362 0   1977/78-
550   Issued by: Instruction and Program Development, 1993-94-
650 0   Private schools ≠z New York (State) ≠x Directories.
650 0   School administrators ≠z New York (State) ≠x Directories.
710 2   University of the State of New York. ≠b Information Center on Education.
710 2   University of the State of New York. ≠b Office of Instruction and Program
         Development.
→ 780 00 ≠t Directory of New York State nonpublic schools and administrators ≠x
         0275-861X ≠w (DLC)sc80002026 ≠w (OCoLC)3591788

DISCUSSION

- In this example, the order of words of the title proper changed from "Directory of New York State nonpublic schools and administrators" to "Directory of nonpublic schools and administrators, New York State," necessitating a separate record under the new title, even though the change does not change the meaning of the title or indicate any change in the subject content of the serial (21.2A1).
- Whenever the title proper has changed, the related preceding entry is given in a note (12.7B7b). A link to the preceding entry is input in field 780. The first indicator is set to value "0" in order to generate a note from the link. The second indicator describes the relationship between the serial being cataloged and the preceding entry. Second indicator value "0" generates a note with the display constant "Continues:" followed by the preceding entry.

J14

PROBLEM CONSIDERED:

Change in the order of title proper and parallel title not necessitating a separate record (LCRI 12.7B5)

RULE(S) CONSULTED:

AACR2R: 1.1B8, 24.3A1
LCRI: 21.2C

TAGGED DATA RECORD (based on OCLC #2407016)

LDR   *****cas_/22*****Ia*4500

00-05	06	07-14	15-17	18	19	20	21	22-28	29	30-32	33	34	35-37	38	39
760831	c	19689999	enk	b	r	l	p	-------	0	///	b	0	eng	-	d

008

022   0023-6438 ≠y 0032-6428 ≠z 0460-1173

→ 041 0   engfreger

→ 245 00 Lebensmittel-Wissenschaft + Technologie = ≠b Science + technologie
          alimentaire = Food science + technology.

246 31 Science + technologie alimentaire

246 31 Food science + technology

246 13 Lebensmittel-Wissenschaft und -Technologie

246 13 Food science & technology

246 13 Science et technologie alimentaire

260   London : ≠b Academic Press, ≠c 1968-

300   v. : ≠b ill. ; ≠c 30 cm.

310   Bimonthly

362 0   Vol. 1, no. 1 (1968)-

500   "International journal for chemistry, biochemistry, microbiology and
         technology of food processing."

→ 500   English title appears first, 1989-

546   English, French or German.

→ 550   Official publication of: Swiss Society of Food Science and Technology.

650 0 Food industry and trade ≠x Periodicals.

→ 710 2 Schweizerische Gesellschaft für Lebensmittel-Wissenschaft und -Technologie.

Lebensmittel-Wissenschaft + Technologie
               ISSN 0023-6438

Science + technologie alimentaire

Food Science + Technology

Published for the Swiss Society of Food Science
and Technology

International Journal for Food Chemistry,
Biochemistry, Microbiology,
Technology and Engineering

Vol. 1 (1968)
No. 1
Academic Press

Cover of first issue

Food Science & Technology

Lebensmittel-Wissenschaft & Technologie
              ISSN 0023-6438

International Journal for Food Chemistry,
Biochemistry, Microbiology,
Technology and Engineering

Published for the Swiss Society of Food Science
and Technology

Vol. 22 (1989)
No. 1
Academic Press

Cover of 1989 issue

DISCUSSION

- This example illustrates another situation in which the title is not considered to have changed. In serials cataloging, it is common for parallel titles to be added or removed, or to appear in varying forms or in different orders on the chief source. When this happens, generally it does not constitute a title change if the languages of the text remain unchanged. This journal has been published as "Lebensmittel-Wissenschaft + Technologie," with French and English parallel titles appearing after the title proper. Because the text of the journal is in English, French, or German, the first title (in German) appearing on the chief source of the first issue is chosen as the title proper and the French and English titles are treated as parallel titles. Only when the text of the item is in a single language may the title proper be chosen according to the language of the text (1.1B8).
- Beginning in 1989, the English version of the title appears first; however, this reversal does not constitute a title change (LCRI 21.2C). Instead, a General 500 Note, such as "Order of titles varies," may be added to the record (LCRI 12.7B5). Another alternative is to provide a note specifically describing the new title arrangement, as has been done in this case.
- Field 550 is used for issuing bodies notes. Such notes explain the bodies' relationships to the publication and justify any 7xx added entries. This work is published by a commercial publisher but is issued as an official publication of the Swiss Society of Food Science and Technology. Therefore, field 550 is used to record that fact and justify an added entry for the Society.
- Field 710 contains corporate names used as added entries, in established catalog entry form. If the name of the corporate body appears on the item in different languages, use the form in the official language of the body (24.3A1). In this case, the German form of the name of the corporate body "Schweizerische Gesellschaft für Lebensmittel-Wissenschaft und -Technologie" should be used rather than the English form, because the official language of the body is German.

J15

PROBLEM CONSIDERED:

Title proper fluctuates (LCRI 21.2C)

RULE(S) CONSULTED:

AACR2R: 21.30J1

Bulletin Metropolitan Museum of Art New York *1942*	The Metropolitan Museum of Art Bulletin Summer 1989
Cover	**Cover of a later issue**

TAGGED DATA RECORD (based on OCLC #1624350)

LDR   *****cas_/22*****Ia*4500

00-05	06	07-14	15-17	18	19	20	21	22-28	29	30-32	33	34	35-37	38	39
008															
750914	c	19059999	nyu	q	r	l	p	-------	0	///	a	0	eng	-	d

022   0026-1521
110 2   Metropolitan Museum of Art (New York, N.Y.)
→ 245 10 Bulletin / ≠c Metropolitan Museum of Art.
→ 246 1   ≠i Some issues have title: ≠a Metropolitan Museum of Art bulletin
260   New York : ≠b The Museum,
300   v. : ≠b ill. ; ≠c 24-26 cm.
310   Quarterly, ≠b <1977->
321   Ten no. a year, ≠b summer 1942-
362 0   Vol. 1 (1905)-v. 37, no. 6 (June 1942) ; new ser., v. 1 (summer 1942)-
500   Title from cover.
520   New ser. v. 6-29 include 77th-100th Annual report of the Trustees of the
        Metropolitan Museum of Art, 1946-1969-70 (previously and subsequently
        published separately)
525   Supplements accompany some numbers.
555   Vols. 1-10, Nov. 1905-Dec. 1915. 1 v.; Vols. 1-22, Nov. 1905-Dec. 1927. 1 v.;
        Vols. 1-36, 1905-42. 1 v.
580   Beginning with 1989, fall issue is called Recent acquisitions, in continuation
        of the title Recent acquisitions, published separately by the Museum
        1985/86-1987/88.
610 20 Metropolitan Museum of Art (New York, N.Y.)
650 0 Art ≠x Periodicals.
710 2   Metropolitan Museum of Art (New York, N.Y.). ≠t Recent acquisitions.
777 1   Metropolitan Museum of Art (New York, N.Y.). Board of Trustees. ≠t Annual
        report of the Trustees of the Metropolitan Museum of Art ≠x 0740-7661 ≠w
        (DLC)5031605 ≠w (OCoLC)2563946
780 15 Metropolitan Museum of Art (New York, N.Y.). ≠t Recent acquisitions ≠g
        1989 ≠x 0889-6585 ≠w (DLC)sn86010490 ≠w (OCoLC)13987056

DISCUSSION

• Sometimes a serial publication may carry two or more titles which fluctuate
  from issue to issue, according to a regular pattern or with no pattern at all. In
  this example, "Bulletin," issued by the Metropolitan Museum of Art, is sometimes entitled "Metropolitan Museum of Art bulletin." According to LCRI
  21.2C, this is not considered to be a title change. In this case, there is no evidence that the publisher intends to change the title. The cataloger should
  choose the title appearing on the earliest issue as the title proper and give the
  other title(s) in a note worded to explain the title fluctuation. In general, because a cataloger can only decide whether a title is fluctuating or not after two
  or three title changes, or when he or she has a complete run of the publication
  in hand, this is an area where sensible judgment is required. One way in which
  to make a sound judgment is to study the intent of the publisher, that is, to see
  whether the title "change" or fluctuation is intentional. If it is intentional, then
  it may not be treated merely as a fluctuating title and a separate record is justified (see also CCM 16.2.4).

- Because treatment as a title change is not justified in this example, a note and an added entry are made under the variant form of title, which is considered necessary for access (21.30J1). Use field 246 to trace the varying form of title. First indicator value "1" indicates that both a note and a title added entry are to be generated from the field. Since a special display is needed in this case, the second indicator should be blank so that the cataloger-constructed display text "Some issues have title:" will be input in subfield ≠i, followed by the varying form of title "Metropolitan Museum of Art bulletin" in subfield ≠a.

J16

PROBLEM CONSIDERED:

Title proper changes from one language to another (LCRI 21.2C)

TAGGED DATA RECORD (based on OCLC #33629499)

LDR   *****cas_/22*****Ia*4500

00-05	06	07-14	15-17	18	19	20	21	22-28	29	30-32	33	34	35-37	38	39
008 951121	c	19959999	au		x		m	---b---	0	///	a	0	eng	-	d

→ 245 00   Austrian studies in English.
   260   Wien : ≠b Braumüller, ≠c 1995-
   300   v. ; ≠c 24 cm.
   310   Irregular
   362 0   Vol. 81 (1995)-
→ 546   Usually published in English.
   650 0   English philology.
   650 0   English literature ≠x History and criticism.
   650 0   English-speaking countries ≠x Civilization.
→ 780 00   ≠t Wiener Beiträge zur englischen Philologie ≠x 0083-9914 ≠w (DLC)85641225 ≠w (OCoLC)1587192

Austrian studies in English Vol. 81 1995 Wien Braumüller	Wiener Beiträge zur englischen Philologie Band 80 1986 Universität Wien Institut für Anglistik und Amerikanistik
Title page	**Title page of an earlier issue**

DISCUSSION

- In this example, the journal changed from the German title "Wiener Beiträge zur englischen Philologie" to the English title "Austrian studies in English."

The German title ceased in 1986 with volume 80 and was continued in 1995 by the English title "Austrian studies in English," which continues the volume designation of the German title. Note that this does not involve a change in the *order* of parallel titles because there is no English parallel title in the earlier issue, nor does a German title appear on the new issues. Also, since the title changed, the text has usually been published in English. This fact is recorded in a field 546 language note. It is clear that the change must be treated as a real title change and entails a separate record (LCRI 21.2C; see also CCM 16.2.2).

- The preceding entry is recorded in field 780. The first indicator is set to value "0" in order to generate a note from the linking entry. The second indicator describes the relationship between the serial being cataloged and the preceding entry. Second indicator value "0" generates the display constant "Continues:". Subfield ≠x (International Standard Serial Number) and subfield ≠w, which is repeatable and contains the system control number of the related record, should be given when available at the time of cataloging.

J17

PROBLEM CONSIDERED:

Section title remains the same and common title changes (LCRI 21.2A)

RULE(S) CONSULTED:

AACR2R: 1.1B9, Appendix D (p. 622)

TAGGED DATA RECORD (based on OCLC #3207494)

LDR   *****cas_/22*****Ia*4500

00-05	06	07-14	15-17	18	19	20	21	22-28	29	30-32	33	34	35-37	38	39
950712	c	19949999	dcu	a	r			---s--f	0	///	a	0	eng	-	d

008

043   n-us---

→ 245 00   FSA commodity fact sheet. ≠p Feed grains / ≠c United States Department of Agriculture, Farm Service Agency.

246 2   Farm Service Agency commodity fact sheet. ≠p Feed grains

246 30   Feed grains

260   [Washington, D.C.] : ≠b The Agency, ≠c [1994-

300   v. ; ≠c 28 cm.

310   Annual

362   1994-

500   Title from caption.

500   "Summary of ... support program and related information."

650   0   Grain as feed ≠x Prices ≠z United States.

650   0   Agricultural price supports ≠z United States.

→ 710 1   United States. ≠b Farm Service Agency.

→ 780 00   ≠t ASCS commodity fact sheet. Feed grains ≠w (DLC)sn87016531 ≠w (OCoLC)1496319

```
┌─────────────────────────────────────────────────────────────────┐
│                                                                   │
│   FSA                  FEED GRAINS        United States           │
│   Commodity             Summary of        Department of           │
│                        1994 Support       Agriculture            │
│   Fact Sheet             Program                                  │
│                        and Related        Farm Service            │
│                        Information         Agency                 │
│                                                                   │
│        ─────────────────────────────────────────────────         │
│                                            February 1995          │
│                                                                   │
└─────────────────────────────────────────────────────────────────┘
```

Caption (to the left of the first box)

```
┌─────────────────────────────────────────────────────────────────┐
│                                                                   │
│   ASCS                 FEED GRAINS        United States           │
│   Commodity             Summary of        Department of           │
│                        1993 Support       Agriculture            │
│   Fact Sheet             Program                                  │
│                        and Related        Agricultural Stabilization│
│                        Information         and Conservation        │
│                                            Service                │
│        ─────────────────────────────────────────────────         │
│                                            February 1994          │
│                                                                   │
└─────────────────────────────────────────────────────────────────┘
```

Caption (to the left of the second box)

DISCUSSION

- A section of a serial is defined in AACR2R as: "A separately published part of a serial, usually representing a particular subject category within the larger serial and identified by a designation that may be a topic, or an alphabetical or numerical designation, or a combination of these" (p. 622, Appendix D). Whenever a title entry consists of a common title and a designation (alphabetical or numerical) or a common title with a combination of a designation and a section title, all these elements should be treated as the title proper (1.1B9). The same form should also be used in linking notes, tracings, reference sources, or added entries.

- In this example, the common title "ASCS commodity fact sheet" changes to "FSA commodity fact sheet," while the section title "Feed grains" remains the same. "ASCS" is the initialism for the corporate body "Agricultural Stabilization and Conservation Service" and "FSA" is the initialism for "Farm Service Agency." According to LCRI 21.2A, when the change is in the name of a body that is part of the title proper and that change requires the creation of a new heading for the body, the title proper is considered to have changed. In the record for "ASCS commodity fact sheet," the heading for the issuing body is "United States. Agricultural Stabilization and Conservation Service." In the current record, the heading for the body is "United States. Farm Service Agency" in field 710. For this reason, a title change is clearly justified, and a new record is required.

J18

PROBLEM CONSIDERED:

Common title remains the same and section title changes or is dropped (21.2A1)

RULE(S) CONSULTED:

AACR2R: 12.1B4

J18a

TAGGED DATA RECORD (based on OCLC #34428029)

LDR   *****cas_/22*****Ia*4500

	00-05	06	07-14	15-17	18	19	20	21	22-28	29	30-32	33	34	35-37	38	39
008	960321	c	19959999	sz	g	r			---s--i	0	///	a	0	eng	-	d

022		≠y 1014-7411
043		e------
→ 245	00	Trade policy review. ≠p European Union.
246	30	European Union
260		Geneva : ≠b World Trade Organization, ≠c 1995-
300		v. : ≠b ill. ; ≠c 30 cm.
310		Biennial
362	0	1995-
515		Issues for 1995- published in 2 vols.
580		Also issued in Spanish and French editions.
651	0	European Union countries ≠x Commercial policy.
651	0	European Union countries ≠x Commerce.
650	0	Foreign trade regulation ≠z European Union countries.
710	2	World Trade Organization.
→ 780	00	≠t Trade policy review. European communities ≠w (DLC)92640005 ≠w (OCoLC)25058793

J18a

World Trade Organization

Trade Policy Review
European Union

1995

Geneva, November 1995
Volume I

Title page

J18a

WORLD
TRADE
ORGANIZATION

TRADE
POLICY
REVIEW

EUROPEAN COMMUNITIES
1993

Title page of an earlier issue

J18b

TAGGED DATA RECORD (based on OCLC #27301079)

LDR   *****cas_/22*****Ia*4500

00-05	06	07-14	15-17	18	19	20	21	22-28	29	30-32	33	34	35-37	38	39
930121	d	19921992	fr	u	u			---s--i	0	///	a	0	eng	-	d

008

043	e-cs---
→ 245 00	Energy policies. ≠p Czech and Slovak Federal Republic.
260	Paris : ≠b OECD/IEA, ≠c 1992.
300	1 v. : ≠b ill., maps ; ≠c 27 cm.
362 0	1992 survey.
650 0	Energy policy ≠z Czechoslovakia.
650 0	Power resources ≠z Czechoslovakia ≠x Statistics.
710 2	Organisation for Economic Co-operation and Development.
710 2	International Energy Agency.
→ 785 00	≠t Energy policies of the Czech Republic ≠w (DLC)95646602 ≠w (OCoLC)31441743

J18b

```
     Energy Policies
    Czech and Slovak
     Federal Republic

           1992
          Survey


           Paris
         OECD/IEA
```

Title page

J18b

```
     Energy Policies
         of the
     Czech Republic

           1994
          Survey


           Paris
         OECD/IEA
```

Title page of a later issue

DISCUSSION

- The serial in example J18a has the common title "Trade policy review" and the section title "European Communities" both appearing in the chief source of pieces published before 1995. Consequently, in keeping with rule 12.1B4, both phrases together are considered to form the title proper. Beginning in 1995, the section title changes to "European Union," even though the common title remains the same. Because the section title is considered to be part of the title proper, a change in the section title constitutes a change in the title proper. The provisions of rule 21.2A1 should also be applied to section title changes.

- In example J18b, the common title "Energy policies" and the section title "Czech and Slovak Federal Republic" together make up the title proper. The publication ceased after just one issue in 1992, and re-emerged in 1994 under a new title "Energy policies of the Czech Republic." Because a change has taken place in the first five important words of the title proper, this should be considered to be a title change, and a new record is justified for the new title (21.2A1).

J19

PROBLEM CONSIDERED:

Parallel title dropped not necessitating a separate record (LCRI 21.2C)

RULE(S) CONSULTED:
AACR2R: 12.7B9
LCRI: 1.4D2

Cover

National Research Council Canada	Conseil national de recherches Canada
Computational Intelligence	**Intelligence informatique**
Volume 7, Number 4, November 1991	Volume 7, numéro 4, novembre 1991

Cover of a later issue

Volume 8, Number 1   February 1992

Computational Intelligence

AN INTERNATIONAL JOURNAL

BLACKWELL PUBLISHERS

TAGGED DATA RECORD (based on OCLC #12073389)

LDR   *****cas_/22*****Ia*4500

00-05	06	07-14	15-17	18	19	20	21	22-28	29	30-32	33	34	35-37	38	39
850523	c	19859999	onc	q	r	4	p	------f	0	///	a	0	eng	-	d

008

022　　　0824-7935
041 0　　engfre
→ 245 00　Computational intelligence = ≠b Intelligence informatique.
246 08　　Comput. Intell.
246 31　　Intelligence informatique
260　　　Ottawa : ≠b National Research Council of Canada, ≠c 1985-
300　　　v. : ≠b ill. ; ≠c 26-28 cm.
310　　　Quarterly
362 0　　Vol. 1, no. 1 (Feb. 1985)-
→ 500　　French title dropped with v. 8, no. 1 (Feb. 1992).
→ 500　　Imprint varies.
546　　　Text in English or French.
650　0　Artificial intelligence ≠x Periodicals.
650　0　Computational linguistics ≠x Periodicals.
710 2　　National Research Council Canada.

DISCUSSION

- The journal "Computational intelligence" was published from 1985 to 1991 with the French parallel title "Intelligence informatique." However, an editorial in the February 1992 issue stated that the journal would be undergoing several changes, including a change in publisher and a change in format, with a new cover and a new size. The language of the text remains the same, but the French parallel title has now been dropped.

- Despite all these changes and the new incarnation the journal was to take, the present case is not a title change. A new record is not required for the subsequent issues lacking the parallel title (LCRI 21.2C). The deletion of the parallel title from the chief source of information in the journal does not affect its scope, coverage, or the language of the text. A general note should be made in field 500 to record this information, and another note should be made to indicate the variation in the publication, distribution, etc., details of the journal (12.7B9). In this case, a general statement such as "Imprint varies" is sufficient, unless the cataloger considers it important to state explicitly that the publisher has now changed to "Blackwell Publishers."

- Although the name of the publisher appears in both English and French in the chief source, the French name is not transcribed as a parallel publisher's name in field 260 (publication, distribution, etc., area). According to LCRI 1.4D2, only the publisher's name in the language corresponding to that of the title proper is transcribed in field 260, and, therefore, "National Research Council of Canada" alone is transcribed as the publisher in field 260 in this record.

J20

PROBLEM CONSIDERED:

Alternating section titles in a single record (LCRI 21.2C)

RULE(S) CONSULTED:

AACR2R: 21.2A1

TAGGED DATA RECORD (based on OCLC #21266025)

LDR   *****cas_/22*****Ia*4500

00-05	06	07-14	15-17	18	19	20	21	22-28	29	30-32	33	34	35-37	38	39
900326	c	19909999	nyu	m	r	l	p	-------	0	///		a	0	eng	-	d

008

022 0	1050-2947 ≠y 0556-2791	
→ 245 00	Physical review. ≠n A, ≠p Atomic, molecular, and optical physics	
→ 246 1	≠i Issued on 15th of the month as: ≠a Physical review. ≠n A, ≠p Statistical physics, plasmas, fluids, and related interdisciplinary topics	
260	New York, N.Y. : ≠b Published by the American Physical Society through the American Institute of Physics, ≠c c1990-	
300	v. : ≠b ill. ; ≠c 29 cm.	
310	Monthly, ≠b 1993-	
321	Semimonthly, ≠b 1990-1992	
362 0	Third ser., v. 41, no. 1 (1 Jan. 1990)-	
→ 500	Numbers for 1990-1992 issued on the 1st of the month called: Atomic, molecular, and optical physics; numbers issued on the 15th of the month called: Statistical physics, plasmas, fluids, and related interdisciplinary topics. Pagination is continuous.	
500	Title from cover.	
515	New vols. start on Jan. 1 and July 1 of each year.	
580	Continues: Physical review. A, General physics.	
580	Continued in part in 1993 by: Physical review. E, Statistical physics, plasmas, fluids, and related interdisciplinary topics.	
580	Indexed by: Physical review and Physical review letters index.	
650 0	Nuclear physics ≠x Periodicals.	
650 0	Statistical physics ≠x Periodicals.	
650 0	Plasma (Ionized gases) ≠x Periodicals.	
650 0	Fluids ≠x Periodicals.	
710 2	American Physical Society.	
710 2	American Institute of Physics.	
780 10	≠t Physical review. A, General physics ≠w 0556-2791 ≠w (DLC)75021361 ≠w (OCoLC)1083925	
→ 785 11	≠t Physical review. E, Statistical physics, plasmas, fluids, and related interdisciplinary topics ≠w 1063-651X ≠w (DLC)93661989 ≠w (OCoLC)26103502	
787 1	≠t Physical review and Physical review letters index ≠x 0094-0003 ≠w (DLC)83642755 ≠w (OCoLC)3811892	

PHYSICAL REVIEW A

ATOMIC, MOLECULAR, AND
OPTICAL PHYSICS

Volume 41   *Third Series*   Number 1

1 JANUARY 1990

Published by
THE AMERICAN PHYSICAL SOCIETY
through the
AMERICAN INSTITUTE OF PHYSICS

Cover of issue on 1st of month

PHYSICAL REVIEW A

STATISTICAL PHYSICS, PLASMAS, FLUIDS,
AND RELATED INTERDISCIPLINARY TOPICS

Volume 41   *Third Series*   Number 2

15 JANUARY 1990

Published by
THE AMERICAN PHYSICAL SOCIETY
through the
AMERICAN INSTITUTE OF PHYSICS

Cover of issue on 15th of month

PHYSICAL REVIEW A

GENERAL PHYSICS

Volume 40   *Series 3*   Number 12

15 DECEMBER 1989

Published by
THE AMERICAN PHYSICAL SOCIETY
through the
AMERICAN INSTITUTE OF PHYSICS

Cover of preceding issue

DISCUSSION

- This example is similar to J15 in that the title proper of the serial fluctuates. However, the fluctuation here is based on a regular pattern. The journal was known as "Physical review. A, General physics" from January 1970 to December 1989. From January 1990 onward, the section title "General physics" has been dropped. A title change is therefore justified (21.2A1).

- It is indicated by the publisher that the issue of the journal published on the first of each month will bear the section title "Atomic, molecular, and optical physics"; the issue published on the fifteenth of each month will have the section title "Statistical physics, plasmas, fluids, and related interdisciplinary topics." This means the same journal "Physical review A" will have alternating section titles on a semimonthly basis, according to its subject matter. However, note that the alternating sections still share the same numerical and chronological designation "Third series, volume 41" of the journal "Physical review A" (as recorded in field 362 of the record), and their pagination is continuous. For these reasons, only a single new record should be created as a result of the title change, i.e., under the title "Physical review. A, Atomic, molecular, and optical physics," which is the title on the earliest issue, and *not two* separate records for the alternating sections of the journal.

- According to LCRI 21.2C, if a serial has two or more titles used on different issues according to a regular pattern, choose as the title proper the title on the earliest issue and give the other title(s) in a note to explain the title fluctuation; and always make an added entry for the title not chosen as the title proper. In this case, a general 500 note field is used to explain the title fluctuation. Field 246 (Variant Title Entry) is used to provide access to the title not chosen as the title proper, i.e., "Physical review. A, Statistical physics, plasmas, fluids, and related interdisciplinary topics."

K. Changes and Problems Considered in Other Areas

During the lifespan of a serial a great many changes can occur in a single publication. In addition to changes in title proper (see section J), corporate name, or issuing body (see section I), there can also be changes in other title information, publisher (see section D), place of publication, frequency, edition statement, series statement (see section G), numbering system (see section F), and physical format (see section Q). Usually these changes can be reflected by a note in the bibliographic record. However, certain changes in other title information, physical format, and numbering system may necessitate the creation of a new record. The following are examples of some changes and problems that one might encounter.

EXAMPLES

K1	Changes in the publisher's name or imprint for a serial
K2	Individual issues and cumulations with different numerical systems and titles
K3	Individual issues and cumulations in one record with the same designation system
K4	Individual issues and cumulations of the same title in a separate record with different numeric system
K5	Works published in bound volume and loose-leaf with the same title
K6	Individual parts do not have their own numbering systems
K7	Individual parts have their own numbering systems and differ in frequency
K8	Individual parts have their own numbering systems but the same frequency
K9	Individual parts with continuous alternate numbering system
K10	Link to a pre-AACR2 record
K11	Identical title related to pre-AACR2 record
K12	Changes in frequency necessitating a separate record
K13	Changes in designations
K14	Place of publication used as qualifier in the uniform title heading changes
K15	Issued alternately with different editions

K1

PROBLEM CONSIDERED:

Changes in the publisher's name or imprint for a serial (LCRI 12.0Bl)

RULE(S) CONSULTED:

AACR2R: 12.7B6, 12.7B9, 21.2C1, 21.3B1
LCRI: 12.0, 12.7B9

<table>
<tr><td rowspan="6" align="right">K1a
Title page
of the
1996
edition</td><td>
THE PRINCETON REVIEW

Hillel Guide To
JEWISH LIFE
ON CAMPUS

1996 Edition

Random House, Inc. New York 1995
</td></tr>
</table>

K1a

TAGGED DATA RECORD (based on OCLC #23174692)

LDR   *****cas_/22*****_a*4500

	00-05	06	07-14	15-17	18	19	20	21	22-28	29	30-32	33	34	35-37	38	39
008	910301	c	19929999	nyu	u	u	l		--r----	0	///	a	0	eng	-	d

022 0	1090-4859	
245 04	The Hillel guide to Jewish life on campus.	
246 18	Jewish life on campus	
→ 260	Washington, D.C. : ≠b B'nai B'rith Hillel Foundations, ≠c c1990-	
300	v. : ≠b ill. ; ≠c 28 cm.	
362 1	1991/1992-	
500	At head of title: The Princeton Review, <1996->	
→ 500	Published: New York, N.Y. : Random House, <1996->	
650 0	Jewish college students ≠z United States ≠x Societies, etc. ≠x Periodicals.	
650 0	Jewish college students ≠z Canada ≠x Societies, etc. ≠x Periodicals.	
710 2	B'nai B'rith Hillel Foundations.	
710 2	Princeton Review (Firm)	
780 00	≠t Jewish life on campus ≠w (DLC)91640220 ≠w (OCoLC)10783477	

K1b

TAGGED DATA RECORD (based on OCLC #7297725)

LDR   *****cas_/22*****_a*4500

00-05	06	07-14	15-17	18	19	20	21	22-28	29	30-32	33	34	35-37	38	39
810402	c	19809999	gw	m	r	z	p	-------	0	///	a	0	eng	-	d

008

022	0173-0835
245 00	Electrophoresis.
→ 260	Weinheim, Germany : ≠b Verlag Chemie, ≠c [1980-
300	v. : ≠b ill. ; ≠c 28 cm.
310	Monthly, ≠b Jan. 1985-
321	Bimonthly, ≠b < Feb. 1982->
362 0	Vol. 1, no. 1 (Apr. 1980)-
→ 500	Publisher (international subscription) varies: VCH Verlagsgesellschaft mbH, Jan. 1985-
→ 500	Imprint varies for USA and Canada subscription: Deerfield Beach, FL : VCH Publishers, Jan. 1985-
550	Official journal of: Electrophoresis Society, 1980-81; International Electrophoresis Society, 1982-
650 0	Electrophoresis ≠x Periodicals.
710 2	Electrophoresis Society.
710 2	International Electrophoresis Society.

DISCUSSION

- The two basic characteristics of serial publications are: (1) they change, and (2) they continue. If a change occurs in the first five words of the title proper of any serial or in the main entry of a serial entered under a name heading, a separate record should be created (21.2C1; 21.3B1). However, if a change occurs in areas other than these, a separate record is usually not justified (LCRI 12.0B1). In examples K1a and K1b, the change occurred in the imprint area and, therefore, no separate record was made; instead, differences in place of publication and publisher were recorded in the note area (12.7B9).

- Note that microforms and reprint editions are cataloged by different rules and are exceptions to the above pattern. For instance, if a microfilm is filmed by an agency that differs from that of an existing record, a separate record should be input. Similarly, if the publisher of a reprinted serial differs from that of the original record, a separate record should be created, even though the title proper might remain the same. On the other hand, no separate record is necessary if both the reprint and the original publication have the same publisher, even though the title proper might differ (LCRI 12.0).

- A field 500 General Note is used for recording changes in the place of publication and changes in commercial publishers (LCRI 12.7B9). This has been done in example K1a. In cases where changes in place of publication and publisher are frequent, as in example K1b, a note with the general statement "Imprint varies" should be input to avoid cluttering the cataloging record with minor changes.

- Note also, that, as may be seen in example K1b, changes involving other corporate bodies associated with the serial or publishers other than commercial publishers should be recorded in field 550 (12.7B6).

K2

PROBLEM CONSIDERED:

Individual issues and cumulations with different numerical systems and titles (LCRI 12.0)

RULE(S) CONSULTED:

AACR2R: 12.7B7

K2a

> **HONG KONG**
> ─────────
> **LAW
> DIGEST**
>
>
> December 1996

Title page of December 1996 issue

K2b

> **HONG KONG
> LAW DIGEST
> YEARBOOK
> 1995**
>
> This volume includes digests of legislation gazetted between 1 January 1995 and 30 December 1995 and judgments received by the editor during the same period (Vol. II of Hong Kong Law Reports for 1995 not included)

Title page of 1995 annual cumulation

K2a

TAGGED DATA RECORD (based on OCLC #20291740)

LDR   *****cas_/22*****Ia*4500

	00-05	06	07-14	15-17	18	19	20	21	22-28	29	30-32	33	34	35-37	38	39
008	890901	d	19891996	hk	m	x			--w----	0	///	a	0	eng	-	d

043	a-hk---
245 00	Hong Kong law digest.
260	Hong Kong : ≠b Hong Kong Legal Publications, ≠c c1989-1996.
300	8 v. ; ≠c 25 cm.
→ 310	Eleven issues yearly
362 1	Jan. 1989-Dec. 1996.
500	Published Jan. 1991- Hong Kong : Longman Group (Far East).
500	Index cumulates with each issue.
→ 580	Has annual cumulation under title: Hong Kong law yearbook, 1985-1993; called: Hong Kong law digest yearbook, 1994-
580	Merged with: Hong Kong Law Reports, to form: Authorised Hong Kong law reports & digests
650 0	Law reports, digests, etc. ≠z China ≠z Hong Kong.
780 00	≠t Hong Kong current law ≠w (DLC)sn86023375 ≠w (OCoLC)12358815
785 17	≠t Hong Kong law reports ≠w (OCoLC)16942221
785 17	≠t Authorised Hong Kong law reports & digests ≠w (OCoLC)37108990
787 1	≠t Hong Kong law yearbook ≠w (DLC)sn87018298 ≠w (OCoLC)15173036
787 1	≠t Hong Kong law digest yearbook ≠w (DLC)sn97033063 ≠w (OCoLC)33327003

K2b

TAGGED DATA RECORD (based on OCLC #33327003)

LDR   *****cas_/22*****Ia*4500

00-05	06	07-14	15-17	18	19	20	21	22-28	29	30-32	33	34	35-37	38	39
951007	c	19949999	hk	a	r			--w----	0	///	a	0	eng	-	d

008

043   a-hk---
245 00 Hong Kong law digest yearbook.
260   Hong Kong : ≠b FT Law & Tax Asia Pacific, ≠c 1995-
300   v. ; ≠c 25 cm.
→ 310   Annual
362 0   1994-
→ 580   Annual cumulation of the monthly publication: Hong Kong law digest.
500   Includes digests of legislation gazetted ... and judgments received for the year.
650 0   Law reports, digests, etc. ≠z China ≠z Hong Kong.
780 00 ≠t Hong Kong law yearbook ≠w (DLC)sn87018298 ≠w (OCoLC)15173036
787 1   ≠t Hong Kong law digest ≠w (DLC)sn89019712 ≠w (OCoLC)20291740

DISCUSSION

- A cumulation of a serial may or may not carry the same title as the serial itself. If the titles of the individual issues and the cumulation differ, separate
records are usually made, unless the cumulation continues the numbering system of the serial (LCRI 12.0), e.g., the December issue for each year is a cumulation of prior issues.

- In example K2a, the serial "Hong Kong law digest" is published monthly from
January to December, with an annual cumulation published at the end of the
year called "Hong Kong law digest yearbook" (see K2b). Since the designation system does not tie the individual issues and the annual cumulation together, separate records should be made (LCRI 12.0).

- A linking note should be made to explain the cumulation's relationship to the
monthly issues (12.7B7). This is recorded in field 580 (Linking Entry Complexity Note), which describes the specific relationship. Use also field 787
(Nonspecific Relationship Entry) for the linking entry, since the related record
does not fit into any of the cases defined in linking fields 765–785.

K3

PROBLEM CONSIDERED:

Individual issues and cumulations in one record with the same designation system (LCRI 12.0)

RULE(S) CONSULTED:

AACR2R: 12.7B1

K3a

TAGGED DATA RECORD (based on OCLC #1490320)

LDR   *****cas_/22*****Ia*4500

00-05	06	07-14	15-17	18	19	20	21	22-28	29	30-32	33	34	35-37	38	39
750730	d	19701987	ilu	q	n	l		--i----	0	///	a	0	eng	-	d

008

022 0	0098-4604
043	n-us---
245 00	Index to U.S. Government periodicals
246 10	U.S. government periodicals
260	[Chicago] : ≠b Infordata International, ≠c 1970-1987.
300	18 v. ; ≠c 26 cm.
→ 310	Quarterly, the 4th issue being the annual cumulation
362 0	1970-1987.
651 0	United States ≠x Government publications ≠x Indexes.
650 0	American periodicals ≠x Indexes.

K3b

TAGGED DATA RECORD (based on OCLC #1536773)

LDR   *****cas_/22*****Ia*4500

00-05	06	07-14	15-17	18	19	20	21	22-28	29	30-32	33	34	35-37	38	39
750812	c	19659999	miu	q	r	l	p	---io--	0	///	a	0	eng	-	d

008

022 0	0524-0581
245 00	Book review index.
260	Detroit : ≠b Gale Research Co.,
300	v. ; ≠c 27 cm.
→ 310	Quarterly, with semiannual and annual cumulations, ≠b 1994-
→ 321	Monthly, with quarterly and annual cumulations, ≠b 1965-
→ 321	Bimonthly, with annual cumulations, ≠b <May/June 1977>-1993
362 0	Vol. 1, no. 1 (Jan. 1965)-
→ 515	Annual cumulative issues lack vol. designation
580	Selected citations also issued under titles: Children's book review index, and: Young adult book review index.
650 0	Books ≠x Reviews ≠x Indexes ≠x Periodicals.
710 2	Gale Research Company.
787 1	≠t Children's book review index ≠x 0147-5681 ≠w (DLC)75027408 ≠w (OCoLC)2306438
787 1	≠t Young adult book review index ≠x 0897-7402 ≠w (DLC)88645812 ≠w (OCoLC)17609918

DISCUSSION

- In example K3a, the publication "Index to U.S. Government periodicals" puts out three quarterly issues per year, with the fourth quarterly issue being an annual cumulation. The quarterly issues and the annual cumulation not only have the same title, but also the same volume numbering system. Therefore, according to LCRI 12.0, a separate record should not be made for the cumulations.

Instead, a Current Frequency Note (using field 310) is used to explain the frequency of the cumulations (12.7B1).

- In example K3b, "Book review index" is published quarterly, with the second issue being a semiannual and the fourth issue being an annual cumulation. Even though the individual issues and the cumulations have different designation systems (i.e., the individual issues have a volume designation, but the fourth issue, which is the annual cumulation, has only a date designation), no separate record should be made for the cumulation. This is because the quarterly issues are cumulated into a permanent volume at the end of each year. If a separate record is made for the last cumulated issue, not only would the designation of the quarterly issues be disrupted, but the bibliographic record for the individual issue would also have an incomplete coverage.

K4

PROBLEM CONSIDERED:

Individual issues and cumulations of the same title in a separate record with different numeric system (LCRI 12.0)

RULE(S) CONSULTED:

AACR2R: 12.7B7

K4a

TAGGED DATA RECORD (based on OCLC #31403847)

LDR   *****cas_/22*****Ia*4500

00-05	06	07-14	15-17	18	19	20	21	22-28	29	30-32	33	34	35-37	38	39
941104	c	19949999	nyu	m	n	l	p	--i----	0	///	a	0	eng	-	d

008

022 0	1079-4719 ≠y 0019-4077
043	n-us---
245 00	Index to legal periodicals & books
246 3	Index to legal periodicals and books
260	Bronx, N.Y. : ≠b H.W. Wilson Co., ≠c 1994-
300	v. ; ≠c 26 cm.
→ 310	Monthly (except Sept.)
→ 362 0	Vol. 88, no. 1 (Oct. 1994)
500	Title from cover.
→ 580	Issued also in an annual cumulation.
580	CD-ROM ed. available.
650 0	Law ≠z United States ≠x Periodicals ≠x Indexes.
650 0	Law ≠x Periodicals ≠x Indexes.
650 0	Law ≠z United States ≠x Bibliography ≠x Indexes.
650 0	Law ≠x Bibliography ≠x Indexes.
710 2	H.W. Wilson Company.
780 00	≠t Index to legal periodicals ≠x 0019-4077 ≠w (DLC)41021689 ≠w (OCoLC)1585611
787 1	≠t Index to legal periodicals & books (Cumulation) ≠w (DLC)sn96034081 ≠w (OCoLC)33500252

K4b

TAGGED DATA RECORD (based on OCLC #33500252)

LDR   *****cas_/22*****Ia*4500

00-05	06	07-14	15-17	18	19	20	21	22-28	29	30-32	33	34	35-37	38	39
951117	c	19959999	nyu	a	r			--i----	0	///	a	0	eng	-	d

008

022   ≠y 1079-4719
043   n-us---
→ 130 0   Index to legal periodicals & books (Cumulation)
245 00   Index to legal periodicals & books
246 3   Index to legal periodicals and books
260   New York : ≠b H.W. Wilson Co., ≠c 1995-
300   v. ; ≠c 26 cm.
→ 310   Annual
→ 362 0   Vol. 34 (Sept. 1994-Aug. 1995)-
→ 580   Cumulation of the monthly publication.
650   0   Law ≠z United States ≠x Periodicals ≠x Indexes.
650   0   Law ≠x Periodicals ≠x Indexes.
650   0   Law ≠z United States ≠x Bibliography ≠x Indexes.
650   0   Law ≠x Bibliography ≠x Indexes.
710 2   H.W. Wilson Company.
780 00   ≠t Index to legal periodicals (Cumulation) ≠w (DLC)sn87018093 ≠w (OCoLC)8593640
787 1   ≠t Index to legal periodicals & books ≠x 1079-4719 ≠w (DLC)95648012 ≠w (OCoLC)31403847

DISCUSSION

- The examples in K4 illustrate cases in which separate records are made for serials and their cumulations. In K4a, the publication "Index to legal periodicals & books" is published monthly except September. It has an annual cumulation under the same title, but with a different designation system. According to LCRI 12.0, when the individual issues and the cumulation have the same title but have different designation systems, separate records should be made.

- Example K4b shows the separate record made for the annual cumulations of "Index to legal periodicals & books." Since the records for the monthly issues and the cumulations both have the same title proper, it is necessary to distinguish between the two records. A uniform title heading is therefore constructed for the title of the cumulations, with the word "Cumulation" as the qualifier.

- A linking note (field 580) should be made to explain the cumulation's relationship to the monthly issues (12.7B7).

K5

PROBLEM CONSIDERED:

Works published in bound volume and loose-leaf with the same title (LCRI 12.0)

RULE(S) CONSULTED:

LCRI: 25.5B

K5a

TAGGED DATA RECORD (based on OCLC #5584901)

LDR   *****cas_/22******Ia*4500

00-05	06	07-14		15-17	18	19	20	21	22-28	29	30-32	33	34	35-37	38	39
008																
791025	c	19uu9999		ilu	a	r			--f----	0	///	a	0	eng	-	d

043   n-us---

110 2   American Institute of Certified Public Accountants.

→ 240 10   AICPA technical practice aids (Bound ed.)

245 10   AICPA technical practice aids.

246 3   American Institute of Certified Public Accountants technical practice aids

→ 250   [Bound ed.]

260   Chicago : ≠b Published for the American Institute of Certified Public Accountants by CCH Inc.,

300   v. ; ≠c 23 cm.

310   Annual

500   Description based on: as of July 1, 1994.

→ 580   This publication is also issued in a loose-leaf format with the same title.

650 0 Accounting ≠x Standards ≠z United States ≠x Handbooks, manuals, etc.

650 0 Auditing ≠x Standards ≠z United States ≠x Handbooks, manuals, etc.

710 2   CCH Incorporated.

787 1   American Institute of Certified Public Accountants. ≠t AICPA technical practice aids ≠w (OCoLC)4357015

K5b

TAGGED DATA RECORD (based on OCLC #4357015)

LDR   *****cas_/22******Ia*4500

00-05	06	07-14		15-17	18	19	20	21	22-28	29	30-32	33	34	35-37	38	39
008																
781108	c	19uu9999		ilu		x			--f----	0	///	a	0	eng	-	d

110 2   American Institute of Certified Public Accountants.

245 10   AICPA technical practice aids.

246 30   Technical practice aids

260   Chicago : ≠b Published for the American Institute of Certified Public Accountants by Commerce Clearing House,

300   v. ; ≠c 26cm.

→ 500   Loose-leaf for updating.

500   Description based on: 1980, v. 1-2.

515   Each edition issued in several vols., each with a distinctive title.

→ 580   This publication is also issued in a bound reprint edition

650 0 Accounting ≠x Handbooks, manuals, etc.

650 0 Accounting ≠x Problems, exercises, etc.

787 1   American Institute of Certified Public Accountants. ≠s AICPA technical practice aids (Bound ed.) ≠w (DLC)96644513 ≠w (OCoLC)5584901

DISCUSSION

- Not all reprinted issues of a serial can be cataloged as separate records; separate records should usually only be made for those that are published by a publisher who was not responsible for the original (LCRI 12.0).
- The publication "AICPA technical practice aids" is issued in both loose-leaf format and reprinted bound edition, and both are published by the same publisher. Note, however, that in spite of the fact that standard practice would be not to create a separate record for issues reproduced by the same publisher, in this example a separate record has been made for the reprinted bound edition. The reason for this is the nature of the reprints; this is not a case where a few isolated issues of the loose-leaf publication have been reprinted, but, rather, the reprint bound volume is issued annually on a regular basis.
- Usually a reprinted serial, such as the one in this case, will carry the same title as the original. According to Library of Congress policy, no uniform title should be established to distinguish the reprint from the original. However, in this case, the uniform title in field 240 has been created not to distinguish between the reproduction and the original, but, rather, to distinguish between the loose-leaf format and the bound edition.
- Note that in K5a the edition statement in field 250 is given in brackets, because it has been supplied by the cataloger. The edition statement is also then used as the qualifier in the 240 uniform title (LCRI 25.5B; see also CCM 9.2.4).

K6

PROBLEM CONSIDERED:

Individual parts do not have their own numbering systems (LCRI 12.0)

RULE(S) CONSULTED:

AACR2R: 12.7B8

Title page of Vol. 1	**HONG KONG'S TRADE BY COUNTRIES** STATISTICAL YEARBOOK 1989 VOLUME 1

Title page of Vol. 2	**HONG KONG'S MAJOR EXPORTS** STATISTICAL YEARBOOK 1989 VOLUME 2 *Research Department* *Hong Kong Trade Development Council*

TAGGED DATA RECORD (based on OCLC #26658469)

LDR   *****cas_/22*****Ia*4500

	00-05	06	07-14	15-17	18	19	20	21	22-28	29	30-32	33	34	35-37	38	39
008	920923	c	19889999	hk	a	r			--s----	0	///	a	0	eng	-	d

043   a-hk---
130 0   Statistical yearbook (Hong Kong Trade Development Council. Research Dept.)
245 00 Statistical yearbook.
246 3   Statistical year book
260   Hong Kong : ≠b Research Dept., Hong Kong Trade Development Council,
300   v. ; ≠c 29 cm.
310   Annual
362 1   Began publication in 1988.
500   Chiefly tables.
→ 515   Issued in 2 vols.: v. 1, Hong Kong's trade by countries; v. 2, Hong Kong's major exports.
500   Description based on: 1989.
651 0 Hong Kong (China) ≠x Commerce ≠x Statistics.
710 2   Hong Kong Trade Development Council. ≠b Research Dept.

DISCUSSION

- When a serial is issued in parts, separate records may or may not be made. This is determined using a number of criteria listed in LCRI 12.0. One of the circumstances under which separate records are generally *not* made is when the individual parts do not have a numbering system or date designation of their own.

- In this example, "Statistical yearbook" is issued in two volumes, i.e., "Volume 1. Hong Kong's trade by countries" and "Volume 2. Hong Kong's major exports." The individual parts do not have a numbering system of their own. Even though every subsequent issue of this serial is published in two volumes with distinctive titles, they are meant to be kept together on the shelf and to be used together (LCRI 12.0). Therefore, no separate record should be made for the individual parts.

- Field 515 (Numbering Peculiarities Note) should be input to indicate that a publication is issued in parts (12.7B8).

K7

PROBLEM CONSIDERED:

Individual parts have their own numbering systems and differ in frequency (LCRI 12.0)

K7a

Journal of Magnetic Resonance
Series A
Vol. 101, no. 1 Jan. 1993

Cover

K7b

Journal of Magnetic Resonance
Series B
Vol. 1, no. 1 Feb. 1993

Cover

K7a

TAGGED DATA RECORD (based on OCLC #26224216)

LDR   *****cas_/22*****Ia*4500

00-05	06	07-14	15-17	18	19	20	21	22-28	29	30-32	33	34	35-37	38	39
920720	c	19931996	cau	m	r	l	p	-------	0	///	a	0	eng	-	d

008

022 0   1064-1858

245 00   Journal of magnetic resonance. ≠n Series A.

260   San Diego : ≠b Academic Press, ≠c 1993-1996.

→ 300   23 v. : ≠b ill. ; ≠c 28 cm.

→ 310   Monthly, ≠b 1994-

321   Monthly (except semimonthly in Feb., June, Oct.), ≠b 1993

→ 362 0   Vol. 101, no. 1 (Jan. 1993)-v. 123, no. 2 (Dec. 1996).

500   Title from cover.

580   Merged with: Journal of magnetic resonance. Series B, to form: Journal of magnetic resonance (San Diego, Calif. : 1997).

650 0   Nuclear magnetic resonance ≠x Periodicals.

780 01   ≠t Journal of magnetic resonance ≠x 0022-2364 ≠w (DLC)70004301 ≠w (OCoLC)1783377

785 17   ≠t Journal of magnetic resonance. Series B ≠x 1064-1866 ≠w (DLC)94657053 ≠w (OCoLC)26224244

785 17   ≠t Journal of magnetic resonance (San Diego, Calif. : 1997) ≠w 1090-7807 ≠w (DLC)sn96002721 ≠w (OCoLC)35454788

K7b

TAGGED DATA RECORD (based on OCLC #26224244)

LDR   *****cas_/22*****Ia*4500

00-05	06	07-14	15-17	18	19	20	21	22-28	29	30-32	33	34	35-37	38	39

008 | 920720 | d | 19931996 | cau | m | x | l | p | ------- | 0 | /// | a | 0 | eng | - | d |

022 0   1064-1866

245 00   Journal of magnetic resonance. ≠n Series B.

260   San Diego : ≠b Academic Press, ≠c 1993-1996.

→ 300   13 v. : ≠b ill. ; ≠c 28 cm.

→ 310   9 no. a year, ≠b 1994-

321   Bimonthly, ≠b 1993

→ 362 0   Vol. 101, no. 1 (Feb. 1993)-v. 113, no. 3 (Dec. 1996).

500   Title from cover.

580   Merged with: Journal of magnetic resonance. Series A, to form: Journal of magnetic resonance (San Diego, Calif. : 1997).

650 0   Nuclear magnetic resonance ≠x Periodicals.

780 01   ≠t Journal of magnetic resonance ≠x 0022-2364 ≠w (DLC)70004301 ≠w (OCoLC)1783377

785 17   ≠t Journal of magnetic resonance. Series A ≠x 1064-1858 ≠w (DLC)94657048 ≠w (OCoLC)26224216

785 17   ≠t Journal of magnetic resonance (San Diego, Calif. : 1997) ≠w 1090-7807 ≠w (DLC)sn96002721 ≠w (OCoLC)35454788

DISCUSSION

- See example K8.

K8

PROBLEM CONSIDERED:

Individual parts have their own numbering systems but the same frequency (LCRI 12.0)

K8a

> EUROPEAN
> JOURNAL OF
> MECHANICS
> A/Solids, Volume 8, no. 1

Cover

K8b

> EUROPEAN
> JOURNAL OF
> MECHANICS
> B/Fluids, Volume 8, no. 1

Cover

K8a

TAGGED DATA RECORD (based on OCLC #19528048)

LDR   *****cas_/22*****Ia*4500

00-05	06	07-14	15-17	18	19	20	21	22-28	29	30-32	33	34	35-37	38	39
890410	c	19899999	fr	b	x		p	-------	0	///	a	0	eng	-	d

008

022 0   0997-7538
245 00   European journal of mechanics. ≠n A, ≠p Solids.
246 30   Solids
246 30   A/Solids
246 3   EJM ≠n A, ≠p Solids
246 3   EJM A/Solids
246 13   E.J.M. ≠n A, ≠p Solids
246 13   E.J.M. A/Solids
246 13   Eur. J. mech. ≠n A, ≠p Solids
260   [Paris] : ≠b Gauthier-Villars, ≠c c1989-
300   v. : ≠b ill. ; ≠c 27 cm.
→ 310   Six no. a year
→ 362 0   Vol. 8, no. 1-
500   Title from cover.
650 0   Mechanics, Analytic ≠x Periodicals.
650 0   Mechanics, Applied ≠x Periodicals.
780 01   ≠t Journal de mécanique théorique et appliquée ≠x 0750-7240 ≠w (DLC)82647192 ≠w (OCoLC)8694169

K8b

TAGGED DATA RECORD (based on OCLC #19538423)

LDR   *****cas_/22*****Ia*4500

00-05	06	07-14	15-17	18	19	20	21	22-28	29	30-32	33	34	35-37	38	39
890412	c	19899999	fr	b	x	0	p	-------	0	///	a	0	eng	-	d

008

022   0997-7546
245 00   European journal of mechanics. ≠n B, ≠p Fluids.
246 30   Fluids
246 3   EJM. ≠p B/Fluids
246 13   E.J.M. ≠p B/Fluids
246 13   B/Fluids
260   [Paris] : ≠b Gauthier-Villars, ≠c c1989-
300   v. : ≠b ill. ; ≠c 27 cm.
→ 310   Six no. a year
→ 362 0   Vol. 8, no. 1-
500   Title from cover.
650 0   Fluid mechanics ≠x Periodicals.
650 0   Mechanics, Analytic ≠x Periodicals.
650 0   Mechanics, Applied ≠x Periodicals.
780 01   ≠t Journal de mécanique théorique et appliquée ≠x 0750-7240 ≠w (DLC)82647192 ≠w (OCoLC)8694169

DISCUSSION

- According to LCRI 12.0, when individual parts of a serial have their own numbering system or date designation, separate records are generally made for them.
- In example K7, the "Journal of magnetic resonance" is issued in two parts, i.e., "Series A" and "Series B." Each series has its own numbering system, and they also differ in frequency, with one being monthly and the other published nine times a year. In this case, two separate records are generally preferred to avoid confusion.
- In example K8, the "European journal of mechanics" is also issued in two parts, i.e., "A" and "B." But here the two parts, unlike those in example K7, are issued with identical frequency. In such a case, the cataloger has separated the two parts into two records. It should be noted, however, that the cataloger had the option to decide to keep the parts together in one record. This choice depends greatly on whether the run of issues in hand during cataloging is sufficient to determine if the frequency of the two parts will remain consistent over time. For this reason LCRI 12.0 also contains a provision stating that whenever in doubt the cataloger should prefer separate records.

K9

PROBLEM CONSIDERED:

Individual parts with continuous alternate numbering system (LCRI 12.0)

RULE(S) CONSULTED:

LCRI: 21.2C

K9a

MATHEMATICAL
PROGRAMMING

A PUBLICATION OF
THE MATHEMATICAL PROGRAMMING SOCIETY

SERIES A

VOLUME 46 (1990)

NORTH-HOLLAND — AMSTERDAM

First volume of the year

K9a

MATHEMATICAL
PROGRAMMING

A PUBLICATION OF
THE MATHEMATICAL PROGRAMMING SOCIETY

SERIES A

VOLUME 47 (1990)

NORTH-HOLLAND — AMSTERDAM

Second volume of the year

K9a

MATHEMATICAL
PROGRAMMING

A PUBLICATION OF
THE MATHEMATICAL PROGRAMMING SOCIETY

SERIES B

VOLUME 48 (1990)

NORTH-HOLLAND — AMSTERDAM

Third volume of the year

K9a

TAGGED DATA RECORD (based on OCLC #27143406)

LDR   *****cas_/22*****Ia*4500

	00-05	06	07-14	15-17	18	19	20	21	22-28	29	30-32	33	34	35-37	38	39
008	921218	c	19719999	ne	m	x		p	-a-----	0	///	a	0	eng	-	d

007	h ≠b d ≠d a ≠e a ≠f b--- ≠g b ≠h a ≠i c ≠j a
022	0025-5610
245 00	Mathematical programming ≠h [microform].
260	Amsterdam : ≠b North-Holland, ≠c 1971-
300	v. : ≠b ill. ; ≠c 24 cm.
310	Nine no. a year
362 0	Vol. 1 (Oct. 1971)-
→ 515	Beginning in 1988 two volumes a year are called Series A and the third vol. is called Series B.
550	Issued by: Mathematical Programming Society.
555	Vols. 1-10 with v. 10. (Includes index to Mathematical programming study, Studies 1-6); Vols. 34-45. (Includes index to Mathematical programming study, v. 26-31) 1 v.
533	Microfilm. ≠b Ann Arbor, Mich. : ≠c University Microfilms International, ≠e microfilm reels ; 35 mm.
650 0	Programming (Mathematics) ≠x Periodicals.
650 0	Mathematical optimization ≠x Periodicals.
630 00	Mathematical programming study ≠x Indexes.
710 2	Mathematical Programming Society (U.S.)
776 1	≠t Mathematical programming ≠x 0025-5610 ≠w (OCoLC)1585989

K9b

TAGGED DATA RECORD (based on OCLC #10846334)

LDR   *****cas_/22*****Ia*4500

00-05	06	07-14	15-17	18	19	20	21	22-28	29	30-32	33	34	35-37	38	39
840615	d	18621965	enk	u	u		p	---a---	0	///	a	0	eng	-	d

008

245 00   Journal of the Chemical Society.

→ 246 1   ≠i Odd-numbered volumes from v. 33 (1878)-v. 123 (1923) have title: ≠a Journal of the Chemical Society. ≠p Transactions

→ 246 1   ≠i Even-numbered volumes from v. 34 (1878)-v. 124 (1923) have title: ≠a Journal of the Chemical Society. ≠p Abstracts ≠g (varies slightly)

246 1   ≠i Vols. 126 and 128 have title: ≠a Abstracts of chemical papers issued by the Bureau of Chemical Abstracts

260   [London : ≠b The Society, ≠c 1862-1965]

300   104 v. : ≠b ill. ; ≠c 20-24 cm.

362 0   Vol. 15 (1862)-v. 128 (1925) ; 1926-1965.

500   Title from caption.

515   Vols. 16-29 called also new ser., v. 1-14; vol. numbering discontinued in 1926.

555   Vols. 1 (1848)-v. 25 (1872). 1 v. ; v. 26 (1873)-v. 42 (1882). 1 v.

580   Vols. for 1915-1956 include the proceedings of the Chemical Society, which resumed separate publication in 1957.

580   Abstracts volumes continue as a separate publication after 1925.

580   Split into: Journal of the Chemical Society. A, Inorganic, physical, theoretical; Journal of the Chemical Society. B, Physical organic; and: Journal of the Chemical Society. C, Organic.

650 0   Chemistry ≠x Periodicals.

650 0   Chemistry ≠x Abstracts ≠x Periodicals.

710 2   Chemical Society (Great Britain)

710 2   Bureau of Chemical Abstracts (Great Britain)

780 00   ≠t Quarterly journal of the Chemical Society of London ≠w (DLC)sn87030177 ≠w (OCoLC)9008959

785 16   ≠t Journal of the Chemical Society. A, Inorganic, physical, theoretical ≠x 0022-4944 ≠w (DLC)sn80000036 ≠w (OCoLC)1034199

785 16   ≠t Journal of the Chemical Society. B, Physical organic ≠x 0045-6470 ≠w (DLC)sn80012043 ≠w (OCoLC)1033993

785 16   ≠t Journal of the Chemical Society. C, Organic ≠x 0022-4952 ≠w (DLC)sn79004445 ≠w (OCoLC)1034188

787 1   Chemical Society (Great Britain). ≠t Proceedings of the Chemical Society ≠w (OCoLC)9199233

DISCUSSION

- In example K9a, from 1988 on, the first two volumes of the serial "Mathematical programming" are called "Series A" and the third volume is called "Series B." This numbering system is continuously alternate, with the first two volumes each year always called "Series A" and the third always called "Series B." According to LCRI 12.0, whenever individual parts have a continuous pagination or enumeration, separate records are generally *not* made. In this case, although the serial is issued in two series, the series are tied together by the numbering system, i.e., continuous alternate numbering. Thus, no separate record should be made.

- Example K9b illustrates a similar case, where some individual parts of a serial have a continuous alternate numbering system, and for which no separate records are made. The odd-numbered volumes of the "Journal of the Chemical Society" from v. 33 to v. 123 have the section title "Transactions"; and the even-numbered volumes from v. 34 to v. 124 have the section title "Abstracts."
- Note also that the two sections in K9b that are tied together with a continuous alternate numbering system should be treated as titles that fluctuate on a regular basis. To explain the title fluctuation, notes are given in field 246, Varying Form of Title. In this case, title added entries are made for both titles. Because the title fluctuation does not start with the first issue of the serial, neither of the section titles could be treated as the title proper in field 245 (LCRI 21.2C).

K10

PROBLEM CONSIDERED:

Link to a pre-AACR2 record (LCRI 21.30G)

K10a
TAGGED DATA RECORD (based on OCLC #3571338)

→ LDR   *****cas_/22*****I_*4500

00-05	06	07-14	15-17	18	19	20	21	22-28	29	30-32	33	34	35-37	38	39
008 780120	d	19741990	th	u	u			------i	0	///	a	0	eng	-	d

043   as-----
→ 110 2   Asian Centre of Educational Innovation for Development.
→ 245 10   ACEID newsletter.
260   Bangkok : ≠b UNESCO Regional Office for Education in Asia, ≠c 1974-1990.
300   36 v. ≠b ill. ≠c 28 cm.
362 0   No. 1-36 ; Feb. 1974-1990.
650 0   Education ≠z Asia, Southeastern ≠x Periodicals.
710 2   Asian Centre of Educational Innovation for Development. ≠t Newsletter.
785 00   ≠t ACEID news ≠w (DLC)sn96017761 ≠w (OCoLC)34785733

K10b
TAGGED DATA RECORD (based on OCLC #34785733)

LDR   *****cas_/22*****Ia*4500

00-05	06	07-14	15-17	18	19	20	21	22-28	29	30-32	33	34	35-37	38	39
008 960524	c	19959999	th	u	u			------i	0	///	a	0	eng	-	d

043   as----- ≠a p------
245 00   ACEID news / ≠c Asia-Pacific Centre of Educational Innovation for Development, UNESCO.
246 3   Asia-Pacific Centre of Educational Innovation for Development news
260   Bangkok, Thailand : ≠b The Centre, ≠c 1995-
300   v. : ≠b ill. ; ≠c 28 cm.
362 0   No. 37 (1995)-

500 Title from caption.
650 0 Education ≠z Asia, Southeastern ≠x Periodicals.
650 0 Education ≠z Pacific Area ≠x Periodicals.
710 2 Asia-Pacific Centre of Educational Innovation for Development.
→780 00 ≠t ACEID newsletter ≠w (DLC)77643897 ≠w (OCoLC)3571338

DISCUSSION

- Whenever linking entries are input using field 76x–78x, the links should always be in the form of the AACR2R choice of main entry, form of heading, and form of title proper (LCRI 21.30G). In example K10b, since the serial "ACEID news" continues "ACEID newsletter," a 780 field is made for the preceding entry. Note, however, that the related record (K10a) is a pre-AACR2 record, and position 18 in the Leader has value blank for "non-ISBD," i.e., the item is not cataloged according to ISBD. The main entry in the related pre-AACR2 record is the corporate name heading "Asian Centre of Educational Innovation for Development," recorded in field 110. Note that this is not the AACR2R choice of entry. Consequently, since the heading in the 780 linking field for the succeeding record (K10b) should follow AACR2R rules for choice of main entry, the entry used in this link (field 780) has been changed to "ACEID newsletter" (i.e., a title main entry), which is in keeping with AACR2R rules for choice of entry.

K11

PROBLEM CONSIDERED:

Identical title related to pre-AACR2 record (LCRI 21.30G)

K11a

TAGGED DATA RECORD (based on OCLC #4802185)

LDR *****cas_/22*****Ia*4500

	00-05	06	07-14	15-17	18	19	20	21	22-28	29	30-32	33	34	35-37	38	39
008	790330	d	19171970	ohu	w	n		p	---s---	0	///	a	0	eng	-	d

043 n-us---
245 04 The National underwriter.
260 Chicago, Ill. : ≠b National Underwriter Co., ≠c 1917-1970.
300 54 v. ≠b ill. ≠c 34 cm.
310 Weekly (except semi-weekly the fourth week of Nov.), ≠b 1964-
321 Weekly, ≠b 1917-63
362 0 -74th year, no. 40 (Oct. 1, 1970).
362 1 Began with: 21st year, no. 1 (Jan. 4, 1917).
500 Description based on: 25th year, no. 1 (Jan. 6, 1921); title from cover.
650 0 Insurance, Casualty ≠x Periodicals.
650 0 Insurance, Fire ≠x Periodicals.
650 0 Insurance ≠z United States ≠x Periodicals.
710 2 National Underwriter Company.
780 00 ≠t Western underwriter ≠w (OCoLC)11072275
→785 00 ≠t National underwriter (Property & casualty insurance ed.) ≠x 0163-8912 ≠w (OCoLC)4537056

K11b

TAGGED DATA RECORD (based on OCLC #4537056)

→ LDR   *****cas_/22*****I**4500

00-05	06	07-14	15-17	18	19	20	21	22-28	29	30-32	33	34	35-37	38	39
790110	d	19701986	ilu	w	r	1	p	-------	0	///	a	0	eng	-	d

008

022 0   0163-8912

→ 245 04   The National underwriter.

→ 250   Property & casualty insurance ed.

260   [Chicago, IL. etc. : ≠b National Underwriter Co.]

300   17 v. : ≠b ill. ; ≠c 34 cm.

310   Weekly, ≠b <July 11, 1980->

321   Weekly, with an extra issue in Dec.

362 0   74th year, no. 41-90th year, no. 51 ; Oct. 9, 1970-Dec. 19, 1986.

530   Available on microfilm from University Microfilms International.

650 0   Insurance ≠x Periodicals.

710 2   National Underwriter Company.

776 1   ≠t National underwriter (Property & casualty insurance ed.) ≠w (OCoLC)6870162

→ 780 00   ≠t National underwriter ≠w (OCoLC)4802185

785 00   ≠t National underwriter (Property & casualty/employee/benefits ed.) ≠x 0898-8897 ≠w (DLC) sn87020428 ≠w (OCoLC)15277852

DISCUSSION

- The record for the serial publication in example K11b is a pre-AACR2 record, i.e., the item is not cataloged according to ISBD. This publication is a continuation of a serial with the same title ("The National underwriter") and for that reason a 780 field is present in the record. Note, however, that in spite of the fact that the current and preceding titles are identical, no uniform title has been made for this record, since uniform titles were generally not used in pre-AACR2 records. Instead, a record was distinguished from other records with the same title by means of an edition statement in field 250.
- The related record in example K11a, which has the same title as its succeeding title (K11b), is an AACR2R record. Note that in creating a link from this record (K11a) to its succeeding record (K11b), LCRI 21.30G should apply. This rule states that a linking entry should be made according to AACR2R choice of entry, form of heading, form of title proper, and uniform title. Therefore, in example K11a, a uniform title heading has been constructed in field 785 with the edition statement from example K11b as the qualifier.

K12

PROBLEM CONSIDERED:

Changes in frequency necessitating a separate record (12.7B1)

RULE(S) CONSULTED:

LCRI: 21.2A

K12a

DIRECTION OF
TRADE
STATISTICS

MARCH 1994
International Monetary Fund

Title page

K12b

DIRECTION OF
TRADE
STATISTICS
QUARTERLY

JUNE 1994
International Monetary Fund

Title page

K12a

TAGGED DATA RECORD (based on OCLC #7154584)

LDR   *****cas_/22*****Ia*4500

00-05	06	07-14	15-17	18	19	20	21	22-28	29	30-32	33	34	35-37	38	39
810225	d	19811994	dcu	q	r	0		--s---i	0	///	a	0	eng	-	d

008

022 0 0252-306X ≠z 0278-9248
→ 245 00 Direction of trade statistics.
260   Washington, D.C. : ≠b International Monetary Fund, ≠c 1981-1994.
300   13 v. ; ≠c 28 cm.
→ 310   Quarterly, ≠b <June 1991>-1994
→ 321   Monthly
362   Jan. 1981-Mar. 1994.
500   Issued also in an annual summary: Yearbook.
→ 530   Also issued on computer tape from the International Monetary Fund.
650 0 Commercial statistics ≠x Periodicals.
710 2   International Monetary Fund.
→ 776 1   ≠t Direction of trade statistics (Computer tape) ≠x 1017-2734 ≠w (DLC)sn85061671 ≠w (OCoLC)13172206
780 00 ≠t Direction of trade (International Monetary Fund. Bureau of Statistics) ≠x 0012-3226 ≠w (OCoLC)1566677 ≠w (DLC)sf82002043
785 00 ≠t Direction of trade statistics quarterly ≠w (DLC)sn95029196 ≠w (OCoLC)31189140
787 1   ≠t Direction of trade statistics. Yearbook ≠x 0252-3019 ≠w (OCoLC)7866916

K12b

TAGGED DATA RECORD (based on OCLC #31189140)

LDR   *****cas_/22*****Ia*4500

00-05	06	07-14	15-17	18	19	20	21	22-28	29	30-32	33	34	35-37	38	39
940928	c	19949999	dcu	q	r			--s---i	0	///	a	0	eng	-	d

008

022   ≠y 0252-306X

→ 245 00 Direction of trade statistics quarterly / ≠c [prepared by Real Sector Division, IMF Statistics Dept.].

246 13 DOTS

246 17 Direction of trade statistics

260   Washington, D.C. : ≠b International Monetary Fund, ≠c c1994-

300   v. ; ≠c 28 cm.

→ 310   Quarterly

362   June 1994-

500   Issued also in an annual summary: Yearbook.

→ 530   Available also on computer tape from the International Monetary Fund.

650 0 Commercial statistics ≠x Periodicals.

710 2   International Monetary Fund. ≠b Real Sector Division.

710 2   International Monetary Fund.

→ 776 1   ≠t Direction of trade statistics (Computer tape) ≠x 1017-2734 ≠w (DLC)sn85061671 ≠w (OCoLC)13172206

780 00 ≠t Direction of trade statistics ≠x 0252-306X ≠w (DLC)81649851 ≠w (OCoLC)7154584

787 1   ≠t Direction of trade statistics. Yearbook ≠x 0252-3019 ≠w (OCoLC)7866916

DISCUSSION

- According to 12.7B1, changes in the frequency of a serial should be recorded in a note. This, however, applies to cases where the change in frequency does not involve a change in title. This example illustrates a case where a change in frequency necessitates a separate record.

- In example K12a, the serial "Direction of trade statistics" is published monthly. It changed its frequency to quarterly some time in 1991. From 1994 onward, this change was affirmed by the addition of the word "quarterly" to the title of the publication. As a result, a separate record under the new title "Direction of trade statistics quarterly" is necessary, since a word has been added within the first five words of the title proper (LCRI 21.2A).

- Whenever the frequency of a serial has changed, input the former frequency in field 321, and the current frequency in field 310.

- In both records in this example, a 530 field for Additional Physical Form Available Note is input noting that this publication is also available on computer tape.

- A corresponding 776 linking field for Additional Physical Form Entry is also provided for both records. Note that the title used in field 776 is, in this case, a uniform title heading in established catalog entry form. When making a linking note to a record entered under a uniform title heading, always refer to the uniform title heading and not to the title proper.

K13

PROBLEM CONSIDERED:

Changes in designations (LCRI 12.3G)

RULE(S) CONSULTED:

AACR2R: 12.7B8
LCRI: 12.7B9

TAGGED DATA RECORD (based on OCLC #6706790)

LDR   *****cas_/22*****Ia*4500

	00-05	06	07-14	15-17	18	19	20	21	22-28	29	30-32	33	34	35-37	38	39
008	800913	d	19361991	nyu	a	x			-------	0	///	a	0	eng	-	d

245 00	New directions in prose and poetry.	
→ 246 1	≠i Some issues have title: ≠a New directions	
→ 246 1	≠i Some issues have title: ≠a New directions in prose & poetry	
246 13	ND ≠f 12-14, 18-55	
260	Norfolk, Ct. : ≠b New Directions, ≠c 1936-1991.	
300	55 v. : ≠b ill. ; ≠c 18-24 cm.	
310	Annual (irregular)	
→ 362 0	1936-1941 ; no. 7 (1942)-no. 55.	
→ 500	Published: New York, N.Y., 1948-1991.	
→ 515	Vols. for 1936-41 lack numbering but constitute no. 1-6; no. 9-55 designated only by no.	
650 0	American literature ≠y 20th century.	
650 0	Literature, Modern ≠y 20th century.	

DISCUSSION

- Very often during the lifetime of a serial publication the designation may change, or parts of the designation may be dropped or added on later issues. As long as the numbering is successive, or the chronological designation accounts for the previously published chronological issues, such a change may be indicated in a field 515 Numbering Peculiarities Note (LCRI 12.3G).

- In this example, the serial "New directions in prose and poetry" was initially designated only by year for the first six issues; then it was designated by both number and year for two issues before assuming only a number designation for the remaining issues from no. 9 through no. 55. Adding or dropping the numerical or chronological designation for a serial should not be considered to constitute the adoption of a new designation system (LCRI 12.3G). Such fluctuations in the numerical designation are recorded in a note in field 515 (12.7B8), instead of in the 362 field (see also CCM 8.6.3).

- Note also that the title of the serial fluctuates and the variant titles are recorded in field 246 for Variant Title Access.

- Changes in the place of publication may be noted in a 500 General Note (LCRI 12.7B9). In this example, the country code in fixed field 008 positions 15–17 has also been updated accordingly.

K14

PROBLEM CONSIDERED:

Place of publication used as qualifier in the uniform title heading changes (LCRI 25.5B)

RULE(S) CONSULTED:

LCRI: 12.7B9; 25.5B, p. 6

TAGGED DATA RECORD (based on OCLC #1785642)

LDR   *****cas_/22*****Ia*4500

00-05	06	07-14	15-17	18	19	20	21	22-28	29	30-32	33	34	35-37	38	39
730907	c	19729999	wau	m	r	l	p	-------	0	///	a	0	eng	-	d

→ 008

022 0	0091-3286
→ 130 0	Optical engineering (Redondo Beach, Calif.)
245 00	Optical engineering : ≠b the journal of the Society of Photo-optical Instrumentation Engineers.
→ 260	Redondo Beach, Calif. ≠b The Society, ≠c 1972-
300	v. : ≠b ill. (some col.) ; ≠c 28 cm.
310	Monthly, ≠b <Jan. 1986->
321	Bimonthly, ≠b 1972-
362 0	Vol. 11, no. 1 (Jan.-Feb. 1972)-
→ 500	Published: Bellingham, WA, <Jan. 1986->
500	Some issues have also a distinctive title.
530	Available also on microform.
550	Journal of SPIE International Society for Optical Engineering, Jan. 1986-
650 0	Optical instruments ≠x Periodicals.
710 2	Society of Photo-optical Instrumentation Engineers.
776 1	≠t Optical engineering (Redondo Beach, Calif.)
780 00	≠t Journal (Society of Photo-optical Instrumentation Engineers) ≠w (OCoLC)8049608

DISCUSSION

- Changes in uniform title qualifiers generally do not necessitate new records, unless the changes involve corporate body headings, conference name headings, or physical format (LCRI 25.5B; see also CCM 5.5.3).
- In this example, "Optical engineering" has been published since 1972 in Redondo Beach. This place name has been used as the qualifier in the uniform title heading. Beginning in 1986, the place of publication changed to Bellingham, so that the place of publication which appears as the uniform title qualifier no longer applies to the publication. However, according to LCRI 25.5B, p. 6, this does not constitute a title change necessitating a new record. Instead, changes in place of publication are recorded in a 500 General Note (LCRI 12.7B9), and the uniform title qualifier remains that of the previous place of publication. In this example, the country code in fixed field 008 positions 15–17 has also been updated accordingly.

K15

PROBLEM CONSIDERED:

Issued alternately with different editions (LCRI 12.0)

TAGGED DATA RECORD (based on OCLC #15214233)

LDR   *****cas_/22*****Ia*4500

00-05	06	07-14	15-17	18	19	20	21	22-28	29	30-32	33	34	35-37	38	39
008	870219	d	1987198u	ilu	m	r	l	p	--r----	0	///	a	0	eng	-	d

022 0   0893-9950
043   n-us---
245 00   Print media editorial calendars : ≠b a monthly publication of Standard Rate & Data Service, Inc.
246 17   Business publication editorial calendars
260   Wilmette, IL : ≠b The Service, ≠c [1987-
300   v. : ≠b ill. ; ≠c 28 cm.
310   Monthly
362 0   Vol. 1, no. 1 (Feb. 10, 1987)-
500   Title from cover.
→ 515   Issues carry alternately designated editions: Business, Newspaper, and Consumer magazine/farm editions which share the same continuous numerical designation.
650 0   American periodicals ≠x Directories.
650 0   Advertising, Magazine ≠z United States ≠x Handbooks, manuals, etc.
710 2   Standard Rate & Data Service.
→ 785 00   ≠t Special issues (Standard Rate & Data Service) ≠x 1043-6863 ≠w (DLC)89641796 ≠w (OCoLC)19462097

DISCUSSION

- As recorded in field 515 for notes on irregularities or peculiarities in number-ing, the monthly serial in this example is issued alternately in different editions called "Business edition," "Newspaper edition," and "Consumer magazine/farm edition." If each edition had its own numerical designation, separate records would be needed for each one. However, in this case, since the various editions share the same continuous numerical designation, no separate records should be made for the individual editions (LCRI 12.0). Their numerical designations are tied together, and to create separate records for each alternately designated edition would disrupt the designation system. The resulting records would then have an incomplete coverage. (In any case, as recorded in field 785, the alternately designated editions were eventually merged to form a publication entitled "Special issues.")

L.   Related Works

In serials cataloging one often has to deal with the problem of how to catalog serials that may be related to one another in diverse ways. Before attempting to catalog a given serial, the cataloger should first determine whether and how this item is related to other serials. Once that relationship has been established, a decision is needed as to whether the item in hand should be cataloged separately or mentioned in a note on the record for the related serial. Because this decision varies with each different type of material involved, each situation must be dealt with separately.

If the decision is made not to treat the item in hand as a separate record, information about that item should be added to the record for the related work, usually in the form of a note. If, as is most often the case, the decision is made to catalog the item in hand in a separate record, linking fields (765–787) must be used to provide machine links between the related works. Each linking field may also be used to provide a machine-generated note based on the linking field entry. A note thus generated consists of the entry itself preceded by a brief term or phrase (i.e., display constant) describing explicitly how one serial relates to another. However, if the existing relationship is too complex to be explained by the available display constants, a Linking Entry Complexity note, field 580, should be used to describe the relationship. If a 580 note is input, the first indicator of the linking field should be set to value "1" to suppress the production of a machine-generated note.

In general, the relationships between a serial and the works related to it may be characterized as either *sequential* or *complementary:*

I. SERIALS IN A SEQUENTIAL RELATIONSHIP (EXAMPLES L1–L10):

A sequential relationship involves changes in the title, issuing body, numbering system, etc., which occur periodically during the life span of the serial. Thus, when the relationship is sequential, a later title, issuing body, etc., either entirely or partially replaces an earlier one. For example, preceding or succeeding titles are serials with sequential relationships.

1. USE OF THE LINKING FIELD 780 FOR PRECEDING ENTRY

The creation of a separate catalog record in serials is required if there is a title change according to the provisions of rules 21.2A1 and 21.2C1 and LCRIs 21.2A and 21.2C; if a change occurs in the corporate body under which an item has been entered (21.3B1); if the enumeration repeats the exact numeric designation without a designation indicated by *new series* or similar wording (LCRI 12.3G); if there is a change in the name of the corporate body used as a qualifier in a uniform title heading (LCRI 21.3B); or if the physical format in which the serial is issued changes (LCRI 21.3B). If one of these criteria is met, the earlier entry is considered to have ceased, and linking notes are created to connect the earlier and later entries.

Field 780 is the linking field for the preceding entry. Determined by the value of the second indicator, the display constant of the 780 field describes the linking relationship between the preceding title(s) and the title being cataloged. The values assigned to the second indicators of the preceding entry are defined as follows:

0 Continues:
1 Continues in part:
2 Supersedes: (no longer used in AACR2 records)
3 Supersedes in part: (no longer used in AACR2 records)
4 Merger of: . . . and: . . .
5 Absorbed:
6 Absorbed in part:
7 Separated from:

2. USE OF THE LINKING FIELD 785 FOR SUCCEEDING ENTRY

When a serial is continued by a subsequently published serial, the original (i.e., preceding serial) title is considered to have ceased. If the cataloger has the first or last issue in hand, then the numeric and/or alphabetic, chronological, or other designation area of the catalog record should be completed, so that it includes not only the designation of the first issue, but also the designation of the last issue (12.3F1). If the cataloger does not have the first or last issue in hand and the information is available, informal notes such as "Began publication in . . . " and/or "Ceased with . . . " should be added to the record. For a completed serial the appropriate number (in Arabic numerals) should also appear in the physical description area preceding the Specific Material Designation (12.5B2). A linking note in the record to the succeeding serial(s) should be included (12.7B7).

Field 785 is the linking field for the succeeding entry. Depending on the values of the second indicator, the display constant of the 785 field describes the linking relationship between the succeeding title(s) and the title being cataloged. The values assigned to the second indicators of the succeeding entry are defined as follows:

0 Continued by:
1 Continued in part by:
2 Superseded by: (no longer used in AACR2 records)
3 Superseded in part by: (no longer used in AACR2 records)
4 Absorbed by:
5 Absorbed in part by:
6 Split into: . . . and: . . .
7 Merged with: . . . to form: . . .

II. SERIALS IN A COMPLEMENTARY RELATIONSHIP (EXAMPLES L11–L28):

Complementary relationships occur between horizontally related works. A serial with a complementary relationship to another serial can be a supplement, a special issue, an index, or a cumulation. It can be a translated work, a language edition, or other serial version. (For microform versions, see section P. For electronic versions, see section R.) A serial issued within a serial is another example. Complementary serial publications may also have nonspecific relationships with other serials or monographs. These may be selections, excerpts of articles from serials, companion volumes, etc.

The linking fields used in records for serials in complementary relationship are chosen on the basis of the precise nature of the relationship, e.g., fields 765 and 767 are defined for an original language entry and a translation, respectively; fields 770 and 772 are used for a supplement/special issue entry and its parent record entry, respectively, etc. Because the appropriate linking fields must be chosen on a case-by-case basis, they will be discussed later in each individual example.

EXAMPLES

SEQUENTIAL RELATIONSHIP

Preceding Entry

L1	Serial continues a previously published serial
L2	Serial continues in part a previously published serial
L3	Serial formed by the union of two or more serials
L4	Serial absorbed a previously published serial
L5	Serial separated from another published serial

Succeeding Entry

L6	Serial continued by a subsequently published serial
L7	Serial continued in part and absorbed in part by other serials
L8	Serial absorbed by a subsequently published serial
L9	Serial split into two or more parts
L10	Serial merged with another to form a new serial

COMPLEMENTARY RELATIONSHIP

Translations

L11	Translation of a previously published serial
L12	Serial published in original language and also in translation

Supplements and Special Issues

L13	Supplement to a serial (cataloged separately)
L14	Supplement updating a serial between editions
L15	Supplement to an individual issue
L16	Parent serial with supplement
L17	Special issue with its own numbering
L18	Special issue numbered in with regular issues

Reprints, Language, and Other Serial Editions

L19	Reprinted serial requiring a separate record
L20	Reprinted serial not requiring a separate record

L21   Serial published in several language editions
L22   Other edition available

Issued with

L23   Serial issued with another serial is also published separately
L24   Serial includes another serial with no separate record

Others

L25   Serial consists of selected material from another serial
L26   Serial as a companion volume to other work
L27   Separately published index to one or more serials
L28   Serial continuing a monograph

L1

PROBLEM CONSIDERED:

Serial continues a previously published serial (12.7B7b)

Mathematica in education
(ceased with: v. 3, no. 4 fall 1994)

Reciprocal note
Continued by: Mathematica in education
and research.

(serial being cataloged)

Mathematica in education and research
(began with: v. 4, no. 1 winter 1995)

Linking note
Continues: Mathematica in education.

TAGGED DATA RECORD (based on OCLC #32824132)

LDR   *****cas_/22*****Ia*4500

00-05	06	07-14	15-17	18	19	20	21	22-28	29	30-32	33	34	35-37	38	39
950714	c	19959999	cau	q	r		p	-------	0	///	a	0	eng	-	d

008

022   ≠y 1065-2965

→ 245 00   Mathematica in education and research.

260   Santa Clara, Calif. : ≠b TELOS, The Electronic Library of Science, ≠c c1994-

300   v. : ≠b ill. ; ≠c 28 cm.

310   Quarterly

362 0   Vol. 4, no. 1 (winter 1995)-

500   Title from cover.

650 0   Mathematics ≠x Computer-assisted instruction ≠x Periodicals.

630 0   Mathematica (Computer file) ≠x Periodicals.

650 0   Mathematics ≠x Data processing ≠x Periodicals.

→ 780 00   ≠t Mathematica in education ≠x 1065-2965 ≠w (DLC)94659118 ≠w (OCoLC)26566859

DISCUSSION

- In this example, the title proper changes from "Mathematica in education" to "Mathematica in education and research." The item in hand is a succeeding title and a separate record must be created under the new name. The preceding title is input in field 780 from which a linking note is to be generated: "Continues: Mathematica in education" (12.7B7b).

L2

PROBLEM CONSIDERED:

Serial continues in part a previously published serial (12.7B7e)

Sensors and actuators

(ceased with: v. 20, no. 3 Dec. 1989)

> Reciprocal note
> Split into: Sensors and actuators. A, Physical,
> and: Sensors and actuators. B, Chemical.

(serial being cataloged)

Sensors and actuators.
A, Physical
(began with: v. A21, no. 1-3 Feb. 1990)

Sensors and actuators.
B, Chemical
(began with: v. B21, no. 1-3 Feb. 1990)

> **Linking note**
> **Continues in part: Sensors and actuators**

TAGGED DATA RECORD (based on OCLC #21400903)

LDR   *****cas_/22*****_a*4500

00-05	06	07-14	15-17	18	19	20	21	22-28	29	30-32	33	34	35-37	38	39
900420	c	19909999	sz	b	r		p	-------	0	///	a	0	eng	-	d

008

022   0924-4247

→ 245 00   Sensors and actuators. ≠n A, ≠p Physical.

246 30   Physical

260   Lausanne, Switzerland : ≠b Elsevier Sequoia, ≠c 1990-

300   v. : ≠b ill. ; ≠c 28 cm.

310   Bimonthly (6 vol. each with 3 issues)

362 0   Vol. A21, no. 1-3 (Feb. 1990)-

500   Title from cover.

650 0   Transducers ≠x Periodicals.

650 0   Actuators ≠x Periodicals.

650 0   Solid state electronics ≠x Periodicals.

→ 780 01   ≠t Sensors and actuators ≠x 0250-6874 ≠w (DLC)82640947 ≠w (OCoLC)7427664

DISCUSSION

- Sometimes a succeeding entry will continue only part of the preceding title, and still another record will continue the rest of the preceding title. This case is illustrated in example L2, where the preceding title "Sensors and actuators" has split into two serials, one of which is the item in hand. In such cases, field 780 second indicator value "1" is used, which is defined for a relationship of partial continuation. The linking note thus generated reads, "Continues in part: Sensors and actuators" (12.7B7e).

L3

PROBLEM CONSIDERED:

Serial formed by the union of two or more serials (12.7B7d)

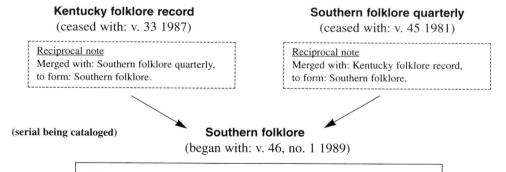

Kentucky folklore record
(ceased with: v. 33 1987)

Reciprocal note
Merged with: Southern folklore quarterly, to form: Southern folklore.

Southern folklore quarterly
(ceased with: v. 45 1981)

Reciprocal note
Merged with: Kentucky folklore record, to form: Southern folklore.

(serial being cataloged)   **Southern folklore**
(began with: v. 46, no. 1 1989)

Linking note
Merger of: Kentucky folklore record, and: Southern folklore quarterly; and continues the vol. numbering of the latter.

TAGGED DATA RECORD (based on OCLC #18176287)

LDR   *****cas_/22*****_a*4500

00-05	06	07-14	15-17	18	19	20	21	22-28	29	30-32	33	34	35-37	38	39
880706	c	19899999	kyu	t	r	l	p	-------	0	///	a	0	eng	-	d

008

022 0   0899-594X ≠y 0889-594X

→ 245 00   Southern folklore.

260   Lexington, Ky. : ≠b University Press of Kentucky for Western Kentucky
University, ≠c 1989-

300   v. : ≠b ill. ; ≠c 23 cm.

310   Three times a year

362 0   Vol. 46, no. 1-

500   Title from cover.

→ 580   Merger of: Kentucky folklore record; and: Southern folklore quarterly; and
continues the vol. numbering of the latter.

650 0   Folklore ≠x Periodicals.

651 0   Southern States ≠x Social life and customs ≠x Periodicals.

650 0   Folklore ≠z Southern States ≠x Periodicals.

650 0   Manners and customs ≠x Periodicals.

710 2   Western Kentucky University.

→ 780 14   Kentucky folklore record ≠x 0023-0227 ≠w (DLC)59030559 ≠w
(OCoLC)2095690

→ 780 14   Southern folklore quarterly ≠x 0038-4127 ≠w (DLC)38017465 ≠w
(OCoLC)1766187

DISCUSSION

- Serials can be formed by the union of two or more serials, as in this example.
The title "Southern folklore" was formed by the merger of "Kentucky folklore
record" and "Southern folklore quarterly." Give the titles of the serials that
were merged in a linking note (12.7B7d). The same note may include other information relevant to the relationship between the new and earlier titles as in
this example, where the note also states that the numbering of one of the
merged serials is being continued by that of the succeeding serial.

- A Linking Entry Complexity Note (field 580) may be input to express the relationship between related publications. The first indicator of field 780 is set to
value "1" to suppress the production of a note, since a note already appears in
field 580. The second indicator is set to value "4" to indicate that the current
publication is a result of the merger of two previously published serials.

L4

PROBLEM CONSIDERED:

Serial absorbed a previously published serial (12.7B7f)

RULE(S) CONSULTED:

LCRI: 12.7B7f

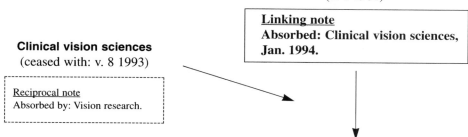

(serial being cataloged)

Vision research
(v. 1 1961)-

Linking note
Absorbed: Clinical vision sciences,
Jan. 1994.

Clinical vision sciences
(ceased with: v. 8 1993)

Reciprocal note
Absorbed by: Vision research.

TAGGED DATA RECORD (based on OCLC #1589794)

LDR   *****cas_/22*****_a*4500

00-05	06	07-14	15-17	18	19	20	21	22-28	29	30-32	33	34	35-37	38	39
750901	c	19619999	enk	s	r	z	p	-------	0	///		a	0	eng	-	d

008

022	0042-6989
041 0	engfreger
→ 245 00	Vision research.
260	Oxford : ≠a New York ; ≠b Pergamon Press, ≠c 1961-
300	v. : ≠b ill. ; ≠c 26-29 cm.
310	Semimonthly, ≠b 1994-
321	Monthly, ≠b 1961-1993
362 0	Vol. 1, no. 1 (June 1961)-
546	English, French, or German, with summaries in three languages.
550	Published for the Association for Research in Vision and Ophthalmology, <1979->
650 0	Vision ≠x Periodicals.
710 2	Association for Research in Vision and Opthalmology.
→ 780 05	≠t Clinical vision sciences ≠g Jan. 1994 ≠x 0887-6169 ≠w (DLC)sn86001128 ≠w (OCoLC)13307264

DISCUSSION

- If a serial publication takes in and incorporates a serial that has been published independently until the time of incorporation, that title is said to have "absorbed" the other. As a result, the absorbing publication continues and the serial being absorbed does not, as illustrated in the preceding diagram. In this example, the serial being absorbed is "Clinical vision sciences," which, in January 1994, upon absorption by "Vision research," ended as a ceased title.
- The serial absorbed is input in a linking note, field 780 (12.7B7f). The second indicator of linking field 780 is set to value "5" to indicate absorption. The date of absorption, whenever readily available, is input in subfield ≠g (LCRI 12.7B7f).

L5

PROBLEM CONSIDERED:

Serial separated from another published serial (12.7B7e)

Survey of current business
(No. 1 Aug. 1, 1921)-

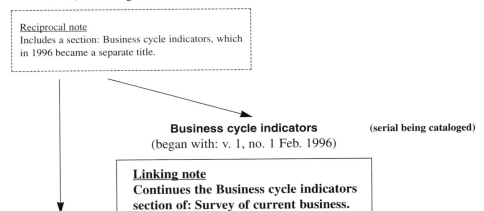

Reciprocal note
Includes a section: Business cycle indicators, which in 1996 became a separate title.

Business cycle indicators   (serial being cataloged)
(began with: v. 1, no. 1 Feb. 1996)

Linking note
Continues the Business cycle indicators section of: Survey of current business.

TAGGED DATA RECORD (based on OCLC #34528173)

LDR   *****cas_/22*****_a*4500

00-05	06	07-14	15-17	18	19	20	21	22-28	29	30-32	33	34	35-37	38	39
960408	c	19969999	nyu	m	r	l	p	---s---	0	///	a	0	eng	-	d

008

022 0	1088-7857
043	n-us---
→ 245 00	Business cycle indicators / ≠c the Conference Board.
246 3	BCI
260	New York, N.Y. : ≠b Conference Board, ≠c 1996-
300	v. : ≠b ill. ; ≠c 28 cm.
310	Monthly
362 0	Vol. 1, no. 1 (Feb. 1996)-
500	Title from cover.
→ 580	Continues the Business cycle indicators section of: Survey of current business.
650 0	Business cycles ≠z United States ≠x Periodicals.
650 0	Economic indicators ≠z United States ≠x Periodicals.
650 0	Business cycles ≠z United States ≠x Statistics ≠x Periodicals.
650 0	Economic indicators ≠z United States ≠x Statistics ≠x Periodicals.
710 2	Conference Board.
→ 780 17	≠t Survey of current business ≠x 0039-6222 ≠w (DLC)21026819 ≠w (OCoLC)1697070

DISCUSSION

- In this example, the serial "Business cycle indicators," formerly a featured section in the serial "Survey of current business," has now become an independent publication. The preceding title "Survey of current business," of which this item was once a part, is input in linking field 780 (12.7B7e). The second indicator of linking field 780 is set to value "7," to indicate a "Separated from:" relationship.
- If the display constant "Separated from:" does not adequately characterize the relationship, describe the relationship explicitly in a Linking Entry Complexity Note, field 580. Such is the case in this example where a more informational note, "Continues the Business cycle indicators section of: Survey of current business," has been preferred.

L6

PROBLEM CONSIDERED:

Serial continued by a subsequently published serial (12.7B7c)

RULE(S) CONSULTED:

AACR2R: 12.3F1
LCRI: 12.7B8

(serial being cataloged)   **Mathematica in education**
                            (ceased with: v. 3, no. 4 fall 1994)

> **Linking note**
> **Continued by: Mathematica in education and research.**

Mathematica in education and research
(began with: v. 4, no. 1 winter 1995)

> Reciprocal note
> Continues: Mathematica in education.

TAGGED DATA RECORD (based on OCLC #26566859)

LDR   *****cas_/22*****_a*4500

	00-05	06	07-14	15-17	18	19	20	21	22-28	29	30-32	33	34	35-37	38	39
008	920909	d	19911994	cau	q	r	1	p	-------	0	///	a	0	eng	-	d

022 0   1065-2965

→ 245 00   Mathematica in education.

260   Rohnert Park, CA : ≠b Dept. of Mathematics, Sonoma State University, ≠c 1991-1994.

300   3 v. : ≠b ill. ; ≠c 28 cm.

310   Quarterly

→ 362 1   Began with v. 1, issue 1 for fall 1991.

→ 362 0   -v. 3, no. 4 (fall 1994).

500   Published: Santa Clara, CA : Electronic Library of Science, winter 1994-fall 1994.

500   Description based on: Vol. 1, no. 3 (spring 1992); title from caption.

650 0   Mathematics ≠x Computer-assisted instruction ≠x Periodicals.

630 00   Mathematica (Computer file) ≠x Periodicals.

650 0   Mathematics ≠x Data processing ≠x Periodicals.

710 2   Sonoma State University. ≠b Dept. of Mathematics.

→ 785 00   ≠t Mathematica in education and research ≠w (OCoLC)32824132

DISCUSSION

- In this example, the title proper has changed from "Mathematica in education and research" to "Mathematica in education." The item in hand is the preceding title. The subsequently published title is input in a linking note (12.7B7c).

- Note that on the record for the serial "Mathematica in education and research," the designation of the first issue has been given in an unformatted 362 field: "Began with v. 1, issue 1 for fall 1991." Apparently the information concerning the beginning date was known but the cataloger did not have the first issue in hand (LCRI 12.7B8). Now that the title has ceased and the cataloger has the last issue in hand, the designation of the last issue should be added to the record in a second, formatted 362 field, "-v. 3, no. 4 (fall 1994)" (12.3F1).

- Field 785 is used for the succeeding entry when a serial is continued by a subsequently published title. The second indicator is chosen on the basis of the relationship of the succeeding entry to the preceding title. In this example, value "0" is used to indicate that the original title is continued by its successor.

L7

PROBLEM CONSIDERED:

Serial continued in part and absorbed in part by other serials (12.7B7e)

(serial being cataloged)

Guide to literary agents & art/photo reps
(ceased in 1994)

Linking notes
**Continued in part by: Guide to
literary agents.
Absorbed in part by: Artist's
& graphic designer's market.
Absorbed in part by:
Photographer's market.**

Artist's market
(ceased in 1994)

**Photographer's
market**
(published since 1978)

Reciprocal note
Absorbed in part: Guide to
literary agents & art/photo
reps, 1995.

**Artist's & graphic
designer's market**
(began in 1995)

Reciprocal note
Continues: Artist's market.
Absorbed in part: Guide to
literary agents & art/photo
reps, 1995.

Guide to literary agents
(began in 1995)

Reciprocal note
Continues in part: Guide to
literary agents & art/photo reps.

TAGGED DATA RECORD (based on OCLC #23239176)

LDR   *****cas_/22*****_a*4500

	00-05	06	07-14	15-17	18	19	20	21	22-28	29	30-32	33	34	35-37	38	39
008	910313	d	19921994	ohu	a	r	l		--r----	0	///	a	0	eng	-	d

022 0   1055-6087

043   n-us--- ≠a n-cn---

→ 245 00 Guide to literary agents & art/photo reps.

    246 3   Guide to literary agents and art photo reps

    246 30 Literary agents & art/photo reps

    260   Cincinnati, Ohio : ≠b F&W Publications, ≠c 1991-1993.

    300   3 v. ; ≠c 24 cm.

    310   Annual

    362 0   1992-1994.

    500   "500 listings of agents who handle novels, short stories, nonfiction books, scripts, textbooks, juvenile books, plays, poetry, and more. Also includes listings of artists' and photographers' representatives"—Cover.

    550   Issued by: Writer's Digest Books.

    650 0   Literary agents ≠z United States ≠x Directories.

    650 0   Literary agents ≠z Canada ≠x Directories.

    650 0   Artists' representatives ≠z United States ≠x Directories.

    650 0   Artists' representatives ≠z Canada ≠x Directories.

    650 0   Photographers' representatives ≠z United States ≠x Directories.

    650 0   Photographers' representatives ≠z Canada ≠x Directories.

    710 2   Writer's Digest Books (Firm)

→ 785 01 ≠t Guide to literary agents ≠x 1078-6945 ≠w (DLC)9565319 ≠w (OCoLC)31162125

→ 785 05 ≠t Artist's & graphic designer's market ≠x 1075-0894 ≠w (DLC)95640723 ≠w (OCoLC)31121153

→ 785 05 ≠t Photographer's market ≠x 0147-247X ≠w (DLC)78643526 ≠w (OCoLC)3469714

DISCUSSION

- In this example, the serial "Guide to literary agents & art/photo reps" split into three parts. One of the parts consists of a new publication entitled "Guide to literary agents," for which no bibliographic record has ever existed. Two other parts are absorbed by two existing serials, "Artist's & graphic designer's market" and "Photographer's market." Thus, three separate linking notes are made on the record for the serial (12.7B7e).

- When one serial absorbs another serial, this normally involves the absorption of the whole publication. However, in this case, the existing serial "Photographer's market" has absorbed only one part of the serial with the title "Guide to literary agents & art/photo reps."

- Another interesting twist to this example involves the fact that when "Artist's market" absorbed part of the Guide, it changed its own title, i.e., it then became "Artist's & graphic designer's market."

- Three separate 785 fields, one for each succeeding entry, are needed on the record for "Guide to literary agents & art/photo reps." The second indicator of the 785 field for the succeeding title "Guide to literary agents" is set to value "1." On the other hand, the second indicator of the 785 field for the succeeding entries "Artist's & graphic designer's market" and "Photographer's market" are set to value "5," because there the relationship is one of absorption.

L8

PROBLEM CONSIDERED:

Serial absorbed by a subsequently published serial (12.7B7f)

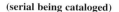

(serial being cataloged)

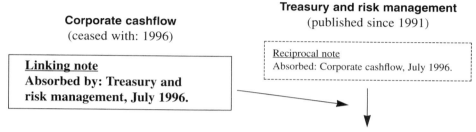

Corporate cashflow
(ceased with: 1996)

Treasury and risk management
(published since 1991)

Linking note
Absorbed by: Treasury and
risk management, July 1996.

Reciprocal note
Absorbed: Corporate cashflow, July 1996.

TAGGED DATA RECORD (based on OCLC #17976195)

LDR   *****cas_/22*****_a*4500

00-05	06	07-14	15-17	18	19	20	21	22-28	29	30-32	33	34	35-37	38	39
008	880519	d	19881996	gau	m	r	l	p	-------	0	///	a	0	eng	-	d

022 0	1040-0311 ≠y 0196-6227	
→ 245 00	Corporate cashflow.	
246 3	Corporate cash flow	
246 3	Cash flow	
260	Atlanta, GA : ≠b Communication Channels, Inc., ≠c 1988-1996.	
300	9 v. : ≠b ill. ; ≠c 28 cm.	
310	Monthly	
362 0	Vol. 9, no 5 (May 1988)-v. 17, no. 7 (June 1996).	
500	Title from cover.	
500	Imprint varies.	
500	Includes an annual special issue called Buyer's guide issue.	
650 0	Cash flow ≠x Periodicals.	
650 0	Cash management ≠x Periodicals.	
740 02	Buyer's guide issue.	
780 00	≠t Cashflow ≠x 0196-6227 ≠w (DLC)85641380 ≠w (OCoLC)5864352	
→ 785 04	≠t Treasury and risk management ≠g July 1996 ≠x 1067-0432 ≠w (DLC)94641899 ≠w (OCoLC)27131223	

DISCUSSION

- In this example, the serial "Corporate cashflow" was absorbed by another serial "Treasury and risk management" in 1996. Note that this is not a *merger* where two or more publications are merged into one, but rather an absorption, because the serial "Treasury and risk management" is still being published under the same name. Had this been a case of merger, a new publication with a new name would have been formed; both of the publications that merged would cease to exist (see also example L4).

- The absorbing serial is input in a linking note, field 785 (12.7B7f); the second indicator value of field 785 is set to "4" to indicate absorption. The date of the absorption is input in subfield ≠g.

L9

PROBLEM CONSIDERED:

Serial split into two or more parts (12.7B7e)

(serial being cataloged)   **Sensors and actuators**
(ceased with: v. 20, no. 3 Dec. 1989)

```
Linking note
Split into: Sensors and actuators. A, Physical,
and: Sensors and actuators. B, Chemical.
```

Sensors and actuators. A, Physical   **Sensors and actuators. B, Chemical**
(began with: v. A21, no. 1-3 Feb. 1990)   (began with: v. B21, no. 1-3 Feb. 1990)

```
Reciprocal note
Continues in part: Sensors and actuators.
```

```
Reciprocal note
Continues in part: Sensors and actuators.
```

TAGGED DATA RECORD (based on OCLC #7427664)

LDR   *****cas_/22*****_a*4500

00-05	06	07-14	15-17	18	19	20	21	22-28	29	30-32	33	34	35-37	38	39
810518	d	19811989	sz	b	r	l	p	-------	0	///	a	0	eng	-	d

008 (as above)

022 0	0250-6874

→ 245 00 Sensors and actuators.
260   Lausanne, Switzerland : ≠b Elsevier Sequoia, ≠c 1981-1989.
300   20 v. : ≠b ill. ; ≠c 24 cm.
310   Bimonthly (6 vol. each with 3 issues), ≠b 1989
321   Monthly (3 vol. each with 4 issues), ≠b <Jan. 1988-1989>
321   Quarterly, ≠b 1981-
362 0   Vol. 1, no. 1 (Mar. 1981)-v. 20, no. 3 (Dec. 1989)
500   Title from cover.
500   Contains papers presented at the NATO Advanced Study Institute on Chemically Sensitive Electronic Devices, Mar. 1981-
650 0 Transducers ≠x Periodicals.
650 0 Actuators ≠x Periodicals.
650 0 Solid state electronics ≠x Periodicals.
710 2   NATO Advanced Study Institute on Chemically Sensitive Electronic Devices
→ 785 06 ≠t Sensors and actuators. A, Physical ≠x 0924-4247 ≠w (DLC)90641633 ≠w (OCoLC)21400903
→ 785 06 ≠t Sensors and actuators. B, Chemical ≠x 0925-4005 ≠w (DLC)90644089 ≠w (OCoLC)21252574

DISCUSSION

- When a serial separates into two or more serials, the titles resulting from the split should be given on the original record in a linking note (12.7B7e).
- In constructing a linking note, the cataloger should be aware that there are certain differences implied by the use of "Split into" versus "Continued in part by" when the separation results in two or more serials. As a rule of thumb, consider the original serial to have split if, as the direct result of the separation, the serial ceases to exist; otherwise, treat the original serial as being continued in part by another title. One way to look at this is to consider "Continued in part by" to be reciprocal to "Separated from"; both cases indicate a one-to-one relationship, as illustrated by examples L5 and L7. The case of one title splitting into two is illustrated in this example, where the original serial "Sensors and actuators" is replaced by two subsequently published serials that, taken together, cover the entire scope of their predecessor.
- Linking field 785 is used for the succeeding entry when the serial being cataloged has ceased. The second indicator of field 785 is set to value "6," which is defined for a "Split into" relationship. If the original serial has split into more than two serials, give the linking relationship in a Linking Entry Complexity Note, field 580, and set the first indicator of the 785 fields to value "1."

L10

PROBLEM CONSIDERED:

Serial merged with another to form a new serial (12.7B7d)

RULE(S) CONSULTED:

AACR2R: 12.3F1, 12.5B2, 21.28A1

(serial being cataloged)

Agri-Practice

(ceased with v. 17, no. 10 Nov./Dec.1996)

> **Linking note**
> Merged with: Large animal veterinarian covering health & nutrition, to form: Large animal practice.

Large animal veterinarian covering health & nutrition

(ceased with v. 51, no. 6 Nov./Dec. 1996)

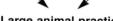

Large animal practice

(began with: v. 18, no. 1 Jan./Feb. 1997)

> Reciprocal note
> Merger of: Large animal veterinarian covering health & nutrition, and: Agri-Practice, and continues the vol. numbering of the latter.

TAGGED DATA RECORD (based on OCLC #9181636)

LDR *****cas_/22*****Ia*4500

	00-05	06	07-14	15-17	18	19	20	21	22-28	29	30-32	33	34	35-37	38	39
008	830202	d	19831996	cau	m	x	l	p	-------	0	///	a	0	eng	-	d

022 0	0745-452X
→ 245 00	Agri-Practice.
246 3	AgriPractice
246 3	Agriculture practice
260	Santa Barbara, CA : ≠b Veterinary Practice Pub. Co., ≠c 1983-1996.
→ 300	16 v. : ≠b ill. ; ≠c 28 cm.
310	Ten no. a year
→ 362 0	Vol. 4, no. 1 (Jan. 1983)-v. 17, no. 10 (Nov./Dec. 1996).
500	Title from cover.
→ 580	Merged with: Large animal veterinarian covering health & nutrition, to form: Large animal practice.
650 0	Cattle diseases ≠x Periodicals.
780 00	≠t Bovine practice ≠x 0199-5456 ≠w (DLC)sn80011161 ≠w (OCoLC)5978747
→ 785 17	≠t Large animal veterinarian covering health & nutrition ≠x 1043-7533 ≠w (DLC)sn89007235 ≠w (OCoLC)18603490
→ 785 17	≠t Large animal practice ≠x 1092-7603 ≠w (DLC)sn97005711 ≠w (OCoLC)36319164

DISCUSSION

- This example shows the record for the serial "Agri-Practice," which has merged with "Large animal veterinarian covering health & nutrition" to form a new title, "Large animal practice." A linking note "Merged with: Large animal veterinarian covering health & nutrition, to form: Large animal practice," is input to provide a link with the two related titles (12.7B7d and 21.28A1).

- In addition, because the last issue of the ceased title is available, the numeric and/or alphabetic, chronological, or other designation area has been completed on the record (12.3F1). For the same reason, the number "16" has been added to the physical description area, preceding the specific material designation (12.5B2).

- Field 785 is used for a succeeding entry when the work in hand has ceased. When a serial has merged with another serial, the "merged with" serial and the resulting serial are entered in separate 785 fields. The "merged with" serial should be input in the first 785 field and the resulting serial in the second 785 field, with first indicator value "0" (in the absence of a 580 note) and second indicator value "7" in both. Note that a 580 note should always be input in lieu of a machine-generated linking note if there is more than one "merged with" title.

L11

PROBLEM CONSIDERED:

Translation of a previously published serial (12.7B7a)

RULE(S) CONSULTED:

AACR2R: 12.2B1, 25.5C1
LCRI: 12.7A2

TAGGED DATA RECORD (based on OCLC #28386631)

LDR   *****cas_/22*****Ia*4500

00-05	06	07-14	15-17	18	19	20	21	22-28	29	30-32	33	34	35-37	38	39
008 930706	c	19919999	gw	u	u		p	-------	0	///	a	0	ger	-	d

→ 041 1   ger ≠h eng
→ 130 0   Synergy (San Diego, Calif.). ≠l German.
  245 10   Synergy.
  260   München : ≠b W. Heyne, ≠c 1991-
  300   v. ; ≠c 18 cm.
  362 0   1 (1991)-
→ 580   Translation of: Synergy (San Diego, Calif.).
  650 0   Science fiction ≠x Periodicals.
  650 0   Science fiction, American ≠x Periodicals.
→ 765 1   ≠t Synergy (San Diego, Calif.) ≠x 0892-449X ≠w (DLC)88640826 ≠w (OCoLC)15194131

DISCUSSION

- This example is a German translation of a serial previously published in English. Note that this is *not* another language edition of the serial (for which see 12.2B1). In general, if the publisher of the related work differs, treat the title as a translation. If both works have the same publisher, treat them as language editions (CCM 14.3.1).
- When it is known that a work has appeared as a translation, a uniform title heading should be established in order to bring together all entries for the same work. The uniform title heading in such cases consists of the title in the original language and the name of the language of the translation (25.5C1). In order to link the two records together, a note should be given describing the original language version (12.7B7a).
- If the specific information regarding the original work is not available or the original work is not represented in the catalog, either give in a note general information, such as "Translation from the French," or cite in a note the entry for the original work that would be used under AACR2R (LCRI 12.7A2).
- Field 130 is used for uniform title headings. Subfield ≠a contains the title in the original language, and subfield ≠l is used for the name of the language of the translation.
- Field 765 is used for the original language entry, providing a machine link to that version when the publication in hand is a translation. First indicator value

"0" is used to generate a note from data in field 765 when *no* corresponding field 580 (Linking Entry Complexity Note) is present. A display text, "Translation of:" will be generated at the beginning of the note. Set the first indicator to value "1" when a linking note is input in field 580, as in this example.

- Field 041 and first indicator value "1" should be used when the work is a translation. Subfield ≠a is used for the languages of the text, and the language from which the work was translated is coded in subfield ≠h.

L12

PROBLEM CONSIDERED:

Serial published in original language and also in translation (12.7B7a)

TAGGED DATA RECORD (based on OCLC #15194131)

LDR   *****cas_/22*****_a*4500

00-05	06	07-14	15-17	18	19	20	21	22-28	29	30-32	33	34	35-37	38	39
008	870213	c	19879999	cau	f	r	l		-------	0	///	a	0	eng	-	d

022 0	0892-449X
→ 130 0	Synergy (San Diego, Calif.)
→ 245 10	Synergy.
260	San Diego : ≠b Harcourt Brace Jovanovich, ≠c 1987-
300	v. ; ≠c 18 cm.
310	Semiannual
362 0	No. 1-
515	No. 1- called also vol. 1-
→ 580	Also available in a German translation.
650 0	Science fiction ≠x Periodicals.
650 0	Science fiction, American ≠x Periodicals.
→ 767 1	≠t Synergy (San Diego, Calif.). German. Synergy ≠w (OCoLC)28386631

DISCUSSION

- Example L12 is an original serial published in English. When the cataloger has an original language version in hand, it is not necessary to search to find out whether translations are available. However, if information concerning translation is given in the item, such information should be included in the record as a note (12.7B7a).
- Field 767 contains the title of the translation when the item in hand is the original language version, providing a machine link to the translation. It is important to note that, whenever a linking field is used, it should refer to the uniform title heading or uniform title if one is present. Notice that the title data in field 767 consist of the uniform title heading from the record for the original version plus the language of the translation plus the title proper from the record for the translation, i.e., "Synergy (San Diego, Calif.). German. Synergy." In this example, the cataloger chose to input a field 580, and set the first indicator of field 767 to value "1" to suppress a note.

L13

PROBLEM CONSIDERED:

Supplement to a serial (cataloged separately) (LCRI 21.28B)

RULE(S) CONSULTED:

AACR2R: 1.5E1, 12.7B7j

<table>
<tr><td rowspan="5">Caption</td><td colspan="2">IDR

Despatches   Volume 1 No. 1 January 1994</td></tr>
<tr><td colspan="2"></td></tr>
<tr><td colspan="2"></td></tr>
<tr><td colspan="2"></td></tr>
<tr><td colspan="2">A monthly supplement to the International Defense Review.</td></tr>
</table>

TAGGED DATA RECORD (based on OCLC #29865049)

LDR   *****cas_/22*****Ia*4500

00-05	06	07-14	15-17	18	19	20	21	22-28	29	30-32	33	34	35-37	38	39
940223	d	19941994	enk	m	r		p	-------	0	///	a	0	eng	-	d

008 (as above)

→ 245 00   IDR despatches.
    246 30   Despatches
    260   Coulsdon, Surrey, U.K. : ≠b Jane's Information Group, ≠c 1994.
    300   1 v. : ≠b ill. ; ≠c 28 cm.
    310   Monthly
    362 0   Vol. 1, no. 1 (Jan. 1994)-v. 1, no. 12 (Dec. 1994).
    500   Title from caption.
    650 0   Military art and science ≠x Periodicals.
    650 0   Military supplies ≠x Periodicals.
    650 0   Armed Forces ≠x Periodicals.
    710 2   Jane's Information Group.
→ 730 0   International defense review.
→ 772 0   ≠t International defense review ≠w (OCoLC)1893800
    785 00   ≠t Despatches ≠w (OCoLC)32305975

DISCUSSION

- In example L13, "IDR despatches" is issued as a supplement to "International defense review." Note that the supplement carries its own numbering system, and does not follow the numeric system of the parent serial, nor does it update that serial. On this basis, it is cataloged in a separate bibliographic record with its own numbering designation (LCRI 21.28B; 1.5E1). A linking note such as "Supplement to:" is derived from linking field 772 to explain its relation to the parent serial "International defense review" (12.7B7j). Because the title proper of the supplement is not identical to the title proper of the related serial, a simple added entry serial should be given for the parent serial (LCRI 21.28B).

- Field 730 is used for the title added entry of a related work under the established catalog entry form. In this example, the related work is the parent serial "International defense review."

L14

PROBLEM CONSIDERED:

Supplement updating a serial between editions (LCRI 21.28B)

RULE(S) CONSULTED:

AACR2R: 12.7B7j
LCRI: 1.5E1; 21.30J, p. 5

Yearbook supplement

HANDBOOK OF
IS MANAGEMENT
1994-95 YEARBOOK
AUERBACH PUBLISHERS Boston and New York

TAGGED DATA RECORD (based on OCLC #26271365)

LDR   *****cas_/22*****_a*4500

	00-05	06	07-14	15-17	18	19	20	21	22-28	29	30-32	33	34	35-37	38	39
008	920728	c	19919999	mau	u	u			--f----	0	///	a	0	eng	-	d

245 00   Handbook of IS management.
246 3   Handbook of information systems management
260   Boston : ≠b Auerbach Publishers, ≠c c1991-
300   v. : ≠ ill. ; ≠c 25 cm.
362 0   3rd ed.-
→ 525   Supplements issued between editions with title: Handbook of IS management ... yearbook.
650 0   Management information systems ≠x Handbooks, manuals, etc.
780 00   ≠t Handbook of MIS management ≠x 1055-5870 ≠w (DLC)90641776 ≠w (OCoLC)17830947

DISCUSSION

- In example L14, the serial has three supplements issued between the third and fourth editions entitled "Handbook of IS management . . . yearbook." These yearbook supplements are expected to be used in conjunction with the main serial and will become superseded, since all the information contained in the supplements will be included in the new edition, in this case, that is, the fourth edition. Do not catalog these updating supplements in separate records (LCRI 21.28B; LCRI 1.5E1). Instead, describe the supplement in a Supplement Note (field 525) on the record for the main work and give an added entry for the supplement title, if such access is warranted (12.7B7j; LCRI 21.30J, p. 5). (See also example N11.)

L15

PROBLEM CONSIDERED:

Supplement to an individual issue (LCRI 21.28B)

RULE(S) CONSULTED:

AACR2R: 12.7B7j

<table>
<tr><td rowspan="5">**Supplement issue**</td><td>**DIRECÇÃO GERALDE MINAS E SERVIÇOS GEOLÓGICOS**</td></tr>
<tr><td>COMUNICAÇÕES
DOS
SERVIÇOS GEOLÓGICOS DE PORTUGAL</td></tr>
<tr><td>**Supplemento ao tomo XXVII**</td></tr>
</table>

TAGGED DATA RECORD (based on OCLC #1382787)

LDR   *****cas_/22*****_a*4500

00-05	06	07-14	15-17	18	19	20	21	22-28	29	30-32	33	34	35-37	38	39
750610	d	19191992	po	a	r	z	p	-------	0	///	b	0	por	-	d

008

022	0037-2730
041 0	porfre
043	e-po---
245 00	Comunicações dos Serviços Geológicos de Portugal.
260	Lisboa : ≠b Serviços Geológicos de Portugal, ≠c 1919-1992.
300	66 v. : ≠ ill. ; ≠c 23-25 cm.
310	Annual, ≠b <1974>-1992
362 0	T. 13 (1919)-t. 78 (1992).
→ 525	Separately-paged supplements accompany some vols.
546	Portuguese and French.
650 0	Geology ≠z Portugal ≠x Periodicals.
780 00	≠t Comunicações da Comissão do Serviço Geológico de Portugal ≠w (OCoLC)25174515
785 00	≠t Comunicações (Instituto Geológico e Mineiro (Portugal)) ≠w (DLC)96649034 ≠w (OCoLC)34201610

DISCUSSION

- Some individual issues of this serial are accompanied by supplements, e.g., "Supplemento ao tomo XXVII" in this example. Usually these occasional supplements are published with a specific theme or a distinctive title and therefore they may be cataloged as monographs. In such cases, the serial is analyzable and the monographic record is an analytical record.
- Regardless of whether the supplement issue is analyzed or not, information about the supplementary material should be input in a Supplement Note (field 525) on the bibliographic record for the parent serial (LCRI 21.28B; 12.7B7j). This note should be worded in general terms to avoid specific information that may not be applicable to other occasional supplements published in the future.

L16

PROBLEM CONSIDERED:

Parent serial with supplement (12.7B7j)

RULE(S) CONSULTED:

AACR2R: 12.1B4
LCRI: 21.28B

L16a

> **ADVANCES IN INDUSTRIAL AND LABOR RELATIONS**
>
> A Research Annual
>
> VOL. 1 1983
>
> **JAI PRESS INC.**

Title page of the parent serial

L16b

> **ADVANCES IN INDUSTRIAL AND LABOR RELATIONS**
>
> A Research Annual
>
> **SUPPLEMENT** 1 1990
>
> **JAI PRESS INC.**

Title page of the supplement issue

L16a

TAGGED DATA RECORD (based on OCLC #10235929)

LDR *****cas_/22*****_a*4500

00-05	06	07-14	15-17	18	19	20	21	22-28	29	30-32	33	34	35-37	38	39
831120	c	19839999	ctu	a	r	l	p	-------	0	///	a	0	eng	-	d

008

022 0 0742-6186

→ 245 00 Advances in industrial and labor relations.

260   Greenwich, Conn. : ≠b JAI Press, ≠c 1983-

300   v. ; ≠c 24 cm.

310   Annual

362 0 Vol. 1 (1983)-

650 0 Industrial relations ≠x Periodicals.

→ 770 0 ≠t Advances in industrial and labor relations. Supplement ≠w
    (DLC)sn91024048 ≠w (OCoLC)23153117

L16b

TAGGED DATA RECORD (based on OCLC #23153117)

LDR *****cas_/22*****_a*4500

00-05	06	07-14	15-17	18	19	20	21	22-28	29	30-32	33	34	35-37	38	39
910225	c	19909999	ctu	a	r		m	-------	0	///	a	0	eng	-	d

008

→ 245 00 Advances in industrial and labor relations. ≠p. Supplement.

260   Greenwich, Conn. : ≠b JAI Press, ≠c 1990-

300   v. ; ≠c 24 cm.

310   Annual

362 0 1 (1990)-

650 0 Industrial relations.

→ 772 0 ≠t Advances in industrial and labor relations ≠x 0742-6186 ≠w
    (DLC)84640984 ≠w (OCoLC)10235929

DISCUSSION

- The serial in example L16a, "Advances in industrial and labor relations," has a supplement that carries a different designation system (i.e., Supplement 1, 1990) from that of the parent record. In such a case, the supplement is cataloged in a separate record (see L16b), as instructed in rule 12.1B4. In L16a, a linking note to the supplement is input on the record for the parent serial (12.7B7j). No title added entry for the supplement is needed, however, since the supplement has a common title that is identical to the parent title (LCRI 21.28B).

- Linking Entry for Supplement, field 770, is used on the record for the parent serial. The display constant of the 770 field is "Has supplement:". (Although the 770 field is paired with the 772 field on the record for the supplement, it is understandably not necessary to provide a link reciprocally from the parent serial to the supplement each time a supplement to the serial is cataloged for the collection.)

L17

PROBLEM CONSIDERED:

Special issue with its own numbering (1.9A1)

RULE(S) CONSULTED:

AACR2R: 12.1B4
LCRI: 21.28B

Cover of the special issue

> **Journal of Coastal Research**
> **Special issue**
> No. 1
> spring 1986
> **CERF**
>
> Late Quaternary Sea-level Changes
> & Coastal Evolution
> edited by
> Paolo A. Pirazzoli, John R. Suter

TAGGED DATA RECORD (based on OCLC #14039239)

LDR   *****cas_/22*****_a*4500

	00-05	06	07-14	15-17	18	19	20	21	22-28	29	30-32	33	34	35-37	38	39
008	860804	c	19869999	flu	u	u		m	-------	0	///	a	0	eng	-	d

→ 245 00   Journal of coastal research. ≠p Special issue / ≠c CERF.
   246 13   JCR
   246 30   Special issue
   260   Fort Lauderdale, Fla. : ≠b Coastal Education and Research Foundation, ≠c 1986-
   300   v. : ≠b ill. ; ≠c 26-29 cm.
   362 0   No. 1 (spring 1986)-
   500   Title from cover.
   500   Each vol. has also a distinctive title.
   650 0   Coasts.
   650 0   Coast changes.
   650 0   Coastal ecology.
   710 2   Coastal Education & Research Foundation (U.S.)
→ 772 1   ≠t Journal of coastal research ≠x 0749-0208 ≠w (DLC)8864955 ≠w (OCoLC)11052665

DISCUSSION

- The item in this example is a special issue that carries its own numbering designation. If a special issue has its own numbering designation, it should be cataloged in a separate record (1.9A1). In this example, the special issue is treated as a subseries of the serial "Journal of coastal research" (12.1B4).

- A machine-linking entry is provided in field 772 for the main serial (LCRI 21.28B). However, the first indicator value of field 772 is set to "1" to suppress a note from being generated, since the display constant "Supplement to:" is not applicable in this situation.

L18

PROBLEM CONSIDERED:

Special issue numbered in with regular issues (1.9B1b)

RULE(S) CONSULTED:

AACR2R: 12.7B7j
LCRI: 21.30J, p. 5

**Cover of the
special issue**

**CORPORATE
CASHFLOW**

THE MAGAZINE OF TREASURY MANAGEMENT

VOL. 17, NO. 2   JANUARY 31, 1996

**Buyers'
Guide
Issue**

TAGGED DATA RECORD (based on OCLC #17976195)

LDR   *****cas_/22*****_a*4500

00-05	06	07-14	15-17	18	19	20	21	22-28	29	30-32	33	34	35-37	38	39
880519	d	19881996	gau	m	r	l	p	-------	0	///	a	0	eng	-	d

008

022 0	1040-0311 ≠y 0196-6227
245 00	Corporate cashflow.
246 3	Corporate cash flow
246 3	Cashflow
260	Atlanta, GA : ≠b Communication Channels, Inc., ≠c 1988-1996.
300	9 v. : ≠b ill. ; ≠c 28 cm.
310	Monthly
362 0	Vol. 9, no. 5 (May 1988)-v. 17, no. 7 (June 1996).
500	Title from cover.
500	Imprint varies.
→ 500	Includes an annual special issue called Buyers' guide issue.
650 0	Cash flow ≠x Periodicals.
650 0	Cash management ≠x Periodicals.
→ 740 02	Buyers' guide issue.
780 00	≠t Cash flow ≠x 0196-6227 ≠w (DLC)85641380 ≠w (OCoLC)5864352
785 04	≠t Treasury and risk management ≠g July 1996 ≠x 1067-0432 ≠w (DLC)94641899 ≠w (OCoLC)27131223

DISCUSSION

- In example L18, the special issue "Buyers' guide issue" is numbered in with the regular issues and does not carry a numbering of its own. Therefore this special issue cannot be cataloged in a separate serial record. Instead, relevant information about the special issue is explained in a general note, "Includes an annual special issue called Buyers' guide issue," on the record for the parent serial (1.9B1b; 12.7B7j).
- If a title added entry is needed for the title of the special issue, as in this example, use field 740 with second indicator value set to "2," since the added entry is for an analytic (LCRI 21.30J, p. 5).

L19

PROBLEM CONSIDERED:

Reprinted serial requiring a separate record (LCRI 12.0)

RULE(S) CONSULTED:

AACR2R: 1.7A3
LCRI: 21.28B; 25.5B, p. 6

TAGGED DATA RECORD (based on OCLC #18403526)

LDR   *****cas_/22*****Ia*4500

00-05	06	07-14	15-17	18	19	20	21	22-28	29	30-32	33	34	35-37	38	39
880825	c	19879999	ilu	g	r			-r-----	0	///		0	eng	-	d

008

043 · n-us---
245 00 Occupational outlook handbook / ≠c compiled by the United States Department. of Labor, [Bureau of Labor Statistics].
260   Lincolnwood, Ill. : ≠b VGM Career Horizons, ≠c 1987-
300   v. : ≠b ill. ; ≠c 28 cm.
310   Biennial
362 0 1986-87 ed.-
→ 580 Reprint. Originally published: Washington, D.C. : U.S. Dept. of Labor, Bureau of Labor Statistics.
650 0 Labor supply ≠z United States.
650 0 Vocational guidance ≠z United States.
651 0 United States ≠x Occupations.
710 1 United States. ≠b Bureau of Labor Statistics.
→ 775 1 ≠t Occupational outlook handbook ≠w 0082-9072 ≠w (DLC)sn88040069 ≠w (OCoLC)1773253

Occupational Outlook Handbook

compiled by the
United States Department of Labor

**Title page of
the reprint**

VGM Career Horizons
1987

DISCUSSION

- Not all reprinted serials can be cataloged as separate records; separate records should be made only for those that are produced by a publisher who was not responsible for the original (LCRI 12.0). Thus, in this example, the reprinted serial was published by VGM Career Horizons and the original was published by the Bureau of Labor Statistics of the U.S. government; therefore, a separate record is made for the reprinted serial. A link to the original serial should also be provided (LCRI 21.28B).

- Usually a reprinted serial will carry the same title as the original. The normal tendency in such a case may be to create a uniform title heading to distinguish between the two. Nevertheless, according to Library of Congress policy, no *uniform title* should be established to distinguish the reprint from the original. In fact, if the original itself has a uniform title heading, that same uniform title heading should be used for the reprinted serial (LCRI 25.5B, p. 6).

- Field 775 is used to provide a machine link to the original serial; the first indicator is set to value "1" so that no linking note is generated. Instead, a Linking Entry Complexity Note (field 580) is input to describe the publishing details of the original serial. The reprint note should be in the formatted style, as instructed in rule 1.7A3.

L20

PROBLEM CONSIDERED:

Reprinted serial not requiring a separate record (LCRI 12.0)

RULE(S) CONSULTED:

AACR2R: 21.30J1

TAGGED DATA RECORD (based on OCLC #9670810)

LDR *****cas_/22*****Ia*4500

00-05	06	07-14	15-17	18	19	20	21	22-28	29	30-32	33	34	35-37	38	39
008	830706	c	19uu9999	txu	q	r	l	p	-------	0	///	a	0	eng	-	d

022 1	0746-004X
043	nccz---
245 04	The Canal Zone philatelist / ≠c Canal Zone Study Group.
→ 246 1	≠i Some issues reprinted with title: ≠a C.Z.S.G. philatelic notes
→ 246 1	≠i Some issues reprinted with title: ≠a Canal Zone philatelic notes
260	Richardson, Tex. : ≠b The Group,
300	v. : ≠b ill. ; ≠c 28 cm.
500	Description based on: Vol. 4, no. 1 (1st quarter, 1968); title from caption.
515	Vols. for 1968- called also no. 6-
515	Publication suspended 1955?-1967.
650 0	Postage stamps ≠z Panama ≠z Canal Zone ≠x Periodicals.
710 2	Canal Zone Study Group.

DISCUSSION

- In cases where a serial was reprinted by the same publisher responsible for the original, no separate record should be made, even when the reprinted issues carry a different title (LCRI 12.0). In this example, the serial "The Canal Zone philatelist" has had some issues reprinted under the titles "C.Z.S.G. philatelic notes" and "Canal Zone philatelic notes." In spite of such changes in title, no separate records are made for the reprints because the reprinted issues were issued by the publisher of the original. Instead, a note is input on the record for the original to provide access to the titles on the reprinted issues (21.30J1).

- Note that the provision of this rule interpretation applies to reprints by the original publisher, whether the reprinted issues represent the whole run of the serial or just a few issues to fill in gaps in the holdings for the original (LCRI 12.0).

- In this example, two 246 fields are input to provide access to the reprinted titles. The source of the title is input in subfield ≠i of each field 246.

L21

PROBLEM CONSIDERED:

Serial published in several language editions (12.7B7g)

RULE(S) CONSULTED:

AACR2R: 12.2B2
LCRI: 25.5B, p. 3

TAGGED DATA RECORD (based on OCLC #29998948)

LDR   *****cas_/22*****_a*4500

00-05	06	07-14	15-17	18	19	20	21	22-28	29	30-32	33	34	35-37	38	39
940322	c	199u9999	bl	b	r		p	-------	0	///		0	eng	-	d

008

→ 130 0   Braudel papers (English ed.)

245 00   Braudel papers : ≠b document of the Fernand Braudel Institute of World Economics.

→ 250   English ed.

260   São Paulo, Brasil : ≠b The Institute,

300   v. : ≠b ill. ; ≠c 43 cm.

310   Bimonthly

500   Description based on: Mar./Apr. 1993; title from caption.

→ 580   Issued also in Portuguese.

650 0   Economic history ≠y 1990- ≠ x Periodicals.

651 0   Brazil ≠x Politics and government ≠y 1985- ≠x Periodicals.

710 2   Instituto Fernand Braudel de Economia Mundial.

→ 775 1   ≠t Braudel papers ≠w (DLC)sn94035148 ≠w (OCoLC)30020595

DISCUSSION

- Some serials may be published in more than one edition, and in that case each edition should be cataloged as a separate record. An edition statement, such as English edition, Northern edition, etc., may or may not appear on the item being cataloged. In this example, a formal edition statement on the item indicates that this is the English edition of a main work issued simultaneously in Portuguese. In such a case, a linking note should be given on each record indicating the availability of the other editions (12.7B7g).

- In this example, since the title of the main edition is the same as that of the edition being cataloged, a uniform title heading should be used in order to distinguish between the two. For this record, the edition statement "English ed." is used as a qualifier in the uniform title heading (LCRI 25.5B, p. 3).

- Note that statements of revision or those merely indicating volume numbering or chronological coverage (such as 1st ed., 1980 ed., etc.) should not be considered to be formal edition statements that require a separate record (12.2B2).

- Field 250 is used only for edition statements appearing on the item being described. Field 775 is used for other available editions. In this example, the first indicator is set to value "1" because the information on the other available edition is given in field 580 (Linking Entry Complexity Note). Note that a linking field should always refer to the uniform title heading if one is present in the record.

L22

PROBLEM CONSIDERED:

Other edition available (12.7B7g)

RULE(S) CONSULTED:

LCRI: 12.7B7g

TAGGED DATA RECORD (based on OCLC #26201828)

LDR   *****cas_/22*****7a*4500

	00-05	06	07-14	15-17	18	19	20	21	22-28	29	30-32	33	34	35-37	38	39
008	920716	c	19uu9999	nyu	w	r	l	p	-------	0	///	a	0	eng	-	d

022 0	1064-0304	
→ 130 0	Time international (Asia ed.)	
245 00	Time international.	
246 13	Time Asia	
→ 250	Asia ed.	
260	New York, N.Y. : ≠b Time, Inc.,	
300	v. : ≠b ill. ; ≠c 28 cm.	
310	Weekly	
500	Description based on surrogate of: Vol. 139, no. 26 (June 29, 1992); title from cover.	
→ 580	Issued also in various regional editions.	
→ 775 1	≠t Time ≠x 0040-781X ≠w (DLC)25011669 ≠w (OCoLC)1767509	
→ 775 1	≠t Time Australia	
→ 775 1	≠t Time (Canada ed.)	
→ 775 1	≠t Time international (Japan ed.) ≠x 1059-9363 ≠w (DLC)sn 910079829	
→ 775 1	≠t Time international (New Zealand ed.)	
→ 775 1	≠t Time international (South Africa ed.) ≠x 0256-3908	
→ 775 1	≠t Time international (United Kingdom ed.) ≠x 0959-5023	

DISCUSSION

- If a serial has other editions that differ in partial contents and/or language, create a link from the title being cataloged to the title of the other edition in an "Other edition available" note (12.7B7g; LCRI 12.7B7g). Other editions of a serial are those issued simultaneously, usually with the same title and intended for a specific audience (CCM 14.3.2). They are also distinguished by the presence of an edition statement, which is input in field 250 if the information is available on the chief source. In this example, the Asia edition of "Time international" is related to "Time," the main magazine, and other regional editions of "Time international." Field 775, Other Edition Available Entry, is used for each of the related titles. Note that the uniform title heading is input in linking field 775. In this example, most of these uniform title headings include the edition statement as qualifier.

- For simplicity, the information regarding multiple editions of a serial may be summarized in a single 580 note, as shown in this example: "Issued also in various regional editions." In this case, the first indicator of field 775 is set to value "1" to suppress a note.

L23

PROBLEM CONSIDERED:

Serial issued with another serial is also published separately (12.7B21)

RULE(S) CONSULTED:

AACR2R: 21.30G1

L23a

TAGGED DATA RECORD (based on OCLC #6836704)

LDR   *****cas_/22*****_a*4500

00-05	06	07-14	15-17	18	19	20	21	22-28	29	30-32	33	34	35-37	38	39
008	801017	d	19801995	fr	w	r		p	-------	0	///	b	0	fre	-	d

245 00   Révolution.

260   Paris : ≠b Société d'édition du journal "Révolution", ≠c 1980-1995.

300   782 v. : ≠b ill. ; ≠c 32 cm.

310   Weekly

362 0   No. 1 (7/13 mars 1980)-no. 782 (23 fév./1 mars 1995).

500   Title from cover.

→ 580   Beginning in 1989 includes: L'Ecole et la nation.

580   Merged with: Avancées, to form: Regards.

→ 730 02 Ecole et la nation.

→ 777 1   ≠t Ecole et la nation ≠w (DLC)sn90022097 ≠w (OCoLC)6679737

780 00 ≠t Nouvelle critique ≠w (DLC)52039091 ≠w (OCoLC)2620165

785 17 ≠t Avancées

785 17 ≠t Regards (Paris, France : 1995) ≠w (DLC)95641819 ≠w (OCoLC)33063122

L23b

TAGGED DATA RECORD (based on OCLC #6679737)

LDR   *****cas_/22*****_a*4500

00-05	06	07-14	15-17	18	19	20	21	22-28	29	30-32	33	34	35-37	38	39
008	800904	d	19511995	fr	q	r		p	-------	0	///	b	0	fre	-	d

043   e-fr---

245 02   L'Ecole et la nation.

260   Paris : ≠b Parti communiste français, ≠c 1951-1995.

300   v. : ≠b ill. ; ≠c 32 cm.

310   Quarterly, ≠b 1991-

321   Monthly, ≠b 1951-90

362 0   No. 1 (oct. 1951)-

362 1   Ceased in 1995.

500   Title from caption.

→ 580   Beginning with no. 402 issue published in: Révolution.

650 0 Education ≠z France ≠x Periodicals.

710 2   Parti communiste français.

→ 730 02 Révolution.

→ 777 1   ≠t Révolution ≠w (DLC)806499227 ≠w (OCoLC)6836704

DISCUSSION

- Occasionally a serial that is issued within another serial can also be described in a separate record. Such is the case illustrated in example L23a, where the serial "L'Ecole et la nation" is issued with "Révolution," the serial being cataloged. Although issued with or included in each other, the two related serials retain their separate numbering designations.

- A linking note is needed for a serial that is issued with or included in the serial being cataloged (12.7B21). Field 777 is the linking field used for this purpose and it should appear on the record for each of the related serials. The linking note generated from the 777 field has the display constant, "Issued with:". However, in most cases, the relationship is better described in a Linking Entry Complexity Note, field 580, as in example L23a, "Beginning in 1989 includes: L'Ecole et la nation," and in example L23b, "Beginning with no. 402 issue published in: Révolution."
- An added entry for the "Issued with" title should be made on each of the separate serial records (21.30G1).
- Field 730 is used for the necessary title added entries, "Ecole et la nation" and "Révolution" in examples L23a and L23b, respectively. Note that the French article is omitted from field 730 in example L23a; the first indicator is set to value "0" as a result.

L24

PROBLEM CONSIDERED:
Serial includes another serial with no separate record (12.7B18)

TAGGED DATA RECORD (based on OCLC #5756229)

LDR   *****cas_/22*****_a*4500

00-05	06	07-14	15-17	18	19	20	21	22-28	29	30-32	33	34	35-37	38	39
791204	d	19781994	onc	b	r	4	p	-------	0	///	a	0	eng	-	d

008

022	0829-772X
043	n-cn---
245 00	Civic public works.
260	Toronto : ≠b Maclean-Hunter, ≠c 1978-1994.
300	17 v. : ≠b ill. (some col.) ; ≠c 29 cm.
310	Bimonthly, ≠b <1993>-1994
321	Monthly, ≠b 1978-<1980>
362 0	Vol. 30, no. 5 (May 1978)-v. 46, no. 5 (fall 1994).
→ 500	Includes an annual no. called: Public works reference manual & buyers guide (varies slightly).
530	Issued also on microform.
580	Vol. for 1978 accompanied by supplement: Wastes handling, which it absorbed in 1979.
650 0	Municipal government ≠z Canada ≠x Periodicals.
650 0	Public works ≠z Canada ≠x Periodicals.
730 0	Wastes handling.
→ 740 02	Public works reference manual & buyers guide.
772 1	≠t Wastes handling ≠g 1978 ≠x 0315-1921 ≠w (DLC)75645935 ≠w (OCoLC)2242756
780 00	≠t Civic ≠x 0315-1972 ≠w (DLC)75647769 ≠w (OCoLC)2243907
780 15	≠t Wastes handling ≠x 0315-1921 ≠w (DLC)75645935 ≠w (OCoLC)2242756
785 04	≠t Heavy construction news ≠x 0017-9426 ≠w (OCoLC)2470737

DISCUSSION

- Sometimes a serial includes another serial for which no separate record can be made—when, for example, the serial-within-a-serial does not have the basic information for description. Example L24 illustrates such a case. It is clear that the annual number of the serial called "Public works reference manual & buyers guide" was not considered to be an independent publication. Apparently no formal title statement for the guide ever appears on the chief source. Likewise, there is no evidence that the issues of this guide have any numbering system except that used by the main serial "Civic public works" (compare this with example L23b, where the included serial continues to have a numbering designation of its own). Therefore, this buying guide should not be cataloged separately as a serial and no linking fields should be made. Instead, give in a general note (usually taken from the introduction) the information on what is contained in the item described (12.7B18).

- Field 500 is used for general notes. In this case an informal scope note is made. Field 740 with a second indicator value "2" is used to provide access for analytical titles of independent works contained within the item.

L25

PROBLEM CONSIDERED:

Serial consists of selected material from another serial (12.7B7)

RULE(S) CONSULTED:

AACR2R: 21.30G1

Title page

> # Recommended
> # Reference Books
>
> ## for Small and Medium-sized
> ## Libraries and Media Centers
> ### 1995
>
> Libraries Unlimited, Inc. • Englewood, Colorado

Introduction page

> ### Introduction
>
> Following the pattern established in 1981 with the first volume, RRB consists of book reviews chosen from the current edition of American Reference Books Annual.

TAGGED DATA RECORD (based on OCLC #7610929)

LDR   *****cas_/22*****Ia*4500

00-05	06	07-14	15-17	18	19	20	21	22-28	29	30-32	33	34	35-37	38	39
810724	c	19819999	cou	a	r	1		---fb--	0	///	a	0	eng	-	d

008 (as above)

022 0	0277-5948	
245 00	Recommended reference books for small and medium-sized libraries and media centers.	
260	Littleton, Colo. : ≠b Libraries Unlimited, Inc., ≠c 1981-	
300	v. ; ≠c 24-26 cm.	
310	Annual	
362 0	1981-	
500	Published: Englewood, Colo., <1991->	
→ 580	Selected from: American reference books annual.	
650 0	Reference books ≠x Bibliography.	
650 0	Reference service (Libraries) ≠x Handbooks, manuals, etc.	
650 0	Instructional materials centers ≠x Handbooks, manuals, etc.	
→ 787 1	≠t American reference books annual ≠x 0065-9959 ≠w (DLC)75120328 ≠w (OCoLC)1028287	

DISCUSSION

- If a serial being cataloged is related to another serial but the relationship does not correspond to any of those defined in 12.7B7, give the entry for the related work in a note (21.30G1). Because there are so many possible relationships between serials, in most cases, a 580 note is added to specifically describe the relationship.

- In this example, the relationship between the serial being cataloged—"Recommended reference books for small and medium-sized libraries and media centers"—and its related serial—"American reference books annual"—is described in field 580, "Selected from: . . . ," and the link to the related serial is input in a Nonspecific Relationship Entry, field 787.

L26

PROBLEM CONSIDERED:

Serial as a companion volume to other work (12.7B7)

<table>
<tr><td>Title page</td><td>

The Year's Work in Critical and Cultural Theory

Vol. 1
1991

Companion to: The Year's Work in English Studies

</td></tr>
</table>

TAGGED DATA RECORD (based on OCLC #30804262)

LDR   *****cas_/22*****Ia*4500

	00-05	06	07-14	15-17	18	19	20	21	22-28	29	30-32	33	34	35-37	38	39
008	940721	c	19919999	enk	a	r	z	p	-------	0	///	a	0	eng	-	d

022 0	1077-4254	
245 04	The Year's work in critical and cultural theory.	
246 14	YWCCT	
260	Oxford : ≠b Published for the English Association by Blackwell Publishers, ≠c c1994-	
300	v. ; ≠c 23 cm.	
310	Annual	
362 0	Vol. 1 (1991)-	
490 0	Blackwell reference	
→ 580	Companion to: The Year's work in English studies.	
650 0	Criticism ≠x Periodicals.	
650 0	Critical theory ≠x Periodicals.	
650 0	Culture ≠x Periodicals.	
710 2	English Association.	
→ 787 1	≠t Year's work in English studies ≠x 0084-4144 ≠w (DLC)22010024 ≠w (OCoLC)1770338	

DISCUSSION

- A serial may be related to another simultaneously published serial simply in that one publication may be of interest to readers of the other because of the similarity of material covered by the two publications. In such a situation it is up to the cataloger to judge whether a note about the companion serial would be valuable. If the decision is made to include such information, give the title of the related work in a note (12.7B7). Field 787, Nonspecific Relationship Entry, is used. Because in cases like this the relationship of the related work must always be spelled out in a Linking Entry Complexity Note, field 580, the first indicator of field 787 is always set to value "1."

L27

PROBLEM CONSIDERED:

Separately published index to one or more serials (LCRI 21.28B)

RULE(S) CONSULTED:

AACR2R: 12.7B7

TAGGED DATA RECORD (OCLC #17360391)

LDR   *****cas_/22*****_a*4500

00-05	06	07-14	15-17	18	19	20	21	22-28	29	30-32	33	34	35-37	38	39
880119	c	19879999	ilu	u	u			--i----	0	///	a	0	eng	-	d

008

245 04		The Policy studies index.
260		Urbana, Ill. : ≠b Policy Studies Organization, ≠c 1987-
300		v. ; ≠c 26 cm.
362 0		1987-
→ 580		Indexes: Policy studies journal; and: Policy studies review.
→ 630 00		Policy studies journal ≠x Indexes.
→ 630 00		Policy studies review ≠x Indexes.
650 0		Policy sciences ≠x Periodicals ≠x Indexes.
710 2		Policy Studies Organization.
→ 787 1		≠t Policy studies journal ≠w (DLC)72625926 ≠w (OCoLC)1316083
→ 787 1		≠t Policy studies review ≠w (DLC)82641149 ≠w (OCoLC)7714805

DISCUSSION

- If an index is published separately and is issued by an entity different from the one responsible for the serial being indexed, a separate bibliographic record should be made for the index (LCRI 21.28B). Also, a separate record should be created for an index that covers two or more different serials, as in this example.

- If the index covers no more than three serials, create a subject heading consisting of the heading for the indexed serial followed by the subdivision "Indexes" (LCRI 21.28B). In this example, two 630 fields are input to provide access to the two serials being indexed—one for "Policy studies journal," and the other for "Policy studies review." No title added entry is needed for the work being indexed.

- If the index covers no more than three serials, a link should also be established to each serial being indexed. Since the relationship is not covered in rule 12.7B7, field 787, Nonspecific Relationship Entry, is used and a Linking Entry Complexity Note, field 580, is made to give the details of the relationship.

L28

PROBLEM CONSIDERED:

Serial continuing a monograph (LCRI 12.0A4e)

RULE(S) CONSULTED:

AACR2R: 21.28A1, 21.28B1

TAGGED DATA RECORD (based on OCLC #29806634)

LDR   *****cas_/22*****Ia*4500

	00-05	06	07-14	15-17	18	19	20	21	22-28	29	30-32	33	34	35-37	38	39
008	930902	c	19919999	ilu	a	r			-------	0	///	a	0	eng		d

043	n-us----- ≠a n-cn---
245 00	Assessment administration practices in the U.S. and Canada.
260	Chicago, Ill. : ≠b International Association of Assessing Officers, ≠c 1991-
300	v. ; ≠c 28 cm.
310	Annual
362 0	Sept. 1991-
→ 580	Continues and updates the monograph published under the title: Taxonomy of administrative and legal features of states and provinces of the United States and Canada.
650 0	Tax assessment ≠z United States.
650 0	Tax assessment ≠z Canada.
710 2	International Association of Assessing Officers.
→ 730 0	Taxonomy of administrative and legal features of states and provinces of the United States and Canada.

DISCUSSION

- Some serial publications may serve as updating supplements to a monograph. If these publications are meant to be kept together and used in conjunction with the main work, do not catalog them as serials (LCRI 12.0A4e); catalog them as serials only if these publications are independent works. Such is the case in this example, where the item is an updating supplement to a monograph but, at the same time, it is a truly independent publication. Thus, it is cataloged in a separate record. For continuity, a note is input to inform users of the related work and an added entry should also be made to provide access to the related title (21.28A1; 21.28B1).

- In this example, a 580 linking note is input to give the linking relationship and provide justification for the title added entry for the related work. However, according to CONSER practice, links are not made between serials and monographs (CCM 14.4.2). Field 730 is used to provide title added entries for related works that are cataloged separately in the catalog, e.g., the monographic title in this example. The second indicator is blank because the added entry is not an analytic.

M. Conference and Exhibition Publications

In a footnote to rule 21.1B1, AACR2R defines conferences as "meetings of individuals or representatives of various bodies for the purpose of discussing and/or acting on topics of common interest, or meetings of representatives of a corporate body that constitute its legislative or governing body." In applying this definition to the interpretation of rule 21.1B1, it must be kept in mind that conferences, projects, and programs are all considered to be corporate bodies.

Rule 21.1B2d states that an item that represents the collective activity of a conference or an exhibition, fair, festival, etc., should be entered under the name of the conference, exhibition, etc., itself. In addition, all the following criteria should be met in order for a conference or exhibition publication to be entered under its own name heading:

1. The conference or exhibition must appear on the chief source of information of the item being cataloged, and not just appear prominently (LCRI 21.1B2, category d).
2. The work must deal with the activities of many persons involved in the conference or exhibition. For example, the collective activities of a conference include proceedings, collected papers, etc. (21.1B2d).
3. The meeting, exhibition, etc., must be named (i.e., it must have a distinctive name). In some cases the "name" of a meeting may consist of a corporate body plus a generic term for meeting (LCRI 24.13 type 6).

EXAMPLES

M1   Named meeting entered directly under its own name
M2   Named meeting entered under the heading for a corporate body plus a generic term
M3   Unnamed or named conference entered under title
M4   Named conference with thematic title
M5   Named conference as title proper
M6   Non-conference work with conference-like title proper
M7   Exhibition entered under the heading for a corporate body
M8   Unnamed exhibition entered under title
M9   Named festival entered under its own name
M10   Unnamed festivals

M1

PROBLEM CONSIDERED:

Named meeting entered directly under its own name (21.1B2d)

RULE(S) CONSULTED:

AACR2R: 12.1B7, 12.7B6, 24.7A1

ACM **PRESS** **RECOMB 97** **Proceedings of the** **First Annual International Conference on** **Computational Molecular Biology** **January 19-22, 1997** **Sponsored by** **ACM SIGACT** **with support from** **SLOAN Foundation** **US Department of Energy**

Title page

TAGGED DATA RECORD (based on OCLC #36577317)

LDR   *****cas_/22*****Ia*4500

00-05	06	07-14	15-17	18	19	20	21	22-28	29	30-32	33	34	35-37	38	39
970319	c	19979999	nyu	a	r			-------	1	///	a	0	eng	-	d

008

→ 111 2   International Conference on Computational Molecular Biology.

→ 245 10   Proceedings of the ... annual International Conference on Computational Molecular Biology.

260   New York, N.Y. ≠b ACM Press, ≠c c1997-

300   v. : ≠b ill. ; ≠c 28 cm.

310   Annual

362 0   1st ('97)-

550   Sponsored by ACM SIGACT with support from SLOAN Foundation and U.S. Dept. of Energy.

650 0   Molecular biology ≠x Mathematics ≠x Congresses.

650 0   Molecular biology ≠x Statistical methods ≠x Congresses.

→ 710 2   ACM Special Interest Group for Automata and Computability Theory.

DISCUSSION

- The publication shown in this example represents the collective activity of the International Conference on Computational Molecular Biology, and the conference's name (which is distinctive) appears in the item's chief source. Therefore, rule 21.1B2d has been applied, and the item is entered directly under the conference's own name heading with the omission of the number "First annual" (24.7A1).
- The conference number embedded in the title proper of this work has been omitted and replaced by the mark of omission (…), since such a date or number will usually vary from issue to issue (12.1B7). Also use the mark of omission if the date or number appears at the end of the title and is grammatically linked with the title.
- In this example, the name of the sponsor of the conference is given in an Issuing Body Note, field 550 (12.7B6). This note explains the body's relationship to the publication and justifies the 710 added entry.
- Field 111 is used for a main entry consisting of the heading for a named conference, meeting, or event, such as an exhibition, a fair, or a festival. The first indicator describes the form of name. First indicator value "2" is used for conferences entered directly under their own names. The second indicator is blank.
- Field 710 is used to provide added entries for corporate names. The first indicator is based on the type of corporate name. First indicator value "2" is used when the corporate body is entered directly under its own name. The second indicator is blank.

M2

PROBLEM CONSIDERED:

Named meeting entered under the heading for a corporate body plus a generic term (LCRI 24.13 type 3; LCRI 24.13 type 6).

Title page	**Research on Agricultural Chemicals in Illinois Groundwater** **Status and Future Directions** **Illinois Groundwater Consortium** **Annual Conference Proceedings**

TAGGED DATA RECORD (based on OCLC #33409626)

LDR   *****cas_/22*****_a*4500

	00-05	06	07-14	15-17	18	19	20	21	22-28	29	30-32	33	34	35-37	38	39
→ 008	951101	c	199u9999	ilu	a	r			-------	1	///	a	0	eng	-	d

043   n-us-il

→ 110 2   Illinois Groundwater Consortium. ≠b Conference.

245 10   Research on agricultural chemicals in Illinois groundwater / ≠c Illinois Groundwater Consortium.

246 13   Annual conference proceedings

246 14   Proceedings of ... annual conference

260   [Carbondale, IL] : ≠b The Consortium,

300   v. : ≠b ill. ; ≠c 28 cm.

310   Annual

500   Description based on: 4th (Mar. 23-24, 1994).

650 0 Agricultural chemicals ≠x Environmental aspects ≠z Illinois ≠x Congresses.

650 0 Groundwater ≠x Pollution ≠z Illinois ≠x Congresses.

780 00 Illinois Groundwater Consortium. Conference. ≠t Proceedings ≠w (OCoLC)30527239

DISCUSSION

- The term "named meeting" does not necessarily refer only to a meeting that has a distinctive name of its own; in certain cases, "named meeting" may also refer to constructions consisting of a corporate name and a generic term, such as "meeting," "conference," "workshop," etc. There are two types of such headings:

  1. The generic term appears on the piece grammatically linked to the corporate body, e.g., "Annual meeting of the American Society of Clinical Oncology" (LCRI 24.13 type 6).

  2. The generic term appears on the piece separate from (i.e., not grammatically linked to) the corporate name, e.g., "Annual Conference" separated typographically from "Illinois Groundwater Consortium" (LCRI 24.13 type 3).

- Such generic name headings are entered in field 110 or 710 rather than field 111 or 711, which are used for named conferences. It should also be noted that the fixed field element 008 position 29 (Conference Publication Indicator) is coded as "1" for conference publication, even though the main entry is entered in field 110.

M3

PROBLEM CONSIDERED:

Unnamed or named conference entered under title (21.5A)

RULE(S) CONSULTED:

AACR2R: 21.1B2d, 21.30E1
LCRI: 21.1B2, category d

M3a

TAGGED DATA RECORD (based on OCLC #30801139)

LDR   *****cas_/22*****_a*4500

00-05	06	07-14	15-17	18	19	20	21	22-28	29	30-32	33	34	35-37	38	39
931026	c	19909999	pau	a	r			-------	1	///	a	0	eng	-	d

008

→ 245 00   Ferroelectric thin films : ≠b symposium.
260   Pittsburg, Pa. : ≠b Materials Research Society, ≠c c1990-
300   v. : ≠b ill. ; ≠c 24 cm.
310   Annual
362 0   [1] (1990)-
490 1   Materials Research Society symposium proceedings
515   Symposium not held in 1992.
650 0   Ferroelectric thin films ≠x Congresses.
→ 710 2   Materials Research Society.
830 0   Materials Research Society symposia proceedings

MATERIALS RESEARCH SOCIETY SYMPOSIUM PROCEEDINGS   VOLUME 200

Ferroelectric Thin Films I

Symposium held April 16-20, 1990, San Francisco, California, U.S.A.

M3a Title page

M3b

TAGGED DATA RECORD (based on OCLC #33268360)

LDR   *****cas_/22*****Ia*4500

00-05	06	07-14	15-17	18	19	20	21	22-28	29	30-32	33	34	35-37	38	39
950801	c	19849999	nyu	u	u			-------	1	///	a	0	eng	-	d

008

→ 245 00   Intersections between particle and nuclear physics.
260   New York : ≠b American Institute of Physics, ≠c 1984-
300   v. : ≠b ill. ; ≠c 25 cm.
362 0   1984-
440 0   AIP conference proceedings
→ 500   Proceedings of the Conference on Intersections of Particle and Nuclear Physics.
515   Vols. for 1986- called 2nd- conference.
650 0   Particles (Nuclear physics) ≠x Congresses.
650 0   Nuclear physics ≠x Congresses.
→ 711 2   Conference on the Intersections between Particle and Nuclear Physics.

M3b
Title page

AIP Conference Proceedings
Number 123

Intersections Between Particle and Nuclear Physics

(Steamboat Springs, 1984)

M3b
Foreword

FOREWORD

The Conference on the Intersections of Particle and Nuclear Physics was organized as one way to bring together . . .

DISCUSSION

• In approaching the cataloging of a conference publication, the cataloger must first determine whether the conference or meeting is considered to be named or unnamed. If the conference is named and also appears in the chief source of information, entry should be made under the heading for the conference (21.1B2d). If the conference is named but does not appear in the chief source, the publication should be entered under title. This is illustrated in example M3a, where the conference lacks a name and the symposium publication is published sequentially under the title "Ferroelectric thin films." Thus, the serial is entered under title with the other title information "symposium" (21.5A). A 710 added entry is made for the corporate body, Materials Research Society, which is both the sponsor of the symposium and the publisher of the proceedings (21.30E1).

• The name of the conference in example M3b is distinctive, and it is thus considered to be a named conference. However, in spite of this, entry for this publication must be made under title, since the name of the conference appears only in the foreword of the publication and not on its chief source (LCRI 21.1B2, category d). A 500 General Note recording the name of the conference is included in the bibliographic description so that an added entry for the conference is justified. Field 711 is used for that added entry.

M4

PROBLEM CONSIDERED:

Named conference with thematic title (LCRI 21.1B1)

RULE(S) CONSULTED:

AACR2R: 1.1E4, 21.1B2d
LCRI: 12.0A

EVOLUTIONARY PROGRAMMING

Conference on Evolutionary Programming
Proceedings of the 4th Annual Conference on
Evolutionary Programming

MIT Press
Cambridge, Massachusetts

Title page (left margin)

TAGGED DATA RECORD (based on OCLC #34728491)

LDR   *****cas_/22*****Ia*4500

00-05	06	07-14	15-17	18	19	20	21	22-28	29	30-32	33	34	35-37	38	39
960514	c	19959999	mau	a	r			-------	1	///	a	0	eng	-	d

008

→ 111 2   Conference on Evolutionary Programming.

→ 245 10   Evolutionary programming : ≠b proceedings of the ... annual Conference on Evolutionary Programming.

246 30   Proceedings of the ... annual Conference on Evolutionary Programming

260   Cambridge, Mass. : ≠b MIT Press, ≠c c1995-

300   v. : ≠b ill. ; ≠c 26-29 cm.

310   Annual

362 0   4th (1995)-

500   Description based on : 4th (1995).

650 0   Evolutionary programming (Computer science) ≠x Congresses.

780 00   Conference on Evolutionary Programming. ≠t Proceedings of the ... annual Conference on Evolutionary Programming

DISCUSSION

- Often a conference publication will have a theme title that may vary from conference to conference. In such a case the publication may always be given monographic cataloging. However, a conference publication may be cataloged as a serial only when the name of the conference and the general title (i.e., Acts of . . . , Proceedings of . . . , etc.) remain constant (LCRI 12.0A). In monographic cataloging, the thematic title is recorded as the title proper; however, in serial cataloging, the recurring general title is recorded as the title proper, and a general note (e.g., Each vol. has also a distinctive title) is included in the record to cover the varying thematic titles.

- In example M4, the "Conference on Evolutionary Programming" is clearly a named conference (LCRI 21.1B1). The name also appears on the title page, which serves as the chief source of information. Therefore, the main entry for the cataloging record is made under the heading for the conference (21.1B2d). The thematic title "Evolutionary Programming," which remains stable from issue to issue, is chosen as the title proper for the serial, while the general title "Proceedings of the . . . annual Conference on Evolutionary Programming" is input as other title information (1.1E4). The conference numbering in the other

284

title information is replaced by the mark of omission, since such data varies with each issue. Title added entries are made to provide access to both the title proper and the other title information.

M5

PROBLEM CONSIDERED:

Named conference as title proper (1.1B3)

RULE(S) CONSULTED:

AACR2R: 1.1E6, 21.1B2d, 21.30J1
LCRI: 21.30J

TAGGED DATA RECORD (based on OCLC #35028060)

LDR   *****cas_/22*****Ia*4500

00-05	06	07-14	15-17	18	19	20	21	22-28	29	30-32	33	34	35-37	38	39
960703	c	19uu9999	nyu	g	r			-------	1	///	a	0	eng	-	d

008

→ 111 2   IEEE ASSP Workshop on Applications of Signal Processing to Audio and Acoustics.

→ 245 00   IEEE ASSP Workshop on Applications of Signal Processing to Audio and Acoustics : ≠b [proceedings].

260   Piscataway, NJ : ≠b IEEE Service Center,

300   v. : ≠b ill. ; ≠c 28 cm.

310   Biennial

500   Description based on surrogate of: 1995.

550   Sponsored by the Signal Processing Society of the IEEE.

650 0   Sound ≠x Recording and reproducing ≠x Mathematics ≠x Congresses.

650 0   Signal processing ≠x Digital techniques ≠x Congresses.

710 2   IEEE Signal Processing Society.

DISCUSSION

- Quite often the publication of a named conference will include in its chief source only the name of the conference and no title proper. In such a case, the name of the conference should be treated as the title proper (1.1B3). Thus, in this example, "IEEE ASSP Workshop on Applications of Signal Processing to Audio and Acoustics" is clearly the name of the meeting, but because no title proper appears on the title page, the name of the meeting "IEEE ASSP Workshop on Applications of Signal Processing to Audio and Acoustics" is treated as the title proper. (Note that capitalization for the title proper is as it appears in the name.) Other title information may be supplied by the cataloger if it is necessary to make the nature of the item clear to users; in this example, "proceedings" is added in brackets as other title information (1.1E6).

- Because this workshop is named, the item is entered under the name of the conference as a corporate body (21.1B2d). When the name of a corporate body is the main entry of a bibliographic record and is also taken as the title proper as in this example, an added entry for the title proper is not needed (21.30J1).

For that reason, the first indicator in field 245 is set to "0." See example N7 for a similar situation in which an added entry **is** made, in keeping with LC practice as stated in LCRI 21.30J.

M6

PROBLEM CONSIDERED:

Non-conference work with conference-like title proper (21.1B2d)

RULE(S) CONSULTED:

AACR2R: 21.1B2a

TAGGED DATA RECORD (based on OCLC #27573890)

LDR   *****cas_/22*****Ia*4500

	00-05	06	07-14	15-17	18	19	20	21	22-28	29	30-32	33	34	35-37	38	39
→008	03-225	c	19909999	mdu	u	u			------s	0	///	a	0	eng	-	d

→ 110 1   Maryland. ≠b Greenways Commission.
→ 245 10   Minutes of the Maryland Greenways Commission meeting.
    260   Annapolis, MD : ≠b The Commission, ≠c 1990-
    300   v. ; ≠c 28 cm.
    362 0   March 5, 1990-
    650 0   Greenways ≠z Maryland.
    650 0   Open spaces ≠z Maryland.
    650 0   Environmental protection ≠z Maryland.
    610 10   Maryland. ≠b Greenways Commission.

DISCUSSION

- Occasionally a cataloger may encounter an item that has a conference-like title proper, but that nevertheless should not be cataloged as a conference publication because it does not have the nature of such (i.e., it is *not* a meeting of individuals or representatives of various bodies gathering for the purpose of discussing and acting on topics of common interest, or a meeting of representatives of a corporate body that constitute its legislative or governing body) (21.1B2d). This distinction is an important one to make, calling for careful examination of the publication by the cataloger. In this example, the title "Minutes of the . . ." looks very much like the title of a conference publication. However, examination of the publication reveals that this is not actually the proceedings of a conference, but, rather, a report on a meeting of an administrative nature dealing with the corporate body, the Maryland Greenways Commission. The cataloger should apply the provisions of rule 21.1B2a rather than rule 21.1B2d to set up the catalog entry for this record. In keeping with this distinction, the serial in this example, the minutes of the Maryland Greenways Commission meeting, should not be treated as a conference publication. Accordingly, fixed field 008 position 29 is coded "0" for Non-Conference Publication.

M7

PROBLEM CONSIDERED:

Exhibition entered under the heading for a corporate body (21.1B2a)

RULE(S) CONSULTED:

AACR2R: 21.1B2

TAGGED DATA RECORD (based on OCLC #29858281)

LDR   *****cas_/22*****Ia*4500

00-05	06	07-14	15-17	18	19	20	21	22-28	29	30-32	33	34	35-37	38	39
008 940222	c	19879999	ctu	a	r			--c----	0	///	a	0	eng	-	d

→ 110 2   New Britain Museum of American Art.
→ 245 10   Invitational / ≠c New Britain Museum of American Art.
260   New Britain, Conn. : ≠b The Museum, ≠c 1987-
300   v. : ≠b ill. ; ≠c 23 cm.
362 0   1st (1987)-
500   Catalog of an annual exhibition.
610 20   New Britain Museum of American Art ≠x Exhibitions.
650 0   Art, Modern ≠y 20th century ≠z United States ≠x Exhibitions.
650 0   Art, American ≠x Exhibitions.

DISCUSSION

- Exhibitions are treated as corporate bodies according to the provisions of rule 21.1B2, category a and category d. Therefore, an exhibition emanating from a corporate body can be defined as a work of administrative nature (21.1B2a). However, this applies only in cases where the items on exhibit are held or owned exclusively by the corporate body. In this example, the catalog of the annual exhibition lists works held by the New Britain Museum of American Art. Because there is no doubt that the items on exhibit are held by the Museum, the record for the exhibition may be entered under the corporate body. In such cases, it makes no difference whether the exhibit itself is named or unnamed.

M8

PROBLEM CONSIDERED:

Unnamed exhibition entered under title (21.1B3)

RULE(S) CONSULTED:

AACR2R: 21.1B2a, 21.1B2d, 21.30E1

TAGGED DATA RECORD (based on OCLC #30349656)

LDR   *****cas_/22*****Ia*4500

	00-05	06	07-14	15-17	18	19	20	21	22-28	29	30-32	33	34	35-37	38	39
008	940429	u	19uuuuuu	nhu	u		u			--c----	0	///	a	0	eng	-	d

→ 130 0   Annual exhibition (New Hampshire Art Association)
→ 245 00   Annual exhibition / ≠c New Hampshire Art Association.
   246 14   Annual exhibition of the New Hampshire Art Association
   260   Manchester, N.H. : ≠b Currier Gallery of Art,
   300   v. : ≠b ill. ; ≠c 20 cm.
   310   Annual
   500   Catalog of the exhibition.
   500   Description based on: 23rd (1969).
   650   0   Art ≠z New England ≠x Exhibitions ≠x Catalogs.
   650   0   Art, Modern ≠y 20th century ≠x Exhibitions ≠x Catalogs.
→ 710 2   New Hampshire Art Association.
   710 2   Currier Gallery of Art.

DISCUSSION

- The exhibition in this example is unnamed, and therefore entry may not be made under the name of the exhibition (21.1B2d). The cataloger must next consider whether the work can be entered under corporate name, "New Hampshire Art Association," which appears in the chief source, in accordance with rule 21.1B2a. One should always bear in mind that very few exhibitions may be entered under the name of a corporate heading because, in most cases, when an exhibition is sponsored by a corporate body, that body does not actually own the objects in the exhibition, and, therefore, rule 21.1B2a cannot be applied. Such is the case in this example. By careful examination of the item, the cataloger has determined that the work falls outside the categories given in 21.1B2a. Therefore, since the work cannot be entered under the name of the exhibition (it is unnamed), nor under the corporate body (the objects are not owned by that body), entry must be made under title (21.1B3). An added entry is made for the sponsoring body "New Hampshire Art Association" (21.30E1).

- A uniform title is constructed for this record to distinguish this item from other serials with the same title.

M9

PROBLEM CONSIDERED:

Named festival entered under its own name (LCRI 21.1B2, category d)

RULE(S) CONSULTED:

AACR2R: 21.1B2, 21.1B2a, 21.1C1c

LCRI: 21.30E; 25.5B, p. 2

TAGGED DATA RECORD (based on OCLC #34928793)

LDR   *****cas_/22*****_a*4500

00-05	06	07-14	15-17	18	19	20	21	22-28	29	30-32	33	34	35-37	38	39
960614	u	19uuuuuu	ohu	a	r			-------	0	///	a	0	eng	-	d

008

→ 111 2   New Music & Art Festival.

→ 245 10   Annual New Music & Art Festival : ≠b [program].

246 3   Annual New Music and Art Festival : ≠b [program]

260   [Bowling Green, Ohio] : ≠b College of Musical Arts, School of Art, Bowling Green State University,

300   v. : ≠b ill. ; ≠c 28 cm.

310   Annual

500   Description based on: 10th (1989); title from cover.

611 20   New Music & Art Festival ≠x Periodicals.

→ 710 2   Bowling Green State University. ≠b College of Musical Arts.

DISCUSSION

- In example M9, the New Music & Art Festival is a named festival and it also appears in the chief source of information; therefore, the work is entered directly under the name of the festival (LCRI 21.1B2, category d). The Bowling Green State University College of Musical Arts is the body that sponsors the festival, and access to it is provided through an added entry (LCRI 21.30E).

- Had the festival not been named, main entry would have been under the sponsoring body, provided it met the condition set forth in rule 21.1B2a. Such is the case in example M10a, where the festival does not meet the conditions for being a named festival. The serial in that example contains programs and notes about an annual activity of the Worcester County Musical Association (i.e., the conditions of 21.1B2a are met), and, therefore, the main entry for the item is under the heading for that body.

- The festival in example M10b is unnamed. Although the Fire Department appears on the chief source as the sponsoring body, the publication is not entirely about the activities of the Fire Department (i.e., none of the conditions of 21.1B2 is met), and, therefore, main entry cannot be made under that body. Instead, entry is made under the title "Annual festival" (21.1C1c). A uniform title heading qualified by the corporate name is used to distinguish this work from others with the same title (LCRI 25.5B, p. 2).

M10

PROBLEM CONSIDERED:

Unnamed festivals (21.1B2)

RULE(S) CONSULTED:

AACR2R: 21.1B2a, 21.1C1c
LCRI: 25.5B, p. 2

M10a
TAGGED DATA RECORD (based on OCLC #11102892)

LDR   *****cas_/22*****Ia*4500

00-05	06	07-14	15-17	18	19	20	21	22-28	29	30-32	33	34	35-37	38	39
840829	u	1873uuuu	mau	a	r			-------	0	///	a	0	eng	-	d

008

043	n-us-ma
→ 110 2	Worcester County Musical Association.
→ 245 10	Annual festival of the Worcester County Musical Association.
246 13	Programmes of concerts and matinees ... Annual festival of the Worcester County Musical Association
260	Worcester, Mass. : ≠b The Association, ≠c 1873-
300	v. : ≠b ill. ; ≠c 23 cm.
310	Annual
362 0	16th (1873)-
→ 500	Consists of programs and historical and descriptive notes.
610 20	Worcester County Musical Association.
650 0	Concerts ≠z Massachusetts ≠z Worcester ≠x Programs.
650 0	Music festivals ≠z Massachusetts ≠z Worcester.

M10b
TAGGED DATA RECORD (based on OCLC #17677465)

LDR   *****cas_/22*****Ia*4500

00-05	06	07-14	15-17	18	19	20	21	22-28	29	30-32	33	34	35-37	38	39
880324	u	19uuuuuu	lau	a	r			-------	0	///	a	0	eng	-	d

008

043	n-us-la
→ 130 0	Annual festival (New Orleans (La.). Fire Dept.)
→ 245 00	Annual festival / ≠c New Orleans Fire Department.
260	New Orleans : ≠b The Dept.,
300	v. : ≠b ill. ; ≠c 30 cm.
310	Annual
500	Description based on: 12th (1919); title from cover.
610 10	New Orleans (La.). ≠b Fire Dept. ≠x Exhibitions.
650 0	Fairs ≠z Louisiana ≠z New Orleans.
650 0	Festivals ≠z Louisiana ≠z New Orleans.
→ 710 1	New Orleans (La.). ≠b Fire Dept.

DISCUSSION

• See example M9.

N. Added Entries

The AACR2R definition of added entry is: "An entry, additional to the main entry by which an item is represented in a catalogue; a secondary entry" (p. 615, Appendix D). There are two kinds of added entry: analytical and simple (LCRI 21.30M).

An analytical added entry is made to provide an access point to the substance of a work *contained* in the item being cataloged. Examples of analytical added entries include those for a running title, caption title, responsible body, name heading/title, etc., as well as entries that refer to a related work that includes or is included in the item being described (i.e., an "Issued with" entry, accompanying supplement not cataloged separately). With regard to tagging of analytical added entries, always use field 246 for a variant form of title added entry and field 700, 710, or 711 for a name heading or name heading/title added entry. For title added entry for a related work included in the item being cataloged, use field 730 if the entry is in the established catalog entry form; otherwise, use field 740.

A simple added entry is made to provide an access point to a related work *other than* an "Issued with" entry. These related works include parent records, supplement records, series, serials from which selected articles are collected, etc. For simple name heading/title added entries, always use field 700, 710, or 711. For simple title added entries for related work not included in the item being cataloged, use field 730 if the entries are in the established catalog entry form; otherwise, use 740 field. For simple series added entries, use 440 or 8xx field.

Added entries are made on the basis of various rules, but they may be made only when they are justified by information contained within the body of the bibliographic record (usually in a note). This information in the note does not have to conform to AACR2R choice or form of entry; it may appear in an abbreviated form, in a different language, etc. However, it is important to note that added entries cited in fields 700, 710, 711, 730, and 8xx must be in accordance with AACR2R.

EXAMPLES

N1   Added entry for varying form of title
N2   Added entry for variant access title
N3   Added entry for portion of title proper
N4   Added entry for title in "At head of title" note
N5   Added entry for parallel title and title on diskette label
N6   Added entry for current and former issuing bodies
N7   Added entry for the name of a conference

N8   Added entries for serials from which articles are selected
N9   Name/title analytical added entry
N10   Name/title added entry no longer given for variant title
N11   Added entry for supplements not in a separate record
N12   Added entry for special issues
N13   Added entry for parent record entry of a supplement
N14   Added entry for a journal title as a sponsoring body
N15   Added entry for a journal title that has the same editor as that of the item being cataloged
N16   Added entry for corporate name in vernacular form
N17   Added entry for title on inverted page
N18   Added entry for title included in the serial with no established catalog entry
N19   Added entry for title included in the serial with established catalog entry
N20   Added entry for related record in uniform title heading

N1

PROBLEM CONSIDERED:

Added entry for varying form of title (21.30J1)

RULE(S) CONSULTED:

LCRI: 21.30J, p. 25

Cover

> **journal of
> studies in
> technical
> careers**
>
> Volume 1   Fall 1978

TAGGED DATA RECORD (based on OCLC #4381548)

LDR   *****nas_/22*****Ia*4500

	00-05	06	07-14	15-17	18	19	20	21	22-28	29	30-32	33	34	35-37	38	39
008	781117	d	19781995	ilu	q	r	l	p	-------	0	///	a	0	eng	-	d

022 0	0163-3252
245 00	Journal of studies in technical careers.
→ 246 17	JSTC ≠f <1988->
260	Carbondale, Ill. : ≠b School of Technical Careers, Southern Illinois University at Carbondale, ≠c 1978-1995.
300	15 v. ; ≠c 23 cm.
310	Quarterly
362 0	Vol. 1, no. 1 (fall 1978)-
362 1	Ceased with v. 15, no. 4 published in Dec. 1995.
500	Title from cover.
550	Issued by: School of Technical Careers, 1978- ; College of Technical Careers, <1988->
650 0	Technical education ≠x Periodicals.
650 0	Vocational education ≠x Periodicals.
710 2	Southern Illinois University at Carbondale. ≠b School of Technical Careers.
710 2	Southern Illinois University at Carbondale. ≠b College of Technical Careers.

DISCUSSION

- In this example, the cover serves as the chief source of information. The title chosen as title proper appears in full form on the cover of the work. However, there is also a running title in the form of an initialism, and an added entry is needed to provide access to this variant title (21.30J1; LCRI 21.30J, p. 25).
- Field 246 is used for a varying form of title. First indicator value "1" is used to specify that the added entry for the variant title is to be derived from the 246 field and a note is needed to explain the type of title in the added entry. The actual working of this note depends on the value assigned to the second indicator. In this example, value "7" is assigned and a note is generated with the display constant "Running title:" followed by the title "JSTC."

N2

PROBLEM CONSIDERED:

Added entry for variant access title (21.30J1)

RULE(S) CONSULTED:

LCRI: 21.30J

```
                                              Products and
                                              Services from

  Cover              ERS-NASS
                                              USDA's
                                              Economics
                                              Agencies
                                              Annual issue 1995
```

TAGGED DATA RECORD (based on OCLC #33902661)

LDR   *****nas_/22*****_a*4500

00-05	06	07-14	15-17	18	19	20	21	22-28	29	30-32	33	34	35-37	38	39
008 951213	c	19959999	dcu	a	r			---bc-f	0	///	a	0	eng	-	d

→ 245 00 Products and services from ERS-NASS
→ 246 2   Products and services from Economic Research Service - National
          Agricultural Statistics Service
→ 246 30 ERS-NASS
→ 246 13 Products and services from USDA's economic agencies
→ 246 17 ERS-NASS catalog
   260   Washington, DC : ≠b U.S. Dept. of Agriculture ; ≠a Herndon, VA : ≠b
          ERS-NASS [distributor], ≠c 1995?-
   300   v. : ≠b ill. ; ≠c 28 cm.
   310   Annual
   362 0 Annual issue 1995-
   500   Title from cover.
   525   Kept up to date between annual issues by 2 or 3 supplements.
   650 0 Agriculture ≠x Economic aspects ≠x Bibliography ≠x Catalogs.
   650 0 Government publications ≠z United States ≠x Bibliography ≠x Catalogs.
   710 1 United States. ≠b Dept. of Agriculture.
   710 1 United States. ≠b Dept. of Agriculture. ≠b Economic Research Service.
   710 1 United States. ≠b National Agricultural Statistics Service.
   780 00 ≠t Agriculture economics reports ≠w (DLC)sn87043050 ≠w
          (OCoLC)11720513

DISCUSSION

- One type of variant access title is one that may not actually appear on the item
  being described, but that might reasonably be considered by some users to be
  the title of the publication, and that, therefore, merits a title added entry to provide access for such users (21.30J1). There are other situations when access
  should be provided for a variant form of title, with the following representing
  the most common: an ampersand in the title proper versus a spelled-out word;
  abbreviated words versus their full forms; initialisms and letters with separating punctuation versus those without separating punctuation; numbers or

dates, signs, and symbols versus spelled-out forms; one-word compounds versus two-word compounds; hyphenated words versus unhyphenated words, etc. All these situations require additional access for the variant form.

- In keeping with the guidelines given in LCRI 21.30J, added entries are made to provide additional access to portion of the title proper ("ERS-NASS"), other title ("Products and services from USDA's economic agencies"), and running title ("ERS-NASS catalog").
- A title added entry with the corresponding spelled-out form of the abbreviated words, "Products and services from Economic Research Service - National Agricultural Statistics Service," is also input (LCRI 21.30J). Field 246 first indicator value "2" is used to suppress a note, at the same time not generating a variant title added entry. This variant title added entry may be useful for online searchability.

N3

PROBLEM CONSIDERED:

Added entry for portion of title proper (LCRI 21.30J, p. 13)

RULE(S) CONSULTED:

LCRI: 21.30J, p. 12

TAGGED DATA RECORD (based on OCLC #34371137)

LDR   *****cas_/22*****_a*4500

00-05	06	07-14	15-17	18	19	20	21	22-28	29	30-32	33	34	35-37	38	39
960314	c	19969999	mdu	q	x	1	p	-------	0	///	a	0	eng	-	d

008

022 0	1091-9856 ≠y 0899-1499
245 00	INFORMS journal on computing.
→ 246 13	JOC
→ 246 3	Institute for Operations Research and the Management Sciences journal on computing
→ 246 30	Journal on computing
260	Linthicum, MD : ≠b INFORMS, ≠c c1996-
300	v. : ≠b ill ; ≠c 28 cm.
310	Four no. a year
362 0	Vol. 8, no. 1 (winter 1996)-
500	Title from cover.
500	"Charting new directions in OR and CS."
650 0	Operations research ≠x Data processing ≠x Periodicals.
710 2	Institute for Operations Research and the Management Sciences.
780 00	≠t ORSA journal on computing ≠x 0899-1499 ≠w (OCoLC)18006127 ≠w (DLC)sf93091641

Cover

Charting New Directions in OR and CS

DISCUSSION

- The cataloger must use discretion in determining whether to make an additional added entry for a portion of a title proper. General guidelines for this practice are found in LCRI 21.30J, p. 13. An added entry for a portion of the title proper should be made when:

  The title proper contains an alternative title.
  The title proper contains a part or designation of a part, or both.
  Some users might consider the portion of a title proper to be the title proper, especially when the title transcription begins with an author or a corporate body's name.

- In this example, the title proper is "INFORMS journal on computing." However, since the word "INFORMS" does not link grammatically with the rest of the title proper, it is possible that some users might consider the phrase "Journal on computing" to be the title of the serial. An added entry, therefore, is made for this phrase. When making an added entry for a portion of the title, use field 246 first indicator value "3" so that no note but a title added entry will be generated from the field. The second indicator value should be set to "0" to indicate that the title in this field is a portion of the full title.

- In this record, two other title added entries are made. The first is for the initialism form of the title. Note that the initialism form of the title, "JOC," appears prominently in the chief source according to typography and layout, and it is thus reasonable to assume that the serial may be known by this initialism. An added entry is made to provide access under this title. Use field 246 second indicator value "3" to generate a display constant "Other title:".

- The other title added entry "Institute for Operations Research and the Management Sciences journal on computing" is used to provide variant access for the title proper. Because the title proper "INFORMS journal on computing" incorporates the initialism of the corporate body, it is necessary to provide variant access for the title proper with the spelled-out form of the initialism (LCRI 21.30J, p. 12).

N4

PROBLEM CONSIDERED:

Added entry for title in "At head of title" note (LCRI 21.30J, p. 21)

TAGGED DATA RECORD (based on OCLC #9883345)

LDR   *****cas_/22*****_a*4500

	00-05	06	07-14	15-17	18	19	20	21	22-28	29	30-32	33	34	35-37	38	39
008	830907	c	19839999	dcu		x	l		---rh--	0	///	a	0	eng	-	d

022 0	0882-2506 ≠y 0065-9827
043	n-us---
110 2	American Psychiatric Association.
245 10	Biographical directory.
→ 246 1	≠i At head of title: ≠a Fellows and members of the American Psychiatric Association
260	Washington, D.C. : ≠b American Psychiatric Association, ≠c c1983-
300	v. ; ≠c 29 cm.
310	Irregular
362 0	1983-
610 20	American Psychiatric Association ≠x Directories.
610 20	American Psychiatric Association ≠x Biography.
650 0	Psychiatrists ≠x Directories.
650 0	Psychiatrists ≠x Biography.
780 00	American Psychiatric Association. ≠t Biographical directory of fellows & members of the American Psychiatric Association ≠x 0065-9827 ≠w (DLC)63012595 ≠w (OCoLC)1325847

Title page

**Fellows and members
of the
American Psychiatric Association**

Biographical Directory
1983

Washington, DC

DISCUSSION

- In this example, the phrase "Fellows and members of the American Psychiatric Association" appears above the title "Biographical directory." The latter has been chosen as the title proper of the journal. But, because users may assume the phrase incorporating the name of the issuing body is the title of the journal, that phrase should be recorded in an "At head of title" note. In addition, this phrase contributes to the identification of the journal. For these reasons, it should be given a title added entry (LCRI 21.30J, p. 21).
- An "At head of title" added entry is input in field 246 when the added entry is for a variant title. Always use first indicator value "1" to generate a note for the

variant title preceded by the text "At head of title:" in subfield ≠i. Second indicator value blank should be used whenever subfield ≠i is used. An "At head of title:" note may be input in a 500 General Note, when the information at the head of the title is a corporate name, or anything other than a variant title.

N5

PROBLEM CONSIDERED:

Added entry for parallel title and title on diskette label (LCRI 21.30J, p. 24)

TAGGED DATA RECORD (based on OCLC #32714672)

LDR   *****cas_/22*****_a*4500

00-05	06	07-14	15-17	18	19	20	21	22-28	29	30-32	33	34	35-37	38	39
950627	c	19959999	onc	a	r			--r---f	0	///	a	0	eng	-	d

008

00	01-04	05	06-08	09	10	11	12-17
m	////	g	---	-	/	0	//////

006   (computer file)

022	1201-611X
041 0	engfre
043	n-cn---
245 00	Symbols and interlibrary loan policies in Canada / ≠c National Library of Canada = Sigles et politiques de prêt entre bibliothèques au Canada / Bibliothèque nationale du Canada.
→ 246 1	≠i Title on English-language diskette label: ≠a Interlibrary loan policies in Canada
→ 246 1	≠i Title on French-language diskette label: ≠a Politiques de prêt entre bibliothèques au Canada
→ 246 31	Sigles et politiques de prêt entre bibliothèques au Canada
260	Ottawa : ≠b National Library of Canada, ≠c 1995-
300	v. ; ≠c 28 cm.
310	Annual
362 0	Jan. 1995-
→ 515	The 1995 issue contains a print version of the library symbols and diskette versions of the Interlibrary loan policies in WordPerfect 5 format.
546	In English and French.
580	Merger of: Interlibrary loan policies in Canada; Politiques de prêt entre bibliothèques au Canada; and: Symbols of Canadian libraries.
650 0	Libraries ≠z Canada ≠x Abbreviations.
650 0	Interlibrary loans ≠z Canada ≠x Policy statements.
650 0	Electronic mail systems ≠z Canada ≠x Directories.
710 2	National Library of Canada.
780 14	≠t Interlibrary loan policies in Canada ≠x 1192-7127 ≠w (DLC)94651219 ≠w (CaOONL)930722418 ≠w (OCoLC)28395969
780 14	≠t Politiques de prêt entre bibliothèques au Canada ≠x 1192-7135
780 14	≠t Symbols of Canadian libraries ≠x 0316-1196 ≠w (OCoLC)02248081 ≠w (DLC)85647019 ≠w (CaOONL)750325755E

Title page

> **Symbols and interlibrary loan policies in Canada**
> **Sigles et politiques de prêt**
> **entre bibliothèques au Canada**
>
> National Library of Canada
> Bibliothèque nationale du Canada
>
> *January/Janvier 1995*

DISCUSSION

- This serial publication "Symbols and interlibrary loan policies in Canada" contains information on interlibrary loan policies issued on two diskettes. One is in French and has a French title, and the other is in English and carries an English title. Since it is reasonable to expect that users may search for the publication under the diskette titles, two variant title added entries are given in the record to provide access to each of the titles on the English- and French-language diskette labels (LCRI 21.30J, p. 24).

- Use field 246 for varying forms of title associated with the item. First indicator value "1" specifies that both a note and a title added entry are to be generated from the field. Since a special display is needed in this case to indicate the type of title recorded in this field, the second indicator is blank, and information about the type of title ("Title on English-language diskette label:") is input in subfield ≠i, followed by the title in subfield ≠a.

- The third 246 field in the record is for the parallel title from field 245. Always use first indicator value "3" to show that no note but a title added entry is to be generated from the field. Second indicator value is "1" for parallel title (LCRI 21.30J, p. 24).

- Field 515 serves several purposes. Besides describing irregularities and peculiarities in numbering or publishing patterns, it may also be used to show that a publication is issued in parts or revised editions. The 1995 issue of this serial contains both a print version and diskette versions of some parts of the item being cataloged, and field 515 is used for the note conveying that information.

N6

PROBLEM CONSIDERED:

Added entry for current and former issuing bodies (21.30E1)

TAGGED DATA RECORD (based on OCLC #10485375)

LDR   *****cas_/22*****Ia*4500

	00-05	06	07-14	15-17	18	19	20	21	22-28	29	30-32	33	34	35-37	38	39
008	840305	c	19759999	azu	u	u	l		--r----	0	///	a	0	eng	-	d

022 0   0749-050X

043   n-us--- ≠a n-cn---

245 00   Directory of information and referral services in the United States and
          Canada.

→ 260   Phoenix, Ariz. : ≠b Alliance of Information and Referral Services, ≠c c1975-

300   v. ; ≠c 22 cm.

362 0   [1975]-

→ 550   Issued by: Alliance of Information and Referral Systems, 1984-

650 0   Social service ≠z United States ≠x Directories.

650 0   Social service ≠z Canada ≠x Directories.

→ 710 2 Alliance of Information and Referral Services (U.S.)

→ 710 2 Alliance of Information and Referral Systems (U.S.)

<table>
<tr><td>Title page
of current issue</td><td>

DIRECTORY
of
Information and Referral Services
in the
United States and Canada
1984

Alliance of Information and Referral Systems

</td></tr>
</table>

DISCUSSION

- When a work is entered under title, make an added entry under the heading for
  a prominently named responsible body (21.30E1). In this example, the corporate body "Alliance of Information and Referral Services" appeared on the
  chief source of information as the issuing body until 1984, and then changed
  to "Alliance of Information and Referral Systems." Added entries should be
  made for each form of the corporate name (see also CCM 4.8.3). Note that
  added entries for corporate bodies should always be justified by their presence

in field 245 (title and statement of responsibility area), field 260 (publication, distribution, etc., area), field 550 (Issuing Body Note), or a 500 General Note.

- Field 710 is used for a corporate name added entry. Use first indicator value "2" for a corporate name in direct order. The second indicator is blank for both entries, since neither of them is for an analytic.

N7

PROBLEM CONSIDERED:

Added entry for the name of a conference (LCRI 21.30J, p. 7)

RULE(S) CONSULTED:

AACR2R: 1.1B3, 21.1B2d, 21.30J1
LCRI: 21.1B2, category d; 21.30E

<table>
<tr><td>Title page</td><td>

**Symposium
for the Marketing of Higher
Education**

1991
Chicago, Illinois
American Marketing Association
</td></tr>
</table>

TAGGED DATA RECORD (based on OCLC #33129378)

LDR   *****cas_/22*****Ia*4500

	00-05	06	07-14	15-17	18	19	20	21	22-28	29	30-32	33	34	35-37	38	39
008	950914	c	19899999	ilu	a	r			-------	1	///	a	0	eng	-	d

043		n-us---
111	2	Symposium for the Marketing of Higher Education.
→ 245	10	Symposium for the Marketing of Higher Education : ≠b [proceedings].
260		Chicago, Ill. : ≠b American Marketing Association,
300		v. : ≠b ill. ; ≠c 28 cm.
310		Annual
362	1	Began in 1989.
490	1	Proceedings series
500		Description based on: 1991.
650	0	Education, Higher ≠z United States ≠x Marketing ≠x Congresses.
650	0	College publicity ≠z United States ≠x Congresses.
650	0	College students ≠x Recruiting ≠z United States ≠x Congresses.
710	2	American Marketing Association.
830	0	Proceedings series (American Marketing Association)

DISCUSSION

- In this example, no title appears on the chief source except the name of the conference "Symposium for the Marketing of Higher Education." Therefore, the name of the conference is treated as the title proper (1.1B3). Since this conference carries its own name and the name appears on the chief source of information, the work is entered under the name of the conference as a corporate body (21.1B2d; LCRI 21.1B2, category d).
- Whenever a work is entered under a name heading, according to Library of Congress practice, a tracing must be made for the title proper, even though the title proper is essentially the same or even identical to the main entry heading (LCRI 21.30J, p. 7). Field 245 first indicator value "1" generates a title added entry, which, in this case, is the same as the conference name. (See example M5 for a case where the provisions of AACR2R 21.30J1 are followed.)
- If a conference publication is not entered under the conference name because the name does not appear on the chief source of information, make an added entry if the name of the conference appears anywhere in the item (LCRI 21.30E).

N8

PROBLEM CONSIDERED:

Added entries for serials from which articles are selected (LCRI 21.28B)

RULE(S) CONSULTED:

AACR2R: 21.30G1

TAGGED DATA RECORD (based on OCLC #8357542)

LDR *****cas_/22*****Ia*4500

008

00-05	06	07-14	15-17	18	19	20	21	22-28	29	30-32	33	34	35-37	38	39
820421	c	19829999	nyu	a	r	z	p	-------	0	///	a	0	eng	-	d

022 0732-4448
043 a-cc---
245 00 Current topics in Chinese science. ≠n Section G, ≠p Medical science.
246 30 Medical science
260 New York : ≠b Gordon and Breach, ≠c 1982-
300 v. : ≠b ill. ; ≠c 25 cm.
310 Annual
362 0 Vol. 1 (1982)-
→580 Selected articles translated from: K'o hsüeh t'ung pao, and Scientia sinica.
650 0 Medicine ≠z China ≠x Periodicals.
650 0 Medicine, Chinese ≠x Periodicals.
→730 0 K'o hsüeh t'ung pao.
→730 0 Scientia sinica.
787 1 ≠t K'o hsüeh t'ung pao ≠w (OCoLC)1643919
787 1 ≠t Scientia sinica ≠w (OCoLC)6494586

DISCUSSION

- Some serials consist of selected articles from one or more other serials. This information should be given in a Linking Entry Complexity Note, field 580. If no more than three related serials are involved, a simple added entry is made for each of them; if four or more different serials are involved, in general no added entry should be made for any of them (LCRI 21.28B).
- This serial publication contains selected articles translated from two related serials "K'o hsüeh t'ung pao" and "Scientia sinica." Two simple added entries are given in the record (21.30G1).
- The field used for an added entry for a related work depends on the form of the entry. If the entry for the related work is under a person, corporate body, or conference name, use field 700, 710, or 711, respectively. If the related work is entered under title, then use field 740 or 730 as appropriate. In this case, the two related works are entered under the established catalog entry form of the title, and, therefore, field 730 is used for the added entries. The first indicator indicates the number of nonfiling characters and is always set to value "0," since Library of Congress practice is to omit initial articles in uniform titles. The second indicator is blank, since the added entry is not analytical.

N9

PROBLEM CONSIDERED:

Name/title analytical added entry (21.30M1)

RULE(S) CONSULTED:

AACR2R: 21.29C, App. D (p. 620)

TAGGED DATA RECORD (based on OCLC #6897148)

LDR   *****cas_/22*****Ia*4500

00-05	06	07-14	15-17	18	19	20	21	22-28	29	30-32	33	34	35-37	38	39
801104	u	1977uuuu	ph	u	u		p	--g----	0	///	a	0	eng	-	d

008

043	a-ph--- ≠a d------
245 00	Law and development.
260	Quezon City, Philippines : ≠b University of the Philippines Law Center, ≠c 1977-
300	v. ; ≠c 26 cm.
362 0	1977-
→ 500	"Journal of the Asian Council for Law and Development."
→ 520	Includes Annual report of the Asian Council for Law and Development.
650 0	Law ≠z Philippines ≠x Periodicals.
650 0	Law ≠z Developing countries ≠x Periodicals.
710 2	University of the Philippines. ≠b Law Center.
→ 710 2	Asian Council for Law and Development.
→ 710 22	Asian Council for Law and Development. ≠t Annual report.

Law and Development

1977

University of the Philippines Law Center
Quezon City, Philippines

Journal of the Asian Council for Law and Development

DISCUSSION

- In this example, "Law and development" is chosen as the title proper. The phrase "Journal of the Asian Council for Law and Development" is not treated as other title information. According to the definition in AACR2R (p. 620, Appendix D), other title information includes any phrase appearing in conjunction with the title proper. Because the phrase in question here appears at the bottom of the chief source, its position could not be considered to be "in conjunction" with the title proper, and, therefore, it is not transcribed in field 245 as other title information but is instead included in a 500 General Note field.
- According to 21.29C, an added entry should be made under the heading for the body, since users may suppose that the journal would be found under the body rather than under the title chosen as main entry (see also CCM 4.8.3).
- Field 710 is used for a corporate name added entry. Since the corporate body "Asian Council for Law and Development" is established in direct order, use first indicator value "2." The second indicator is blank since the added entry here is not for an analytic.
- However, a second added entry is made in this record for an analytic. Note that the summary note states: "Includes Annual report of the Asian Council for Law and Development." In accordance with 21.30M1, when an item being cataloged contains another work, make an analytical added entry for the other work. In this example, "Law and development" includes "Annual report of the Asian Council for Law and Development," and, therefore, an analytical added entry should be made for the annual report. Since the annual report is entered under the corporate name "Asian Council for Law and Development," the added entry given is a name/title analytical added entry, using field 710 with second indicator value "2" (see also CCM 7.5.1). For discussion of a title analytical added entry, see examples N18 and N19.

N10

PROBLEM CONSIDERED:
Name/title added entry no longer given for variant title (LCRI 21.30J, p. 14)

RULE(S) CONSULTED:
AACR2R: 21.1B2d

TAGGED DATA RECORD (based on OCLC #3490335)

LDR   *****cas_/22*****Ia*4500

00-05	06	07-14	15-17	18	19	20	21	22-28	29	30-32	33	34	35-37	38	39
008 771214	c	19779999	nyu	a	r	1		-------	1	///	a	0	eng	-	d

022 0   0149-645X

111 2   IEEE MTT-S International Microwave Symposium.

→ 245 10   IEEE MTT-S International Microwave Symposium digest.

→ 246 3   Digest

246 1   ≠i Other title: ≠a IEEE MTT International Microwave Symposium digest

260   New York : ≠b Institute of Electrical and Electronic Engineers, ≠c 1977-

300   v. : ≠b ill. ; ≠c 28 cm.

362 0   1977-

500   Published as: IEEE MTT International Microwave Symposium digest, 1988.

515   Some vols. issued in parts.

650 0   Microwaves ≠x Congresses.

650 0   Microwave devices ≠x Congresses.

710 2   Institute of Electrical and Electronics Engineers.

780 00   IEEE MTT-S International Microwave Symposium. ≠t IEEE MTT-S International Microwave Symposium digest of technical papers ≠x 0149-6298 ≠w (DLC)77645127 ≠w (OCoLC)3509048

Title page

1996 IEEE MTT-S INTERNATIONAL MICROWAVE SYMPOSIUM DIGEST

Volume 1

June 17 - 21, 1996
Moscone Convention Center
San Francisco, California

DISCUSSION

• In this example, the work is entered under the name of the symposium, since the name "IEEE MTT-S International Microwave Symposium" appears on the title page (21.1B2d). The title proper "IEEE MTT-S International Microwave Symposium Digest" is transcribed as it actually appears in the chief source. A title added entry is needed for "Digest," a portion of the title proper (LCRI 21.30J, p. 14), and field 246 is used for this purpose. Because the work is entered under the conference name, one might assume that added entries for the variant forms of title should also be entered under the conference name.

Name/title added entries such as these are no longer given in catalog records (see CCM 7.5.3).

- Although name/title added entries are not currently used only for variant titles, they are used for related works entered under corporate or conference names. Since fields 730 and 740 cannot generate a name/title added entry, whenever a name/title added entry is needed, a 700, 710, or 711 field must be used (see example N9).

N11

PROBLEM CONSIDERED:

Added entry for supplements not in a separate record (LCRI 21.28B)

RULE(S) CONSULTED:

AACR2R: 12.7B7j
LCRI: 12.0A4e; 21.30J, p. 5

TAGGED DATA RECORD (based on OCLC #3226184)

LDR   *****cas_/22*****Ia*4500

00-05	06	07-14	15-17	18	19	20	21	22-28	29	30-32	33	34	35-37	38	39
770829	c	19699999	miu		x	l		-------	0	///	a	0	eng	-	d

008

022 0	0737-7843 ≠z 0730-546X
245 00	Periodical title abbreviations.
260	Detroit, Mich. : ≠b Gale Research Co., ≠c 1969-
300	v. ; ≠c 23-29 cm.
310	Irregular
362 0	[1st ed.]-
500	"Covering periodical title abbreviations in science, the social sciences, the humanities, law, medicine, religion, library science, engineering, education, business, art and many other fields."
→ 515	Issued in two or more vols.: v. 1, By abbreviation; v. 2, By title; v. 3, New periodical title abbreviations
→ 525	Kept up to date by an annual supplement: New periodical title abbreviations, 3rd ed.-
650 0	Periodicals ≠x Abbreviations of titles.
710 2	Gale Research Company.
→ 740 02	New periodical title abbreviations.

Vol. 1

ISSN 0737-7843

Periodical Title Abbreviations: By Abbreviation

Covering: Periodical Title Abbreviations, Database
Abbreviations, and Selected Monograph Abbreviations
in Science, the Social Sciences, the Humanities, Medicine,
Religion, Library Science, Engineering, Education,
Business, Art and Many Other Fields

NINTH EDITION

Volume 1

Gale Research Inc. DETROIT•WASHINGTON, D.C.•LONDON

Vol. 2

ISSN 0737-7843

Periodical Title Abbreviations: By Title

Covering: Periodical Title Abbreviations, Database
Abbreviations, and Selected Monograph Abbreviations
in Science, the Social Sciences, the Humanities, Medicine,
Religion, Library Science, Engineering, Education,
Business, Art and Many Other Fields

NINTH EDITION

Volume 2

Gale Research Inc. DETROIT•WASHINGTON, D.C.•LONDON

Vol. 3

ISSN 0737-7843

New Periodical Title Abbreviations

**Volume 3 of
Periodical Title Abbreviations, Ninth Edition
Supplement**

Covering: Periodical Title Abbreviations, Database
Abbreviations, and Selected Monograph Abbreviations
in Science, the Social Sciences, the Humanities, Medicine,
Religion, Library Science, Engineering, Education,
Business, Art and Many Other Fields

Entries Arranged both by Abbreviations and by Title

Gale Research Inc. DETROIT•WASHINGTON, D.C.•LONDON

DISCUSSION

- In this example, the annual supplement carries its own title "New periodical title abbreviations" and is issued as volume 3 of the parent serial "Periodical title abbreviations."
- The annual nature of this supplement would be justification for describing it in a separate record; however, because the publisher called the supplement "volume 3," it appears that the intention was for it to be kept together with the two main volumes. For that reason, a separate record is not created for the supplement (LCRI 12.0A4e). Instead, a supplement note is included in the record for the parent serial (12.7B7j). Field 525 is used for a supplement note when the supplement is not separately described.
- An added entry is made for a supplement with a different title from the parent serial that is not cataloged in a separate record (LCRI 21.28B). (Note that an

added entry is not necessary for a supplement cataloged in a separate record, but in that case a linking field 770 is required.) Field 740 should be used for the added entry (LCRI 21.30J, p. 5). First indicator value "0" is used when no initial articles are present in the title entry. Second indicator value "2" is used for an analytical added entry, since the supplement is issued as part of and contained in the parent serial.

N12

PROBLEM CONSIDERED:

Added entry for special issues (21.30M1)

TAGGED DATA RECORD (based on OCLC #2250813)

LDR   *****cas_/22*****Ia*4500

00-05	06	07-14	15-17	18	19	20	21	22-28	29	30-32	33	34	35-37	38	39
760620	c	19689999	enk	m	r	z	p	-------	0	///	a	0	eng	-	d

008

022   0010-4485
245 00   Computer aided design.
246 3   Computer-aided design ≠f <1985->
246 13   CAD
260   Oxford : ≠b Butterworth-Heinemann, ≠c 1968-
300   v. : ≠b ill. ; ≠c 30 cm.
310   Monthly, ≠b <Jan. 1992->
321   Quarterly
321   Bimonthly, ≠b <1981->
321   10 no. a year, ≠b <1985->
362 0   Vol. 1, no. 1 (autumn 1968)-
→ 500   Issues for Dec. <1985-> have also title: Computer-aided design international directory.
650   0 Engineering design ≠z Data processing ≠z Periodicals.
650   0 Computer graphics ≠x Periodicals.
→ 730 02 Computer-aided design international directory.

DISCUSSION

• When a work being cataloged contains another work, an analytical added entry should be made to provide access to that other work (21.30M1). In this example, "Computer-aided design international directory" is a special issue contained within the December 1985 issue of the serial publication "Computer aided design." Note that this is not a question of a variant title for the publication, which would require an added entry in field 246, with subfields ≠i and ≠a. Rather, in this case, the name of the special issue should be recorded in the note area and given an analytical added entry. Also note that, since no linking entry is made for this record, field 580 (Linking Entry Complexity Note), should not be used; instead, such information is noted in field 500.

• The next task of the cataloger is to decide whether the added entry should be entered in field 700, 710, 711, 730, or 740. The field used depends on the form of the entry. If the entry for a work is under a person, corporate body, or conference name, use field 700, 710, or 711, respectively. If it is entered under title, then use field 740 or 730 as appropriate. In this case, "Computer-aided design international directory" is entered under title in catalog entry form (i.e., an established heading is available for this title in the catalogs), and, therefore, field 730 is used for the added entry. The first indicator is for the number of nonfiling characters and is always set to value "0," since Library of Congress practice is to omit initial articles in uniform titles. Second indicator value "2" is used for an analytical added entry.

N13

PROBLEM CONSIDERED:

Added entry for parent record entry of a supplement (21.30G1)

RULE(S) CONSULTED:

LCRI: 21.28B

TAGGED DATA RECORD (based on OCLC #20942966)

LDR   *****cas_/22*****Ia*4500

00-05	06	07-14	15-17	18	19	20	21	22-28	29	30-32	33	34	35-37	38	39
900123	d	19891994	dcu	a	r	0		------i	1	///	a	0	eng	-	d

(008 field)

022	1014-7268
043	d------
111 2	World Bank Conference on Development Economics.
245 10	Proceedings of the World Bank Annual Conference on Development Economics.
260	Washington, D.C. : ≠b International Bank for Reconstruction and Development/World Bank, ≠c c1990-c1995.
300	6 v. : ≠b ill. ; ≠c 26 cm.
310	Annual
362 0	1989-1994.
500	Title from cover.
515	Vols. for 1989-1994 called also 1st-6th annual conference.
530	Also available on microfilm from University Microfilms.
→ 580	Supplement to: World Bank economic review, and: World Bank research observer.
651 0	Developing countries ≠x Economic conditions ≠x Congresses.
651 0	Developing countries ≠x Economic policies ≠x Congresses.
710 2	World Bank.
→ 730 0	World Bank economic review.
→ 730 0	World Bank research observer.
→ 772 1	≠t World Bank economic review ≠x 0258-6770 ≠w (DLC)86659557 ≠w (OCoLC)13534968
→ 772 1	≠t World Bank research observer ≠x 0257-3032 ≠w (DLC)86643528 ≠w (OCoLC)12303480
785 00	World Bank Conference on Development Economics. ≠t Annual World Bank Conference on Development Economics ≠x 1020-4407 ≠w (DLC)96657620 ≠w (OCoLC)34530077

> **Proceedings of the World Bank
> Annual Conference
> on
> Development Economics**
>
> **1989**
>
> *Supplement to The World Bank Economic Review
> and The World Bank Research Observer*

Cover

DISCUSSION

- When cataloging a supplement that is closely related to another work, always make an added entry under the heading for the related work (21.30G1). However, on the record for the related work, do not make an added entry for the supplement. On that record, make a linking entry for the supplement in field 770 (LCRI 21.28B).

- In this example, the work "Proceedings of the World Bank Annual Conference on Development Economics" is issued as a supplement to two other works, "World Bank economic review" and "World Bank research observer." This information is recorded in field 580 (Linking Entry Complexity Note). Because neither of the related works is contained in the item being cataloged, simple added entries under the headings for these two related publications should be made (21.30G1).

- Field 730 is used for an added entry in established catalog entry form. First indicator value "0" is used for an added entry without an initial article. Second indicator value blank is used for a simple added entry.

- A link is made in field 772 for the parent publication when the item in hand is a supplement or special issue cataloged as a separate record. First indicator value "1" is used so that no note will be generated, since a note for display is already recorded in field 580. The second indicator is undefined. Because the two publications are entered directly under title, subfield ≠t is used. Subfield ≠x (International Standard Serial Number) and subfield ≠w (Record Control Number) should also be input whenever available at the time of cataloging.

N14

PROBLEM CONSIDERED:

Added entry for a journal title as a sponsoring body (21.30H1)

RULE(S) CONSULTED:

AACR2R: 12.7B6

TAGGED DATA RECORD (based on OCLC #7626119)

LDR   *****cas_/22*****Ia*4500

00-05	06	07-14	15-17	18	19	20	21	22-28	29	30-32	33	34	35-37	38	39
810729	c	19819999	nju	a	r	1		-------	1	///	a	0	eng	-	d

008

022 0   0739-1471
111 2   National Online Meeting.
245 10   Proceedings / ≠c National Online Meeting.
246 14   Proceedings of the ... National Online Meeting
260   Medford, NJ : ≠b Learned Information, ≠c c1981-
300   v. : ≠b ill. ; ≠c 25 cm.
310   Annual
362 0   2nd (1981)-
500   Abstracts from the first National Online Information Meeting, Mar. 25-27, 1980, were published as: National Online Information Meeting: collected abstracts. Papers from that meeting were not published in the form of a proceedings volume.
→ 550   Sponsored by: On-line review.
650 0   Online data processing ≠x Congresses.
→ 730 0   On-line review.

Title page

> **2nd National
> ONLINE
> MEETING**
>
> **PROCEEDINGS—1981**
>
> *Sponsored by*
> **On-line Review**
>
> Learned Information, Inc.
> Medford, NJ

DISCUSSION

- It is common for conferences to be associated with one or more sponsoring corporate bodies or even another journal. When the names of such sponsors do not appear in the title and statement of responsibility area, make notes on them (12.7B6). Also make added entries under their respective headings if they provide important access points for the identification of the item being cataloged (21.30H1).
- Use field 550 (Issuing Body Note) to record information about conference sponsors. In this case, the proceedings of the National Online Meeting are sponsored by "On-line review," the international journal of On-line Information Systems. An added entry is made for the journal using field 730, since a catalog entry form has been established for the journal.

N15

PROBLEM CONSIDERED:

Added entry for a journal title that has the same editor as that of the item being cataloged (21.30G1).

TAGGED DATA RECORD (based on OCLC #30655416)

LDR   *****cas_/22*****Ia*4500

	00-05	06	07-14	15-17	18	19	20	21	22-28	29	30-32	33	34	35-37	38	39
008	940623	c	19939999	dcu	a	r			---fs--	0	///	a	0	eng	-	d

043		n-us---
245	04	The Aviation & aerospace almanac.
246	3	Aviation and aerospace almanac
260		Washington, D.C. : ≠b Aviation Week Group Newsletters, McGraw-Hill, ≠c c1993-
300		v. ; ≠c 23 cm.
310		Annual
362	0	1993 ed.-
→ 550		Compiled by the editors of Aviation daily and Aerospace daily.
650	0	Aeronautics ≠z United States ≠x Handbooks, manuals, etc.
650	0	Airlines ≠z United States ≠x Handbooks, manuals, etc.
650	0	Aerospace industries ≠z United States ≠x Handbooks, manuals, etc.
650	0	Aeronautics ≠x Handbooks, manuals, etc.
650	0	Airlines ≠x Handbooks, manuals, etc.
650	0	Aerospace industries ≠x Handbooks, manuals, etc.
→ 730	0	Aviation daily.
→ 730	0	Aerospace daily.

DISCUSSION

- This serial publication is compiled by the editors of two other related journals (see field 550). In cases where the item being cataloged is indirectly related to another, an added entry may be made under the heading for the related work (21.30G1). Hence, two added entries are made in this record under the headings for the related journals "Aviation daily" and "Aerospace daily" (see also CCM 7.5.2b).

- Because the titles of both the related journals are entered in established catalog entry form, field 730 is used for the added entries.

N16

PROBLEM CONSIDERED:

Added entry for corporate name in vernacular form (24.3A1)

RULE(S) CONSULTED:

LCRI: 21.30E

TAGGED DATA RECORD (based on OCLC #1624094)

LDR   *****cas_/22*****Ia*4500

00-05	06	07-14	15-17	18	19	20	21	22-28	29	30-32	33	34	35-37	38	39
750914	c	19649999	dk	f	r	z	p	-------	0	///	b	0	eng	-	d

008

022 0	0078-5326
043	e-dk---
245 00	Ophelia.
→ 260	Helsingør, Denmark : ≠b Marine Biological Laboratory, ≠c 1964-
300	v. : ≠b ill. ; ≠c 26 cm.
310	Vol. 1 (May 1964)-
→ 500	At head of title, 1964-75: University of Copenhagen.
500	"International journal of marine biology."
650 0	Marine biology ≠x Periodicals.
→ 710 2	Københavns universitet. ≠b Marinbiologiske laboratorium.
770 0	≠t Ophelia. Supplementum ≠x 0107-5896 ≠w (DLC)sn82021674 ≠w (OCoLC)7085670

Title page

University of Copenhagen

O P H E L I A

International Journal of Marine Biology

VOL. 1

OPHELIA PUBLICATIONS
MARINE BIOLOGICAL LABORATORY, HELSINGØR, DENMARK
May 1964

DISCUSSION

- In this example, the journal "Ophelia" is entered under title. "University of Copenhagen" appears prominently at the head of the title from 1964–75 (see field 500). "Marine Biological Laboratory," which is a subordinate body of the University, is the issuing body and is given as publisher in the publication, distribution, etc., area in field 260. In this case, an added entry should be made under the heading for a prominently named corporate body to provide additional access to the item (LCRI 21.30E).
- Note that only one corporate name added entry is made and that is under the heading for the Laboratory, which is established as a subordinate body under the University. When both parent and subordinate bodies appear in the heading, there is no need to make an added entry under the heading for the parent body by itself, i.e., Københavns universitet, in this case (see also CCM 4.8.3c).
- The name of the Laboratory appears in English on the item. However, when a field 710 added entry is being established, the heading for the body should be in the form in the official language of the body (24.3A1). In this case, the official language of the Laboratory is Danish, and, therefore, the heading is established in Danish, i.e., "Københavns universitet. Marinbiologiske laboratorium."

N17

PROBLEM CONSIDERED:

Added entry for title on inverted page (21.29C)

RULE(S) CONSULTED:

AACR2R: 1.4D2

TAGGED DATA RECORD (based on OCLC #21095111)

LDR   *****cas_/22*****Ia*4500

00-05	06	07-14	15-17	18	19	20	21	22-28	29	30-32	33	34	35-37	38	39
008	900220	c	19899999	onc	q	r	4	p	---s--f	0	///	a	0	eng	-	d

	022 0	0843-7548
	041 0	engfre
	043	n-cn---
	245 00	Focus on culture.
→	246 15	Culture en perspective
→	260	Ottawa : ≠b Statistics Canada, ≠c 1989-
	300	v. ; ≠c 28 cm.
	310	Quarterly
	362 0	Vol. 1, no. 1 (autumn 1989)-
	525	Supplements accompany some numbers.
→	546	Text in English and French with French text on inverted pages.
	651 0	Canada ≠x Popular culture ≠x Statistics ≠x Periodicals.
	710 2	Statistics Canada.

FOCUS ON CULTURE	LA CULTURE EN PERSPECTIVE
Autumn 1989 Volume 1, No. 1	Automne 1989 Volume 1, No. 1
Statistics Statistique Canada Canada	Statistics Statistique Canada Canada
Title page	**Inverted title page**

DISCUSSION

- In bilingual serials, it is quite common for a publication to have two title pages in different languages facing each other or on a separate added title page. The text and added title pages may be inverted. In such cases, make an added entry for the title not chosen as title proper (21.29C). In this example, the English title page is chosen as the chief source, and, therefore, an added entry is made for the French title.
- Use field 246 to record a title appearing on an added title page that has not been chosen as the chief source. First indicator value "1" will generate both a note and an added entry from the field. Use second indicator value "5" to set the display constant to "Added title page title:" (see also CCM 7.2.2e).
- Note that in the publication, distribution, etc., area in field 260, only the English name of the publisher is transcribed, although both the English and French names appear on the chief source. According to 1.4D2, when the publisher's name is given in more than one language or script, use the form that is in the language or script of the title proper (see also CCM 10.2.1c). In this example, the language of the title proper is English.

N18

PROBLEM CONSIDERED:

Added entry for title included in the serial with no established catalog entry (21.30M1)

RULE(S) CONSULTED:

AACR2R: 12.7B2, 21.29C

TAGGED DATA RECORD (based on OCLC #1645538)

LDR   *****cas_/22*****Ia*4500

	00-05	06	07-14	15-17	18	19	20	21	22-28	29	30-32	33	34	35-37	38	39
008	750921	d	19551992	nyu	b	r	l	p	-------	0	///	a	0	eng	-	d

022 0	0020-725X
→ 041 0	eng ≠b frespa
245 00	International journal of fertility.
260	Port Washington, NY : ≠b MSP International Inc., ≠c 1955-1992.
300	37 v. : ≠b ill. ; ≠c 25 cm.
310	Bimonthly
362 0	Vol. 1 (Oct./Dec. 1955)-v. 37 (Nov./Dec. 1992).
→ 520	Most issues include Current bibliography index of mammalian reproduction.
→ 546	Summaries in English, French, and Spanish.
→ 550	Official publication: International Fertility Association, Oct./Dec. 1955-1969; United States International Foundation for Studies in Reproduction, 1970- ; The Scandinavian Association for Studies in Fertility and the International Federation of Fertility Societies, 1971, no.3- ; Falloppius International Society and the International Society of Reproductive Medicine, Jan./Feb. 1992-Nov./Dec. 1992.
650 0	Reproduction ≠x Periodicals.
650 0	Fertility ≠x Periodicals.
→ 710 2	International Fertility Association.
→ 710 2	United States International Foundation for Studies in Reproduction.
→ 710 2	Scandinavian Association for Studies in Fertility.
→ 710 2	Falloppius International Society.
→ 710 2	International Society of Reproductive Medicine.
→ 710 2	International Federation of Fertility Societies.
→ 740 02	Current bibliography index of mammalian reproduction.
785 00	≠t International journal of fertility and menopausal studies ≠x 1069-3130 ≠w (DLC)sn93004904 ≠w (OCoLC)27702532

DISCUSSION

- This serial publication "International journal of fertility" includes a separately named section with the title "Current bibliography index of mammalian reproduction" (field 520). When a work being cataloged contains another work, an analytical added entry should be made under the heading for the other work (21.30M1).

- In this example, the analytical added entry for "Current bibliography index of mammalian reproduction" is entered in field 740, since this heading is not in established catalog entry form, i.e., an authority record for it has not been found in OCLC or in other bibliographic utilities. Second indicator value "2" is used for an analytical added entry.

- Because the journal has summaries in more than one language, a note on this should be input in field 546 (12.7B2). A corresponding field 041 (Language Code) is also entered. Use subfield ≠a to code the original language of the text and subfield ≠b for the languages of the summaries. It is not necessary to repeat a language code in subfield ≠b if that language code already appears in subfield ≠a.

- During its lifetime, this journal had been issued as an official publication to various corporate bodies. This information is recorded in an Issuing Body Note in field 550. Added entries are made for the various corporate bodies (field 710) to provide additional access to the journal (21.29C).

N19

PROBLEM CONSIDERED:

Added entry for title included in the serial with established catalog entry (21.30M1)

TAGGED DATA RECORD (based on OCLC #1124917)

LDR   *****cas_/22*****Ia*4500

00-05	06	07-14	15-17	18	19	20	21	22-28	29	30-32	33	34	35-37	38	39
008 741230	c	19609999	ilu	w	x	l	p	-------	0	///	a	0	eng	-	d

022 0	0098-7484 ≠y 0002-9955
245 00	JAMA : ≠b the journal of the American Medical Association.
→ 246 30	Journal of the American Medical Association
246 17	J.A.M.A.
260	Chicago : ≠b American Medical Association, ≠c 1960-
300	v. : ≠b ill., ports. ; ≠c 28 cm.
310	Four issues per month, ≠b <Mar. 21, 1980->
321	Weekly
362 0	Vol. 173, no. 9 (July 2, 1960)-
500	Title from caption.
530	Available in microform from University Microfilms International.
→ 580	Vols. for 1960-1981 contain annually: Continuing education courses for physicians, also issued separately; vols. for 1982- contain semiannually: Continuing education opportunities for physicians, also issued separately as: Continuing education opportunities for physicians for the period ...
580	Other editions available: JAMA. French. JAMA, and: JAMA en Español.
650 0	Medicine ≠x Periodicals.
710 2	American Medical Association.
→ 730 02	Continuing education courses for physicians.
→ 730 02	Continuing education opportunities for physicians for the period ...
775 1	≠t JAMA. French. JAMA ≠e fre ≠x 0221-7678 ≠w (OCoLC)6371173
775 1	≠t JAMA en Español ≠e spa ≠x 0221-4445
777 1	≠t Continuing education courses for physicians ≠w (OCoLC)6474422
777 1	≠t Continuing education opportunities for physicians for the period ... ≠w (OCoLC)9818071
780 00	≠t Journal of the American Medical Association ≠x 0002-9955 ≠w (DLC)07037314 ≠w (OCoLC)1480379

DISCUSSION

- Similar to example N18, some volumes of this serial publication "JAMA : the journal of the American Medical Association" contain certain publications that are also issued separately, as recorded in field 580 (Linking Entry Complexity Note). In cases like this, analytical added entries should be made under the headings for those separate works (21.30M1).

- The two related publications for which analytical entries should be made are: "Continuing education courses for physicians" and "Continuing education opportunities for physicians for the period . . . ." These are both entered in field 730, rather than field 740 as in N18, since both headings here are in established catalog entry form, i.e., records for each have been found in OCLC or in other bibliographic utilities. Second indicator value "2" is used for an analytical added entry.

- A variant form of title is entered in field 246 to provide access to the full form of title that has been recorded as other title information, in this case, "Journal of the American Medical Association" (see also CCM 6.3.4).

N20

PROBLEM CONSIDERED:

Added entry for related record in uniform title heading (21.30G1)

RULE(S) CONSULTED:

AACR2R: 12.7B7j
LCRI: 21.30J, p. 9; 25.5B, p. 1

TAGGED DATA RECORD (based on OCLC #33019778)

LDR   *****cas_/22*****Ia*4500

00-05	06	07-14	15-17	18	19	20	21	22-28	29	30-32	33	34	35-37	38	39
008 950821	c	19949999	ohu	a	r	1		-------	0	///	a	0	eng	-	d

022 0   1084-2896
043   n-us---
→ 245 00 Shortcut2 markets.
→ 246 3   Shortcut two markets
260   Cincinnati, OH : ≠b National Underwriter Co.,
300   v. : ≠b ill. ; ≠c 28 cm.
310   Annual
362 1   Began in 1994?
500   Description based on: 1995; title from cover.
→ 580   "A supplement to National Underwriter."
650 0   Insurance ≠z United States.
710 2   National Underwriter Company.
→ 730 0   National Underwriter (Property & casualty/risk & benefits management edition)
→ 772 1   ≠t National Underwriter (Property & casualty/risk & benefits management edition) ≠w (OCoLC)19106506

```
┌─────────────────────────────────────────┐
│  A supplement to                         │
│  National                                │
│  Underwriter                             │
│                                          │
│                   1995                   │
│                Shortcut2                  │
│                Markets                   │
│                                          │
│                                          │
│              Cincinnati, OH              │
│                                          │
└─────────────────────────────────────────┘
```

Cover

DISCUSSION

- The title of this publication "Shortcut2 markets" includes an Arabic numeral. Because some users may reasonably assume that the numeral is spelled out in words in the source, make a title added entry substituting the corresponding spelled-out form of the number in the language of the title proper (LCRI 21.30J, p. 9). The varying form of title is input in field 246 (see also CCM 7.2.3e).
- Because this serial is issued as a supplement to another serial, enter a 580 (Linking Entry Complexity Note) recording the name of the parent serial (12.7B7j).
- According to 21.30G1, when cataloging a work that is closely related to another, the cataloger should generally include an added entry under the heading for the related work. Since a uniform title heading has been established for the parent serial, that form is used in linking field 772 (Parent Record Entry) (LCRI 25.5B, p. 1). Field 730 is used for a title added entry in established catalog entry form. The second indicator value is blank since the added entry is not for an analytic.

O. Uniform Title Headings and Uniform Titles

In serials cataloging, a uniform title serves one of two main purposes: It is used to distinguish between different works with the same title, or it is used to bring together all entries for the same work when different manifestations of that work (i.e., translations, editions) have appeared under different titles.

The most significant impact of AACR2R on serials cataloging may be seen in the increased number of serials that must be entered under title. This increase results from the fact that many serials do not deal directly with the corporate body responsible for them and must therefore, according to AACR2R, be entered under title (21.1B3 and 21.1C1). Frequently such items have nondistinctive titles, such as Bulletin, Research Report, Newsletter, etc., and require the construction of a uniform title heading to distinguish them from all others with the same title. Even serials with distinctive titles must occasionally be distinguished from other serials with the same title by means of a uniform title heading.

A uniform title for a serial entered under title is made up of the title proper plus a qualifier in parentheses. A uniform title for a serial entered under a name heading is made up of the title proper along with a parenthetical term consisting of date, other title information, an "edition" statement, or any other term or combination of terms as appropriate (LCRI 25.5B7c). The parenthetical terms used to qualify the title proper, as prescribed by LCRI 25.5B, follow:

> Place of publication
> Corporate body
> Date
> Place and date or corporate body and date
> Edition statement, other title information, etc.

Note that these terms are not given in priority order; catalogers are urged to exercise judgment in choosing the most appropriate term for the title under consideration. However, making a choice between qualifiers such as place of publication and corporate body may be a challenge for novice catalogers. Generally, prefer place over corporate body as the qualifying term. Use corporate body as the exception, for example, with a title proper consisting solely of an indication of type of publication or periodicity, or when place alone as qualifier is inadequate to break a conflict between two serial titles. Following the premises of the provisions for choosing place or body alone, LCRI 25.5B further illustrates the use of combining either place and date or corporate body and date.

The use of uniform titles may be summarized as follows:

1. In serials cataloging the basic purpose for using uniform titles is to distinguish between identical serial titles. Guidelines for constructing uniform titles for such purposes of differentiation are found in LCRI 25.5B. If a uniform title is used in a serial record under a name heading, it is input in field 240. The name heading (i.e., a personal, corporate, or conference name) and the uniform title in field 240 together comprise the main entry of the cataloging record. A uniform title created for a serial record entered under title is input in field 130, and that uniform title heading serves as the main entry of the cataloging record.

2. A uniform title is created only when the title proper of the item in hand is identical to the title proper of another serial found in a catalog, in a database, or in a reference source, or when the title proper of the item in hand is identical to a title proper appearing as a simple added entry or in a linking note for a related work in another bibliographic record. If no such entry is found, do not predict a conflict. In making this decision, do not take into account variant titles on a bibliographic record, such as running titles, cover titles, etc.

3. A uniform title is added only to the bibliographic record for the serial being cataloged; do not add a uniform title to a record for a serial cataloged earlier or to a pre-AACR2 record.

4. Once a uniform title has been created as a uniform title heading in field 130, the same form should be used in added entries, subject entries, linking notes, and linking fields referring to that title.

For uniform titles in special physical formats, such as cartographic materials, sound recordings, visual materials, etc., see section Q; for uniform titles in computer files, see section R.

EXAMPLES

O1   Uniform title heading qualified by place of publication
O2   Uniform title heading qualified by place and date of publication
O3   Uniform title heading qualified by corporate name
O4   Uniform title heading qualified by corporate name in vernacular form
O5   Uniform title heading qualified by edition statement
O6   Uniform title heading qualified by frequency
O7   Uniform title heading qualified by "Series"
O8   Uniform title heading qualified by "Series" and corporate name
O9   Uniform title heading for other language edition
O10   Uniform title heading in record with parallel title
O11   Uniform title entered under a name heading
O12   Uniform title in legal material
O13   Uniform title heading in record for reprint
O14   Uniform title heading in record for reproduction microform
O15   Uniform title heading in record for original microform
O16   Common title and section title in uniform title heading
O17   Common title in uniform title form with section title
O18   Common title and section title without an initial article as uniform title heading
O19   Linking relationship with the uniform title for another language edition
O20   Linking relationship with the uniform title entered under a name heading

O1

PROBLEM CONSIDERED:

Uniform title heading qualified by place of publication (LCRI 25.5B, p. 2)

Cover page

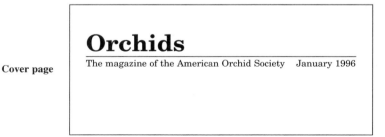

Orchids

The magazine of the American Orchid Society   January 1996

TAGGED DATA RECORD (based on OCLC #34000653)

LDR   *****cas_/22*****_a*4500

00-05	06	07-14	15-17	18	19	20	21	22-28	29	30-32	33	34	35-37	38	39
960108	c	19969999	flu	m	r	l	p	---b---	0	///	a	0	eng	-	d

008

022   1087-1950 ≠y 0003-0252
→ 130 0   Orchids (West Palm Beach, Fla.)
245 00   Orchids : ≠b the magazine of the American Orchid Society.
260   West Palm Beach, Fla. : ≠b The Society, ≠c 1996-
300   v. : ≠b ill. ; ≠c 24 cm.
310   Monthly
362 0   Vol. 65, no. 1 (Jan. 1996)-
500   Title from cover.
650 0   Orchid culture ≠x Periodicals.
710 2   American Orchid Society.
780 00   ≠t American Orchid Society bulletin ≠x 0003-0252 ≠w (DLC)36030994 ≠w (OCoLC)148050375

DISCUSSION

- When constructing a uniform title heading for an item whose title proper is not a generic term, give preference to place of publication over publisher as qualifier, as illustrated in this example. Here the serial has the distinctive title proper "Orchids." Because other serial publications in the catalog bear the same title proper, a uniform title heading must be established to distinguish the current publication from the others in the catalog (LCRI 25.5B, p. 2). The place of publication, "West Palm Beach, Fla.," is chosen as the qualifier.
- When the place of publication is being used as the qualifying term in a uniform title heading, choose the place that appears on the first issue or the first available issue of the item. If the place of publication changes on later issues, no separate record should be created.

O2

PROBLEM CONSIDERED:

Uniform title heading qualified by place and date of publication (LCRI 25.5B, p. 3)

TAGGED DATA RECORD (based on OCLC #20639870)

LDR *****cas_/22*****Ia*4500

	00-05	06	07-14	15-17	18	19	20	21	22-28	29	30-32	33	34	35-37	38	39
008	891113	c	19889999	ne	m	r	z	p	-------	0	///	a	0	eng	-	d

022 0166-218X
→ 130 0 Discrete applied mathematics (Amsterdam, Netherlands : 1988)
245 00 Discrete applied mathematics.
260 Amsterdam : ≠b North Holland,
300 v. : ≠b ill. ; ≠c 24 cm.
310 Monthly
362 1 Began with v. 21, no. 1 in 1988.
500 Description based on: Vol. 22, no. 1, published in 1989.
515 Issues frequently published in combined form.
555 Vols. 31 (1991)-40 (1992) in 1 v.
650 0 Mathematics ≠x Periodicals.
650 0 Combinatorial analysis ≠x Periodicals.
650 0 Mathematics ≠x Data processing ≠x Periodicals.
650 0 Combinatorial analysis ≠x Data processing ≠x Periodicals
→ 780 00 ≠t Discrete applied mathematics and combinatorial operations research ≠x 0166-218X ≠w (DLC)86657513 ≠w (OCoLC)14217949

DISCUSSION

- This serial—"Discrete applied mathematics"—has gone through several title changes. It went from "Discrete applied mathematics" (v. 1–10) to "Discrete applied mathematics and combinatorial operations research" (v. 11–20) and now back to its original title "Discrete applied mathematics" (v. 21–).
- This is a title change necessitating the creation of a new record. To catalog this latest title with "Discrete applied mathematics" as the title proper would result in a title conflict with another serial publication bearing the same title proper (i.e., the serial's own former title) in the catalog, and, therefore, a uniform title heading must be established.
- When constructing a uniform title heading for an item, generally prefer the place of publication as the qualifying term. However, in this example, since both titles in conflict are published in the same place, the use of place as a qualifying term is inadequate to resolve the conflict. A double qualifier combining place and date of publication is therefore preferred (LCRI 25.5B, p. 3). Use the beginning date of publication for the date element. Hence, the qualifying term in the uniform title heading for the current publication is "Amsterdam, Netherlands : 1988."

O3

PROBLEM CONSIDERED:

Uniform title heading qualified by corporate name (LCRI 25.5B, p. 2)

RULE(S) CONSULTED:

AACR2R: 21.1B2

TAGGED DATA RECORD (based on OCLC #35315103)

LDR   *****cas_/22*****Ia*4500

00-05	06	07-14	15-17	18	19	20	21	22-28	29	30-32	33	34	35-37	38	39
960828	c	19969999	enk	u	u		p	-------	0	///	a	0	eng	-	d

008

022	≠y 0952-2832
043	e-uk---
→ 130 0	Research bulletin (British Library. Research and Innovation Centre)
→ 245 00	Research bulletin / ≠c The British Library, Research and Innovation Centre.
260	London : ≠b The Centre, ≠c 1996-
300	v. : ≠b ill. ; ≠c 30 cm.
362 0	Issue 14 (summer 96)-
500	Title from caption.
610 20	British Library. ≠b Research and Innovation Centre ≠x Periodicals.
650 0	Libraries ≠x Research ≠z Great Britain ≠x Periodicals.
710 2	British Library. ≠b Research and Innovation Centre.
→ 780 00	≠t Research bulletin (British Library. Research and Development Dept.) ≠x 0952-2832 ≠w (DLC)sn88013075 ≠w (OCoLC)17340722

DISCUSSION

- The serial publication "Research bulletin" is entered under title, since it does not fall into any of the categories given in 21.1B2. Its title proper, however, is also used by other publications in the catalog, among which is its own previous title (field 780). Therefore, a uniform title heading must be constructed to distinguish it from other publications with the same title.

- Since the title proper consists solely of an indication of type of publication (i.e., "Research bulletin"), the heading for the corporate body with which the publication originated or by which it was issued or published is used as the qualifier in the uniform title heading (LCRI 25.5B, p. 2). In this case, the corporate body that issues the work appears in the publication as "British Library Research and Innovation Centre." The established heading for this body (i.e., "British Library. Research and Innovation Centre") is used as the qualifier in the uniform title heading.

O4

PROBLEM CONSIDERED:

Uniform title heading qualified by corporate name in vernacular form (LCRI 25.5B, p. 2)

RULE(S) CONSULTED:

AACR2R: 24.1A, 24.1B1

TAGGED DATA RECORD (based on OCLC #28906652)

LDR   *****cas_/22*****Ia*4500

00-05	06	07-14	15-17	18	19	20	21	22-28	29	30-32	33	34	35-37	38	39
930929	c	19939999	cc	j	x		p	------f	0	///	a	0	eng	-	d

008

043   a-cc---

→ 130 0   Newsletter (China. Kuo chia k'o wei)

→ 245 00 Newsletter / ≠c the State Science and Technology Commission, People's Republic of China.

246 1   ≠i At head of title: ≠a China science and technology

260   Beijing, China : ≠b The Commission, ≠c 1993-

300   v. ; ≠c 29 cm.

310   Three or 4 no. a month

362 0   No. 1 (June 10, 1993)

650 0   Science ≠z China ≠x Periodicals.

650 0   Science and state ≠z China ≠x Periodicals.

650 0   Technology ≠z China ≠x Periodicals.

650 0   Technology and state ≠z China ≠x Periodicals.

710 1   China. ≠b Kuo chia k'o wei.

Caption

CHINA SCIENCE AND TECHNOLOGY
NEWSLETTER
The State Science and Technology Commission
People's Republic of China

No. 1	June 10, 1993

DISCUSSION

- Similar to the example in O3, the title proper here consists solely of an indication of type of publication, i.e., "Newsletter." In order to distinguish it from other publications in the catalog with the same title, the heading for the corporate body with which the publication originated or by which it was issued or published is used as the qualifier in the uniform title heading (LCRI 25.5B, p. 2).

- The corporate body that issues the newsletter is the "State Science and Technology Commission, People's Republic of China." The formal heading for this body should be the name by which it is commonly identified in items issued by that body in its own language (24.1A), which, in this case, is Chinese. Furthermore, rule 24.1B1 also applies when the name of the body is in a language written in a nonroman script, and the name should be romanized according to the table adopted by the cataloging agency for that language. According to Library of Congress practice, the established heading is "China. Kuo chia k'o wei" using Wade-Giles romanization. This established heading should be used as the qualifier in the uniform title heading in field 130.

O5

PROBLEM CONSIDERED:

Uniform title heading qualified by edition statement (LCRI 25.5B, p. 3)

RULE(S) CONSULTED:

AACR2R: Appendix B

O5a

TAGGED DATA RECORD (based on OCLC #25908131)

LDR *****cas_/22*****Ia*4500

	00-05	06	07-14	15-17	18	19	20	21	22-28	29	30-32	33	34	35-37	38	39
008	920529	c	19929999	mdu	a	r	1		-------	0	///	a	0	eng	-	d

022 1063-1690
→ 130 0 Statistical abstract of the United States (Enlarged print ed.)
245 00 Statistical abstract of the United States / ≠c U.S. Dept. of Commerce, Economics and Statistics Administration, Bureau of the Census.
→ 250 Enlarged print ed.
260 Lanham, Md. : ≠b Bernan Press, ≠c 1992-
300 v. ; ≠c 29 cm.
310 Annual
362 0 112th ed. (1992)-
500 "The national data book."
580 Near exact reprint of: Statistical abstract of the United States.
651 0 United States ≠x Statistics.
710 1 United States. ≠b Economics and Statistics Administration.
710 1 United States. ≠b Bureau of the Census.
775 1 ≠t Statistical abstract of the United States ≠x 0081-4741 ≠w (DLC)04018089 ≠w (OCoLC)1193890

O5b

TAGGED DATA RECORD (based on OCLC #27330784)

LDR *****cas_/22******Ia*4500

00-05	06	07-14	15-17	18	19	20	21	22-28	29	30-32	33	34	35-37	38	39
930127	c	19929999	txu	a	r			-------	0	///	a	0	eng	-	d

008 (as tabled above)

043	n-us---
→ 130 0	Statistical abstract of the United States (Reference Press ed.)
245 00	Statistical abstract of the United States.
→ 250	Reference Press ed.
260	Austin, Tex. : ≠b The Reference Press, ≠c 1992-
300	v. : ≠b ill. ; ≠c 24 cm.
310	Annual
362 0	112th ed. (1992)-
550	Issued by: Bureau of the Census.
580	Commercial ed. of publication sold by U.S. Government Printing Office.
651 0	United States ≠x Statistics.
710 1	United States. ≠b Bureau of the Census.
775 1	≠t Statistical abstract of the United States ≠x 0081-4741 ≠w (DLC)04018089 ≠w (OCoLC)1193890

DISCUSSION

- Usually the presence of an edition statement on an item implies the existence of other editions sharing the same title proper. Therefore, whenever an edition statement is included in a record, it is usually necessary to construct a uniform title heading to distinguish the serial in hand from other editions with the same title proper. In such a case, construct the uniform title heading by using the title proper qualified by the edition statement (LCRI 25.5B, p. 3).

- In examples O5a and O5b, the original edition of "Statistical abstract of the United States" was published in 1878. Beginning with the 112th edition, there have also been two other editions called "Reference Press edition" and "Enlarged print edition." These editions are therefore used as the qualifiers in the uniform title headings to distinguish them from the original edition.

- Note that standard abbreviations from AACR2R Appendix B should be used in all areas of the cataloging record except in the title and statement of responsibility area. In this example, "Enlarged print edition" and "Reference Press edition" are therefore transcribed as "Enlarged print ed." and "Reference Press ed." in the edition statement (field 250) and in the qualifier for the uniform title heading (field 130).

O6

PROBLEM CONSIDERED:

Uniform title heading qualified by frequency (LCRI 25.5B, p. 3)

RULE(S) CONSULTED:

LCRI: 25.5B, p. 1

O6a
TAGGED DATA RECORD (based on OCLC #11652018)

LDR   *****cas_/22*****Ia*4500

00-05	06	07-14	15-17	18	19	20	21	22-28	29	30-32	33	34	35-37	38	39
008	850204	c	19849999	azu	m	r	l	p	-------	0	///	a	0	eng	-	d

022 0	8756-7687 ≠y 0736-5071
→ 130 0	AI trends (Monthly)
→ 245 00	AI trends.
246 13	AI trends newsletter
260	Scottsdale, Ariz. : ≠b DM Data, Inc., ≠c 1984-
300	v. : ≠b ill. ; ≠c 28 cm.
→ 310	Monthly
362 0	Vol. 1, no. 1 (Oct. 1984)-
500	"The newsletter of the artificial intelligence industry."
500	Title from cover.
650 0	Artificial intelligence ≠x Periodicals.
780 00	≠t Technology trends newsletter ≠x 0736-5071 ≠w (OCoLC)9145889

O6b
RELATED TAGGED DATA RECORD (based on OCLC #12765168)

LDR   *****cas_/22*****Ia*4500

00-05	06	07-14	15-17	18	19	20	21	22-28	29	30-32	33	34	35-37	38	39
→ 008	851106	d	19uu19uu	azu	a	r			p	---rs--	0	///	a	0	eng	-	d

043	n-us---
→ 245 00	AI trends.
260	Scottsdale, Ariz. : ≠b DM Data Inc.,
300	v. : ≠b ill. ; ≠c 28 cm.
→ 310	Annual
500	Description based on: 1985.
520	"A comprehensive annual report on the artificial intelligence industry."
650 0	Computer industry ≠z United States ≠x Technological innovations ≠x Periodicals.
650 0	Speech processing systems industry ≠z United States ≠x Technological innovations ≠x Periodicals.
650 0	Artificial intelligence ≠x Periodicals.
650 0	Market surveys ≠z United States ≠x Periodicals.
710 2	DM Data Inc.
785 00	≠t Artificial intelligence (Scottsdale, Ariz.) ≠x 1060-0639 ≠w (OCoLC)24416901 ≠w (DLC)sn91032114

DISCUSSION

- The publications in O6 share the same title, and, therefore, must be distinguished from one another. Because they both have the same place of publication and issuing body, i.e., "DM Data Inc.," a uniform title heading using either the place of publication or the corporate body as qualifier would be inadequate to resolve the title conflict.
- According to LCRI 25.5B, p. 3, the cataloger may use as qualifier any element or combination of elements extracted from the description of the work that will serve to distinguish it from other works. In this case, since the titles in conflict are published with different frequencies, the frequency of the publication is used as the qualifier (see also CCM 5.3.4).
- A uniform title heading is usually created only for the serial being cataloged; it is not necessary to add one also to the record for a serial cataloged earlier. However, these two examples were cataloged in 1985 without uniform title and the earlier cataloged record (O6a) was updated and replaced in 1987. For that reason, the uniform title, qualified by "Monthly," was added to the earlier record (LCRI 25.5B, p. 1).

O7

PROBLEM CONSIDERED:

Uniform title heading qualified by "Series" (LCRI 25.5B, p. 7)

RULE(S) CONSULTED:

AACR2R: 1.1B3, 21.1B2, 21.1C1c

TAGGED DATA RECORD (based on OCLC #1604878)

LDR   *****cas_/22*****Ia*4500

00-05	06	07-14	15-17	18	19	20	21	22-28	29	30-32	33	34	35-37	38	39
750907	c	18999999	enk		x		m	-------	0	///	a	0	eng	-	d

008 (as above)

043	e-ie---
→ 130 0	Irish Texts Society (Series)
→ 245 00	Irish Texts Society : ≠b [publications].
260	London : ≠b The Society,
300	v. ; ≠c 25cm.
310	Irregular
362 1	Began in 1899.
500	Description based on: Vol. 55, published in 1991.
500	Each issue has also a distinctive title.
650 0	Irish literature ≠x Criticism, Textual.
650 0	Irish literature ≠x Translations into English.
710 2	Irish Texts Society.

DISCUSSION

- When the title proper consists solely of the name of a corporate body responsible for the work, use that name as the title proper (1.1B3). Thus, in this example, "Irish Texts Society" is treated as the title proper. Because this work does not meet the conditions for entry under corporate body (21.1B2), it must be entered under title (21.1C1c). According to LCRI 25.5B, p. 7, whenever a record is entered under a title that is identical to the name of a corporate body (including corporate name initials and acronyms) found in a heading, in a reference, or on the item being cataloged, a uniform title heading that consists of the title qualified by the term "Series" should be assigned even though there is no conflict with another series or serial title. Therefore, the work in this example is entered under the uniform title heading "Irish Texts Society (Series)" (see also CCM 5.5.2).

O8

PROBLEM CONSIDERED:

Uniform title heading qualified by "Series" and corporate name (LCRI 25.5B, p. 7)

RULES (S) CONSULTED:

LCRI: 25.5B, p. 2

TAGGED DATA RECORD (based on OCLC #14955355)

LDR   *****cas_/22*****Ia*4500

00-05	06	07-14		15-17	18	19	20	21	22-28	29	30-32	33	34	35-37	38	39
008	861211	u	1986uuuu	nyu	u	u		m	-------	0	///	a	0	eng	-	d

→ 130 0   DE (Series) (American Society of Mechanical Engineers. Design Engineering Division)

→ 245 00   DE.

260   New York, N.Y. : ≠b American Society of Mechanical Engineers, ≠c c1986-

300   v. : ≠b ill. ; ≠c 28 cm.

362 0   Vol. 1-

550   Issued by the Design Engineering Division, ASME.

580   Vol. 21 also issued as PED (Series) v. 36.

650   0   Engineering design.

710 2   American Society of Mechanical Engineers. ≠b Design Engineering Division.

787 1   ≠t PED (Series) ≠x 0887-6150 ≠w (OCoLC)10832162

DISCUSSION

- According to LCRI 25.5B, p. 7 (Series Titles Identical to Corporate Names), if a new series title is identical to both a corporate name (including corporate name initials and acronyms) and a series title that has been qualified by the term "Series," the qualifier for the new title's uniform title heading should be "Series" followed, within its own set of parentheses, by another qualifier selected to resolve the conflict between the two titles.
- In this example, the title on the serial being cataloged is "DE." This title is identical to one that is already present in the catalog and that has been cata-

loged with the uniform title heading "DE (Series)." In order to distinguish the new title from the earlier one, a uniform title heading must be constructed. In keeping with the above rule interpretation, the first qualifier used is "Series." A second qualifier must also be used. In this case, the second qualifier is the heading for the issuing corporate body "American Society of Mechanical Engineers. Design Engineering Division." This is sufficient to distinguish between the two titles in conflict, since they are issued by different bodies. The whole uniform title heading is thus "DE (Series) (American Society of Mechanical Engineers. Design Engineering Division)."

- Note that in cases such as this where a corporate name is treated as the title proper, the form of that name actually found on the item is used as the basis for the uniform title heading—not necessarily the AACR2R form of heading for the body, e.g., DE, which is an initialism for Design Engineering Division (LCRI 25.5B, p. 7). However, when a name is used as a qualifier in a uniform title heading, then the AACR2R form of heading should be used (LCRI 25.5B, p. 2). Therefore, the second qualifier in the uniform title in this example is an established AACR2R form.

O9

PROBLEM CONSIDERED:

Uniform title heading for other language edition (25.3C2–25.3C3)

RULE(S) CONSULTED:

AACR2R: 12.7B7g, 25.5C1

TAGGED DATA RECORD (based on OCLC #26569378)

LDR *****cas_/22*****Ia*4500

008

00-05	06	07-14	15-17	18	19	20	21	22-28	29	30-32	33	34	35-37	38	39
920910	c	19909999	cc	a	r		p	-------	0	///	a	0	eng	-	d

043 a-cc---
→ 130 0 Chung-kuo chin jung nien chien. ≠l English.
→ 245 10 Almanac of China's finance and banking.
→ 250 English ed.
260 [Peking] : ≠b China's Financial Pub. House, ≠c 1991-
300 v. : ≠b col. ill. ; ≠c 26 cm.
310 Annual
362 0 1990-
500 Publisher: People's China Publishing House, <1993->
→ 580 Issued also in Chinese: Chung-kuo chin jung nien chien.
650 0 Banks and banking ≠z China ≠x Periodicals.
650 0 Finance ≠z China ≠x Periodicals.
650 0 Financial institutions ≠z China ≠x Periodicals.
710 2 Chung-kuo chin jung ch'u pan she.
775 1 ≠t Chung-kuo chin jung nien chien ≠w (DLC)89641028 ≠w (OCoLC)20216471

ALMANAC

OF

CHINA'S FINANCE AND BANKING

(ENGLISH EDITION)

1990

China's Financial Publishing House

Title page

DISCUSSION

- Occasionally a work is published simultaneously in different languages and under different titles. According to rule 25.3C2–25.3C3, the title of one of the editions should be chosen and used in the uniform title of all other editions. The uniform title should consist of the title in the language of the original edition, or primary edition, plus the name of the language of the item spelled out in full (25.5C1).

- In this example, "Chung-kuo chin jung nien chien" was first published in 1987 in Chinese. Since 1991, it has also been issued simultaneously in an English edition under the title "Almanac of China's finance and banking." Because the Chinese edition was the one first published, its title should be used as the uniform title for the English edition. Note that the uniform title had to be established in romanized form, because the title in the original edition is in Chinese.

- Field 130 is used for uniform title headings. Subfield ≠l should be input with the language of the work in hand spelled out in full.

- A 580 linking note, such as "Issued also in Chinese: Chung-kuo chin jung nien chien," should be added to the record. If the exact title of the serial in the other languages is not known, then a general note, such as "Also published in Chinese edition," should be given (12.7B7g).

O10

PROBLEM CONSIDERED:

Uniform title heading in record with parallel title (LCRI 25.5B, p. 1)

RULE(S) CONSULTED:

AACR2R: 1.1B8

TAGGED DATA RECORD (based on OCLC #33120952)

LDR   *****cas_/22*****Ia*4500

00-05	06	07-14	15-17	18	19	20	21	22-28	29	30-32	33	34	35-37	38	39
008 950912	c	19959999	at	f	r	-	p	---o---	0	///	a	0	eng	-	d

022	1324-9347 ≠y 0156-7365
043	a-cc--- ≠a c-ch--- ≠a a-hk---
→ 130 0	China journal (Canberra, A.C.T.)
→ 245 04	The China journal = ≠b Chung-kuo yen chiu.
246 31	Chung-kuo yen chiu
260	Canberra, ACT, Australia : ≠b Contemporary China Centre, Research School of Pacific and Asian Studies, Australian National University, ≠c [1995-
300	v. : ≠b ill. ; ≠c 25 cm.
310	Semiannual (in Jan. and July)
362 0	34 (July 1995)-
500	Title from cover.
530	Issued also in microform by University Microfilms.
651 0	China ≠x Periodicals.
651 0	Taiwan ≠x Periodicals.
651 0	Hong Kong (China) ≠x Periodicals.
710 2	Australian National University. ≠b Contemporary China Centre.
780 00	≠t Australian journal of Chinese affairs ≠x 0156-7365 ≠w (DLC)81641441 ≠w (OCoLC)5895676

Cover

中
國
研
究

The
China
Journal

Formerly The Australian Journal of Chinese Affairs

34
July 1995

DISCUSSION

• The chief source of information for this serial publication bears titles in two languages: Chinese and English. Because the text of the serial is in English, the English title "The China journal" is chosen as the title proper (1.1B8), although the Chinese title appears on the chief source just as typographically prominent as the English title. The Chinese title in this case is recorded as the parallel title. It is recorded in romanized form in subfield ≠b in field 245.

- The chosen title proper of the serial "The China journal" clashes with another serial bearing the same title in the catalog. When a uniform title heading is being established for the serial, the title proper "China journal" is used and not the parallel title. In this case, the qualifier used in the uniform title is the place of publication (LCRI 25.5B, p. 1).
- Note that the initial article "The" is omitted from the uniform title heading, because, according to Library of Congress policy, initial articles are omitted in formulating uniform title headings. Thus, the first indicator value in field 130 for a uniform title heading is always set to "0."

O11

PROBLEM CONSIDERED:

Uniform title entered under a name heading (LCRI 25.5B)

RULE(S) CONSULTED:

LCRI: 25.5B, p. 5

TAGGED DATA RECORD (based on OCLC #21120889)

LDR   *****cas_/22*****Ia*4500

00-05	06	07-14	15-17	18	19	20	21	22-28	29	30-32	33	34	35-37	38	39
900224	d	19871987	ke	a	r			---s--f	0	///	a	0	eng	-	d

008

043	f-ke---
→ 110 2	National Housing Corporation.
→ 240 10	Annual report (1987)
→ 245 00	Annual report / ≠c National Housing Corporation, NHC.
260	[Nairobi] : ≠b NHC, ≠c [1987]
300	1 v. : ≠b ill. ; ≠c 30 cm.
310	Annual
362 0	1986/1987.
500	Title from cover.
515	Report year ends June 30.
610 20	National Housing Corporation.
650 0	Housing ≠z Kenya.
650 0	Housing policy ≠z Kenya.
→ 780 00	National Housing Corporation. ≠t Biennial report - National Housing Corporation ≠w (DLC)80647637 ≠w (OCoLC)7631755
785 00	National Housing Corporation. ≠t Triennial report ≠w (DLC)95983320 ≠w (OCoLC)31898830

DISCUSSION

- If an item being cataloged is entered under a name heading and the title proper is identical to the title proper of another work entered under the same name heading, a uniform title should be constructed by adding a qualifying term in parentheses to the title proper (LCRI 25.5B).

- In this example, the main entry is under the corporate name "National Housing Corporation." Although it is not discernible from the one record included here, the title proper has, in fact, changed many times, from "Annual report" to "Biennial report" and then back to "Annual report" again. To distinguish between the present publication and the earlier one with the same title, i.e., "Annual report," a uniform title should be made. In this case, since both conflicting titles are published in the same place and by the same body, the uniform title is constructed by adding a date in parentheses to the title proper "Annual report" in order to distinguish it from its predecessor with the same title proper entered under the same name heading (LCRI 25.5B, p. 5). When using a date as the qualifier, use the publishing date (field 260, subfield ≠c) and not the chronological designation (see also CCM 5.3.3).
- When a record is entered under a name heading and a uniform title is required, the uniform title is entered in field 240.

O12

PROBLEM CONSIDERED:
Uniform title in legal material (25.15A2)

RULE(S) CONSULTED:
AACR2R: 21.1B2b
LCRI: 25.15A2

TAGGED DATA RECORD (based on OCLC #34587001)

LDR   *****cas_/22*****Ia*4500

00-05	06	07-14	15-17	18	19	20	21	22-28	29	30-32	33	34	35-37	38	39
960417	c	198u9999	ilu	u	u			------s	0	///	a	0	eng	-	d

008 (above table)

043   n-us-il
→ 110 1   Illinois.
→ 240 10 Illinois Dead Animal Disposal Act.
→ 245 10 Illinois Dead Animal Disposal Act (with regulations) / ≠c administered by Illinois Department of Agriculture, Bureau of Animal Welfare.
246 30   Dead animal disposal act
260   [Springfield, Ill.] : ≠b The Bureau,
300   v. ; ≠c 28 cm.
500   Description based on: 1996; title from cover.
550   Issued by: Illinois Dept. of Agriculture, Division of Animal Industries, [1989-1994].
610 10   Illinois. ≠b Bureau of Animal Welfare.
650 0   Veterinary public health ≠x Law and legislation ≠z Illinois.
650 0   Communicable diseases in animals ≠x Law and legislation ≠z Illinois.
710 1   Illinois. ≠b Bureau of Animal Welfare.
710 1   Illinois. ≠b Dept. of Agriculture.

Cover

**ILLINOIS
DEAD ANIMAL
DISPOSAL ACT**

(WITH REGULATIONS)

**Administered by the
ILLINOIS DEPARTMENT
OF AGRICULTURE**

Bureau of Animal Welfare

DISCUSSION

- This example involves legal materials. In accordance with rule 21.1B2b, the work is entered under the corporate body, i.e., "Illinois." Because the work being cataloged is a single legislative enactment, the official short title or citation title is used as the uniform title according to the order of preference in 25.15A2.
- When using the official short title or citation title in a uniform title, give the complete short title or citation title, regardless of whether that title includes the name of the jurisdiction (LCRI 25.15A2). Therefore, in this case, the uniform title constructed for the single legislative enactment is the complete citation title "Illinois Dead Animal Disposal Act," and not "Dead Animal Disposal Act."

O13

PROBLEM CONSIDERED:

Uniform title heading in record for reprint (LCRI 25.5B, p.6)

TAGGED DATA RECORD (based on OCLC #32171919)

LDR   *****cas_/22*****Ia*4500

00-05	06	07-14	15-17	18	19	20	21	22-28	29	30-32	33	34	35-37	38	39
950320	d	18921894	nhu	m	r		p	-r-----	0	///	a	0	eng	-	d

→ 008

→ 130 0   Organ (Boston, Mass.)

245 04   The Organ.

260   Harrisville, N.H. : ≠b Boston Organ Club Chapter of the Organ Historical
Society, ≠c c1995.

300   1 v. : ≠b ill., music ; ≠c 32 cm.

362 0   Vol. 1, no. 1 (May 1892)-v. 2, no.12 (Apr. 1894).

500   "A monthly journal devoted to the king of instruments."

515   Vol. 2, no. 1-v. 2, no. 12 also called whole no. 13-24.

→ 580   Reprint. Originally published monthly: Boston, Mass. : E.E. Truette, 1892-1894.

650 0   Organ ≠x Periodicals.

650 0   Organ music ≠x Periodicals.

700 1   Truette, Everett E. ≠q (Everett Ellsworth), ≠d 1861-1933.

710 2   Organ Historical Society. ≠b Boston Organ Club Chapter.

→ 775 1   ≠t Organ (Boston, Mass.) ≠w (OCoLC)16556553

DISCUSSION

- When a serial reappears as a reprint or as a microform copy, etc., Library of
Congress policy states that *no* uniform title should be constructed to distinguish
one of these secondary manifestations from the original (LCRI 25.5B, p. 6).
However, if the original itself has a uniform title in the bibliographic record,
use that same uniform title in all records for secondary manifestations (i.e.,
reprints, microreproductions, etc.). The purpose of this practice is to bring together different manifestations of the same work.

- The item in O13 is a reprint. A note (field 580) in the record provides information on the original. The bibliographic record for the original has a uniform
title heading "Organ (Boston, Mass.)," as may be seen in field 775 (Other Edition Available Entry). Thus, the bibliographic record for the reprint should also
have that same uniform title heading (field 130).

- Since the item is a reprint, character position 23 (Form of Item) in field 008
(Fixed-Length Data Elements) for serials should be coded "r" for "Regular
Print Reproduction."

- The same rule applies to the record in example O14. The item being described
is a reproduction microform. Since the bibliographic record for the original
work has a uniform title heading, the record for the reproduction microform
should also have the same uniform title heading (field 130).

- Note that the bibliographic description is based on the originally published
item, with the general material designation "microform" recorded in subfield
≠h in field 245. A corresponding physical description fixed field 007 for micro-

form should also be given. Position 23 (Form of Item) in field 008 (Fixed-Length Data Elements) for serials should be coded "a" for "Microfilm."

- A note describing the reproduction is added to the record in field 533 (Reproduction Note). The reproduction in this example was published as two series, i.e., "Research collections in labor studies" and "Labor union periodicals. Part 1, The Metal trades." The series statements are also included in this note using repeatable subfield ≠f. An added entry for each series is made using field 830.

O14

PROBLEM CONSIDERED:

Uniform title heading in record for reproduction microform (LCRI 25.5B, p. 6)

TAGGED DATA RECORD (based on OCLC #24987717)

LDR   *****cas_/22*****Ia*4500

	00-05	06	07-14	15-17	18	19	20	21	22-28	29	30-32	33	34	35-37	38	39
→ 008	911217	u	1926uuuu	miu	m	r		p	-a-----	0	///	a	0	eng	-	d

→ 007   h ≠b d ≠d a ≠e f ≠f a--- ≠g b ≠h a ≠i c ≠j a   (microfilm)

→ 130 0   Fisher body worker (Workers (Communist) Party of America. Shop Nucleus.)

→ 245 00   Fisher body worker ≠h [microform].

260   [Detroit, Mich.] : ≠b Workers (Communist) Party Shop Nucleus, ≠c 1926-

300   v. ; ≠c 28 cm.

310   Monthly

362 0   Vol. 1, no. 3 (Nov. 1926)-

515   Some numbers issued in combined form.

550   Published by the Shop Nucleus of the Workers (Communist) Party in the Fisher Body Plants of Detroit.

→ 533   Microfilm. ≠m 1926-1927. ≠b Bethesda, Md. : ≠c University Publications of America, ≠d 1990. ≠e 1 microfilm reel ; 35 mm. ≠f (Research collections in labor studies) ≠f (Labor union periodicals. Part 1, The Metal trades).

580   Filmed with: Auto workers news.

500   Source note: The collection was filmed from the holdings of the State Historical Society of Wisconsin.

610 20   Workers (Communist) Party of America. ≠b Shop Nucleus.

650 0   Trade-unions ≠x Metal-workers ≠z United States ≠x Periodicals.

650 0   Trade-unions ≠x Automobile industry workers ≠z United States ≠x Periodicals.

710 2   Workers (Communist) Party of America. ≠b Shop Nucleus.

730 02   Auto workers news.

780 04   ≠t Workers bulletin (Workers (Communist) Party of America. Shop Nucleus (Fisher Body Plant 10).) ≠w (OCoLC)24987534

780 04   ≠t Fisher body worker (Workers (Communist) Party of America. Shop Nucleus (Fisher Plant 18).) ≠w (OCoLC)24987609

→ 830 0   Research collections in labor studies.

→ 830 0   Labor union periodicals. ≠n Part 1, ≠p Metal trades.

DISCUSSION

- See example O13.

O15

PROBLEM CONSIDERED:

Uniform title heading in record for original microform (LCRI 21.3B)

RULE(S) CONSULTED:

LCRI: 25.5B, p. 3, p. 6

TAGGED DATA RECORD (based on OCLC #12112462)

LDR   *****cas_/22*****Ia*4500

00-05	06	07-14	15-17	18	19	20	21	22-28	29	30-32	33	34	35-37	38	39
850603	d	19841988	mau	q	r	l		bb-ibc-	0	///	a	0	eng	-	d

008

007   h ≠b e ≠d b ≠e m ≠f u--- ≠g b ≠h u ≠i u ≠j u   (microfiche)

022   0190-3373

→ 130 0   Anthropological literature (Microfiche)

→ 245 00 Anthropological literature ≠h [microform].

260   Cambridge, Mass. : ≠b Tozzer Library, ≠c [c1984-1988]

→ 300   93 microfiches : ≠b negative ; ≠c 11 x 15 cm.

310   Quarterly, with annual cumulation.

362 0   Vol. 6 (1984)-v. 10, no. 4 (fall 1988).

500   Title from eye-readable header.

515   Vol. 6 issued in annual cumulation only.

530   Also available in a CD-ROM ed. with title: Anthropological literature on disc.

→ 580   Continues: Anthropological literature, and continued by: Anthropological literature (Cambridge, Mass. : 1989), both issued in print format.

650 0   Anthropology ≠x Indexes.

610 20 Tozzer Library ≠x Periodicals ≠x Catalogs.

650 0   Anthropology ≠x Periodicals ≠x Bibliography.

650 0   Anthropology ≠x Periodicals ≠x Catalogs.

710 2   Tozzer Library.

776 1   ≠t Anthropological literature on disc ≠w (DLC)sn96031173 ≠w (OCoLC)30703805

780 10 ≠t Anthropological literature ≠w 0190-3373 ≠w (DLC)79649261 ≠w (OCoLC)4818564

785 10 ≠t Anthropological literature (Cambridge, Mass. : 1989) ≠w 0190-3373 ≠w (DLC)89643992 ≠w (OCoLC)20386569

DISCUSSION

- Unlike the example in O14 (reproduction microform), the serial in this example was issued originally in microform. The item "Anthropological literature" was first published in print copy, and during 1984–1988 it changed to the microform format. The change in physical format has necessitated a new record (LCRI 21.3B; LCRI 25.5B, p. 6). Note that the Physical Description Area in field 300 pertains to the microform, as the item was originally issued as such.

- Because the microform format has the same title as its preceding title, a uniform title is required to distinguish between the two. In this example, the Specific Material Designation "Microfiche" is used as the qualifier, instead of the General Material Designation "microform" (LCRI 25.5B, p. 3).

O16

PROBLEM CONSIDERED:

Common title and section title in uniform title heading (LCRI 25.5B, p. 4)

TAGGED DATA RECORD (based on OCLC #25636708)

LDR   *****cas_/22*****Ia*4500

00-05	06	07-14	15-17	18	19	20	21	22-28	29	30-32	33	34	35-37	38	39
920413	c	19929999	enk	m	r		p	--a----	0	///	a	0	eng	-	d

008

022   ≠y 0001-9852
043   f------
→ 130 0 Africa research bulletin. ≠p Economic, financial, and technical series (1992)
→ 245 00 Africa research bulletin. ≠p Economic, financial, and technical series.
246 30   Economic, financial, and technical series
260   Oxford, England : ≠b Blackwell, ≠c 1992-
300   v. ; ≠c 26 cm.
310   Monthly
362 0   Vol. 29, no. 1 (Jan. 16th-Feb. 15th 1992)-
500   Title from caption.
651 0   Africa ≠x Economic conditions ≠x Abstracts ≠x Periodicals.
→ 780 00 ≠t Africa research bulletin. Economic series ≠w (DLC)sn85015170 ≠w (OCoLC)12032734

DISCUSSION

- Whenever the title proper of a serial consisting of a common title with a section number or with a section title, or with both, is identical to the title proper of another record, a uniform title heading should be constructed by placing an appropriate qualifier at the end of the title proper (LCRI 25.5B, p. 4).

- In this example, the title proper "Africa research bulletin. Economic, financial, and technical series" is identical to the title proper of another work, so a uniform title heading is required to resolve the conflict. The next task of the cataloger is to decide on the appropriate qualifier to use for the uniform title heading. Some bibliographic searching of the catalog reveals that this title has undergone several changes. It was first published between 1965 and 1985 as "Africa research bulletin. Economic, financial, and technical series." In February 1985 the section title became "Economic series" and then, in 1992, the section title changed back to its original form. This necessitated a separate record with a uniform title. Because the new title is published in a different city, the place of publication was a possible choice as the qualifier in the uniform title. However, in this case, the place of publication was not chosen by the cataloger. Instead, the date was apparently considered to be more useful for distinguishing this new serial from its predecessor, which was published in a different period. Therefore, the publication date "1992" is used as the qualifier and placed at the end of the title proper, which in this case consists of the common title and section title together.

O17

PROBLEM CONSIDERED:

Common title in uniform title form with section title (LCRI 25.5B, p. 5)

O17a
TAGGED DATA RECORD (based on OCLC #20289017)

LDR   *****cas_/22******Ia*4500

	00-05	06	07-14	15-17	18	19	20	21	22-28	29	30-32	33	34	35-37	38	39
008	890831	d	198719uu	sp	a	r			---bc-f	0	///	b	0	spa	-	d

022	0214-4441
043	e-sp---
→ 130 0	Bibliografía española (Madrid, Spain : 1958). ≠p Suplemento de cartografía.
→ 245 00	Bibliografía española. ≠p Suplemento de cartografía.
246 30	Suplemento de cartografía
260	Madrid : ≠b Ministerio de Cultura, Dirección General del Libro y Bibliotecas, ≠c 1989-
300	v. ; ≠c 24 cm.
310	Annual
362 0	1980-1987-
500	At head of title: Biblioteca Nacional.
651 0	Spain ≠x Maps ≠x Bibliography.
651 0	Spain ≠x Bibliography.
710 2	Biblioteca Nacional (Spain)
710 1	Spain. ≠b Dirección General del Libro y Bibliotecas.
→ 772 0	≠t Bibliografía española (Madrid, Spain : 1958) ≠x 0523-1760 ≠w (DLC)60044645 ≠w (OCoLC)1519739
785 00	≠t Bibliografía española (Madrid, Spain : 1958). Cartografía ≠x 1133-9519 ≠w (DLC)96655585 ≠w (OCoLC)32298886

O17b

TAGGED PARENT RECORD (based on OCLC #1519739)

LDR   *****cas_/22*****Ia*4500

00-05	06	07-14	15-17	18	19	20	21	22-28	29	30-32	33	34	35-37	38	39
750807	d	19581992	sp	m	r			--b---f	0	///	b	0	spa	-	d

008

022	0523-1760 ≠z 0525-3675
043	e-sp---
→ 130 0	Bibliografía española (Madrid, Spain : 1958)
245 00	Bibliografía española.
260	Madrid : ≠b Ministerio de Educación Nacional, Dirección General de Archivos y Bibliotecas, Servicio Nacional de Información Bibliográfica, ≠c 1959-1992.
300	v. ; ≠c 24-30 cm.
310	Monthly, ≠b 1982-
321	Annual, ≠b 1958-1968
321	Monthly, ≠b 1969-Sept. 1976
321	Annual, ≠b 1977-1978
362 0	1958-dic. 1992.
515	Suspended 1964-1966, 1979-1981, 1986, 1991.
550	Issued by: Spain, Servicio Nacional de Información Bibliográfica, 1958-1970; by: Instituto Bibliográfica Hispánico, 1971-1982; by: Ministerio de Cultura, Dirección General del Libro y Bibliotecas, 1983-<oct.-dic. 1984>; by: Biblioteca Nacional, <1987->1992.
651 0	Spain ≠x Bibliography.
650 0	Spanish literature ≠x Bibliography.
710 2	Biblioteca Nacional (Spain)
710 1	Spain. ≠b Ministerio de Cultura.
710 1	Spain. ≠b Dirección General del Libro y Bibliotecas.
710 2	Instituto Bibliográfica Hispánico.
710 1	Spain. ≠b Servicio Nacional de Información Bibliográfica.
→ 770 0	≠t Bibliografía española (Madrid, Spain : 1958). Suplemento de cartografía ≠x 0214-4441 ≠w (DLC)89645647 ≠w (OCoLC)20289017
770 0	≠t Bibliografía española (Madrid, Spain : 1958). Cartografia ≠x 1135-9519 ≠w (DLC)96655585 ≠w (OCoLC)32298886
770 0	≠t Bibliografía española (Madrid, Spain : 1958). Suplemento de música impresa ≠x 1130-1392 ≠w (DLC)91655665 ≠w (OCoLC)23134037
770 0	≠t Bibliografía española (Madrid, Spain : 1958). Suplemento de publicaciones periódicas ≠x 0210-8372 ≠w (DLC)83640688 ≠w (OCoLC)8380936
780 0	≠t Boletín del depósito legal de obras impresas ≠x 0006-6362 ≠w (DLC)60021620 ≠w (OCoLC)5580333 ≠g 1969
785 0	≠t Bibliografía española. Monografías ≠x 1133-858X ≠w (DLC)96655589 ≠w (OCoLC)32873083

DISCUSSION

- If a title proper consists of a common title with a section number or with a section title, or with both, and the common title itself is a main series (i.e., it is also issued as a separate publication with its own bibliographic record) with a uniform title heading, then all its subseries (such as special issues, supplements, etc.) should have a uniform title heading consisting of the common title in its uniform title form plus the section number, section title, or both (LCRI 25.5B, p. 5).

- The title proper of this record consists of the common title "Bibliografía española" and the section title "Suplemento de cartografía." Since the common title has a separate bibliographic record with a uniform title heading (see parent record O17b), the record for its supplement (i.e., the item now being described) should also have a uniform title heading consisting of that same heading "Bibliografía española (Madrid, Spain : 1958)," plus the section title "Suplemento de cartografía." In other words, in the construction of a uniform title for the supplement now being described, the qualifier for the parent record, i.e., "(Madrid, Spain : 1958)," is retained even though the date "1958" pertains to the parent record and the supplement was first published in 1989.

O18

PROBLEM CONSIDERED:

Common title and section title without an initial article as uniform title heading (LCRI 25.5B, p. 4)

TAGGED DATA RECORD (based on OCLC #21655238)

LDR   *****cas_/22*****Ia*4500

00-05	06	07-14	15-17	18	19	20	21	22-28	29	30-32	33	34	35-37	38	39
008	900531	c	19899999	sz	g	r	l	p	------i	0	///	a	0	eng	-	d

022	1014-7411
043	n-us---
→ 130 0	Trade policy review. ≠p United States of America.
→ 245 00	Trade policy review. ≠p The United States of America.
246 14	Trade policy review. ≠p United States
260	Geneva : ≠b General Agreement on Tariffs and Trade, ≠c [1990-
300	v. ; ≠c 30 cm.
310	Biennial
362 0	1989-
515	Issues for 1992- published in 2 vols.
651 0	United States ≠x Commercial policy ≠x Periodicals.
651 0	United States ≠x Commerce ≠x Periodicals.
650 0	Foreign trade regulation ≠z United States ≠x Periodicals.
710 2	General Agreement on Tariffs and Trade (Organization)

DISCUSSION

- The title proper in this example consists of a common title "Trade policy review" and a section title with an initial article "The United States of America." According to LCRI 25.5B, p. 4, with regard to the construction of uniform titles for common/section titles, whenever a section title includes an initial article, a uniform title should be created to delete the initial article from the section title. The example here illustrates this rule interpretation.

- Notice that the uniform title heading in this record is identical to the title proper "Trade policy review. The United States of America," except that it leaves out the initial article from the section title.

O19

PROBLEM CONSIDERED:

Linking relationship with the uniform title for another language edition (LCRI 25.5C)

RULE(S) CONSULTED:

AACR2R: 25.3C2–25.3C3, 25.5C1

O19a

TAGGED DATA RECORD (based on OCLC #23666199)

LDR   *****cas_/22*****Ia*4500

	00-05	06	07-14	15-17	18	19	20	21	22-28	29	30-32	33	34	35-37	38	39
008	910430	c	19uu9999	cl	a	r		p	--s---i	0	///	b	0	spa	-	d

022   1014-7810

043   cl-----

→ 245 00   Balance preliminar de la economía de América Latina y el Caribe / ≠c Comisión Económica para América Latina y el Caribe.

260   [Santiago de Chile] : ≠b La Comisión,

300   v. : ≠b ill. ; ≠c 28 cm.

310   Annual

500   Description based on: 1990; title from cover.

→ 580   Issued also in English ed.

651 0   Latin America ≠x Economic conditions ≠y 1982- ≠x Statistics.

650 0   Economic indicators ≠z Latin America.

651 0   Caribbean Area ≠x Economic conditions ≠y 1945- ≠x Statistics.

650 0   Economic indicators ≠z Caribbean Area.

710 2   United Nations. ≠b Economic Commission for Latin America and the Caribbean.

→ 775 1   ≠t Balance preliminar de la economía de América Latina y el Caribe. English. Preliminary overview of the economy of Latin America and the Caribbean ≠x 1014-7802 ≠w (DLC)92645995 ≠w (OCoLC)21256666

780 00   ≠t Balance preliminar de la economía latinoamericana ≠w (DLC)87654712 ≠w (OCoLC)16813193

O19b

TAGGED DATA RECORD (based on OCLC #21256666)

LDR   *****cas_/22*****Ia*4500

00-05	06	07-14	15-17	18	19	20	21	22-28	29	30-32	33	34	35-37	38	39
008	900322	c	19899999	cl	a	r			--s---i	0	///	a	0	eng	-	d

022	1014-7802
043	cl----- ≠a cc-----
→ 130 0	Balance preliminar de la economía de América Latina y el Caribe. ≠l English.
→ 245 10	Preliminary overview of the economy of Latin America and the Caribbean / ≠c Economic Commission for Latin America and the Caribbean.
260	Santiago, Chile : ≠b The Commission, ≠c 1989-
300	v. : ≠b ill. ; ≠c 28 cm.
310	Annual
362 0	1989-
500	Title from cover.
580	Issued also in Spanish ed.
651 0	Latin America ≠x Economic conditions ≠y 1982- ≠x Statistics.
650 0	Economic indicators ≠z Latin America.
651 0	Caribbean Area ≠x Economic conditions ≠y 1945- ≠x Statistics.
650 0	Economic indicators ≠z Caribbean Area.
710 2	United Nations. ≠b Economic Commission for Latin America and the Caribbean.
775 1	≠t Balance preliminar de la economía de América Latina y el Caribe ≠x 1014-7810 ≠w (DLC)93663042 ≠w (OCoLC)23666199
780 00	≠t Balance preliminar de la economía latinoamericana. English. Preliminary overview of the Latin American economy during ... ≠w (DLC)90661483 ≠w (OCoLC)18619552

DISCUSSION

- The serial publication in example O19a is published in Spanish. However, it is also issued simultaneously in an English edition under an English title (see field 580). According to LCRI 25.5C, one of the editions should be chosen to serve as the original edition, and the title of that edition should be used in the uniform title on the other language edition (see example O19b). The name of the language of the item should also be added to the uniform title (25.5C1). Generally in cases such as this, the first edition cataloged is considered to be the original (see CCM 5.6.2) as long as none of the rules in 25.3C2–25.3C3 for choosing the primary title apply. In this example, the Spanish edition is chosen as the original, since the preceding title of the Spanish edition was cataloged in 1987 and the preceding title of the English edition was cataloged in 1988.

- When providing a field 775 (Other Edition Available Entry) link to the record for the other language edition, the entry should consist of the uniform title heading (field 130), plus the name of the language (subfield ≠l), and the title proper (field 245) of the other language edition.

O20

PROBLEM CONSIDERED:

Linking relationship with the uniform title entered under a name heading (25.3C2)

O20a

TAGGED DATA RECORD (based on OCLC #9311486)

LDR   *****cas_/22*****Ia*4500

00-05	06	07-14	15-17	18	19	20	21	22-28	29	30-32	33	34	35-37	38	39
830315	d	19811981	sa	a	r			------f	0	///	a	0	eng	-	d

008

043	f-sa---
→ 110 1	South Africa. ≠b Dept. of Agriculture and Fisheries.
→ 245 10	Annual report of the Director General, Agriculture and Fisheries for the period ... / ≠c Republic of South Africa.
246 13	Report of the Director General, Agriculture and Fisheries for the period ...
246 04	Annual report
260	[Pretoria] : ≠b Dept. of Agriculture and Fisheries, ≠c [1981?].
300	1 v. : ≠b ill., maps ; ≠c 30 cm.
310	Annual
362 0	1 Apr. 1980 to 31 Mar. 1981.
→ 580	Also issued in Afrikaans as: Jaarverslag van die Direkteur-generaal Landbou en Visserye vir die tydperk ...
610 10	South Africa. ≠b Dept. of Agriculture and Fisheries.
650 0	Agriculture ≠z South Africa.
650 0	Fisheries ≠z South Africa.
→ 775 1	South Africa. Dept. of Agriculture and Fisheries. ≠s Annual report of the Director General, Agriculture and Fisheries for the period ... Afrikaans. ≠t Jaarverslag van die Direkteur-generaal Landbou en Visserye vir die tydperk ... ≠w (DLC)83647962 ≠w (OCoLC)10220925
780 00	South Africa. Dept. of Agricultural Technical Services. ≠t Annual report of the Secretary for Agricultural Technical Services ≠w (DLC)67005675 ≠w (OCoLC)3019809
785 00	South Africa. Dept. of Agriculture and Fisheries. ≠t Annual report of the Director General, Agriculture for the period ... ≠w (DLC)84640486 ≠w (OCoLC)10227928

O20b

TAGGED DATA RECORD FOR AFRICAANS EDITION (based on OCLC #10220925)

LDR   *****cas_/22*****Ia*4500

00-05	06	07-14	15-17	18	19	20	21	22-28	29	30-32	33	34	35-37	38	39
831215	d	19811981	sa	a	r			------f	0	///	b	0	afr	-	d

008

043   f-sa---

→ 110 1   South Africa. ≠b Dept. of Agriculture and Fisheries.

→ 240 10   Annual report of the Director General, Agriculture and Fisheries for the period … ≠l Afrikaans.

→ 245 10   Jaarverslag van die Direkteur-generaal Landbou en Visserye vir die tydperk …

246 14   Jaarverslag Departement van Landbou en Visserye

260   Pretoria : ≠b Die Departement, ≠c 1981?

300   1 v. : ≠b ill. ; ≠c 30 cm.

310   Annual

362 0   1 Apr. 1980 tot 31 Maart 1981.

580   Also issued in English.

610 1   South Africa. ≠b Dept. of Agriculture and Fisheries.

650 0   Agriculture ≠z South Africa.

650 0   Fisheries ≠z South Africa.

775 1   South Africa. Dept. of Agriculture and Fisheries. ≠t Annual report of the Director General, Agriculture and Fisheries for the period … ≠w (DLC)83641940 ≠w (OCoLC)9311486

DISCUSSION

- Similar to the example in O19, this example also involves a publication issued in another language edition. The serial here is published in English (O20a) and is also issued in an Afrikaans edition (O20b). Neither of these editions is known to be the original. Therefore, since the work is entered under the heading for a corporate body and English is the language used in that heading, the English edition is treated as the original and its title is used as the uniform title (25.3C2).

- In the record O20a for the original English version, a field 775 (Other Edition Available Entry) link is provided to the record for the Afrikaans edition. This linking entry consists of the main entry heading (field 110) in subfield ≠a, uniform title (field 240 including subfield ≠l, the name of the language) in subfield ≠s, and the title proper (field 245) of the Afrikaans edition in subfield ≠t.

P. Microforms

Microforms may be original publications or they may be reproductions. Original microforms include those that are first issued in microformat, usually in microfiche, as well as those that once were issued in hard copy and now are issued in microformat only. Microforms that are issued simultaneously with their print counterparts by the same source are considered to be original. Microform sets of unrelated titles (including serials) grouped together for the purpose of publication in microform are also considered to be original. Reproduction microforms, on the other hand, refer to works with a preexisting bibliographic and/or physical identity. Reproduction is considered to be a mechanical rather than an intellectual process. For that reason, reproduction microforms may be further categorized in terms of filming generation, such as a first-generation master (for preservation), service copy (for end user), and print master copy (for generating the service copy).

According to AACR2R, Chapter 11, microform serials—original publications (micropublications) and reproductions (microreproductions)—are cataloged in the same manner. However, the Library of Congress has taken a different stand on the guidelines for creating records for microreproductions of serials. As a result, catalogers for institutions whose cataloging policy for microform serials is to follow CONSER practice should first determine whether they are dealing with a microreproduction or a micropublication before applying the appropriate rules. If the item in hand is a preservation master microform, the treatment may depend on whether the institution chooses to adhere to CONSER guidelines for reproduction microforms (see CEG Appendix M).

As mentioned earlier, original microform serials are cataloged according to AACR2R, Chapter 11, which calls for the item in hand to be the basis for the bibliographic description for the catalog record. A uniform title is input if needed, in accordance with LCRI 25.5B, p. 3, and the qualifying term for the uniform title is the same as the Specific Material Designation (SMD) used within the record.

The CONSER guidelines for cataloging serials of reproductions of preexisting textual material may be summarized as follows:

1. Create a separate record for the reproduction based on the record for the original (LCRI Chapter 11).
2. No uniform title is needed for the reproduction to distinguish it from the printed copy.
3. Give the details of the reproduction in a Reproduction Note, field 533 (AACR2R, Chapter 11 may be applied to form the note.) Input the 533 field as the last note following all 5xx fields relating to the original. In OCLC-MARC format, an optional 539 field (Fixed-Length Data Elements of Reproduction Note), may be given following the 533 field.

4. For service copies, a link to the record for the original is optional. For preservation master microforms, the link between the reproduction and the hard copy (original) is mandatory if there is a record for the original in the database.

5. Code in field 008 (Fixed-Length Data Elements—Serials) for the original title the data elements except for character position 23 (Form of Item), which is coded for the reproduction.

6. Input one 007 field (Physical Description Fixed Field—Microform) in each record. If the record is for a preservation master, input additional 007 fields, as appropriate, for other generations of the microform produced by the same filming process.

EXAMPLES

P1	Original microfiche serial
P2	Paper format continued in microfiche format
P3	Microfilm reproduction of an existing print serial (service copy)
P4	Microfilm reproduction of an existing print serial (service copy and preservation master)
P5	Microfilm reproduction issued as a part of a series

P1

PROBLEM CONSIDERED:

Original microfiche serial (Chapter 11)

RULE(S) CONSULTED:

AACR2R: 11.0B1, 11.1C1

TAGGED DATA RECORD (based on OCLC #22457003)

→ LDR   *****nas_/22*****Ia*4500

00-05	06	07-14	15-17	18	19	20	21	22-28	29	30-32	33	34	35-37	38	39
901001	c	19uu9999	vau	a	r			bb-----	0	///	a	0	eng	-	d

→ 008

→ 007   h ≠b e ≠d u ≠e m ≠f u--- ≠g b ≠h a ≠i u ≠j a   (microfiche)

043   n-us---

→ 245 00   Buckmaster's Franchise 500 product ≠h [microform].

246 30   Franchise 500 product

260   Mineral, Va. : ≠b Buckmaster Pub.,

→ 300   microfiches : ≠b ill. ; ≠c 11 x 15 cm.

310   Annual

500   Description based on: 1990; title from brochure.

650 0   Franchises (Retail trade) ≠z United States ≠x Periodicals.

710 2   Buckmaster Publishing.

DISCUSSION

• This example is a serial issued in microfiche only, and therefore it is cataloged as an original microform serial according to the provisions in AACR2R Chapter 11. The bibliographic description is based on information taken from the original microform.

- In this example, in the absence of the title frame and the microfiche header, the chief source of information is the brochure (eye-readable accompanying material) (11.0B1). The source of the title proper is given in a 500 General Note.
- The General Material Designation (GMD) "microform" is added immediately following the title proper (11.1C1), preceding a parallel title, other title information, or the statement of responsibility, if such is present.
- The Specific Material Designation "microfiches" is given in the Physical Description field 300.
- In leader position 6 (Type of Record), code "a" for Language Material. In fixed field 008, position 22 (Form of Original Item), use "b" for Microfiche. In fixed field 007 (Physical Description Fixed Field—Microform) is coded "he_umu---baua." Code "h" is for Microform; "e" for Original Microfiche; "u" for Polarity Unknown; "m" for Size 11 × 15 cm; "u---" for Reduction Ratio Unknown; "b" for Monochrome; "a" for Silver Halide Base Emulsion; "u" for Generation Unknown; and "a" for Safety Base Film.

P2

PROBLEM CONSIDERED:

Paper format continued in microfiche format (Chapter 11)

RULE(S) CONSULTED:

LCRI: 21.3B, 25.5B

P2a

TAGGED DATA RECORD (based on OCLC #26614315)

→ LDR   *****nas_/22*****_a*4500

00-05	06	07-14	15-17	18	19	20	21	22-28	29	30-32	33	34	35-37	38	39
920916	c	19909999	stk	a	r			bb-cb-f	0	///	a	0	eng	-	d

008 (as above)

007   h ≠b e ≠d b ≠e m ≠f u--- ≠g b ≠h u ≠i c ≠j a   (microfiche: service copy)

→ 130 0   Bibliography of Scotland (Microfiche)

→ 245 00   Bibliography of Scotland ≠h [microform].

260   Edinburgh : ≠b National Library of Scotland, ≠c c1991-

300   microfiches ; ≠c 11 x 15 cm. + ≠e 1 loose-leaf index (32 cm.)

310   Annual

362 0   1988-1990-

500   Title from eye-readable header.

500   Issued in loose-leaf binder with introduction and index.

→ 580   Continues the former printed edition of: Bibliography of Scotland.

651 0   Scotland ≠x Imprints ≠x Catalogs.

610 20   National Library of Scotland ≠x Catalogs.

710 2   National Library of Scotland.

→ 780 10   ≠t Bibliography of Scotland ≠w (DLC)81640330 ≠w (OCoLC)5655996

P2b

TAGGED DATA RECORD (based on OCLC #5655996)

→ LDR   *****nas_/22*****_a*4500

	00-05	06	07-14	15-17	18	19	20	21	22-28	29	30-32	33	34	35-37	38	39
008	791106	d	19771987	stk	a	r			---cb-f	0	///	a	0	eng	-	d

245 00	Bibliography of Scotland / ≠c National Library of Scotland.	
260	Edinburgh : ≠b H.M.S.O., ≠c c1978-c1990.	
300	11 v. ; ≠c 25 cm.	
310	Annual	
362 0	1976-77-1987.	
→ 580	Continued in microfiche format with the same title.	
651 0	Scotland ≠x Imprints ≠x Catalogs.	
610 20	National Library of Scotland ≠x Catalogs.	
710 2	National Library of Scotland.	
→ 785 10	≠t Bibliography of Scotland (Microfiche) ≠w (DLC)sn94017713 ≠w (OCoLC)26614315	

DISCUSSION

- When the physical format of a serial changes, e.g., from print format to micro-fiche, this constitutes reason to create a new record for the new format (LCRI 21.3B). Such is the case in this example, where the item "Bibliography of Scotland" is cataloged as an original microfiche (example P2a) because it is no longer published in print format (example P2b).
- A uniform title heading must be created for the new record in the microform format even though the title proper remains the same. LCRI 25.5B gives no specific guidelines with regard to choosing a qualifier for the uniform title in such situations, except for instructions to use any word(s) sufficient to distin-guish between the serials. However, the Specific Material Designation of the physical format is generally considered to be the most appropriate choice as qualifier (CCM 5.2.4). Thus, the uniform title heading in example P2a is qual-ified by the term "Microfiche."
- In example P2a the preceding title is input in field 780. Reciprocally, in exam-ple P2b, the succeeding title is input in field 785. The two linking fields (780 and 785) both have first indicator value "1" so that no note is generated; in-stead, a Linking Entry Complexity Note, field 580, is input for each record.

P3

PROBLEM CONSIDERED:

Microfilm reproduction of an existing print serial (service copy) (LCRI Chapter 11)

RULE(S) CONSULTED:

AACR2R: 1.1C2, 11.4–11.7
LCRI: 12.0B1, 25.5B

TAGGED DATA RECORD (based on OCLC #8648595)

→ LDR   *****nas_/22*****_a*4500

00-05	06	07-14	15-17	18	19	20	21	22-28	29	30-32	33	34	35-37	38	39
820802	c	19729999	dcu	m	x		p	-a-----	0	///	a	0	eng	-	d

→ 008

→ 007   h ≠b d ≠d a ≠e f ≠f b--- ≠g b ≠h u ≠i c ≠j u   (microfilm: service copy)

022   ≠y 0013-189X

043   n-us---

→ 130 0   Educational researcher (Washington, D.C. : 1972)

→ 245 00   Educational researcher ≠h [microform]: ≠ b a publication of the American Educational Research Association.

260   Washington, D.C. : ≠ b The Association, ≠c c1972-

300   v. : ≠b ill. ; ≠c 28 cm.

310   9 no. a year, ≠b <Apr. 1987->

321   Monthly, ≠b Jan. 1972-

362 0   Vol. 1, no. 1 (Jan. 1972)-

500   Title from cover.

→ 533   Microfilm. ≠b Ann Arbor, Mich. : ≠c University Microfilms International, ≠e microfilm reels ; 35 mm.

650 0   Education ≠z United States ≠x Periodicals.

610 20   American Educational Research Association ≠x Periodicals.

710 2   American Educational Research Association.

→ 776 1   ≠c Original ≠w (DLC)87657066 ≠w (OCoLC)1775556

780 00   ≠t Educational researcher ≠x 0013-189X ≠w (DLC)87657065 ≠w (OCoLC)1567611

DISCUSSION

- This example is a reproduction microform of a preexisting print serial. The choice and form of access points and the bibliographic description are based on the originally published item (LCRI Chapter 11). For this reason, cataloging of reproduction microforms may be accomplished by (1) cloning an online record for the print version, as in this example; (2) transcribing the information from a catalog card; or (3) originally cataloging the title page of the print version, as reproduced in the microform format. If a source other than the reproduced title page in the microform serves as the chief source, make a source of title note (LCRI 12.0B1). When cloning or transcribing from a cataloging card, the choice of main entry and transcription of the title statement should be the same as on the record for the original.
- If a uniform title heading has already been established in the record for the print version, that heading should also be transcribed onto the record for the reproduction. Thus, the uniform title heading in this example, "Educational researcher (Washington, D.C. : 1972)," has been input because it appeared on the record for the original and not (as prescribed in LCRI 25.5B) for the purpose of resolving a title conflict.
- The General Material Designation (GMD) "microform" is input, in brackets, immediately following the title proper (1.1C2).
- The catalog record for the reproduction microform must have a field 533 in which the details of reproduction are given. The data elements of this note may be formulated as instructed in rules 11.4–11.7 in AACR2R Chapter 11. They include: Type of reproduction; Date of publication and/or sequential designa-

tion of issues reproduced; Place of reproduction; Agency responsible for re-production; Date of micropublishing; Physical description of reproduction; Series statement of the reproduction; and Notes about the reproduction.

- Field 776 is used to link the reproduction to the print version. According to CONSER guidelines for cataloging reproduction microforms, construction of a link is optional if the microform is a service copy, but is mandatory if the microform is a preservation master (CCM 32.3.2m). Unlike other linking fields, only subfield ≠c (Qualifying Information) and subfield ≠w (Record Control Number) are required for field 776 in the record for the reproduction.
- Coded data elements for the microform format are input in fixed field 008 character position 23 (Form of Item) and in field 007 (Physical Description Fixed Field—Microform). In this example, field 007 is coded "hd_afb---bucu." Code "h" is for Microform; "d" for Microfilm; "a" for Positive Polarity; "f" for Size 16 mm.; "b---" for Normal Reduction Ratio; "b" for Monochrome; "u" for Emulsion Unknown; "c" for Service Copy Generation; "u" for Base of Film Unknown.

P4

PROBLEM CONSIDERED:

Microfilm reproduction of an existing print serial (service copy and preservation master) (LCRI Chapter 11)

RULE(S) CONSULTED:

AACR2R: 1.1C2, 11.4–11.7

TAGGED DATA RECORD (based on OCLC #29937255)

LDR   *****nas_/22*****Ka*4500

	00-05	06	07-14	15-17	18	19	20	21	22-28	29	30-32	33	34	35-37	38	39
008	800318	c	19019999	nyu	m	r		p	-a-----	0	///	a	0	eng	-	d

→ 007   h ≠b d ≠d a ≠e f ≠f u--- ≠g b ≠h a ≠i c ≠j a   (microfilm: service copy)

→ 007   h ≠b d ≠d b ≠e f ≠f u--- ≠g b ≠h a ≠i a ≠j a   (microfilm: preservation master)

→ 245 00   International musician ≠h [microform].

260   Newark, N.J. : ≠b [s.n.],

300   v. : ≠b ill. ; ≠c 30-43 cm.

310   Monthly

362 1   Began publication in 1901.

550   Official journal of the American Federation of Musicians of the United States and Canada.

500   Vols. for 1919-23 include the official proceedings of its annual convention.

525   Includes occasional supplements.

→ 533   Microfilm. ≠m v.1-64 (1901-1969) ≠b New York : ≠c New York Public Library, ≠d [19—]. ≠e 7 microfilm reels ; 35mm.

650 0   Trade-unions ≠x Musicians ≠z United States ≠x Periodicals.

710 2   American Federation of Musicians.

710 2   American Federation of Musicians. ≠t Proceedings of the convention.

→ 776 1   ≠c Original ≠w (DLC)ca14000421 ≠w (OCoLC)1753645

DISCUSSION

- As in example P3, the record in this example is cloned from the online record for the original. However, since this record represents both the presentation master and the service copy of the reproduction, two 007 fields are input. The first 007 field is for the positive service copy (subfield ≠i is coded "c" for Service Copy). The second 007 field is for the preservation master negative (subfield ≠i is coded "a" for Preservation Master Copy).

- The General Material Designation (GMD) "microform" is added in brackets immediately following the title proper (1.1C2).

- The physical description of the microform is given in a Reproduction Note, field 533, which should be constructed according to rules 11.4–11.7 (LCRI Chapter 11).

  Subfield ≠m of field 533 was introduced in the early 1990s for recording holdings data according to the national standards (ANSI/NISO Z39.71-199x) in a form different from field 362 as prescribed by AACR2R. Subfield ≠m is optional in records for service copies but is required for preservation masters. Holdings data in subfield ≠m are given *not* in the form used for field 362 but in the form of enumeration and/or chronology, e.g., v.1-3 (1900-1902); 1960-1968; 7th-14th (1906/1907-1913/1914); v.1-10 (1900-1909): [Gaps]; v.1-10 (1900-1909):[Lacks v.3:no.4-8]; <v.2-3 (1984-Dec.1987)>- etc. (CEG 533 Reproduction Note Subfield ≠m).

  Subfields ≠b and ≠c of field 533 contain the place and name of the agency responsible for the reproduction. Both subfields are repeatable. The name of a distributor or a contractor, if known and considered important, may also be transcribed.

  Subfield ≠d of field 533 contains the dates of filming. If the information is not available or is incomplete, omit this subfield and input a period at the end of subfield ≠c.

  Subfield ≠e of field 533 contains the physical description of the reproduction. The extent of the item is given in terms of the Specific Material Designation (SMD), which is "microfilm reels" in this example. Add the term "negative" or "positive" only if it is considered helpful, such as for a negative service copy, etc.

- For a preservation master reproduction, a link must be made to the record for the original, and vice versa (CCM 32.3.2m). In this example, field 776 is used, but only subfield ≠c and subfield ≠w are needed to provide the link.

P5

PROBLEM CONSIDERED:

Microfilm reproduction issued as a part of a series (LCRI Chapter 11)

RULE(S) CONSULTED:

AACR2R: 12.6

```
                        ┌──────────────────────────────────────────┐
                        │     19th Century American Music Periodicals │
                        │                                            │
     Microfilm          │   Southern Musical Advocate and Singer's   │
     box label          │            Friend 274-1                    │
                        │     Vol: 1-2 July 1859-April 1861          │
                        │                                            │
                        │   Reel 1-Title #274              9066      │
                        └──────────────────────────────────────────┘
```

TAGGED DATA RECORD (based on OCLC #22937620)

LDR   *****nas_/22*****_a*4500

00-05	06	07-14	15-17	18	19	20	21	22-28	29	30-32	33	34	35-37	38	39
910109	d	18591867	vau	u	u		p	-a-----	0	///	a	0	eng	-	d

008

007   h ≠b d ≠d a ≠e f ≠f u--- ≠g b ≠h a ≠i c ≠j a   (microfilm: service copy)

→ 245 04   The Southern musical advocate and singer's friend ≠h [microform].

260   Mountain Valley, Va. : ≠b J. Funk & Sons, ≠c 1859-1867.

300   9 v. : ≠b ill., music ; ≠c 26 cm.

362 0   Vol. 1, no. 1 (July 1859)-

362 1   Ceased in 1867.

500   Title from caption.

→ 533   Microfilm. ≠b Alexandria, Va. : ≠c Chadwyck-Healey, ≠e microfilm reels ; 35 mm. ≠f (19th century American music periodicals)

650 0   Music ≠x Periodicals.

776 1   ≠c Original ≠w (OCoLC)10870617

785 00   ≠t Musical advocate and singer's friend ≠w (DLC)sf92095634 ≠w (OCoLC)22937682

→ 830 0   19th century American music periodicals.

DISCUSSION

- According to LCRI Chapter 11, the cataloging for reproduction microforms is based on the original work being reproduced. When the original work belongs to a series, the series statement should be transcribed within the bibliographic description in the same manner as on the record for the original, as instructed in rule 12.6.

- If the microform is issued as part of a series, the series statement for the microform is included in a Reproduction Note, field 533, subfield ≠f, enclosed in parentheses. If a series added entry is needed, field 8xx must be used to provide access. Note that the entry in the 8xx field must be the authority form for the series. In this example, the microform series is input in parentheses in field 533, subfield ≠f, and a series added entry "19th century American music periodicals" is input in field 830.

Q. Nonprint Serials and Multiformat Accompanying Materials

Many types of nonprint materials may be issued serially. Such nonprint publications can appear in the form of videorecordings (videocassette, videodisc, film reel, etc.), sound recordings (sound cassette, compact disc, sound tape reel, etc.), maps (map, atlas, chart, etc.), graphic materials (slide, poster, etc.), interactive multimedia, direct-access electronic journals (CD-ROM or computer disk) or remote-access electronic journals (see section R), and microforms (see section P).

The cataloging of nonprint serials was affected by the implementation of the final phase of format integration in early 1996. Although the serial MARC record format was used for all nonprint serials *before* format integration, such materials are now cataloged using the appropriate MARC record format according to their physical format. This entails the use of an appropriate code in character position 06 of the leader for Type of Record, e.g., "g" (Projected Medium) may be used for a serial video-recording or a serial slide, "e" (Printed Cartographic Material) for a serial atlas, "j" (Musical Sound Recording) for a serial musical sound recording, etc.

An appropriate field 008 (Fixed-Length Data Elements) must be included in each record, with the choice of coding depending on the physical format of the item. Also, the cataloging record should include field 007 (Physical Description Fixed Field), again with coding chosen according to the physical format of the item as well as to any accompanying materials, e.g., 007 for maps, 007 for computer files, 007 for visual materials, etc. (see USMARC Format for Bibliographic Data for details).

Perhaps the most significant change brought about by format integration on the cataloging of nonprint serials is the obligatory use of field 006 (Fixed-Length Data Elements—Additional Material Characteristics), which contains 18 character positions (00–17) used to code information about special aspects of the item being cataloged that cannot be coded in field 008. As a result of format integration, field 008 records characteristics pertaining to the physical format of a nonprint serial, and, consequently, the serial aspects (frequency, regularity, etc.) of the item have to be coded separately in field 006.

Another function of field 006 is to record the characteristics of any materials that might accompany a serial publication. This function is used quite frequently, since it is not uncommon for a publisher to issue accompanying materials in a format that differs from that of the main item.

Accompanying materials are defined as "materials issued with, and intended to be used with, the item being cataloged" (AACR2R, p. 615). The treatment of accompanying materials is covered in AACR2R 1.5E1 and LCRI 1.5E1. In serials cataloging, these rules should be applied in conjunction with AACR2R 12.5E1. Generally, if accompanying material is issued regularly, then its details are recorded at the end of the physical description in field 300, subfield ≠e. If it is issued irregularly or is issued only once, then it is described in a 500 General Note field (with an open-ended date), or ignored (see also CCM 11.4).

For nonprint serials, the presence of accompanying materials in a different format generally results in a second 006 field, in addition to the obligatory 006 field configured for serials, also being input. This applies to accompanying materials recorded in field 300, subfield ≠e, or in the 500 General Note field; to supplements recorded in field 525 (Supplement Note) not cataloged separately; and to accompanying materials described in other 5xx fields, which are not cataloged separately. However, it should be noted that use of field 006 for the purpose of recording the characteristics of accompanying materials is optional and depends on the cataloging policy of individual libraries; some libraries may choose not to supply this field except in cases of exceptionally significant accompanying materials.

In general, when cataloging nonprint serials, use the MARC fields that are relevant to the particular physical format. For example, for a serial map, use field 255 for cartographic mathematical data, with subfield ≠a for scale and subfield ≠b for projection; for a serial videorecording, use field 508 for a Creation/Production Credits Note and field 511 for a Participant or Performer Note. However, note that such information should be recorded only when it applies to all issues or if it is likely to remain constant.

Supplements or indexes may either be cataloged separately or described in a 525 note field (for supplements) or a 555 note field (for indexes) when these are issued as an integral part of a serial. Separately cataloged supplements or indexes should not be treated as accompanying material in serials cataloging.

EXAMPLES

Q1   Journal on videocassette continues journal on videocassette
Q2   Journal on sound disc continues journal on sound cassette with the same title
Q3   Journal on slides
Q4   Nonmusical sound recording journal accompanied by kit
Q5   Musical sound recording journal issued as a supplement
Q6   Printed music material issued as a serial
Q7   Map/atlas/chart issued as a serial
Q8   Mixed materials issued as a serial
Q9   Print serial accompanied by CD-ROM
Q10   Print serial accompanied by computer disk
Q11   Print serial accompanied by microform
Q12   Print serial accompanied by sound cassette supplements
Q13   Print serial indexed by diskette
Q14   Electronic journal accompanied by print material

Q1

PROBLEM CONSIDERED:

Journal on videocassette continues journal on videocassette

RULE(S) CONSULTED:

AACR2R: 21.2A1

Q1a
TAGGED DATA RECORD (based on OCLC #34724094)

LDR   *****cgs_/22*****Ia*4500   (projected medium serial)

(visual materials: videorecording)

00-05	06	07-14	15-17	18-20	21	22	23-27	28	29-32	33	34	35-37	38	39
921022	c	19919999	nyu	---	/	f	r----	-	////	v	u	eng	-	d

008

00	01	02	03	04	05	06	07	08-10	11	12	13-15	16	17
s	q	r		p	-	-	-	---	-	0	///	a	0

→ 006   (serial)

00	01-04	05	06	07-10	11	12	13	14	15	16	17
a	a---	f	-	----	-	0	0	0	/	0	-

→ 006   (book)

→ 007   v ≠b f ≠d m ≠e b ≠f a ≠g h ≠h o ≠i u   (videocassette)

245 00 VideoUrology times ≠h [videorecording].

246 3 Video urology times

260 New York, NY : ≠b VideoUrology Times, ≠c [1991-

300 videocassettes : ≠b sd., col. with b&w ; ≠c 1/2 in. + ≠e guides

310 Quarterly

362 0 Vol. 4, program 1-

650 0 Urologic diseases ≠x Periodicals.

→ 780 00 ≠t VideoUrology ≠x 0898-4352 ≠w (OCoLC)17811183

Q1b

TAGGED DATA RECORD (based on OCLC #17811183)

LDR   *****cgs_/22*****Ia*4500   (projected medium serial)

(visual materials: videorecording)

00-05	06	07-14	15-17	18-20	21	22	23-27	28	29-32	33	34	35-37	38	39
880419	d	1988199u	nyu	---	/	f	-----	-	////	v	u	eng	-	d

008

00	01	02	03	04	05	06	07	08-10	11	12	13-15	16	17
s	q	r	1	p	-	-	-	---	-	0	///	a	0

006   (serial)

007   v ≠b f ≠d c ≠e b ≠f a ≠g h ≠h o ≠i u   (videocassette)

022 0   0898-4352

245 00   VideoUrology ≠h [videorecording].

246 3   Video urology

260   New York, N.Y. : ≠b P.C. Communications, ≠c [1988-199-?].

300   videocassettes : ≠b sd., col. ; ≠c 1/2 in.

310   Quarterly

362 0   Vol. 1, program 1-v. 3, program 4.

650 0   Urologic diseases ≠x Periodicals.

785 00   ≠t VideoUrology times ≠w (OCoLC)34724094

DISCUSSION

- A video issued as a serial should be cataloged according to its physical format, i.e., position 06 (Type of Record) in the leader is coded "g" for Projected Medium. Field 008 (Visual Materials) is used, with the addition of a 006 field to express the serial nature of the videos. A 007 Physical Description Fixed Field for videorecordings is also required to code the physical characteristics of the videocassettes.

- Though the physical format remains the same, the title in this example has changed from "VideoUrology" to "VideoUrology times." A separate record is therefore created for the succeeding title (21.2A1).

- In the two examples in Q1, field 008 position 33 (Type of Visual Material) is coded "v" for Videorecording. Positions 18–20 (Running Time for Motion Pictures and Videorecordings) are coded "blank" for Unknown, since at the time of cataloging the cataloger did not have the complete run of the videocassettes in hand; otherwise, if the video journal had completed its run, a more accurate code should have been provided.

- Note that in Q1a the catalog record contains two 006 fields. The first is a 006 field for serials, with most of the information relating to the serial nature of the videocassettes. The second is a 006 field for books, used here to code the characteristics of the guides that accompany the videocassettes. Again, the cataloger will need to examine the physical items to be able to provide accurate values for the required codes.

Q2

PROBLEM CONSIDERED:

Journal on sound disc continues journal on sound cassette with the same title

RULE(S) CONSULTED:

LCRI: 21.3B

Q2a

TAGGED DATA RECORD (based on OCLC #18697613)

LDR   `*****cjs_/22*****Ia*4500`   (musical sound recording serial)

(music)

00-05	06	07-14	15-17	18-19	20	21	22	23	24-29	30-31	32-34	35-37	38	39
881101	c	19889999	wau	uu	n	/	g	-	h-----	--	///	N/A	-	d

→008

00	01	02	03	04	05	06	07	08-10	11	12	13-15	16	17
s	a	r		p	-	-	-	---	-	0	///	a	0

→006   (serial)

00	01-04	05	06	07-10	11	12	13	14	15	16	17
a	a---	g	-	----	-	0	0	0	/	0	-

→006   (book)

→007   s ≠b d ≠d f ≠e s ≠f n ≠g g ≠h n ≠i n   (sound disc)

022   0031-6016

130 0   Perspectives of new music (Compact disc)

245 00   Perspectives of new music ≠h [sound recording].

246 30   PNM

260   Seattle, WA : ≠b Perspectives of New Music, ≠c p1988-

300   sound discs : ≠b digital, stereo ; ≠c 4 3/4 in. + ≠e disc information booklet

310   Annual

362 0   Vol. 26 (1988)-

500   Mastered by Nimbus.

→500   Accompanies serial of the same title in conjunction with the last issue of the year, beginning with v. 26 no. 2 (summer 1988).

500   Contents and program notes for disc in each volume of printed serial.

→538   Compact disc.

→580   Continues same title in audio tape cassette format.

650 0   Music ≠y 20th century ≠x History and criticism ≠x Periodicals.

772 1   ≠t Perspectives of new music ≠x 0031-6016 ≠w (OCoLC)1762140 ≠w (DLC)66089176

780 00   ≠t Perspectives of new music (Sound cassette) ≠x 0031-6016 ≠w (OCoLC)15976038

Q2b

TAGGED DATA RECORD (based on OCLC #15976038)

LDR   *****cjs_/22*****Ia*4500   (musical sound recording serial)

(music)

00-05	06	07-14	15-17	18-19	20	21	22	23	24-29	30-31	32-34	35-37	38	39
870615	d	19841987	nyu	uu	n	/	g	-	------	--	///	eng	-	d

→ 008

00	01	02	03	04	05	06	07	08-10	11	12	13-15	16	17
s	a	r		p	-	-	-	---	-	0	///	-	0

→ 006   (serial)

→ 007   s ≠b s ≠d l ≠e s ≠f n ≠g j ≠h l ≠i n ≠j m ≠n u   (sound cassette)

245 00   Perspectives of new music ≠h [sound recording].

260   [Annandale-on-Hudson, N.Y.] : ≠b Perspectives of New Music, ≠c 1984-1987.

300   sound cassettes (58 min.) : ≠b analog, 1 7/8 ips, stereo., Dolby processes ; ≠c 4 1/4 x 2 3/4 in., 1/8 in. tape

310   Annual

362 0   Vol. 22 (1984)-v. 25 (1987)

→ 500   Accompanies serial of the same title in conjunction with the last issue of the year, beginning with v. 22 nos. 1 & 2.

500   Contents and program notes for cassettes in each volume of serial.

→ 580   Continued by the same title in compact disc format.

650 0   Music ≠y 20th century ≠x History and criticism ≠x Periodicals.

785 00   ≠t Perspectives of new music (Compact disc) ≠x 0031-6016 ≠w (OCoLC)18697613

DISCUSSION

- Example Q2a is a serial in compact disc format, which happens to be a continuation of the same title in sound cassette format (example Q2b). Though the title remains the same, a separate record is created for the succeeding publication in compact disc format, since a new record is required whenever there is a change in the physical format in which the serial is issued (LCRI 21.3B).

- Both serials in Q2 are cataloged according to their physical format, i.e., character position 06 (Type of Record) in the leader is coded "j" for Musical Sound Recording. Field 008 is used for music, with the addition of a 006 field for serials to express the serial nature of the sound recording. A 007 Physical Description Fixed Field for sound recordings is also required for each record to code the physical characteristics of the sound disc and the sound cassette respectively.

- In example Q2a, two 006 fields are entered. The first is a 006 field for serials; the second 006 field is for the characteristics of the accompanying "disc information booklet" as recorded in field 300, subfield ≠e. Note that field 007 corresponds to the information given in the description in field 300 and in the 538 note field, i.e., "Compact disc."

Q3

PROBLEM CONSIDERED:

Journal on slides

TAGGED DATA RECORD (based on OCLC #23251517)

LDR   *****cgs_/22*****Ia*4500   (projected medium serial)

(visual materials: slide)

00-05	06	07-14	15-17	18-20	21	22	23-27	28	29-32	33	34	35-37	38	39
910315	c	19919999	enk	nnn	/	f	-----	-	////	s	n	eng	-	d

008

00	01	02	03	04	05	06	07	08-10	11	12	13-15	16	17
s	b	r	z	p	-	-	-	---	-	0	///	a	0

→ 006   (serial)

→ 007   g ≠b s ≠d m ≠e j ≠h j ≠i u   (slide)

022 0   1055-6567

245 00   Slide atlas of current radiology ≠h [slide].

260   London, UK : ≠b Current Science, ≠c c1991-

300   slides + ≠e binder

310   Bimonthly

362 0   Update 1 (Feb. 1991)-

500   Binder issued annually.

→ 580   Slides of the illustrations contained in Current opinion in radiology.

650 0   Radiography ≠x Periodicals.

→ 787 1   ≠t Current opinion in radiology ≠x 1040-869X ≠w (DLC)90649331 ≠w (OCoLC)18553447

DISCUSSION

- Similar to serial videorecordings, serial slides should be cataloged according to physical format, i.e., character position 06 (Type of Record) in the leader should be coded "g" for Projected Medium. Field 008 for visual materials is used, with the addition of a 006 field for serials to express the serial nature of the slides. In field 008, position 33 (Type of Visual Material) is coded "s" for Slide.

- Note that a 007 Physical Description Fixed Field for Projected Graphic is also required in this case to code the physical characteristics of the slides.

- Since the publication in this example contains slides that were made from the illustrations in the print journal "Current opinion in radiology," field 580 (Linking Entry Complexity Note) is used to express the relationship between the slide publication and the print journal. Linking entry field 787 (Nonspecific Relationship Entry) is entered to link the record for the slides to the related print journal record. An added entry for the print journal may be entered in field 730.

Q4

PROBLEM CONSIDERED:

Nonmusical sound recording journal accompanied by kit

RULE(S) CONSULTED:

AACR2R: Appendix D (p. 619)

TAGGED DATA RECORD (based on OCLC #20496682)

LDR   *****cis_/22*****Ia*4500   (nonmusical sound recording serial)

                                                      (music)

→008

00-05	06	07-14	15-17	18-19	20	21	22	23	24-29	30-31	32-34	35-37	38	39
891016	c	19899999	alu	nn	n	/	f	-	r-----	i-	///	eng	-	d

→006

00	01	02	03	04	05	06	07	08-10	11	12	13-15	16	17
s	b	r	l	p	-	-	-	---	-	0	///	a	0

                                                           (serial)

→006

00	01-03	04	05	06-10	11	12-15	16	17
o	nnn	/	f	-----	-	////	b	n

                                      (visual materials: kit)

→007   s ≠b s ≠d l ≠e u ≠f n ≠g j ≠h l ≠i c ≠j m ≠n u   (sound cassette)

022 0   1046-7076

245 00   Practical reviews in dermatology ≠h [sound recording].

260   Birmingham, AL : ≠b Educational Reviews, Inc.,

→300   sound cassettes : ≠b 1 7/8 ips + ≠e quizzes and study cards, guides

310   Bimonthly

362 0   Began in 1989.

500   Recorded on both sides.

500   Includes study guide consisting of table of contents and post-test.

500   Approved for continuing education AAD Category 1 credit.

500   Description based on: Vol. 1, no. 4 (July/Aug. 1989).

550   Sponsored by: Albert Einstein College of Medicine/Montefiore Medical Center.

650 0   Skin diseases ≠x Periodicals.

710 2   Education Reviews, Inc.

710 2   Montefiore Medical Center.

DISCUSSION

- This example is a nonmusical sound recording issued in sound cassette format. Similar to Q2, it is cataloged according to the format for sound recordings. Character position 06 (Type of Record) in the leader is coded "i" for Nonmusical Sound Recording. Field 008 for music is used, with the addition of a 006 field for serials to express the serial nature of the sound recording. A 007 Physical Description Fixed Field for Sound Recording is also required to code the physical characteristics of the cassette.
- This sound recording journal is accompanied by quizzes, study cards, guides, etc. The presence of these is recorded in field 300, subfield ≠e, and the cata-

loger has also supplied a second 006 field to code the characteristics of these accompanying materials. Because the accompanying materials consist of a mixture of educational test materials that are *issued together as a single unit* with none of them predominating, they are treated as a kit. A 006 field for Visual Materials is used. Position 00 in field 006 is coded "o" to denote Kit, and position 16 (Type of Visual Material) is also coded "b" for Kit (for definition of "kit" see AACR2R, p. 619, Appendix D).

Q5

PROBLEM CONSIDERED:

Musical sound recording journal issued as a supplement

RULE(S) CONSULTED:

LCRI: 21.28B

Q5a

TAGGED DATA RECORD (based on OCLC #14880383)

LDR   *****cjs_/22*****Ia*4500   (musical sound recording serial)

(music)

	00-05	06	07-14	15-17	18-19	20	21	22	23	24-29	30-31	32-34	35-37	38	39
→ 008	861126	u	1984uuuu	cau	uu	n	/	g	-	------	--	///	N/A	-	d

	00	01	02	03	04	05	06	07	08-10	11	12	13-15	16	17	
→ 006	s	m	r		p	-	-	-	---	-	0	///	-	0	(serial)

→ 007   s ≠b d ≠d b ≠e s ≠f m ≠g b ≠h n ≠i n ≠j u ≠k p ≠l l ≠m u ≠n u   (sound disc)

→ 245 00   Soundpage ≠h [sound recording].

260   Cupertino, CA : ≠b Keyboard Magazine, ≠c 1984-

300   sound discs : ≠b analog, 33 1/3 rpm, stereo. ; ≠c 5 in.

310   Monthly

362 0   Began in 1984.

500   Description based on: #46 (July 1988).

→ 580   Supplements articles in: Keyboard (Cupertino, Calif.)

500   Eva-tone soundsheet.

650 0   Keyboard instrument music ≠x Periodicals.

730 0   Keyboard (Cupertino, Calif.)

772 1   ≠t Keyboard (Cupertino, Calif.) ≠x 0730-0158 ≠w (DLC)81649762 ≠w (OCoLC)7628273

Q5b

TAGGED DATA RECORD (based on OCLC #7628273)

LDR   *****cas_/22*****Ia*4500   (print serial)

                                             (serial)

00-05	06	07-14	15-17	18	19	20	21	22-28	29	30-32	33	34	35-37	38	39
810730	c	19819999	cau	m	r	l	p	---o---	0	///	a	0	eng	-	d

008

022 0	0730-0158 ≠y 0361-5820
130 0	Keyboard (Cupertino, Calif.)
245 00	Keyboard.
260	Cupertino, Calif. : ≠b GPI Publications, ≠c 1981-
300	v. : ≠b ill. ; ≠c 28 cm.
310	Monthly
362 0	Vol. 7, no. 7 (July 1981)-
500	Title from cover.
500	Published: San Francisco, CA : Miller Freeman Publications, <May '90->
→ 580	Articles supplemented by separately numbered sound recordings: Soundpage, Nov. 1984-
650 0	Piano ≠x Periodicals.
770 1	≠t Soundpage ≠w (DLC)sn96048643 ≠w (OCoLC)14880383
780 00	≠t Contemporary keyboard ≠x 0361-5820 ≠w (DLC)76641315 ≠w (OCoLC)2246955

DISCUSSION

- The example in Q5a is a sound recording journal issued as a supplement to certain articles found in a print journal (field 580). The supplement here has the title "Soundpage" and is cataloged separately from its parent print journal, which has a different title, "Keyboard." In example Q5a, position 06 (Type of Record) in the leader is coded "j" since the item being cataloged is a musical sound recording. Accordingly, field 008 for music is used, with the addition of a 006 field for serials to express the serial nature of the sound recording. A 007 Physical Description Fixed Field for Sound Recording is also required to code the physical characteristics of the sound disc.

- Example Q5b shows the record for the parent print journal. Note that field 580 (Linking Entry Complexity Note) is used for information about the supplement in sound recording format (LCRI 21.28B). No 006 field is required in this case for the sound disc, since the sound recording supplement is cataloged separately and has not been recorded as accompanying material.

Q6

PROBLEM CONSIDERED:

Printed music material issued as a serial

TAGGED DATA RECORD (based on OCLC #1566831)

LDR   *****ncs_/22*****_a*4500   (printed music serial)

(music)

00-05	06	07-14	15-17	18-19	20	21	22	23	24-29	30-31	32-34	35-37	38	39
750824	c	19559999	gw	mu	a	/	f	-	------	n-	///	ger	-	d

008

00	01	02	03	04	05	06	07	08-10	11	12	13-15	16	17
s		x	z	m	-	-	-	---	-	0	///	-	0

→ 006   (serial)

022	0417-805X
041 0	gerlat
245 00	Documenta musicologica. ≠n 2. Reihe, ≠p Handschriften-Faksimiles.
246 3	Documenta musicologica. ≠n Zweite Reihe, ≠p Handschriften-Faksimiles
246 30	Handschriften-Faksimiles
260	Kassel : ≠b Bärenreiter-Verlag, ≠c 1955-
300	v. of music ; ≠c 25-32 cm.
310	Irregular
362 0	1-
546	German or Latin.
550	Issued by: Internationale Gesellschaft für Musikwissenschaft, and: Association internationale des bibliothèques musicales, 1955- ; by: Association internationale des bibliothèque musicales, archives et centres de documentation musicaux, and Internationale Gesellschaft für Musikwissenschaft, <1996->
650 0	Music ≠x Manuscripts ≠x Facsimiles.
710 2	International Musicological Society.
710 2	International Association of Music Libraries.
710 2	International Association of Music Libraries, Archives, and Documentation Centres.

DISCUSSION

- This example involves printed music scores issued as a serial. A 008 fixed field for music should be used, with the addition of a 006 field configured to express the serial nature of the publication.
- Character position 06 (Type of Record) in the leader is coded "c" for Printed Music. In field 008 for music, positions 18–19 (Form of Composition) are coded "mu," since the scores are for various different types of music. Because this serial publication is a full score, position 20 (Form of Music) is accordingly coded "a."

Q7

PROBLEM CONSIDERED:

Map/atlas/chart issued as a serial

RULE(S) CONSULTED:

AACR2R: 3.7B1, 3.7B18

Q7a

TAGGED DATA RECORD (based on OCLC #22865536)

LDR   *****ces_/22*****Ia*4500   (map serial)

                                                                  (atlas)

00-05	06	07-14	15-17	18-21	22-23	24	25	26-27	28	29-30	31	32	33-34	35-37	38	39
901217	c	19919999	nyu	----	--	-	e	//	-	//	0	/	--	eng	-	d

008

00	01	02	03	04	05	06	07	08-10	11	12	13-15	16	17
s	u	u		p	-	-	-	---	-	0	///	a	0

→ 006   (serial)

→ 007   a ≠b d ≠d c ≠e a ≠f n ≠g u ≠h n   (atlas)

022 0   1054-4127

043   n------

245 00 Gousha trucker's road atlas ≠h [map].

246 14 Truckers road atlas

260   New York, NY : ≠b H.M. Gousha, ≠c c1991-

300   v. : ≠b col. maps ; ≠c 39 cm.

362 0   1991-

650 0 North America ≠x Maps ≠x Periodicals.

650 0 Trucks ≠x Routes ≠z North America ≠x Periodicals.

710 2   H.M. Gousha (Firm)

Q7b
TAGGED DATA RECORD (based on OCLC #25240411)

LDR   *****ces_/22*****Ia*4500   (map serial)

(map)

	00-05	06	07-14	15-17	18-21	22-23	24	25	26-27	28	29-30	31	32	33-34	35-37	38	39
008	920207	c	19919999	ilu	----	--	-	c	//	s	//	0	/	--	eng	-	d

	00	01	02	03	04	05	06	07	08-10	11	12	13-15	16	17	
→006	s	q	r			-	-	-	---	s	0	///	a	0	(serial)

→007   a ≠b j ≠d a ≠e a ≠f n ≠g z ≠h n   (map)
→034 0   a ≠d W0913000 ≠e W0873000 ≠f N0423000 ≠g N0370000
110 1   Illinois. ≠b Dept. of Transportation.
245 10   Illinois interstate road work alert ≠h [map].
→255   Scale not given ≠c (W 91°30′—W 87°30′/N 42°30′—N 37°00′).
260   [Springfield, Ill.] : ≠b The Dept., ≠c 1991-
300   maps ; ≠c on sheet 46 x 40 cm. folded to 23 x 10 cm.
310   Quarterly
362 1   Began with summer 1991.
500   Panel title.
500   "Funded in part by the Illinois Tollway Authority."
500   Inset: Metro East Area.
500   Text and inset of Chicago area on verso.
500   Indexed to description of projects with time estimates.
650 0   Interstate Highway System ≠z Illinois ≠x Maps.
650 0   Roads ≠z Illinois ≠x Design and construction ≠x Periodicals.
650 0   Roads ≠z Illinois ≠x Design and construction ≠x Maps.

Q7c

TAGGED DATA RECORD (based on OCLC #20719903)

LDR   *****ces_/22*****Ia*4500   (map serial)

                                              (map)

00-05	06	07-14	15-17	18-21	22-23	24	25	26-27	28	29-30	31	32	33-34	35-37	38	39
891201	c	19uu9999	dcu	acg-	cc	-	c	//	f	//	0	/	--	eng	-	d

008

00	01	02	03	04	05	06	07	08-10	11	12	13-15	16	17
s	f	r		p	-	-	-	---	f	0	///	a	0

→ 006   (serial)

→ 007   a ≠b j ≠d c ≠e a ≠f n ≠g z ≠h n   (map)

→ 034 1   a ≠b 500000 ≠d W0880000 ≠e W0810000 ≠f N0360000 ≠g N0320000

110 1   United States. ≠b National Ocean Service.

245 10   Sectional aeronautical chart. ≠p Atlanta [map].

246 30   Atlanta

246 3   Atlanta, sectional aeronautical chart

→ 255   Scale 1:500,000 ; ≠b Lambert conformal conic proj., standard parallels 33°20′ and 38°40′ ≠c (W 88°--W 81°/N 36°--N 32°).

260   Washington, D.C. : ≠b U.S. Dept. of Commerce, National Oceanic and Atmospheric Administration, National Ocean Service,

300   maps : ≠b both sides, col. ; ≠c 96 x 133 cm. sheets 52 x 151 cm. folded to 26 x 13 cm.

310   Semiannual

→ 500   Relief shown by contours, tints, and spot heights.

→ 500   Includes location map and gradient tints diagram, <1989->

500   Description based on: 42nd ed. (Apr. 6, 1989); title from panel.

515   Vols. For <Apr. 6, 1989-> have topographic data corrected to <Dec. 1988-> and include airspace amendments effective <Apr. 6, 1989-> and other aeronautical data received by <Feb. 9, 1989->; chart becomes obsolete for use in navigation upon publication of next ed.

580   Vols. For <1989-> consult appropriate issue of Notices to airmen, NOTAMs, and flight information publications for supplemental data and current information.

650 0   Aeronautical charts ≠z South Atlantic States ≠x Periodicals.

650 0   Aeronautical charts ≠z Southern States ≠x Periodicals.

787 1   ≠t Notices to airmen ≠w (DLC)sn87042677 ≠w (OCoLC)4276638

DISCUSSION

- Most maps and atlases are issued as monographs because only a very few of them can be treated as serials. When cataloging cartographic materials, whether they are monographs or serials, the cataloger should use fixed field 008 for maps. If the cartographic material is a serial publication, i.e., issued in successive parts bearing numerical or chronological designations and intended to be continued indefinitely, fixed field 006 for serials should be added to the record to express the serial nature of the publication.
- The three serials in this example all consist of cartographic materials. In keeping with this, code "e" for Cartographic Material is used in character position

06 in the leader, and code "s" is used in position 07 to indicate that the cartographic material described is a serial publication.

- Position 25 in fixed field 008 for maps specifies the type of cartographic material: in example Q7a, code "e" is used because the publication is an atlas,
and, in examples Q7b and Q7c, "c" is used for Maps.
- The Cartographic Mathematical Data is given in field 255, with the appropriate codes assigned in field 008. In example Q7c, field 255, subfield ≠b, records
the projection statement "Lambert conformal conic proj.," with corresponding
code "cc" for Lambert's Conformal Conic in fixed field 008 positions 22–23
(Projection).
- When the textual form of data is entered in field 255, field 034 should also be
added to code data concerning the scales, coordinates, and equinox of cartographic materials. (See the 034 field in examples Q7b and Q7c.)
- In example Q7c, the first 500 note is used to describe the nature and scope of
the item (3.7B1). Accordingly, positions 18–21 (Relief) in fixed field 008 are
coded "acg" to correspond with the description for contours, tints, and spot
heights. The second 500 note lists the contents of the item (3.7B18). For the
bibliographic description in the cataloging of maps, atlases, charts, etc., refer
to AACR2R Chapter 3.

Q8

PROBLEM CONSIDERED:

Mixed materials issued as a serial

TAGGED DATA RECORD (based on OCLC #35553213)

LDR   *****npc_/22*****_a*4500   (mixed materials collection)

00-05	06	07-14	15-17	18-22	23	24-34	35-37	38	39

→ 008

| 960913 | i | 19301982 | inu | ////// | - | ////////// | eng | - | d | (mixed material)

00	01	02	03	04	05	06	07	08-10	11	12	13-15	16	17

→ 006

| s | m | x | | p | - | - | - | --- | - | 0 | /// | a | 0 | (serial)

→ 007   zu   (physical form unspecified)

043   n-us-in

110 2   Sigma Delta Pi.

245 10 Records, ≠f 1930-1982.

300   1 ≠f box.

→ 351   ≠b Arranged by type of material, then chronologically.

→ 545   Organized in 1906 at the Teachers College of Indianapolis as a professional sorority for teachers. In 1923 it became a national organization and continues today to promote and elevate teaching as a profession.

520   Primarily issues of the LINK OF SIGMA DELTA PI, 1930-1982. Also included are the organization's history and constitution, information on its business ritual, two Teachers College of Indianapolis booklets (1929-1930), and a Butler University bulletin (1930-1931).

→ 555 0 Collection guide ≠b available in library : ≠c folder level control.

610 20 Sigma Delta Pi ≠x Periodicals.

610 20 Teachers College of Indianapolis.

610 20 Butler University.

630 00 Link of Sigma Delta Pi.

650 0 Teachers ≠z United States ≠x Societies, etc.

650 0 Greek letter societies ≠z Indiana ≠x Periodicals.

DISCUSSION

- The item in this example is cataloged as mixed materials using "p" (Mixed Material) for position 06 (Type of Record) in the leader. Position 07 (Bibliographic Level) is coded "c" (Collection), since the item is a made-up group of items not originally published, distributed, or produced together. Fixed field 008 for Mixed Materials is used.

- When an item being cataloged has components in different formats or material categories, fixed field 007 is repeated for each different format. Alternatively, however, instead of inputting separate 007 fields to code the physical characteristics of individual parts of the multipart collection, a cataloging agency can use a single 007 field, i.e., 007 for unspecified. In this case, according to USMARC Bibliographic Format, "z" should be used for Unspecified in position 00 (Category of Material), and "u" should be used for Physical Form Unspecified in position 01 (Specific Material Designation).

- Field 351 is used for information about the organization and arrangement of a collection of items. Subfield ≠b contains terms to describe the pattern of arrangement of materials within a unit, in this case, by type of material and then chronologically.
- Field 545 (Biographical or Historical Note) records biographical information about an individual or historical information about an institution or event used as the main entry for the item being cataloged. In this example, this field is used to record information about the organization "Sigma Delta Pi."
- Field 555 is used for a Cumulative Index or Finding Aids Note. Subfield ≠b contains the availability source, which refers to the organizational unit—in this case, the holding library itself—from which finding notes may be obtained. Subfield ≠c specifies the extent of administrative, bibliographic, or physical control available over the described materials.

Q9

PROBLEM CONSIDERED:

Print serial accompanied by CD-ROM

RULE(S) CONSULTED:

AACR2R: 12.5E1, 12.7B16
LCRI: 1.5E1

Q9a

TAGGED DATA RECORD (based on OCLC #20310704)

LDR   *****cas_/22*****Ia*4500   (print serial)

(serial)

00-05	06	07-14	15-17	18	19	20	21	22-28	29	30-32	33	34	35-37	38	39
890907	c	19909999	dcu	g	r	l		---hs-f	0	///		a	0	eng	-	d

008 (as above)

022 0	1064-6809
043	n-us---
245 00	Congressional Quarterly's politics in America.
246 30	Politics in America
260	Washington, D.C. : ≠b CQ Press, ≠c c1989-
300	v. : ≠b ill. ; ≠c 27 cm.
310	Biennial
362 0	1990-
→ 530	Vols. for 1996- also available in CD-ROM edition which contains additional data; inserted in book pocket.
580	Has companion publication: Who's who in Congress.
610 10	United States. ≠b Congress ≠x Biography.
610 10	United States. ≠b Congress ≠x Committees.
610 10	United States. ≠b Congress ≠x Election districts.
650 0	Election districts ≠z United States.
710 2	Congressional Quarterly, inc.
→ 776 1	≠t Congressional Quarterly's politics in America (CD-ROM) ≠w (OCoLC)33061167
780 00	≠t Politics in America ≠w (DLC)96645179 ≠w (OCoLC)8013625
787 1	≠t Who's who in Congress ≠w (DLC)92657325 ≠w (OCoLC)23021609

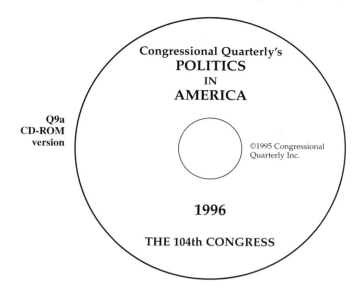

Q9a
CD-ROM
version

Congressional Quarterly's
POLITICS
IN
AMERICA

©1995 Congressional
Quarterly Inc.

1996

THE 104th CONGRESS

Q9b

TAGGED DATA RECORD (based on OCLC #35090040)

LDR   *****cas_/22*****Ia*4500   (print serial)

(serial)

	00-05	06	07-14	15-17	18	19	20	21	22-28	29	30-32	33	34	35-37	38	39
008	960716	c	19979999	enk	a	r		p	--r----	0	///	a	0	eng	-	d

→ 007   c ≠b o ≠d u ≠e g   (CD-ROM)

245 04   The Big official UCAS guide to university & college entrance.

246 13   UCAS guide to university & college entrance

246 13   University & college entrance

260   London : ≠b UCAS in association with the Independent & Letts Study
         Guides, ≠c 1996-

→ 300   v. : ≠b ill. ; ≠c 30 cm. + ≠e computer laser optical disc ; (4 3/4 in.)

310   Annual

362 0   1997-

→ 500   Includes: "STUDYlink: the biggest multimedia guide to undergraduate
         education in the UK" on CD-ROM.

538   System requirements for accompanying disc: Windows: 5 MB of available RAM;
         14″ 256 colour monitor; Windows 3.1 or Windows 95; 35 MB of free hard-disk
         space; CD-ROM drive; 8-bit sound card; Quicktime for Windows 2.0 (included).
         Macintosh: 5.MB of available RAM; 14″ colour monitor; System 7.0 or higher;
         35 MB of free hard-disk space; CD-ROM drive; Quicktime 2.1 (included).

650 0   Universities and colleges ≠z Great Britain ≠x Entrance requirements ≠x Directories.

710 2   Universities & College Admission Service.

780 10   ≠t University & college entrance ≠w (OCoLC)28646516

→ 740 02 STUDYlink.

DISCUSSION

- From 1996 on, issues of the publication in example Q9a are accompanied by a CD-ROM inserted in a book pocket. Information about the CD-ROMs has been recorded in field 530 (Additional Physical Form Available Note), since they are in a physical form different from that of the print serial (12.7B16). Note, however, that even though the CD-ROMs are inserted in book pockets in individual issues of the print serial, they should not be treated as accompanying material per se. This is because the CD-ROMs contain not only the text of the print serial but also additional data and, as such, can be used independently of the print serial. A separate cataloging record should therefore be made for the CD-ROMs, and, consequently, no 006 fixed field (Additional Material Characteristics) for computer file is included in the record for the print serial.

- The publication in example Q9b is accompanied by a CD-ROM that is intended to be used together with the main work. Moreover, every future issue of the print serial is likely to be accompanied by a CD-ROM. For these reasons the CD-ROMs are treated as accompanying material, and information about them is therefore recorded at the end of the physical description area in field 300, subfield ≠e (12.5E1; LCRI 1.5E1).

- According to USMARC Bibliographic Format, field 007 has been made valid for accompanying materials. Therefore, in example Q9b, field 007 Physical Description Fixed Field for Computer File may be added to code information concerning the accompanying CD-ROM.

Q10

PROBLEM CONSIDERED:

Print serial accompanied by computer disk

RULE(S) CONSULTED:

AACR2R: 12.7B11

TAGGED DATA RECORD (based on OCLC #32512203)

LDR   *****cas_/22*****Ia*4500   (print serial)

                                                                    (serial)

00-05	06	07-14	15-17	18	19	20	21	22-28	29	30-32	33	34	35-37	38	39
890907	c	199u9999	dcu	a	r	l		---hs--	0	///	a	0	eng	-	d

008

→ 007   c ≠b j ≠d a ≠e a   (computer disk)

245 04   The Dodge unit cost book / ≠c Marshall & Swift.

260   New York : ≠b McGraw-Hill,

300   v. ; ≠c 28 cm.

310   Annual

500   Description based on: 1996.

→ 525   Vols. for 1996-   accompanied by computer disks containing estimating forms and other ready-to-use documents with title Dodge cost estimation guide.

580   Continues in part: Dodge unit cost data.

650 0   Building ≠x Estimates ≠z United States.

650 0   Building ≠x Estimates ≠z Canada.

710 2   Marshall & Swift (Firm)

→ 740 02   Dodge cost estimation guide.

780 11   ≠t Dodge unit cost data ≠w (OCoLC)15028874 ≠w (DLC)sn87019627

DISCUSSION

- Volumes of the serial in this example have been accompanied by computer disks since 1996. The disks have their own title, "Dodge cost estimation disk." Since the documents and forms contained in the disks should be used with the main work, the disks are not cataloged separately; instead, they are treated as accompanying material. Field 525 (Supplement Note) is used to record information about the accompanying disks (12.7B11).

- According to USMARC Bibliographic Format, field 007 is also valid for accompanying materials, and, therefore, a 007 field for computer file may be added to this record.

- An added entry for the accompanying material entitled "Dodge cost estimation guide" is recorded in field 740, with first indicator value "0" and second indicator value "2" for Uncontrolled Related Analytical Title.

Q11

PROBLEM CONSIDERED:

Print serial accompanied by microform

RULE(S) CONSULTED:

AACR2R: 12.7B11

TAGGED DATA RECORD (based on OCLC #1589690)

LDR   *****cas_/22*****Ia*4500   (print serial)

(serial)

00-05	06	07-14	15-17	18	19	20	21	22-28	29	30-32	33	34	35-37	38	39
008 750901	c	19599999	dcu	q	r	l	p	-------	0	///	a	0	eng	-	d

→ 007   h ≠b e ≠d u ≠e m ≠f u--- ≠g b ≠h u ≠i u ≠j c ≠k a   (microfiche)

022 0   0021-9568

245 00   Journal of chemical and engineering data.

260   [Washington : ≠b American Chemical Society], ≠c 1959-

300   v. : ≠b ill. ; ≠c 29 cm.

310   Quarterly

362 0   Vol. 4 (Jan. 1959)-

→ 525   Some issues for <1978-> accompanied by supplementary material on microfiche.

650 0   Chemistry ≠x Periodicals.

650 0   Chemical engineering ≠x Periodicals.

710 2   American Chemical Society.

780 00   ≠t Chemical & engineering data series ≠x 0095-9146 ≠w (DLC)sn89005870 ≠w (OCoLC) 1421231

DISCUSSION

- Some issues of the journal in this example are accompanied by supplementary material in microfiche format. This information is recorded in a field 525, Supplement Note (12.7B11).

- The characteristics coded in fixed field 008 are those of the serial publication. Because field 008 is not repeatable, fixed field elements for accompanying materials in a different format are presented in field 006. In this case, field 006 for serials is not used, because the supplementary material is a microform serial. Field 007, Physical Description Fixed Field—Microform, may be added to the record to code data for the accompanying material.

Q12

PROBLEM CONSIDERED:

Print serial accompanied by sound cassette supplements

RULE(S) CONSULTED:

AACR2R: 12.7B11

TAGGED DATA RECORD (based on OCLC #11269602)

LDR   *****cas_/22*****Ia*4500   (print serial)

(serial)

00-05	06	07-14	15-17	18	19	20	21	22-28	29	30-32	33	34	35-37	38	39
841016	c	19849999	enk	t	r	-	p	---ob--	0	///	a	0	eng	-	d

008

00	01-02	03	04	05	06	07-12	13-14	15-17
j	mu	n	/	-	-	------	--	///

→ 006   (musical sound recording)

→ 007   s ≠b s ≠d l ≠e m ≠f n ≠g o ≠h l ≠i c ≠j m ≠k n ≠l n ≠m n ≠n e   (sound cassette)

022   0265-0517
245 00   British journal of music education : ≠b BJME.
246 30   BJME
260   Cambridge [England] : ≠b Cambridge University Press, ≠c 1984-
300   v. : ≠b ill. ; ≠c 25 cm.
310   Three times a year
362 0   Vol. 1, no. 1 (Mar. 1984)-
500   Title from cover.
→ 525   Has also audiocassette supplements.
555   Vols. 1 (1984)-5 (1988). 1 v. ; Indexed abstracts: v. 6 (1989)-10 (1993). 1 v.
650   0 Music ≠x Instruction and study ≠x Periodicals.

DISCUSSION

- The publication "British journal of music education" has audiocassette sup-plements, and this is recorded in field 525 (12.7B11). Because the accompany-ing material in this case is in the form of audiocassettes, a 006 field for music is used.

- Character position 00 (Form of Material) of field 006 is coded "j" for Musical Sound Recording. Positions 01–02 (Form of Composition) are coded "mu" for Multiple Forms, since the cassettes contain a variety of forms of composition. Field 007 for Sound Recording may also be added, since, according to USMARC Bibliographic Format, it is also valid for accompanying materials.

Q13

PROBLEM CONSIDERED:

Print serial indexed by diskette

RULE(S) CONSULTED:

AACR2R: 12.7B17

TAGGED DATA RECORD (based on OCLC #24706701)

LDR   *****cas_/22*****Ia*4500   (print serial)

                                                                     (serial)

	00-05	06	07-14	15-17	18	19	20	21	22-28	29	30-32	33	34	35-37	38	39
008	911107	c	19919999	vau	u	u			---acr-	0	///	a	0	eng	-	d

245	00	Healthcare videodisc directory.
246	30	Videodisc
246	14	Interactive healthcare directory. ≠p Videodisc
246	17	Videodisc directory
260		Alexandria, Va. : ≠b Stewart Pub., ≠c 1991-
300		v. ; ≠c 28 cm.
362	0	1991-
→ 555		Indexed by diskette entitled: Interactive healthcare directories.
650	0	Video recordings ≠x Directories.
650	0	Videodiscs ≠x Directories.
650	0	Medical care ≠x Computer programs ≠x Directories.
650	0	Medicine ≠x Computer-assisted instruction ≠x Directories.
780	01	≠t Interactive healthcare directory ≠w (DLC)sn91033395 ≠w (OCoLC)22185935
→ 787	1	≠t Interactive healthcare directories ≠w (DLC)sn96047853 ≠w (OCoLC)35519855

DISCUSSION

- In this example, "Healthcare videodisc directory" is a print serial that is indexed by a diskette. The diskette carries the title "Interactive healthcare directories," which differs from that of the print serial. Moreover, the diskette indexes, in addition to "Healthcare videodisc directory," various other print and nonprint serials. Because of this, the index cannot be simply treated as accompanying material but must be cataloged in a separate record. Consequently, no 006 field (Data Elements for Additional Material Characteristics) is required in the record for the print serial. Field 555 (Cumulative Index/Finding Aids Note) should be input whenever there is an index to a serial, regardless of whether that index is issued as an integral part of the serial (in which case it is treated as accompanying material) or whether it is issued separately and cataloged in a separate record (12.7B17).

Q14

PROBLEM CONSIDERED:

Electronic journal accompanied by print material

RULE(S) CONSULTED:

AACR2R: 12.5E1

TAGGED DATA RECORD (based on OCLC #29950438)

LDR *****cas_/22*****Ia*4500   (language material serial)

(print serial)

00-05	06	07-14	15-17	18	19	20	21	22-28	29	30-32	33	34	35-37	38	39
008	940311	c	19939999	dcu	u		u		p	ss-----	0	///	a	0	eng	-	d

00	01-04	05	06	07-10	11	12	13	14	15	16	17
→ 006	a	----	g	-	----	-	0	0	0	/	0	-	(book)

→ 007   c ≠b o ≠d u ≠e g ≠f u   (CD-ROM)

245 00 Astrophysics on disc ≠h [computer file].

256   Document.

260   Washington, D.C. : ≠b American Astronomical Society, ≠c 1993-

300   computer laser optical discs ; ≠c 4 3/4 in.

362 0   Vol. 1 (1993)-

440 0 AAS CD-ROM series

538   System requirements: Can be used by practically every computer and operating
        system since AAS CD-ROM is formatted for the ISO 9660 Standard, Data
        Interchange Level 1. IBM PC or compatibles, Macintosh or Unix machine.

500   Title from disc label

→ 516   Text (Articles), data (Tables), graphic (Line art and imagery)

→ 556 8 Accompanied by booklets.

520   Contains selected tabular data from: Astronomical journal, the Astrophysical
        journal, Astrophysical journal supplement series and publications of the
        Astronomical Society of the Pacific.

650 0 Astrophysics ≠x Periodicals.

650 0 Astronomy ≠x Periodicals.

650 0 Spectrum analysis ≠x Periodicals.

710 2   American Astronomical Society.

710 2   Astronomical Society of the Pacific.

730 0   Astronomical journal.

730 0   Astrophysical journal.

730 0   Astrophysical journal. ≠p Supplement series.

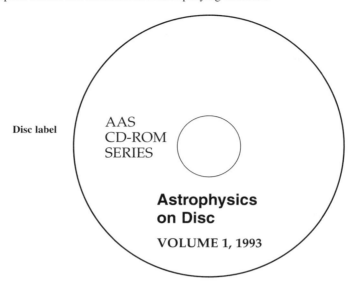

DISCUSSION

- Computer files are often accompanied by documentation, such as user's guides, manuals, contents, etc., and/or search and retrieval software on separate computer diskettes. When these accompany each issue of the serial, that information should be recorded in the physical description area in field 300, subfield ≠e (12.5E1; see also CCM 30.12.4). However, if such material is released only occasionally to accompany particular issues of the serial, then documentation information is input in field 556 and search and retrieval software is described in a 500 General Note field (see also CCM 30.14.7).

- In accordance with format integration, a 006 field should be entered to describe the physical characteristics of accompanying materials that cannot be coded in field 008. For this computer file serial, the booklets described in field 556 are given a corresponding 006 field. Character position 00 (Form of Material) is coded "a" for Language Material, and the remaining positions 01–17 follow field 008/18–34 configuration for Book Format. First indicator value "8" in field 556 is used to specify that no display constant is to be generated. Field 007, Physical Description Fixed Field for Computer File, is also required.

- Field 516, Type of Computer File or Data Note, is used in this record to elaborate on the characteristics of the computer file, since the cataloger feels that this information is not obtainable from other parts of the bibliographic description, such as field 538 (System Details Note) or field 520 (Summary Note).

- In leader character position 06 is coded "a" for Language Material; in fixed field 008 character position 22 (Form of Original Item) and character position 23 (Form of Item) are coded "s" for Electronic.

R   Computer Files

As of the current writing, computer file serials are cataloged using the computer files format together with Bibliographic Level code "s" for serial and Type of Record code "m" for computer file. In addition, field 006 for serial characteristics and field 007 for computer file characteristics are present in the record. This practice reflects cataloging treatment based on the carrier and not on the content of the resource. Type of Record code "m" is used to indicate that the content of the record was for a body of information encoded in a manner that allows it to be processed by a computer, that is, a computer file carrier.

Many changes in the practice of computer file cataloging have taken place while this book was being written. A change approved by MARBI, the USMARC Advisory Group, in June 1997 *(Update No. 3 to the USMARC Bibliographic Format, July 1997)* revised the definition of code "m" to allow for computer files to be coded for their most significant aspect. As a result, Type of Record code "m" is used only for the following classes of electronic resources:

> Computer software (including programs, games, fonts)
> Numeric data
> Computer-oriented multimedia
> Online systems or services

Other classes of electronic resources which require the use of a computer are coded for their most significant aspect, e.g., language material, cartographic material, projected medium, sound recording, etc. Field 007 for Computer File is mandatory for all electronic resources, and, in fact, multiple 007s can be used in a record in order to provide information on the carrier of the primary material, the carrier of one part of mixed material, or the carrier of accompanying material. Field 007 may also be added to the original record in a single-record approach, where field 856 is used to point to the electronic version of the resource described by the record (see *Draft Interim Guidelines for Cataloging Electronic Resources, January 1998,* prepared by the Cataloging Policy and Support Office of the Library of Congress).

At the 1998 ALA Midwinter meeting, MARBI approved the addition of yet another new value, value "s" (electronic), to fixed field 008 character position 23 (Form of Item) and fixed field 006 character position 06 in the USMARC Bibliographic Formats for Books, Serials, Music, and Mixed Materials. In addition, the same value also applies to fixed field 008 character position 22 (Form of Original Item) and fixed field 006 character position 05 in Serials format. The General Material Designation in field 245 is "computer file" for such electronic resources, although this is optional. Because the new provisions have already been approved, the examples in this section have been updated to reflect changes, even though they have not yet been implemented by the Library of Congress and OCLC at the time of writing.

According to LCRI 25.5B, p. 11, a computer file serial should not be considered to be a reproduction of its paper counterpart, and, therefore, the computer file serial should be treated as a separate work, requiring a separate record. CONSER's interim guideline is to prefer to create separate records, although its members may choose not to catalog the online version separately, but to adopt a "single-record" approach instead (i.e., they may note the existence of the electronic version in field 530 and add the electronic location of the online version in field 856 in the record for its print counterpart, instead of creating a separate record). For the discussions in this section, both separate-record and single-record approaches are given whenever appropriate. For the Library of Congress's policy on applying the single/separate record approach, see its *Draft Interim Guidelines for Cataloging Electronic Resources.* The discussions in this section follow the provisions in AACR2R Chapters 9 and 12; Library of Congress Rule Interpretations; the guidelines given in the CONSER Cataloging Manual (CCM), modules 30 and 31 (last revised November 1996); the *Guidelines for the Use of Field 856,* revised August 1997, prepared by the Network Development and MARC Standards Office of the Library of Congress; and the *Draft Interim Guidelines for Cataloging Electronic Resources, January 1998.*

BIBLIOGRAPHIC DESCRIPTION
SPECIFIC TO COMPUTER FILE SERIALS

Computer files are categorized according to whether access is direct or remote.

DIRECT ACCESS:

Computer file serials that are available or stored via a physical carrier, to be inserted into a computer, such as CD-ROMs, floppy disks, laser optical discs, etc.

REMOTE ACCESS:

Computer file serials that are available through an electronic network such as the Internet.

CHIEF SOURCE OF INFORMATION
(9.0B1; 12.0B1; CCM MODULE 31)

DIRECT ACCESS:

Use the title screen(s) of the first issue published or earliest issue available. If there is no title screen, take the information from other formally presented internal evidence, such as main menus or program statements. If no internal title information is available or the cataloger does not have access to the necessary equipment, take the information from the following external sources (in this order of preference): the physical carrier or its label; accompanying material; or the container issued by the publisher, distributor, etc.

REMOTE ACCESS:

Use the title screen of the first issue published or earliest issue available. If a title screen is not available, take the information from any formal statement, either at the beginning or the end of the serial. If no formal statement exists, take information on the title, publisher and/or designation of the serial from anywhere within the body of the serial. If no information is available from the serial itself, take it from other published descriptions of the serial, if available, e.g., a printout of an issue or issues.

With archived issues or multiple files of a single issue, take the title screen from a file representing one complete issue. If this is not available, prefer files containing any introductory matter or the "README" file.

SYSTEM DETAILS NOTE (FIELD 538)

DIRECT ACCESS:

The System Details Note was once treated as the first note in the bibliographic record; however, CEG Update 5 states that, with the exception of field 533 and 539, 5xx notes should be input in numeric tag order. This note describes the computer system requirements and any software not included with the subscription that is necessary for use of the computer file (9.7B1). Also use a 538 note to describe other formats in which the contents of the computer file have been issued (9.7B16).

538 System requirements: NEC 9801, IBM PC or compatible; 640K RAM;
        DOS 3.1 or higher; hard and floppy disk drives.
538 Also issued for Macintosh systems.

REMOTE ACCESS:

This note is used to describe the equipment or operating systems or any special software needed to capture and/or print the remote access computer file (9.7B1).

538 System requirements: Acrobat Reader required to view and print files.

MODE OF ACCESS (FIELD 538)

DIRECT ACCESS:

Not applicable.

REMOTE ACCESS:

All remote access serial records must have at least one Mode of Access 538 note. This note follows the System Details Note, if one is present. Being a free-text note, the 538 note is able to provide more detailed or precise information on how the serial can be accessed than information recorded in formatted style in field 856, Electronic Location and Access. Catalogers may choose to include access method information here for clarity or for the sole purpose of display on an OPAC.

538 Mode of access: Electronic file transfer (FTP) via the Internet.
538 Mode of access: Internet email, FTP, and World Wide Web.

538 Mode of access: Internet email and World Wide Web. For online subscription, mail to listserv@mitvma.mit.edu, with the message: subscribe mini-air [firstname lastname].

538 Mode of access: World Wide Web. URL: http://www.cdc.gov/ncidod/WID/eid.htm.

FILE CHARACTERISTICS AREA (FIELD 256)

CONSER practice is not to use this field for either direct or remote access computer file serials because it is either too specific or not useful for serials.

FILE CHARACTERISTICS/TYPE OF COMPUTER FILE OR DATA (FIELD 516)

LC/CONSER practice is to provide this type of note only when the pertinent information is not available or otherwise clear in the record and, if such a note is necessary, to keep it brief. For remote access computer file serials, this field is used most frequently under the following two circumstances: It is used to describe the type of file (e.g., electronic journal) if it is not clear in the record; and it is used to note the availability of multiple-file formats if a serial has been issued as such.

DIRECT ACCESS:
516 8 Disc characteristics: CD-ROM (ISO 9660 standard).
516 8 Raw data in uncompressed ASCII form.

REMOTE ACCESS:
516   Text (electronic journal)
516 8 Available in ASCII, Acrobat, and PostScript file formats.

ELECTRONIC LOCATION AND ACCESS (856)

DIRECT ACCESS:
Not applicable.

REMOTE ACCESS:
This field is used for locating an electronic item and contains information needed to retrieve or transfer files electronically, connect to an electronic resource, or subscribe to an electronic journal or newsletter. Information for this field may be taken from anywhere in the item or other sources, but preferably from the most recent issue of the serial, since access information is likely to change.

The first indicator describes the access method through which the resource is available, i.e., email, FTP, Telnet, Dial-up, or HTTP, or any other method specified in subfield ≠2 (such as gopher). The second indicator, which used to be undefined and blank, has now been defined to accommodate the various types of relationships between the electronic resource recorded in the field 856 and the resource described in the record. The proposed changes in the first and second indicators of field 856 have been approved (MARBI Proposal No. 97-1), but not yet implemented, by the Library of Congress and OCLC at the time of writing. However, in the interests of future practice and keeping up with rule changes, all examples for remote access computer files in this section have been updated to reflect these new provisions and may therefore be different from existing records in OCLC. Catalogers should follow the current practice for the time being, until the new provisions have been implemented.

The values and definitions for the first and second indicators in field 856, as they appear in MARBI Proposal No. 97-1, follow:

First Indicator: Access Method

0 - Email

Access to the electronic resource is through electronic mail (email). Includes subscribing to an electronic journal or electronic forum through software intended to be used by an email system.

1 - FTP

Access to the electronic resource is through the File Transfer Protocol (FTP). Additional information in other subfields may enable the user to transfer the resource electronically.

2 - Remote login (Telnet)

Access to the electronic resource is through remote login (Telnet). Additional information in subfields of the record may enable the user to connect to the resource electronically.

3 - Dial-up

Access to the electronic resource is through a conventional telephone line (dial-up). Additional information in subfields of the record may enable the user to connect to the resource.

4 - HTTP

Access to the electronic resource is through the HyperText Transfer Protocol.

7 - Method specified in subfield ≠2

Access to the electronic resource is through a method other than the defined values and for which an identifying code is given in subfield ≠2 (Source of access).

Second Indicator: Relationship to Source

This indicator position contains a value that defines the relationship between the electronic resource at the location in field 856 and the resource described in the record. Subfield ≠3 is used to provide further information about the relationship if it is not a one-to-one relationship.

- No information provided.

Value # indicates that no information is provided about the relationship of the electronic resource to the bibliographic item described by the record.

Display constant: *Electronic resource:*

0 - Resource
> Value 0 indicates that the electronic location in the field is for the same re-source described by the record as a whole. In this case, the item represented by the bibliographic record is an electronic resource. If the data in field 856 relates to a constituent unit of the resource represented by the record, sub-field ≠3 is used to specify the portion(s) to which the field applies.
>
> Display constant: *Electronic resource:*

1 - Version of resource
> Value 1 indicates that the location in field 856 is for an electronic version of the resource described by the record. In this case, the item represented by the bibliographic record is not electronic but an electronic version is available. If the data in field 856 relates to a constituent unit of the resource represented by the record, subfield ≠3 is used to specify the portion(s) to which the field applies.
>
> Display constant: *Electronic version:*

2 - Related resource
> Value 2 indicates that the electronic location in field 856 is for an electronic resource that is related to the item described by the record. In this case, the item represented by the bibliographic record is not the electronic resource itself. Subfield ≠3 is used to further characterize the relationship between the electronic item identified in field 856 and the item represented by the bibliographic record as a whole.
>
> Display constant: *Related electronic resource:*

8 - No display constant generated

Although field 856 allows for a total of 26 subfield codes, no single subfield is mandatory, and not all subfields will be needed in every case. In most instances, the choice of subfields depends on the access method indicated by the first indicator or in subfield ≠2 (when the first indicator is "7"). The most common use of this field is sim-ply to record the Uniform Resource Locator (URL) in subfield ≠u. Field 856 is repeated if an electronic serial is available by more than one access method (such as gopher and World Wide Web), or if there are multiple file formats with different file names or groups of files. However, do not input separate 856 fields for different file formats if they are available by the same access method. Instead use a wild-card character (*) in the file name and explain the multiple formats in a subfield ≠z.

There is no prescribed order for coding the subfields in field 856, although sub-field ≠2 (Access Method) is usually input as the last subfield. If subfield ≠3 (Materials Specified) is present, then it is usually input as the first one. The other subfields ≠a to ≠z normally appear in alphabetical order. Alternatively, the data elements may be parsed into separately defined subfields. If a URL is used, Library of Congress practice is not to use a group of specific subfields to record the location and access information again.

Very often a URL may contain an underscore (_) or a spacing tilde (~), or a blank space. At the time of writing, the major bibliographic utilities and the Library of Congress have not yet implemented character set changes to allow for these character sets to be input directly. The Library of Congress and CONSER's interim practice until these characters are accommodated in the USMARC character set is to replace them with their corresponding hex code preceded by the percent sign (%). Thus, input "%5F" for an underscore, input "%7E" for a tilde, and input "%20" for a blank space.

Note that in a record having multiple 856 fields it is not necessary to expect each to pair with a 538 field, Mode of Access. Although an 856 field must be given for each of the primary modes of access, a cataloger may choose to consolidate the access instructions (e.g., FTP via Internet and subscribing to a listserv) into one single Mode of Access note, field 538.

For the convenience of the reader, a table with details of the valid codes for 007 (Physical Description Fixed Field for Computer File) in both OCLC and USMARC Bibliographic Formats follows.

007 Physical Description Fixed Field for Computer File

OCLC Subfields	USMARC Character Positions	Codes	
≠a	00	**Category of material**	
		c	Computer file
≠b	01	**Specific material designation**	
		a	Tape cartridge
		b	Chip cartridge
		c	Computer optical disc cartridge
		f	Tape cassette
		h	Tape reel
		j	Magnetic disc
		m	Magneto-optical disc
		o	Optical disc
		r	Remote
		u	Unknown
		z	Other
≠c	02	**Original vs. reproduction aspect***	
		f	Facsimile
		o	Original
		r	Reproduction
		u	Unknown
		*Do not use for OCLC.	
		Use fill character for USMARC.	
≠d	03	**Color**	
		a	One color
		c	Multicolored
		g	Grey scale
		m	Mixed
		n	Not applicable
		u	Unknown
		z	Other

≠e	04	**Dimensions**			
		a	3½ in.	n	Not applicable
		e	12 in.	o	5¼ in.
		g	4¾ in. or 12 cm.	u	Unknown
		i	1⅛ x 2⅜ in.	v	8 in.
		j	3⅞ x 2½ in.	z	Other

≠f	05	**Sound**	
		(blank)	No sound (silent)
		a	Sound on medium
		b*	Sound separate from medium
		u	Unknown
			For OCLC only.

EXAMPLES

R1	Direct access original computer file (CD-ROM)
R2	Direct access original computer file (computer disks)
R3	CD-ROM index to print journal
R4	CD-ROM serial of print copy with the same title
R5	CD-ROM serial of print copy with a different title
R6	CD-ROM serial of print copy with an existing uniform title
R7	CD-ROM serial qualified by edition statement
R8	Diskette version of print copy with the same title
R9	Diskette version of remote access electronic journal
R10	Remote access electronic journal of print copy with the same title
R11	Remote access electronic journal of print copy with a different title
R12	Remote access original electronic journal
R13	Remote access electronic journal continues print copy with the same title
R14	Print serial continued by remote access electronic version (single-record approach)
R15	Remote access computer file has the same title as that of an unrelated publication
R16	Remote access electronic newspaper
R17	Remote access electronic version of the table of contents of a print serial (single-record approach
R18	Remote access site related to print serial
R19	Related publication in remote access electronic version (single-record approach)
R20	Remote access synopsis of videorecording (single-record approach)

R1

PROBLEM CONSIDERED:

Direct access original computer file (CD-ROM)

RULE(S) CONSULTED:

AACR2R: 9.7B1b, 21.30G1, 21.30M
LCRI: 21.30J, p. 20

TAGGED DATA RECORD (based on OCLC #32814978)

LDR *****cas_/22*****Ia*4500   (language material serial)

(print serial)

00-05	06	07-14	15-17	18	19	20	21	22-28	29	30-32	33	34	35-37	38	39
950714	c	199u9999	nyu	a	r			ss-bci-	0	///	a	0	eng	-	d

008

| 007 | c ≠b o ≠d u ≠e g ≠f u   (CD-ROM) |

245 00   Black studies on disc ≠h [computer file].
260   [New York?] : ≠b G.K. Hall,
300   computer laser optical discs ; ≠c 4 3/4 in.
310   Annual
500   Description based on: 1995 disc; title from disc label.
→ 520   Information on materials by and about African Americans, Africa and peoples of African ancestry. Includes catalog of the Schomburg Center for Research in Black Culture and citations from the Index to Black periodicals, 1989-
→ 538   System requirements: IBM PC or compatible; 640K RAM; MS DOS extensions version 2.0 or higher.
550   Produced by: G.K. Hall & Co. and the Schomburg Center for Research in Black Culture.
→ 556 8 Accompanied by technical reference manual and reference table both titled: Black studies on CD-ROM.
650 0   Afro-Americans ≠x Study and teaching.
650 0   Blacks ≠x Study and teaching.
610 20   Schomburg Center for Research in Black Culture ≠x Catalogs.
650 0   Blacks ≠x Bibliography ≠x Catalogs.
650 0   Afro-Americans ≠x Bibliography ≠x Catalogs.
650 0   Afro-American periodicals ≠x Indexes.
650 0   Afro-Americans ≠x Periodicals ≠x Indexes.
710 2   Schomburg Center for Research in Black Culture.
710 2   G.K. Hall & Company.
→ 730 0 Index to Black periodicals.
→ 740 02 Black studies on CD-ROM.

Note that until the implementation of the proposed coding, the leader and fixed fields should be coded as follows:

LDR *****cms_/22*****Ia*4500   (computer file)
008   for computer file with appropriate values
006   for seriality
007   for CD-ROM

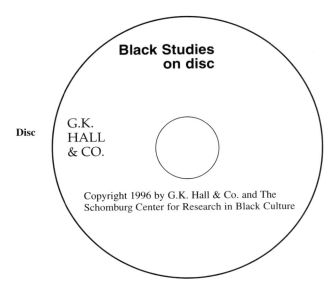

Disc

Black Studies
on disc

G.K.
HALL
& CO.

Copyright 1996 by G.K. Hall & Co. and The
Schomburg Center for Research in Black Culture

DISCUSSION

- This is an original (i.e., not a reproduction) publication CD-ROM containing information on materials by and about African Americans, Africa, and peoples of African ancestry. That information is recorded in a Summary Note, field 520. The CD-ROM is accompanied by documentation with the distinctive title "Black studies on CD-ROM," which is described in a field 556, Information About Documentation Note. The first indicator value for that note is set to "8" so that no display constant will be generated.
- According to 21.30M, an analytical added entry should be made under the heading for a work contained within the item being cataloged (see also CCM 7.5.1). LCRI 21.30J, p. 20 provides guidelines for making title added entries for titles borne by an item. In this example, the accompanying item "Black studies on CD-ROM" is treated as an independent work contained within the item being cataloged. Because the independent title "Black studies on CD-ROM" has not been established in catalog entry form, an uncontrolled title added entry using field 740 with indicator values "0" and "2" is made. The first indicator, indicating the number of nonfiling characters, is always set to value "0" according to Library of Congress practice, which omits initial articles. Second indicator value "2" is used for an analytical entry, i.e., the item being cataloged contains the work represented by the added entry.
- This CD-ROM includes citations from the "Index to Black periodicals." This is another publication that bears a relationship to the CD-ROM being cataloged. According to 21.30G1, an added entry for a related work should be made (see also CCM 7.5.2b). Field 730 is used for a uniform title added entry. The first indicator, which represents the number of nonfiling characters, again is always set to value "0" for the same reason stated earlier for field 740. The second indicator value is blank when the added entry is not for an analytic or when no information is provided as to whether it is for an analytic.
- Field 538, which gives information on the system requirements of the file, presents these characteristics in preferred order (9.7B1b): the make and model of

the computer(s) on which the file is designed to run; the amount of memory required; the name of the operating system; the software required; any required or recommended peripherals.

- Field 007, Physical Description Fixed Field for Computer File, is mandatory for electronic resources. In leader character position 06 is coded "a" for Language Material; in fixed field 008 character position 22 (Form of Original Item) and character position 23 (Form of Item) are coded "s" for Electronic.

R2

PROBLEM CONSIDERED:

Direct access original computer file (computer disks)

RULE(S) CONSULTED:

AACR2R: 12.7B7

TAGGED DATA RECORD (based on OCLC #18578455)

LDR   *****cas_/22*****Ia*4500   (language material serial)

                                                    (print serial)

00-05	06	07-14	15-17	18	19	20	21	22-28	29	30-32	33	34	35-37	38	39
881007	c	19859999	cau	q	r	l	p	ss-----	0	///	a	0	eng	-	d

008

00	01-04	05	06	07-10	11	12	13	14	15	16	17
a	----	g	-	----	-	0	0	0	/	0	-

→ 006   (book)

007	c ≠b j ≠d u ≠e o ≠f u	(computer disk)

022	1045-0564
→ 245 00	World cultures ≠h [computer file].
246 13	World cultures electronic journal
260	La Jolla, Calif. : ≠b World Cultures Publishers, ≠c 1989, c1987-
300	computer disks ; ≠c 5 1/4 in. + ≠e codebook (28 cm.)
310	Quarterly
362 0	Vol. 1, no. 1 (Mar. 1985)-
500	Title from title screen.
500	Issue diskettes accompanied by separate program and data diskettes MAPTAB and program and data utility diskettes MAP and SORT.
516	Disk characteristics: Double sided, double density, 320+ KB.
538	System requirements: DOS 3.3; 256K RAM; disk drive.
→ 580	Has companion publication: World cultures quorum.
650 0	Cross-cultural studies ≠x Periodicals.
650 0	Comparative civilization ≠x Periodicals.
→ 787 1	≠t World cultures quorum ≠x 1045-2656 ≠w (DLC)sn89003026 ≠w (OCoLC)19414386

Note that until the implementation of the proposed coding, the leader and fixed fields should be coded as follows:

LDR   *****cms̲/22*****Ia*4500   (computer file)
008   for computer file with appropriate values
006   for seriality
006   for codebook
007   for computer disk

Title screen

```
c:\WORLD\1#1>echo off


                        WORLD CULTURES

            Electronic Journal of Cross-Cultural Studies


            © 1985, 1986, 1987 World Cultures Publishers
```

DISCUSSION

- This serial, "World cultures," is an original publication (not a reproduction) in computer diskette format. It has a companion publication called "World cultures quorum," which is a print version. This information is recorded in a note, according to 12.7B7, which prescribes that a note be made describing the relationship between the serial being cataloged and any immediately preceding, succeeding, or simultaneously published serial. (Note, however, that the relationship between "World Cultures" and "World cultures quorum" is not one of those specifically defined in rule 12.7B7.) Field 580, Linking Entry Complexity Note, is used here to specify the relationship between the two serials.

- In this example, a machine link is made to the companion publication "World cultures quorum" using field 787 (Nonspecific Relationship Entry), since the related record does not fit into any of the cases defined in linking fields 760–785. First indicator value "1" indicates that a note is not to be generated from the data in the field, since a Linking Entry Complexity Note is already provided by field 580 (see also CCM 30.16.3).

- Because the main publication is accompanied by a codebook, a 006 field is supplied to describe the characteristics of the accompanying material. Character position 00 (Form of Material) is coded "a" for Print Language Material, and the remaining positions, 01–17, follow the field 008 positions 18–34 configuration for books format.

- In leader character position 06 (Type of Record), code "a" is used for Language Material, since the electronic resource contains only a textual document. In fixed field 008 character positions 22-23, code "s" is used for Electronic.

R3

PROBLEM CONSIDERED:

CD-ROM index to print journal

RULE(S) CONSULTED:

AACR2R: 9.7B1, 12.7B7

TAGGED DATA RECORD (based on OCLC #34488341)

LDR	*****cas_/22*****Ia*4500	(language material serial)

(print serial)

00-05	06	07-14	15-17	18	19	20	21	22-28	29	30-32	33	34	35-37	38	39
960329	c	19949999	cau	u	u			ssi----	0	///	a	0	eng	-	d

008

00	01-04	05	06	07-10	11	12	13	14	15	16	17
a	a---	f	-	i---	-	0	0	0	/	0	-

006   (book)

```
007       c ≠b o ≠d c ≠e g                                    (CD-ROM)
022       0076-6879
→ 245 00  Methods in enzymology index ≠h [computer file].
  246 13  Methods in enzymology index CD-ROM
  260     San Diego, Calif. : ≠b Academic Press ; ≠a San Francisco, Calif. : ≠b
          Lightbinder, ≠c c1995-
→ 300     computer laser optical discs : ≠b col. ; ≠c 4 3/4 in. + ≠e 1 guide (6 p. : ill. ;
          12 cm.)
→ 362 0   CD-ROM 1 (1955/1994)-
  500     "Prepared by Lightbinders, Inc. using Dynatext system developed by
          Electronic Book Technologies, Inc."—P.[2] of guide.
  500     Title from disc label.
→ 538     System requirements (IBM): IBM PC or compatible with 80386SX
          processor or higher; MS-DOS 4.1 or higher; MS Windows 3.1 or higher in
          enhanced mode with virtual memory; 8 MB RAM and 8 MB free hard-disk
          space; VGA monitor is minimum requirement for use with the browser;
          super VGA driver (256 colors) and 800 x 600 resolution is recommended;
          CD-ROM drive with MSCDEX 2.0 or higher.
→ 538     System requirements (Macintosh): Macintosh computer with 4 MB of RAM;
          5 MB hard-disk space; Macintosh-compatible CD-ROM drive with Foreign
          File Access installed and System 7 or higher with Color Quickdraw; a color
          display (256 colors) and 800 x 600 resolution is recommended; for computer
          with less than 8 MB of RAM, the virtual memory option should be enabled.
  580     CD-ROM index to: Methods in enzymology.
  630 00  Methods in enzymology ≠x Indexes.
  650  0  Enzymes ≠x Periodicals ≠x Indexes.
  710 2   Academic Press.
  710 2   Lightbinders, Inc.
  787 1   ≠t Methods in enzymology ≠w (OCoLC)2239135
```

Until the implementation of the proposed coding, the leader and fixed fields should be coded as follows:

LDR   *****cms_/22*****Ia*4500   (computer file)
008   for computer file with appropriate values
006   for seriality
006   for guide
007   for CD-ROM

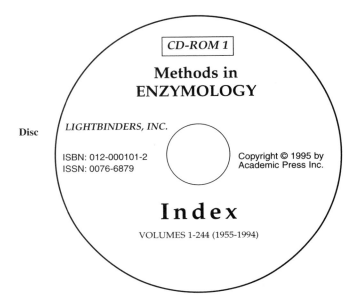

DISCUSSION

- Serials may be related to other serials in many different ways under various circumstances. In addition to the relationships mentioned in 12.7B7 (such as continuation, merging, absorption, editions, supplements, etc.), there are other possible miscellaneous relationships that are not defined in the rule. This example illustrates one of those other miscellaneous relationships between serial records, which is that of an index in computer file format related to a print journal.
- "Methods in enzymology index" is a CD-ROM index to a print journal entitled "Methods in enzymology." In the record for the CD-ROM index, a Linking Entry Complexity Note is given in field 580 to describe the relationship between the two serials. Field 787, Nonspecific Relationship Entry, should be used for a related record that does not fit into any of the cases defined in linking fields 760–785. First indicator value "1" indicates that a note is not to be generated from the data in the field, since a note for display is already recorded in field 580 (see also CCM 30.16.3).
- Although AACR2R Chapters 9 and 12 do not specify the prescribed source of information for the designation of computer file serials, it is reasonable to take the designation information from the chief source of information prescribed

for the item. The words "CD-ROM 1" appear at the top of the label on the disc, and "Volumes 1–244 (1955–1994)" appear at the bottom. The numeric designation "CD-ROM 1" and the chronological designation "1955–1994" are transcribed and then joined with the appropriate punctuation to form the designation in field 362. First indicator value "0" means that the designation is input in formatted style. The cataloger must have the first issue or last issue in hand in order to input this field with first indicator value "0."

- The field 538 System Details Note describes the hardware and software necessary to run the computer file (9.7B1). If the computer file is issued for use with multiple platforms (such as Windows, DOS, Macintosh, etc.) and cataloged in one record, then this field is repeated, with one 538 note for each platform, as is the case in this example (see also CCM 30.14.1).
- Field 007, Physical Description Fixed Field for Computer File, is mandatory for electronic resources. For the use of code "a" in leader character position 06 and the coding of "s" in fixed field 008 character positions 22-23, see discussion in R1.

R4

PROBLEM CONSIDERED:
CD-ROM serial of print copy with the same title

RULE(S) CONSULTED:
LCRI: 1.1C, 9.5B1, 25.5B

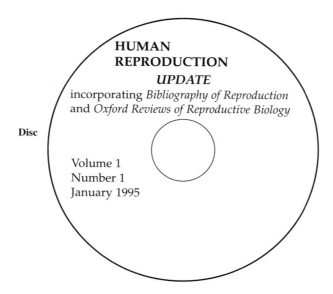

TAGGED DATA RECORD (based on OCLC #34531324)

LDR   *****nas̷_/22*****Ia*4500   (language material serial)

(print serial)

00-05	06	07-14	15-17	18	19	20	21	22-28	29	30-32	33	34	35-37	38	39
960408	c	19959999	enk	b	r			-s-----	0	///	a	0	eng	-	d

008

→ 007   c ≠b o ≠d m ≠e g   (CD-ROM)
→ 130 0   Human reproduction update (CD-ROM)
→ 245 00 Human reproduction update ≠h [computer file].
   260   Oxford : ≠b published in association with ESHRE by Oxford University Press, ≠c 1995-
→ 300   computer laser optical discs ; ≠c 4 3/4 in. + ≠e installation manual
   310   Bimonthly
   362 0   Vol. 1, no. 1 (Jan. 1995)-
   500   Title from title screen.
→ 500   Contains same textual information as print equivalent in addition to color graphics and black and white video clips.
→ 530   Print version also available.
→ 538   System requirements: for Microsoft Windows, CD-ROM drive, 386-class PC compatible, 4 MB RAM, 15 MB free hard-disk space, MS-DOS v. 5.0, Windows v. 3.1, Windows CD-ROM extensions (MSCDEX) v. 2.0; for UNIX, CD-ROM drive, HP, RS6000, Alpha, Sun4, Solaris, or OSF, 15 MB free hard-disk space; for Apple Macintosh, CD-ROM drive, Apple Macintosh IIfx, Centris 650, Quadra 700, or 950, 4 MB RAM (2 MB allocated to WorldView), 10 MB of free hard-disk space, 3.5″ high-density floppy-disk drive, and Apple Macintosh System Software v. 7.1.
   580   Incorporating Bibliography of reproduction and Oxford reviews of reproductive biology.
   650 0 Human reproduction ≠x Periodicals.
   650 0 Embryology ≠x Periodicals.
   710 2   European Society of Human Reproduction and Embryology.
→ 776 1   ≠t Human reproduction update ≠x 1355-4786 ≠w (OCoLC)32055602 ≠w (DLC)95657574
   780 14 ≠t Bibliography of reproduction ≠x 0006-1565 ≠w (OCoLC)1532761 ≠w (DLC)sn88003024
   780 14 ≠t Oxford reviews of reproductive biology ≠x 0260-0854 ≠w (OCoLC)6321542 ≠w (DLC)0648347
   780 01 ≠t Human reproduction (Oxford, England) ≠x 0268-1161 ≠w (OCoLC)13829792 ≠x (DLC)sn87008073

Note that until the implementation of the proposed coding, the leader and fixed fields should be coded as follows:

LDR   *****nms̷_/22*****Ia*4500   (computer file)
008   for computer file with appropriate values
006   for seriality
007   for CD-ROM

DISCUSSION

- According to LCRI 25.5B, a uniform title is needed to resolve the conflict if a computer file serial is also issued in another physical format with the same title. Therefore, in this example, the CD-ROM version of the print journal "Human reproduction update" is given a uniform title heading with the physical medium, "CD-ROM," as qualifier. (Note that the CD-ROM version of the print journal is *not* treated as a reproduction.)

- According to LCRI 1.1C, the General Material Designation (GMD), "computer file," is the prescribed term for computer files. The GMD, enclosed in brackets, is added at the end of the title proper in field 245.

- For the Extent of Item (field 300, subfield ≠a) in the physical description area, the Specific Material Designation (SMD) for CD-ROM products is "computer laser optical discs" (LCRI 9.5B1; CCM 30.11.1). Because the terminology used in the SMD provides pertinent information on file characteristics, the File Characteristics Note (field 516) should be reserved only for information other than the type of file storage.

- The System Details Note (field 538) describes the hardware and software necessary to use the computer file. Prefer to give information on minimum system requirements; because technology so quickly becomes outdated, extremely specific information should be avoided. Note that unlike example R3, where multiple 538 fields are used to record the system details for various platforms, here the cataloger has used one single 538 field to note the multiple platforms on which the CD-ROM runs, i.e., Microsoft Windows, UNIX, Apple Macintosh.

- If a computer file serial is also available in another format, give that information in note field 530. Record the titles of other physical formats in field 776, Additional Physical Form Entry.

- Note that, because its primary content consists of an online version of a print serial, the item in this example is treated as electronic textual material, even though the CD-ROM version includes graphic materials and video clips.

- Field 007, Physical Description Fixed Field for Computer File, is mandatory for electronic resources. In field 008 character position 23 (Form of Original Item), code "s" is used for Electronic.

R5

PROBLEM CONSIDERED:

CD-ROM serial of print copy with a different title

RULE(S) CONSULTED:

AACR2R: 9.0B1, 9.7B16, 12.2B2

TAGGED DATA RECORD (based on OCLC #31626480)

LDR   *****cas_/22*****Ia*4500   (language material serial)

(print serial)

00-05	06	07-14	15-17	18	19	20	21	22-28	29	30-32	33	34	35-37	38	39
941207	c	19959999	mau	f	r	1		-sr----	0	///	a	0	eng	-	d

008

→ 007   c ≠b o ≠d u ≠e g ≠f u   (CD-ROM)

022   1079-9516

→ 245 00   Profiles in business and management ≠h [computer file].

246 1   ≠i At head of title: ≠a Harvard business reference

260   Boston, Mass : ≠b Harvard Business School Pub., ≠c c1995-

300   computer laser optical discs ; ≠c 4 3/4 in. + ≠e user guide

310   Semiannual

→ 362 0   Version 1.0 (fall/winter 1995)-

500   An international directory of scholars and their research.

500   Title from title screen.

→ 530   Also available in a print ed. with title: International directory of business and management scholars and research.

→ 538   System requirements: IBM 386 or compatible; 4 MB RAM; DOS 5.0; VGA monitor; CD-ROM drive.

→ 538   System requirements: IBM 386 or compatible; 4 MB RAM; Windows 3.1; DOS 5.0; VGA monitor; CD-ROM drive.

→ 538   System requirements: Macintosh; 4 MB RAM; System 7.0; CD-ROM drive.

650 0   Business teachers ≠x Directories.

650 0   Finance teachers ≠x Directories.

650 0   Industrial psychologists ≠x Directories.

650 0   Economists ≠x Directories.

650 0   College teachers ≠x Directories.

650 0   Business ≠x Research.

650 0   Management ≠x Research.

710 2   Harvard Business School Publishing Corporation.

→ 776 1   ≠t International directory of business and management scholars and research ≠x 1079-9508 ≠w (DLC) 95649719 ≠w (OCoLC)31626431

Note that until the implementation of the proposed coding, the leader and fixed fields should be coded as follows:

LDR   *****cms_/22*****Ia*4500   (computer file)

008   for computer file with appropriate values

006   for seriality

007   for CD-ROM

```
                                              Version 1.0
                                              Fall/Winter
                                              1995

                    Profiles in Business and Management

 Title screen
                             An international directory of
                             scholars and their research


                            © Harvard Business School Publishing
                                   Boston, Massachusetts
```

DISCUSSION

- AACR2R 9.0B1 stipulates the chief source of information for computer files, with the preferred source being the title screen(s) or other internal sources. Accordingly, the title of this CD-ROM is taken from the title screen and transcribed as "Profiles in business and management" (see also CCM 30.3.2a). As a result, the title proper of this serial is different from that of its print counterpart (see field 530), and, therefore, no uniform title heading is needed to distinguish between the two.

- Because this CD-ROM serial is also available in another physical format, that information should be given in a note (9.7B16). Use field 530, Additional Physical Form Available Note, to record such details (see also CCM 30.14.5).

- Field 776, Additional Physical Form Entry, is used to provide links to works in a different physical format. First indicator value "1" indicates that a note is not to be generated from the field, since a note for display is already recorded in field 530 in this case. Subfields ≠x (International Standard Serial Number) and ≠w (Record Control Number) should be included whenever possible (see also CCM 30.16.2).

- "Version 1.0" is not recorded in the edition statement in field 250 because this field is used only for edition information that applies to the serial as a whole. In this case, the version of the computer file serial is treated as the numerical designation system and therefore input in field 362 (12.2B2). Because the software-related version number changes over time, it may also be given in a System Details Note (see also CCM 30.10).

- Field 007, Physical Description Fixed Field for Computer File, is mandatory for electronic resources. For the use of code "a" in leader character position 06 and the coding of "s" in fixed field 008 character position 23, see discussion in R1.

R6

PROBLEM CONSIDERED:

CD-ROM serial of print copy with an existing uniform title

RULE(S) CONSULTED:

AACR2R: 9.7B16, 25.5B
LCRI: 25.5B, p. 11–12

TAGGED DATA RECORD (based on OCLC #30064530)

LDR   *****cas_/22*****Ia*4500   (language material serial)

(print serial)

00-05	06	07-14	15-17	18	19	20	21	22-28	29	30-32	33	34	35-37	38	39
940401	c	19919999	nyu	a	r			-ss---i	0	///	a	0	eng	-	d

008

(CD-ROM)

007	c ≠b o ≠d c ≠e g ≠f u
022	1020-1114
041 0	engfre
→ 130 0	Statistical yearbook (United Nations. Statistical Division : CD-ROM)
245 00	Statistical yearbook ≠h [computer file].
246 3	SYB CD
246 3	Statistical yearbook compact disc
246 1	≠i Added title screen title: ≠a United Nations statistical yearbook
246 17	SYB-CD
→ 250	CD-ROM ed.
260	New York : ≠b United Nations, ≠c c1993-
300	computer laser optical discs : ≠b col. ; ≠c 4 3/4 in.
310	Annual
362 0	38th issue (1990/91)-
500	Title from title screen.
500	Documentation is also available as SYB-CD quick reference guide.
→ 530	Also available in print edition with the same title.
538	System requirements: minimum configuration of PC8088 with 640 KB RAM; 2.5 MB free HDD or higher, VGA or SVGA display recommended; HP Laserjet, HP Deskjet or Epson compatible printer; CD-ROM reader (ISO 9660).
546	English and French.
550	Prepared by: the Statistical Division, Dept. for Economic and Social Information and Policy Analysis.
→ 556 8	Accompanied by user manual.
650 0	Statistics.
710 2	United Nations. ≠b Statistical Division.
→ 776 1	≠t Statistical yearbook (United Nations. Statistical Division) ≠w (DLC)95641266 ≠w (OCoLC)30065137

Note that until the implementation of the proposed coding, the leader and fixed fields should be coded as follows:

LDR   *****cms_/22*****Ia*4500   (computer file)
008   for computer file with appropriate values
006   for seriality
007   for CD-ROM

Title screen

```
                                              CD ROM edition
                                              38th issue


                        Statistical Yearbook
                              1990-91




                     Prepared by the United Nations
                     Department for Economic and
                     Social Information and Policy Analysis
                           Statistical Division
```

DISCUSSION

- In this example, the serial is issued as a CD-ROM edition of the print version. The edition statement "CD-ROM ed.," which appears on the chief source, is transcribed in field 250. Both the CD-ROM and the print version have the same title proper, and, therefore, a uniform title heading has been established for this record (25.5B).

- According to the guidelines in LCRI 25.5B, p. 11–12 on the choice of uniform title qualifier for computer file serials, terms that describe the physical medium of the serial are to be preferred over place or corporate body. Because the print version itself is entered under a uniform title heading, and the existing uniform title heading "Statistical yearbook (United Nations. Statistical Division)" is qualified by a corporate name, a double qualifier is needed to distinguish the CD-ROM serial from its print version. In this case, the Specific Material Designation "CD-ROM" is added as a second qualifier. The two qualifiers are separated by a colon; hence, the complete uniform title heading is "Statistical yearbook (United Nations. Statistical Division : CD-ROM)" (see also CCM 5.3.5).

- Use field 130 for a uniform title heading used as the main entry. The first indicator represents the number of nonfiling characters. According to Library of Congress practice, initial articles are omitted from uniform titles, so the first indicator is always set to value "0." The second indicator is undefined and blank.

- Field 530, Additional Physical Form Available Note, is used to record information about the availability of the print edition of the CD-ROM serial being cataloged (9.7B16). It is important to note the difference between field 530 and field 580, which expresses a complex relationship between the item described in the record and other items that cannot be adequately generated from the linking entry fields 760–787.
- Field 776, Additional Physical Form Entry, is used to link multiple physical format records of the same work (see also CCM 30.16.2). In this example, the print edition of the serial "Statistical yearbook (United Nations. Statistical Division)" is input in field 776 to provide a link. First indicator value "1" indicates that a note is not to be generated, since a note for display is already recorded in field 530. Subfields ≠x (International Standard Serial Number) and ≠w (Record Control Number) should be included whenever possible.
- Field 007, Physical Description Fixed Field for Computer File, is mandatory for electronic resources. In leader character position 06 (Type of Record), code "a" is used, since the electronic resource is language material in nature. In fixed field 008, character position 23 is coded "s" for Electronic, and position 24 (Nature of Entire Work) is "s" for Statistics.

R7

PROBLEM CONSIDERED:
CD-ROM serial qualified by edition statement

RULE(S) CONSULTED:
AACR2R: 9.7B16, 12.2B1, 12.2B2, 25.5B
LCRI: 25.5B, p. 11–12

Disc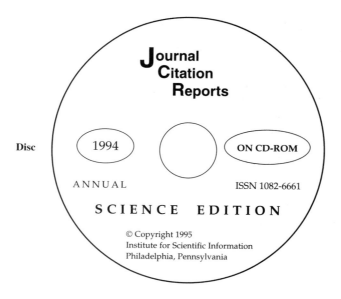

TAGGED DATA RECORD (based on OCLC #32525529)

LDR   *****cas_/22*****Ia*4500   (language material serial))

                                                                      (print serial)

	00-05	06	07-14	15-17	18	19	20	21	22-28	29	30-32	33	34	35-37	38	39
008	950523	c	19959999	pau	a	r	1		sss----	0	///	a	0	eng	-	d

→ 007   c ≠b o ≠d u ≠e g ≠f u   (CD-ROM)

    022   1082-6661

→ 130 0   Journal citation reports on CD-ROM (Science ed.)

    245 00 Journal citation reports on CD-ROM ≠h [computer file] : ≠b JCR.

    246 30 JCR

→ 250   Science ed.

    260   Philadelphia, Pa. : ≠b Institute for Scientific Information, ≠c c1995-

    300   computer laser optical discs ; ≠c 4 3/4 in.

    310   Annual

    362 0   1994-

    500   Description based on surrogate; title from disc label.

    520   A resource tool for journal evaluation, containing bibliometric analysis of over 4,500 journals in areas of science and technology worldwide.

→ 530   Also available on microfiche with title: SCI JCR.

    538   System requirements: IBM PC/compatible PC 386 or higher; minimum 6 MB free hard-disk space; minimum 4 MB RAM (8 MB recommended); MS-DOS 3.3 or higher (5.0 or higher recommended); MS-Windows version 3.1 or higher; CD-ROM drive; EGA monitor (VGA recommended); mouse; printer (optional).

    580   Formerly issued in paper format with title: SCI journal citation reports.

    580   Analyzes citations found in: Science citation index.

    630 00 Science citations index ≠x Statistics.

    650 0   Science ≠x Periodicals ≠x Statistics.

    650 0   Bibliographical citations ≠x Statistics.

    710 2   Institute for Scientific Information.

    730 0   SCI JCR

    730 0   SCI journal citation reports

→ 775 0   ≠t Journal citation reports on CD-ROM (Social sciences ed.) ≠x 1082-6653 ≠w (DLC)sn 95004830

→ 776 1   ≠t SCI JCR ≠w (DLC)93640547 ≠w (OCoLC)23953801

Note that until the implementation of the proposed coding, the leader and fixed fields should be coded as follows:

LDR   *****nms_/22*****Ia*4500   (computer file)

008   for computer file with appropriate values

006   for seriality

007   for CD-ROM

DISCUSSION

- This CD-ROM serial was first issued in paper format. It then became available in microfiche, and is now also published in a CD-ROM version in two different editions: the Social sciences edition and the Science edition. The example discussed here is the Science edition.
- Both the Science edition and the Social sciences edition of this CD-ROM have the same title proper, "Journal citation reports on CD-ROM." Therefore, a uniform title heading is required to differentiate between the two different editions (25.5B). According to LCRI 25.5B, p. 11–12, when choosing a uniform title qualifier for a computer file serial, the cataloger should prefer the term describing the physical medium of the serial. Alternately, the qualifying term may be taken from an edition statement or other title information. The preferred uniform title qualifier for the Science edition is taken from the edition statement (see also CCM 30.5). Usually the presence of an edition statement on an item implies the existence of other editions sharing the same title proper. Whenever an edition statement is included in a record, it is usually necessary to construct a uniform title heading to distinguish the serial in hand from other editions with the same title proper. In such a case, construct the uniform title heading by using the title proper qualified by the edition statement.
- Field 250 is used for edition statements. In serials cataloging, edition statements to be input in this field are formal statements, such as: international edition, cumulative edition, annual edition, Internet edition, etc. (12.2B1). In this case, "Science edition" is a formal statement relating to edition and should be recorded in field 250. Statements indicating volume, numerical or chronological designation, or revision (e.g., 1st ed., 1994 ed.) are not considered to be formal edition statements and should be recorded in the numeric and/or alphabetic, chronological, or other designation area (12.2B2).
- To provide a link to the Social sciences edition, use field 775, Other Edition Available Entry. Field 775 is used only when the other edition is in the same medium as the item being cataloged.
- Because this CD-ROM is also available in microfiche format, a field 530, Additional Physical Form Available Note, is made to indicate the availability of the microfiche (9.7B16; see also CCM 30.14.5). In conjunction with field 530, a corresponding 776 field, Additional Physical Form Entry, should be entered. This field is used to link multiple physical format records of the same work (see also CCM 30.16.2). First indicator value "1" indicates that a note is not to be generated, since a note for display is already recorded in field 530. Subfields ≠x (International Standard Serial Number) and ≠w (Record Control Number) should be included whenever possible.
- In the leader character position 06 is coded "a" for language material, even though the electronic resource contains some computer programs in addition to the text.
- Field 007, Physical Description Fixed Field for Computer File, is mandatory for electronic resources. In field 008 character position 22 (Form of Original Item) and character position 23 (Form of Item), code "s" is used for Electronic.

R8

PROBLEM CONSIDERED:

Diskette version of print copy with the same title

RULE(S) CONSULTED:

AACR2R: 9.7B8, 9.7B16
LCRI: 25.5B, p. 11–12

TAGGED DATA RECORD (based on OCLC #32800475)

LDR   *****cas_/22*****Ia*4500   (language material serial)

(print serial)

	00-05	06	07-14	15-17	18	19	20	21	22-28	29	30-32	33	34	35-37	38	39
008	950711	c	19uu9999	fr		x			-s----i	0	///	a	0	eng	-	d

→ 007   c ≠b j ≠d u ≠e a ≠f u   (computer disk)
041 0   eng ≠g engfre
→ 130 0   Education at a glance (Paris, France : Diskette)
245 00   Education at a glance ≠h [computer file].
→ 246 1   ≠i French title on disk label: ≠a Regard sur l'education
260   Paris, France : ≠b OECD,
300   computer disks ; ≠c 3 1/2 in. + ≠e manual
310   Irregular
500   "OECD Statistics/Statistiques de l'OCDE."
500   At head of title: CREDES & OECD present, 1985-1991-
500   Accompanied by decompression/installation software: OECD TRANS.
500   Description based on: 1985-1991, published in 1994; title from title screen.
→ 516   Files are OECD-compressed databases.
→ 530   Data also available in print publication of the same title.
→ 538   System requirements: IBM-PC or compatible system; MS-DOS v. 3.3 or later; 640K RAM; 11 MB hard-disk space.
515   Preceded by 1988 issue published in 1992 which lacks title screen.
→ 556 8   Accompanied by technical documentation.
650 0   Educational indicators ≠x Cross-cultural studies.
650 0   Education ≠x Evaluation ≠x Statistics ≠x Cross-cultural studies.
710 2   Organisation for Economic Co-operation and Development.
710 2   Centre for Educational Research and Innovation.
→ 776 1   ≠t Education at a glance (Paris, France) ≠w (DLC)95650514 ≠w (OCoLC)29585874

Note that until the implementation of the proposed coding, the leader and fixed fields should be coded as follows:

LDR   *****cms_/22*****Ia*4500   (computer file)
008   for computer file with appropriate values
006   for seriality
007   for computer disk

```
┌─────────────────────────────────────────────┐
│                                               │
│              CREDES & OECD                    │
│                present                        │
│                                               │
│                                               │
│            Education at a Glance              │
│                1985-1991                      │
│                                               │
│                                               │
│      OECD Statistics / Statistique de l'OCDE  │
│                                               │
│                                               │
│                  © OECD                       │
│               Paris, France                   │
│                                               │
└─────────────────────────────────────────────┘
```

Title screen

DISCUSSION

- This is an example of a diskette version of a print serial. The computer file serial "Education at a glance" has exactly the same title as that of its print counterpart, and, consequently, it is necessary for the cataloger to establish a uniform title heading to distinguish between the computer file serial and its print version. Since the print version already has an existing uniform title with place as qualifier, i.e., "Education at a glance (Paris, France)," a double qualifier must be used to establish a unique uniform title heading for the computer file serial.
- According to the guidelines in LCRI 25.5B, p. 11–12, on choosing a uniform title qualifier for computer file serials, terms that describe the physical medium of the serial are to be preferred over place or corporate body. The Specific Material Designation "Diskette" is added to the existing qualifier. The two qualifiers are separated by a colon to form "Education at a glance (Paris, France : Diskette)" (see also CCM 5.3.5).
- Although the title proper of this computer file serial is taken from the title screen, which is the chief source of information, a French title appears on the disk label. Because it is reasonable to expect that users may search for the serial using that title, a field 246 title added entry is made for it. The first indicator is set to "1" to provide both a note and a title added entry. The second indicator value is blank, and subfield ≠i is input to display the following text as a note: "French title on disk label:".
- In this example, because the information is not available elsewhere in the record, field 516 is used to provide information about data or file characteristics (9.7B8).
- Field 530 is used to record details about other physical formats in which the item is available (9.7B16). A field 776, Additional Physical Form Entry, is used to provide a link to the print version of the serial. First indicator value "1" is used, since a note for display is already recorded in field 530. Subfield ≠x (International Standard Serial Number) and subfield ≠w (Record Control Number) should be used when the relevant information is available.

- The fact that this computer file serial is accompanied by technical documentation is recorded in field 556, Information About Documentation Note. First indicator value "8" specifies that no display constant is to be generated, since the text of the note itself is self-explanatory.
- Field 007, Physical Description Fixed Field for Computer File, is mandatory for electronic resources. For the use of code "a" in leader character position 06 and the coding of "s" in fixed field 008 character position 23, see discussion in R1.

R9

PROBLEM CONSIDERED:

Diskette version of remote access electronic journal

RULE(S) CONSULTED:

AACR2R: 9.7B16
LCRI: 25.5B, p. 11–12

TAGGED DATA RECORD (based on OCLC #28863760)

LDR   *****cas_/22*****Ia*4500   (language material serial)

(print serial)

00-05	06	07-14	15-17	18	19	20	21	22-28	29	30-32	33	34	35-37	38	39
930921	c	19909999	ncu	t	r		p	-s-----	0	///	a	0	eng	-	d

008

007	c ≠b j ≠d u ≠e a ≠f u (computer disk)
007	c ≠b r ≠d u ≠e n (computer file: remote)
022	1053-1920
→ 130 0	Postmodern culture (Diskette)
245 00	Postmodern culture ≠h [computer file].
246 3	PMC
250	DOS version.
260	Cary, N.C. : ≠b Oxford,
300	computer disks ; ≠c 3 1/2 in.
310	Three no. a year
362 1	Began publication in 1990.
500	"Oxford electronic journal"
500	Description based on: Vol. 3, no. 2; title from disk label.
→ 530	Available also online and on microfiche.
538	System requirements: IBM-PC or compatibles; MS-DOS version 3.0 or later.
650 0	Postmodernism ≠x Periodicals.
→ 776 1	≠t Postmodern culture ≠x 1053-1920 ≠w (DLC)sn9003259 ≠w (OCoLC)22471982
→ 776 1	≠t Postmodern culture (Microfiche) ≠w (DLC)sn9019114 ≠w (OCoLC)23234647
→ 856 41	≠u http://www.press.jhu.edu/journals/postmodern%5Fculture/
→ 856 41	≠3 Current issue only: ≠u http://www.iath.virginia.edu/pmc/

Note that until the implementation of the proposed coding, the leader and fixed fields should be coded as follows:

LDR   *****cms_/22*****Ia*4500   (computer file)
008   for computer file with appropriate values
006   for seriality
007   for computer disk
007   for computer file: remote

Disk label

POSTMODERN CULTURE

Volume 3, Number 2

DOS VERSION

DISCUSSION

- This serial, "Postmodern culture," issued originally as an online journal, is also available in diskette and microfiche formats. Because these all share the same title proper, it is necessary to create uniform title headings to distinguish among these identical titles proper. In choosing the qualifier to be used in the uniform title heading, the cataloger should refer to LCRI 25.5B, p. 11–12, which says to prefer terms that "describe the physical medium of the serial rather than place or corporate body." Thus, the Specific Material Designation "Diskette" is used as the qualifier in the uniform title for the diskette version of this serial (see also CCM 30.5).
- Use field 130 for a uniform title heading used as the main entry. The first indicator represents the number of nonfiling characters, and Library of Congress practice is always to set the first indicator value to "0," since initial articles are omitted from uniform titles. The second indicator is undefined and blank.
- If the item is also available in other physical formats, this information should be given in a note (9.7B16). Field 530, Other Physical Form Available Note, is used (see also CCM 30.14.5).
- Because a note is made to indicate the availability of the item in other formats, a corresponding 776 linking field should also be made. Field 776 is an Additional Physical Form Entry that is used to link multiple physical format records of the same work (see also CCM 30.16.2). In this example, two 776 fields are given. The first 776 field provides a link to the online version of the serial

"Postmodern culture." (Note that this electronic journal is not entered under a uniform title heading because the journal itself was originally issued online.) The second 776 field is linked to the microfiche edition of the serial. Note that the microfiche edition is entered under a uniform title heading qualified by the Specific Material Designation "Microfiche." First indicator value "1" indicates that a note is not to be generated, since a note for display is already recorded in field 530. Subfield ≠x (International Standard Serial Number) and subfield ≠w (Record Control Number) should be given when available for the related titles.

- Likewise, the bibliographic record for the online version of the serial (OCLC #22471982) has two 776 fields containing links to the diskette version and the microfiche edition of the serial.
- Field 856, Electronic Location and Access, may be added to this record to facilitate access to the electronic resource if the library's OPAC has the capability of linking directly to the resource on the Internet. First indicator value "4" indicates that access to the electronic resource is through the HyperText Transfer Protocol. Second indicator value "1" is used whenever the electronic version in the field is the same resource as the one described in the record, but not in an online format. In this example, "Postmodern culture" described in the record is in computer disks, and the content of the resource given in field 856 is essentially the same, but in online format. The display constant "Electronic version:" may be generated for this value.
- Field 007, Physical Description Fixed Field for Computer File, is mandatory for electronic resources. For the use of code "a" in leader character position 06 and the coding of "s" in fixed field 008 character position 23, see discussion in R1.

R10

PROBLEM CONSIDERED:
Remote access electronic journal of print copy with the same title

RULE(S) CONSULTED:
AACR2R: 1.2B1
LCRI: 25.5B, p. 11–12

PUBLISHED BY THE AMERICAN SOCIETY FOR BIOCHEMISTRY AND MOLECULAR BIOLOGY

Journal of Biological Chemistry

Current issue: 29 November 1996; 271 (48)

© 1996 by The American Society for Biochemistry and Molecular Biology, Inc.
ISSN 1083-351X

Journal homepage

TAGGED DATA RECORD (based on OCLC #32808313)

LDR   *****cas_/22*****Ia*4500   (language material serial)

(print serial)

00-05	06	07-14	15-17	18	19	20	21	22-28	29	30-32	33	34	35-37	38	39
950713	c	19959999	mdu	w	r	1	p	-s-----	0	///	a	0	eng	-	d

008

→ 007   c ≠b r ≠d c ≠e n ≠f u   (computer file: remote)

022   1083-351X

→ 130 0   Journal of biological chemistry (Online)

245 00   Journal of biological chemistry ≠h [computer file].

246 13   JBC online

246 30   JBC

260   Bethesda, Md. : ≠b American Society for Biochemistry and Molecular Biology, ≠c 1995-

310   Weekly

→ 362 0   Vol. 270, no. 1 (Jan. 1995)-

500   World Wide Web version co-published with: Highwire Press, the electronic imprint of Stanford Libraries.

500   Title from journal homepage.

→ 506   Full contents available to subscribing institutions only.

516   Text and hypertext.

530   Online version of the print publication from 1995; available also in CD-ROM: Vol. 267, no. 1-9 (Jan.-Mar. 1992)-

→ 538   System requirements: Ability to display images.

→ 538   Mode of access: World Wide Web: http://www.jbc.org; for fast access from certain countries use URL: http://intl.jbc.org.

650 0   Biochemistry ≠x Periodicals.

710 2   American Society for Biochemistry and Molecular Biology.

776 1   ≠t Journal of biological chemistry ≠x 0021-9258 ≠w (OCoLC)1782222

776 1   ≠t Journal of biological chemistry ≠x 1067-8816 ≠w (DLC)sn93004795 ≠w (OCoLC)26477144

→ 856 40   ≠u http://www-mbc.org

→ 856 40   ≠u http://intl.jbc.org ≠z For faster access from Australia, Brazil, France, Germany, Hong Kong, Israel, Japan, Russia, Singapore, South Korea, Taiwan, UK, China

---

Note that until the implementation of the proposed coding, the leader and fixed fields should be coded as follows:

LDR   *****cms_/22*****Ia*4500   (computer file)

008   for computer file with appropriate values

006   for seriality

007   for computer file: remote

DISCUSSION

- This is an example of an online version of a print serial. Since the online version has the same title proper as its print counterpart, a uniform title has to be established for the online version to avoid conflict with the latter. LCRI 25.5B, p. 11–12 states that terms that describe the physical medium of the serial should be used when choosing a uniform title qualifier for a computer file serial. In cases where the computer file serial is a remote access serial, the term "Online" may be used to distinguish between the online version and its print counterpart (see also CCM 31.6). Note that if the computer file serial is in CD-ROM format, then the term "CD-ROM" should be used as the qualifier. No edition statement, such as "Online edition" or "CD-ROM edition," should be given in field 250 if the statement does not appear on the source (1.2B1).

- Note that, as is recorded in field 362, the online version of the journal began with volume 270, number 1, published in January 1995. However, the homepage changes regularly. Only the numbering of the current issue is displayed in the homepage, which serves as the chief source of information. The first available issue or all previous issues imaged may be listed in the content page for access when the imaged issues are archived in the homepage.

- Field 506 is used for Restrictions on Access Note. In this example, this note is necessary to alert users to the fact that the full contents of this serial are available on the World Wide Web to subscribing institutions only.

- In this example, the field 538 System Details Note contains a general statement about the requirements needed in order to view the journal online. This is followed by another 538 field for Mode of Access, specifically describing how to access the table of contents.

- The first and second 856 fields record the URL through which the journal can be accessed. Since access is via http, the first indicator is set to value "4." Second indicator value "0" indicates that the URL in field 856 is for the same resource described by the record with the display constant "Electronic resource:". Note that the second 856 field is an alternative URL, for faster access from certain countries, and this information is recorded in subfield ≠z (public note) for display.

- Field 007, Physical Description Fixed Field for Computer File, is mandatory for electronic resources. For the use of code "a" in leader character position 06 and the coding of "s" in fixed field 008 character position 23, see discussion in R1.

R11

PROBLEM CONSIDERED:

Remote access electronic journal of print copy with a different title

TAGGED DATA RECORD (based on OCLC #31492939)

LDR   *****cas_/22*****Ia*4500   (language material serial)

(print serial)

00-05	06	07-14	15-17	18	19	20	21	22-28	29	30-32	33	34	35-37	38	39
008	941121	c	19959999	mau	w	r	l	p	-s-----	0	///	a	0	eng	-	d

→ 007   c ≠b r ≠d c ≠e n ≠f u   (computer file: remote)

022 0   1079-7114

→ 245 00   Physical review letters online ≠h [computer file].

246 13   PRL online

260   College Park, MD : ≠b American Physical Society,

310   Weekly

362 1   Began publication in July 1995.

500   Description based on printout of: Apr. 1, 1996; title from title screen.

515   Includes issues published in print format for Sept. 1994-

516   Hypertext (Electronic journal).

→ 530   Online version of the print publication: Physical review letters; Issued also in CD-ROM annual ed.

→ 538   Mode of access: http://ojps.aip.org/prlo/

→ 538   Mode of access: Table of contents and abstracts available on the Internet from the American Physical Society. http://ojps.aip.org/journals/doc/PRLTAO-home/textentry.html

650 0   Physics ≠x Periodicals.

710 2   American Physical Society.

→ 776 1   ≠t Physical review letters ≠x 0031-9007 ≠w (DLC)59067543 ≠w (OCoLC)1715834

776 1   ≠t Physical review letters (CD-ROM) ≠x 1092-0145 ≠w (DLC)sn96027543 ≠w (OCoLC)35157254

→ 856 40   ≠u http://ojps.aip.org/prlo/

856 40   ≠3 Table of contents and abstracts ≠u http://ojps.aip.org/journals/doc/PRLTAO-home/textentry.html

---

Note that until the implementation of the proposed coding, the leader and fixed fields should be coded as follows:

LDR   *****cms_/22*****Ia*4500   (computer file)

008   for computer file with appropriate values

006   for seriality

007   for computer file: remote

Access a Graphical Version of this Entry Page

Physical Review Letters online

Published by The American Physical Society

This online journal delivers <u>PDF</u> and is optimized <u>for Netscape and other modern browsers</u>.

Use of APS online journals implies that the user has read and agrees
to the Terms and Conditions in the <u>Subscription Agreement</u>.

Journal title screen

DISCUSSION

- The publication in this example, "Physical review letters online," is an online version of a print serial titled "Physical review letters." However, since the title proper of the online version is different from that of its print counterpart, no uniform title has to be established for the online version. Information about the print version should be recorded in field 530 (Other Physical Form Available Note) and a link should be made to the record for the print version using field 776 (Additional Physical Form Entry).

- When an online serial requires a login ID and/or password for access, a note should generally be made in field 506 (Restrictions on Access Note) to inform the user. However, in this case, since the need for an ID and password applies only to the full text journal and *not* to its table of contents and abstracts, which can be accessed without any password, the login information is recorded in a field 538 Mode of Access Note.

- The first 856 field records the URL of the journal and the second 856 field records the table of contents and abstracts of the journal. The first indicator value "4" is used for http for both 856 fields. Second indicator value "0" is used to indicate that the electronic resource and the table of contents and abstracts that the two URLs point to in the fields are the same as the resource being described in the record.

- Field 007, Physical Description Fixed Field for Computer File, is mandatory for electronic resources. For the use of code "a" in leader character position 06 and the coding of "s" in fixed field 008 character position 23, see discussion in R1.

R12

PROBLEM CONSIDERED:

Remote access original electronic journal

RULE(S) CONSULTED:

LCRI: 21.30G

TAGGED DATA RECORD (based on OCLC #32808359)

LDR   *****cas_/22*****Ia*4500   (language material serial)

(print serial)

	00-05	06	07-14	15-17	18	19	20	21	22-28	29	30-32	33	34	35-37	38	39
008	950713	c	19959999	dcu	w	r		p	ss-----	0	///	a	0	eng	-	d

→ 007   c ≠b r ≠d c ≠e n ≠f u   (computer file: remote)

→ 245 00   Academe this week ≠h [computer file].

260   Washington, D.C. : ≠b Chronicle of Higher Education, ≠c 1995-

310   Weekly

→ 500   Not archived. A new edition is available every Tuesday at noon, Eastern time (USA).

500   Description based on: Dec. 12-18, 1995; title from title screen.

→ 516   Hypertext (electronic journal)

520   Provides summaries of articles as well as the full text of its classified job notices appearing in the corresponding issue of the Chronicle of higher education.

→ 538   Mode of access: World Wide Web: http://www.chronicle.merit.edu

650 0   Education, Higher ≠x Periodicals.

650 0   College teachers ≠x Employment ≠x Periodicals.

650 0   College administrators ≠x Employment ≠x Periodicals.

650 0   Universities and colleges ≠x Employees ≠x Employment ≠x Periodicals.

→ 730 0   Chronicle of higher education.

→ 856 40   ≠u http://www.chronicle.merit.edu/

Note that until the implementation of the proposed coding, the leader and fixed fields should be coded as follows:

LDR   *****nms_/22*****Ia*4500   (computer file)

008   for computer file with appropriate values

006   for seriality

007   for computer file: remote

The Chronicle of Higher Education

Homepage

Academe This Week

DISCUSSION

- This example, "Academe this week," is a remote access electronic journal. A service of The Chronicle of Higher Education, the journal provides summaries of articles and other items of interest from that journal. The title "Academe this week" appears on the journal homepage or title screen and is transcribed as the title proper.

- In this example, field 538, Mode of Access, contains the access method, which is the World Wide Web, and the URL. The electronic location and access are described in an 856 field, where first indicator value "4" indicates that the access method is via http. The URL is recorded in subfield ≠u (Uniform Resource Locator), which may be used for coding any information required to locate and retrieve an electronic resource, to connect to a service, or to subscribe to an electronic newsletter or journal, and is also used to provide machine links for OPACs.

- A field 500 note is made to indicate that this electronic journal is not archived. On the other hand, in cases where an electronic journal is archived, this information should be given in a 538 field as a Mode of Access Note. Such a note should provide detailed information on how and where to locate or retrieve back issues or archival files.

- Field 516, Type of Computer File or Data Note, contains information that characterizes the computer file. Although Library of Congress or CONSER practice is to keep this note brief or skip it altogether, in this example the note is made, since the information that characterizes the computer file is not clear from other parts of the record.

- Because "Academe this week" contains items appearing in the corresponding issue of the "Chronicle of higher education," a title added entry should be made for the related work (LCRI 21.30G). In this case, since the title "Chronicle of higher education" is entered in catalog entry form, field 730 is used for the title added entry (see also CCM 7.5.2b). The first indicator shows the number of nonfiling characters and is always set to value "0," since initial articles are always omitted in uniform titles according to Library of Congress practice. The second indicator is left blank to show that the added entry is not for an analytic. (Field 730 with second indicator value "2" is used to make an analytical added entry in established catalog entry form for a publication within the publication being cataloged.)

- Field 007, Physical Description Fixed Field for Computer File, is mandatory for electronic resources. For the use of code "a" in leader character position 06 and the coding of "s" in fixed field 008 character positions 22-23, see discussion in R1.

R13

PROBLEM CONSIDERED:

Remote access electronic journal continues print copy with the same title

RULE(S) CONSULTED:

LCRI: 25.5B, p. 11–12

TAGGED DATA RECORD (based on OCLC #33941255)

LDR   *****cas_/22*****Ia*4500   (language material serial)

(print serial)

00-05	06	07-14	15-17	18	19	20	21	22-28	29	30-32	33	34	35-37	38	39
951219	c	19959999	mbc	w	r		p	ss-----	0	///	a	0	eng	-	d

008

→ 007   c ≠b r ≠d c ≠e n ≠f u   (computer file: remote)
022   1201-9364
→ 130 0   CM (Computer file)
245 00   CM ≠h [computer file].
246 30   Canadian materials
260   Winnipeg : ≠b Manitoba Library Association, ≠c 1995-
310   Biweekly
321   Weekly
362 0   Vol. 1, no. 1 (June 16, 1995)-
500   "An electronic reviewing journal of Canadian materials for young people."
500   Title from homepage.
500   Archived, 1971-94.
515   Vol. 1 consists of 18 issues: June 16-Oct. 13, 1995.
516   Text (electronic journal)
→ 538   Mode of access: Internet. URL: http://www.mbnet.mb.ca/cm
→ 538   Mode of access: Send email to: listproc@mbnet.mb.ca. In the body of email message type: subscribe cmlist, <your email address>
650 0   Children's literature, Canadian (English) ≠x Book reviews ≠x Periodicals.
710 2   Manitoba Library Association
→ 780 00   ≠t CM ≠x 0821-1450 ≠w (OCoLC)6583908 ≠w (DLC)sn83039037
856 42   ≠u http://www.mbnet.mb.ca/cm
→ 856 0   mbnet.mb.ca ≠h listproc ≠i subscribe cmlist
→ 856 0   cm@mts.net

Note that until the implementation of the proposed coding, the leader and fixed fields should be coded as follows:

LDR   *****cms_/22*****Ia*4500   (computer file)
008   for computer file with appropriate values
006   for seriality
007   for computer file: remote

CM

Homepage

Published by
The Manitoba Library Association
ISSN 1201-9364

cm@mts.net

DISCUSSION

- The magazine "CM" was published in print format (OCLC #6583908) until December 1994. From June 1995 on, the magazine was continued by its online version, available on the World Wide Web. Since the online version also assumes the name "CM," a uniform title heading is required to distinguish it from its former print version.
- When choosing a qualifier for the uniform title for computer file serials, refer to LCRI 25.5B, p. 11–12, which states that terms which describe the physical medium of the serial should be used. In this case, where the serial in question is a remote access computer file, the qualifier "Computer file" may be used to distinguish the electronic version from the preceding print version (see also CCM 31.6).
- The URL of the electronic journal is recorded in unformatted text in field 538 (Mode of Access Note). In cases where the individual library's OPAC doesn't display field 856, the cataloger may choose to specify the URL in field 538 instead, so that users can view the mode of access in detail. A corresponding 856 field for electronic location and access should also be input. First indicator value "4" indicates that the access method is via http and subfield ≠u contains the URL.
- Because the online version of "CM" continues its print version, a 780 linking field should be made for the preceding title. First indicator value "0" specifies that a note is to be generated from this field, with a display constant based on the second indicator value. In this example, the second indicator value is set to "0" to generate the display constant "Continues:". Subfield ≠w (Record Control Number), which is repeatable, should be given when the information is available.
- The second and third 856 fields record the individual email addresses through which the electronic journal can be subscribed. First indicator value "0" indicates that access is through email. The second indicator is blank. The display constant is generated as "Electronic resource:". The address and subscription commands are parsed into various subfields: subfield ≠a contains the hostname "mbnet.mb.ca"; subfield ≠h (Processor of request) contains the username, or processor of the request, generally the data preceding the @ in the host address

(in this case, "listproc"); subfield ≠i (Instruction) contains the instruction or command (i.e., "subscribe cmlist") needed for the remote host to process a request.

- Field 007, Physical Description Fixed Field for Computer File, is mandatory for electronic resources. For the use of code "a" in leader character position 06 and the coding of "s" in fixed field 008 character position 23, see discussion in R1.

R14

PROBLEM CONSIDERED:

Print serial continued by remote access electronic version (single-record approach)

TAGGED DATA RECORD (based on OCLC #34730070)

LDR   *****cas_/22*****Ia*4500   (language material serial)

(print serial)

00-05	06	07-14	15-17	18	19	20	21	22-28	29	30-32	33	34	35-37	38	39
008															

008 | 960919 | d | 19931996 | vtu | | x | | p | ------- | 0 | /// | a | 0 | eng | - | d |

007   c ≠b r ≠d c ≠e n   (computer file: remote)
043   n-us-vt
→ 245 00   @uvm.edu : ≠b the newsletter of Computer and Information Technology at the University of Vermont.
246 3   At uvm.edu : ≠b the newsletter of Computer and Information Technology at the University of Vermont
246 30 Newsletter of Computer and Information Technology at the University of Vermont
260   Burlington, Vt. : ≠b University of Vermont, University Computing Services, ≠c c1993-1996.
300   v. : ≠b ill. ; ≠c 28 cm.
310   Irregular
321   Quarterly, ≠b spring 1996-
362 0   Vol. 16, no. 3 (Mar./Apr. 1993)-v. 19, no. 2 (Spring 1996).
530   Some issues available online through the Internet.
→ 500   Ceased printed publication with Spring 1996; continued solely as an electronic publication, <1996->
610 20 University of Vermont. ≠b Computing and Information Technology.
650 0 Data processing service centers ≠z Vermont ≠z Burlington ≠x Periodicals.
710 2   University of Vermont. ≠b Computing and Information Technology.
780 00 ≠t University computing newsletter ≠w (OCoLC)35589320
→ 856 42   ≠3 succeeding entry ≠u http://www.uvm.edu/cit/newsletter/

DISCUSSION

- In this example, the title "@uvm.edu" was originally a printed publication. Beginning with the issue for spring 1996, the printed publication ceased and was continued in a digital form.
- Field 856, Electronic Location and Access, may be added to this record to provide access to the electronic version. First indicator value "4" is used to indicate that access to the electronic resource is through http. Second indicator value

"2" is used for the related electronic resource, since the electronic version continues its printed version and the content of these two are not the same. The display constant "Related electronic resource:" may be generated for this value.

- Note that field 785, Succeeding Entry, is not used in the record, because it is not necessary to create a linking field in the single-record approach, and because there is no separate record available for the electronic version. Also, note that subfield ≠3, Succeeding Entry, in field 856 is added to further characterize the relationship between the electronic item identified in the field and the item described in the record, even though the use of second indicator value "2" will generate the display constant "Related electronic resource:".

R15

PROBLEM CONSIDERED:

Remote access computer file has the same title as that of an unrelated publication

RULE(S) CONSULTED:

LCRI: 25.5B, p. 1, p. 11-12

R15a

TAGGED DATA RECORD (based on OCLC #32727244)

LDR   *****cas_/22******Ia*4500   (language material serial)

(print serial)

00-05	06	07-14	15-17	18	19	20	21	22-28	29	30-32	33	34	35-37	38	39
950628	c	19949999	nhu	m	n	l	p	-s-----	0	///	a	0	eng	-	d

008

→ 007   c ≠b r ≠d c ≠e n ≠f u   (computer file: remote)
022   1083-1908
→ 130 0   Metaphysical review (Durham, N.H.)
245 00   Metaphysical review ≠h [computer file].
260   Durham, N.H. : ≠b T.P. Smith, ≠c 1994-
310   Monthly with an annual cumulation
362 0   Vol. 1, no. 1 (July 1, 1994)-
500   Title from homepage.
516   Text (electronic journal)
→ 516   Available in plain text, revTeX, .dvi, and PostScript file formats.
538   Mode of access: Internet. Internet email and World Wide Web.
650 0   Metaphysics ≠x Periodicals.
→ 856 0   unh.edu ≠h metaphysical.review ≠z Request subscription via email in a message which includes your email address, name, institution, and preferred file format (plain text, revTeX, .dvi, or PostScript)
856 40   ≠u http://www.meta.unh.edu

419

Note that until the implementation of the proposed coding, the leader and fixed fields should be coded as follows:

LDR   *****cms_/22*****Ia*4500   (computer file)
008   for computer file with appropriate values
006   for seriality
007   for computer file: remote

R15b

UNRELATED PUBLICATION (OCLC #12259632)

LDR   *****cas_/22*****Ia*4500

00-05	06	07-14	15-17	18	19	20	21	22-28	29	30-32	33	34	35-37	38	39
850712	u	1984uuuu	at				p	-------	0	///	a	0	eng	-	d

008 (row above labelled 008)

022   0814-8805
130 0 Metaphysical review (Melbourne, Vic. : 1984)
245 04 The Metaphysical review.
246 17 TMR ≠f Nov. 1987-
260   Melbourne, Vic., Australia : ≠b B. Gillespie, ≠c 1984-
300   v. : ≠b ill. ; ≠c 30 cm.
310   Irregular
362 0 No. 1 (July, 1984)-
500   Title from cover.
650 0 Science fiction ≠x Periodicals.
650 0 Fanzines ≠x Periodicals.

Metaphysical Review

Essays on the Foundations of Physics

Metaphysics: The study of the fundamental or primary causes and the underlying nature of things

Homepage

Inquiries

The e-mail address of Metaphysical review is:
metaphysical.review@unh.edu

DISCUSSION

- When assigning uniform title headings for computer file serials to distinguish them from their print counterparts, always refer to LCRI 25.5B, p. 11–12. According to this rule interpretation, the preferred qualifying term is a word that describes the physical medium of the serial. Hence, to distinguish between computer file serials and their print counterparts, the qualifier is "CD-ROM," "Diskette," or "Online." However, this is not the case if the computer file serial and the print serial sharing the same title proper are, in fact, unrelated publications, i.e., the computer file serial is *not* an equivalent of the print serial, though they both have the same title proper. In such cases, conflict resolution for the computer file serial and the unrelated print serial should follow the routine treatment prescribed in LCRI 25.5B, p. 1. That is, use place of publication, corporate body, etc., as the qualifying term(s) in the uniform title heading (see also CCM 30.5).

- In this example, the computer file serial "Metaphysical review" has the same title proper as another print serial in the database (R15b). The print serial "Metaphysical review," published in Melbourne, Australia, is unrelated to the computer file serial "Metaphysical review." Since they both have identical titles proper, a uniform title heading must be established for the computer file serial in order to resolve the conflict. In this case though, instead of using the term "Online" as the qualifier in the uniform title heading for the computer file serial, the cataloger should choose the qualifying term according to the rule interpretation dealing with routine conflict resolution. In keeping with that rule interpretation, the first and most appropriate choice of qualifying term for the uniform title heading of the computer file serial is the place of publication. Therefore, the uniform title heading for the computer file serial is "Metaphysical review (Durham, N.H.)" and *not* "Metaphysical review (Online)."

- Field 516, Type of Computer File or Data, is repeatable if necessary. This record has two 516 fields, the first of which describes the type of computer file serial, since this information is not clear elsewhere in the record. The second 516 field is used to note the availability of multiple file formats (plain text, revTeX, .dvi, and PostScript in this case) for the computer file serial. Note that CONSER policy is to create only one record for computer file serials that have been issued in various document formats, using a field 516 note to list the various formats available (see CCM 31.3.4 and 31.15.3).

- Because this electronic journal is available via Internet email, the first 856 field records the electronic location and access information through which the user can access the journal online. First indicator value "0" shows the access method is via email. Subfield ≠a records the host name; subfield ≠h contains the processor of the request, generally the user name or the data that precede the "at" sign (@) in the host address; subfield ≠z is for information that is intended for public display. The second indicator is blank.

- In the second 856 field, the second indicator value "0" is used to indicate that the electronic location in the field is for the same source described in the record. The display constant generated is "Electronic resource:".

- Field 007, Physical Description Fixed Field for Computer File, is mandatory for electronic resources. For the use of code "a" in leader character position 06 and the coding of "s" in fixed field 008 character position 23, see discussion in R1.

R16

PROBLEM CONSIDERED:

Remote access electronic newspaper

RULE(S) CONSULTED:

LCRI: 25.5B

TAGGED DATA RECORD (based on OCLC #33022890)

LDR   *****nas_/22*****Ia*4500   (language material serial)

00-05	06	07-14	15-17	18	19	20	21	22-28	29	30-32	33	34	35-37	38	39
008 950822	c	199u9999	nyu	d	r		n	s------	0	///	a	0	eng	-	d

→ 007   c ≠b r ≠d c ≠e n ≠f u   (computer file: remote)
→ 130 0   TimesFax (Internet ed.)
  245 00   TimesFax ≠h [computer file].
→ 250   Internet ed.
  260   New York, N.Y. : ≠b New York Times,
  310   Daily
→ 500   Description based on printout as of: July 29, 1995; title from title screen.
  500   Not archived.
  516 8   Available in Acrobat format.
  520   Presents highlights of front page articles from the New York times, including top foreign, national and business news, sports, selected editorials, and crossword puzzle.
  538   System requirements: Acrobat reader required to view and print files.
→ 538   Mode of access: available through the Internet World Wide Web. URL:http://nytimesfax.com.
→ 580   Prior to Mar. 31, 1991 issued in print form.
  650 0   History, Modern ≠y 1945- ≠x Newspapers.
→ 752   United States ≠b New York ≠c New York ≠d New York.
→ 780 10   ≠t TimeFax (Special ed.) ≠w (OCoLC)26092043
→ 856 40   ≠u http://nytimesfax.com

Note that until the implementation of the proposed coding, the leader and fixed fields should be coded as follows:

LDR   *****nms_/22*****Ia*4500   (computer file)
008   for computer file with appropriate values
006   for seriality
007   for computer file: remote

```
                    Monday
                    April 22, 1996
Caption on
title screen                              TimesFax
                    ┌─────────────────────┐        FROM
                    │  Internet Edition   │   The New York Times
                    └─────────────────────┘
```

DISCUSSION

- The electronic version of the newspaper "TimesFax" carries an edition statement, "Internet edition," to distinguish it from its print counterpart. According to LCRI 25.5B, a uniform title is needed if a publication is issued in more than one physical medium with the same title. In this example, the qualifier is taken from the edition statement in field 250. In the absence of an edition statement, the qualifying term would be "Online."

- Records for computer file serials should always contain a general note citing the source of the title proper. This note may be combined with a Description Based On Note.

- Normally, the availability of the print form is recorded in field 530. It should be noted, however, that in this case where it is necessary to include a note describing a complex relationship with other editions or formats, field 580 is used instead.

- When cataloging newspapers, whether print or electronic, always make an added entry presenting a hierarchical form of geographical access using field 752 (Added Entry—Hierarchical Place Name). The hierarchical form of geographic name should refer to the name of the community served by the newspaper being cataloged. Subfield codes are assigned depending on the hierarchy, as appropriate in each case. In this example, the subfield codes for recording the hierarchy of geographic names would be subfield ≠a for Country (i.e., United States); subfield ≠b for State, Province, Territory (i.e., New York); subfield ≠c for County, Region, Islands Area (i.e., New York); subfield ≠d for City (i.e., New York).

- In the leader character position 06 is coded "a" for language material. Field 007, Physical Description Fixed Field for Computer File, is mandatory for electronic resources. In field 008 character position 22 (Form of Original Item), code "s" is used for Electronic.

423

R17

PROBLEM CONSIDERED:

Remote access electronic version of the table of contents of a print serial (single-record approach)

TAGGED DATA RECORD (based on OCLC #36152461)

LDR   *****cas_/22*****Ia*4500   (language material serial)

(print serial)

00-05	06	07-14	15-17	18	19	20	21	22-28	29	30-32	33	34	35-37	38	39
008	970103	c	19969999	enk	m	r		p	-------	0	///	a	0	eng	-	d

007   c ≠b r ≠d a ≠e n   (computer file: remote)
022   1367-5435 ≠y 0169-4146
245 00   Journal of industrial microbiology & biotechnology.
246 3   Journal of industrial microbiology and biotechnology
246 30   Industrial microbiology & biotechnology
260   Houndmills, Basingstoke, Hampshire, UK : ≠b Published by Stockton Press
on behalf of the Society for Industrial Microbiology, ≠c c1996-
300   v. : ≠b ill. ; ≠c 28 cm.
310   Monthly
362 0   Vol. 17, no. 3/4 (Sept./Oct. 1996)-
500   Title from cover.
515   Some no. issued in combined form.
550   Issued by: Society for Industrial Microbiology, 1996-
→ 530   Current table of contents available online.
650   0   Industrial microbiology ≠x Periodicals.
650   0   Biotechnology ≠x Periodicals.
710 2   Society for Industrial Microbiology (U.S.)
780 00   ≠t Journal of industrial microbiology ≠x 0169-4146 ≠w (DLC)sn87024327
≠w (OCoLC)13509063
→ 856 4   ≠3 Current table of contents ≠u http://www.stockton-press.co.uk/jim/
index.html

DISCUSSION

- Publishers nowadays frequently capitalize on the timeliness of the Internet to make available electronically article abstracts or tables of contents for print journals. The questions that arise in dealing with these are similar to those that arise in choosing one-record versus separate-record cataloging in the case of online journals and their print equivalents, in that a cataloger may choose to catalog an online table of contents or set of abstracts as a separate record, or to use the one-record approach and simply note their existence in the record for the print serial.
- In this example, the cataloger has chosen to describe the electronically available table of contents in the form of a field 530 (Additional Physical Form Available Note) on the record for the print serial. A corresponding field 856 is

also made to record the URL of the table of contents. The second indicator is blank, since the electronic location in the field is for the current table of contents of the print version described in the record, i.e., the print version of the journal in field 245.

- Note that the URL in subfield ≠u is preceded by subfield ≠3 (Materials Specified), which specifies the part of the bibliographic item to which the field applies. (In this case, the URL applies to the current table of contents only.)

R18

PROBLEM CONSIDERED:

Remote access site related to print serial

TAGGED DATA RECORD (based on OCLC #32623231)

LDR   *****cas_/22*****Ia*4500   (language material serial)

(print serial)

	00-05	06	07-14	15-17	18	19	20	21	22-28	29	30-32	33	34	35-37	38	39
008	950609	c	19969999	ctu	b	r	l	p	-------	0	///	a	0	eng	-	d

007   c ≠b r ≠d c ≠e n   (computer file: remote)
022 0   1082-9415
245 00   WEB developer.
260   Westport, CT : ≠b Mecklermedia Corp., ≠c c1995-
300   v. : ≠b col. ill. ; ≠c 28 cm.
310   Bimonthly, ≠b <May/June 1996->
321   Quarterly, ≠b spring 1996-
362 0   Vol. 1, no. 1 (winter 1996)-
500   Title from cover.
500   Related Web site available on Internet.
→ 530   Also available on the Internet via World Wide Web.
650   0   World Wide Web (Information retrieval system) ≠x Periodicals.
650   0   Internet (Computer network) ≠x Periodicals.
→ 856 41   ≠u http://www.webdeveloper.com/

DISCUSSION

- The serial in this example has a related Web site available. In such a case, the cataloger has the option of choosing to make a separate bibliographic record for the Web site or to record information about its availability via remote access on the record for the serial.
- The record here shows the single-record approach. Two fields have been added to the record for the serial: a 500 General Note, which informs the user of the availability of the electronic resource via remote access; and an 856 field (Electronic Location and Access), which records that information (Uniform Resource Locator) in subfield ≠u. Because access is via http, the first indicator value is set to "4." Second indicator value "1" shows that the electronic

location in this field is for a related electronic resource described in the record (i.e., the print serial being described here). This also generates the display constant "Related Electronic resource:". The use of second indicator value "2" is mostly associated with the separate-record approach, that is, one in which a separate record is created for the electronic resource. However, some institutions may prefer the option of single record approach, as shown in this example, for their environment and users.

R19

PROBLEM CONSIDERED:

Related publication in remote access electronic version (single-record approach)

TAGGED DATA RECORD (based on OCLC #19282362)

LDR   *****cas_/22*****Ia*4500   (language material serial)

(print serial)

00-05	06	07-14	15-17	18	19	20	21	22-28	29	30-32	33	34	35-37	38	39
890301	c	19889999	onc	a	r	4	p	-------	0	///	a	0	eng	-	d

008

007   c ≠b r ≠d c ≠e n   (computer file: remote)

022   0838-3553

041 0   engfre

245 00   Canadian thesaurus = ≠ b Thésaurus canadien.

246 31   Thésaurus canadien

260   Toronto : ≠b Info Globe, ≠c c1988-

300   v. ; ≠c 28 cm.

310   Annual

362 0   1st ed. (1988)-

→ 500   "A guide to the subject headings used in the Canadian periodical index and CPI online."

500   Published: Toronto : Globe and Mail Pub., 1993?-

515   Not published every year although frequency states as annual.

546   Text in English and French.

650 0   Subject headings ≠x Periodicals.

650 0   Subject headings, French ≠x Periodicals.

650 0   Subject headings ≠z Canada ≠x Periodicals.

787 1   ≠t Canadian periodical index ≠x 0008-4719 ≠w (DLC)49002133 ≠w (OCoLC)2336854

787 1   ≠t CPI.Q ≠w (OCoLC)38087773

→ 856 42   ≠3 CPI.Q ≠u http://galenet.gale.com/db/cpi/ ≠z Requires login username and password

DISCUSSION

- In this example the serial "Canadian thesaurus," which is a printed publication, has two related publications, i.e., Canadian periodical index and CPI online, which are described in the 500 field. Two 787 Nonspecific Relationship Entry linking fields are made: one for the the title "Canadian periodical index" and one for the "CPI online" under title: "CPI.Q."

- Field 856, Electronic Location and Access, is added, with first indicator value "4" for http. Second indicator value "2" is for the related electronic resource. Subfield ≠3 is also used to provide additional information about the relationship of the electronic resource to the record. In this case, since the related electronic resource in this field is "CPI.Q," it is essential to alert users that the URL in subfield ≠u points to "CPI.Q" and not to "Canadian periodical index," which is also mentioned as a related resource in field 500.

R20

PROBLEM CONSIDERED:

Remote access synopsis of videorecording (single-record approach)

TAGGED DATA RECORD (based on OCLC #35045359)

LDR   *****cgs_/22*****Ia*4500   (projected medium serial)

(visual materials: videorecording)

→ 008

00-05	06	07-14	15-17	18-20	21	22	23-27	28	29-32	33	34	35-37	38	39
960709	c	19959999	mdu	---	/	g	-----	-	////	v	1	eng	-	d

→ 006

00	01	02	03	04	05	06	07	08-10	11	12	13-15	16	17
s		x		-	-	-	---	-	0	///	a	0	

(serial)

→ 007	v ≠b f ≠d c ≠e b ≠f a ≠g h ≠h o ≠i u (videocassette)
007	c ≠b r ≠d a ≠e n (computer file: remote)
043	n-us---
245 00	Internet roadside café ≠h [videorecording].
260	Towson, MD : ≠b ALA Video/Library Video Network, ≠c c1995-
300	videocassettes (ca. 30 min. each) : ≠b sd., col. ; ≠c 1/2 in.
362 0	#1-
538	VHS
520	Provides introductions, reviews, critiques and demonstrations of Internet services.
530	Synopsis also available on World Wide Web: http://www.bcpl.lib.md.us/~inlib/catalogt.html
550	Videocassette release of a UWTV television production.
650 0	Internet (Computer network)
710 2	UWTV (Television station : Seattle, Wash.)
710 2	ALA Video.
710 2	Library Video Network.
→ 856 4	≠3 Synopsis in text only listing ≠u http://www.bcpl.lib.md.us/%7Einlib/catalogt.html

DISCUSSION

- In this example, the "Internet roadside café" is a video serial and is cataloged according to the videorecording format, with character position 06 (Type of

427

Record) coded "g" for Projected Medium, 008 Fixed-Length Data Elements for Visual Materials, and 007 Physical Description Fixed Field for Videorecording.

- The synopsis of this videorecording serial is available on the World Wide Web within the homepage of ALA Video. Therefore, the cataloger has noted this information by adding the URL of the synopsis in field 856 of the record. The first indicator is coded "4" for HTTP; the second indicator is blank. Note that the URL points only to the online synopsis of the videorecording, and not to an online version of the videorecording serial itself. The use of a subfield ≠3 (Materials Specified) in the 856 field is essential in cases like this to specify the part of the bibliographic item to which the URL applies.

Appendix A

Display of Leader, 006 Field, and 008 Field as Appearing in OCLC, RLIN, DRA, and INNOPAC

LEADER

Bytes	Element	OCLC	RLIN	DRA	INNOPAC
00-04	Logical record length				
05	Record status	Rec stat	MS		Rec Stat
06	Type of record	Type	Leader/06-07 BLT	Type	Rec Type
07	Bibliographic level	Blvl		Bib l	Bib levl
08	Type of control	Ctrl			ARC CTRL
09	Undefined				
10	Indicator count				
11	Subfield code count				
12-16	Base address of data				
17	Encoding level	Elvl	EL	Enc l	Enc levl
18	Descriptive cataloging form	Desc	DCF	Desc	Cat Form
19	Linked record requirement				
20-23	Entry map				

ALL FORMATS

008	Element	OCLC	RLIN	DRA	INNOPAC
00-05	Data entered on file		AD		Date Ent
06	Type of date/ publication status	DtSt	PC (non-serial) PSC (serial)	Dat tp (non-serial) Pub s (serial)	Pub stat
07-10	Date 1/beginning date of publication	Dates	008/11-14 PD (non-serial) D (serial)	Dates	Date one
11-14	Date 2/ending date of publication	Dates		Dates	Date two
15-17	Place of publication, production, or execution	Ctry	CP (non-visual materials) CPR (visual materials)	Ctry	Country
35-37	Language	Lang	L	Lang	Language
38	Modified record	Mrec	MOD	Mod	Modified
39	Cataloging source	Srce	CSC	Srce	Cat Srce

BOOK

008 bytes	Element	006	OCLC	RLIN	DRA	INNOPAC
	Type of 006 code a book t manuscript language material	00	T006			
18-21	Illustrations	01-04	Ills	ILC	Ill	Illustr
22	Target audience	05	Audn	INT	Audience	Audience
23	Form of item	06	Form	REP	Form	Form Itm
24-27	Nature of contents	07-10	Cont	CON	Cont	Contents
28	Government publication	11	Gpub	GPC	Gvt	Govt Pub
29	Conference publication	12	Conf	CPI	Cnf	Conf Pub
30	Festschrift	13	Fest	PSI	Fst	Festsch
31	Index	14	Indx	II	Ind	Index
32	Undefined	15				
33	Fiction	16	Fict	FIC	Fic	Fiction
34	Biography	17	Biog	BIO	Bio	Biog

SERIALS

008 bytes	Element	006	OCLC	RLIN	DRA	INNOPAC
	Type of 006 code s	00	T006			
18	Frequency	01	Freq	FRQ	Freq	Freq
19	Regularity	02	Regl	REG	Reg	Regular
20	ISDS center	03	ISSN	ISDS	ISDS	ISDS Ctr
21	Type of serial	04	SrTp	TYP	Ser t	Ser type
22	Form of original item	05	Orig	PHY	Orig f	Form Ori
23	Form of item	06	Form	REP	Form	Form Itm
24	Nature of entire work	07	EntW	IS c	Entire c	NatureWk
25-27	Nature of contents	08-10	Cont	CNC	Cont	NatureCt
28	Government publication	11	Gpub	GPC	Gvt	Govt Pub
29	Conference publication	12	Conf	CPI	Cnf	Conf Pub
30-32	Undefined	13-15				
33	Original alphabet or script of title	16	Alph	ALPH	Alpha	Orig alp
34	Successive/latest entry	17	S/L	SL	S/L	S/L entr

COMPUTER

008 bytes	Element	006	OCLC	RLIN	DRA	INNOPAC
	Type of 006 code m	00	T006			
18-21	Undefined	01-04				
22	Target audience	05	Audn	AUD	Audience	Audience
23-25	Undefined	06-08				
26	Type of computer file	09	File	TMDF		File Type
27	Undefined	10				
28	Government publication	11	Gpub	GPC	Gvt	Govt Pub
29-34	Undefined	12-17				

MIXED MATERIALS

008 bytes	Element	006	OCLC	RLIN	DRA	INNOPAC
	Type of 006 code p Mixed material	00	T006			
18-22	Undefined	01-05				
23	Form of item	06	Form	REP	Form	Form
24-34	Undefined	07-17				

VISUAL MATERIALS

008 bytes	Element	006	OCLC	RLIN	DRA	INNOPAC
	Type of 006 code g Projected medium k Two-dimensional o Kit r Three-dimensional artifact or naturally occurring object	00	T006			
18-20	Running time for motion pictures and video recordings	01-03	Time	RUN	Run t	
21	Undefined	04				
22	Target audience	05	Audn	INT	Audience	Audience
23-27	Accompanying matter	06-10	AccM	ACMP	Accomp m	Accmping
28	Government publication	11	Gpub	GPC	Gvt	Govt Pub
29-32	Undefined	12-15				
33	Type of visual material	16	Tmat	TYPE	Mat t	
34	Technique	17	Tech	TEQ	Tech	

MAPS

008 bytes	Element	006	OCLC	RLIN	DRA	INNOPAC

	Type of 006 code
	  e Printed map
	  f Manuscript map
		00	T006			

18-21	Relief	01-04	Relf	RLF	Relief	Relief
22-24	Projection/Prime meridian	05-07	Proj (first 2 positions) Prme (last position)	PRJ	Project (first 2 positions) Prime (last position)	Project Prime Md
25	Cartographic material type	08	CrTp	GRP	Mat t	Cart Type
26-27	Undefined	09-10				
28	Government publication	11	Gpub	GPC	Gvt	Govt Pub
29-30	Undefined	12-13				
31	Index	14	Indx	II	Ind	Index
32	Undefined	15				
33-34	Special format characteristics	16-17	SpFm	FMT	Sp form	Sp Format

MUSIC

008 bytes	Element	006	OCLC	RLIN	DRA	INNOPAC
	Type of 006 code c Printed music d Manuscript music i Nonmusical sound recording j Musical sound recording	00	T006			
18-19	Form of composition	01-02	Comp	FCP	Comp	Form Comp
20	Format of music	03	Fmus	SCO	Format	Format
21	Undefined	04				
22	Target audience	05	Audn	INT	Audience	Audience
23	Form of item	06	Form	REP	Form	Form Itm
24-29	Accompanying matter	07-12	AccM	AMC	Accomp m	Accmping
30-31	Literary text for sound recordings	13-14	Ltxt	LIT	Lit	Lit text
32-34	Undefined	15-17				

Appendix B

Cataloging Descriptive Areas and Tracings in 3″ × 5″ Image of a Bibliographic Record

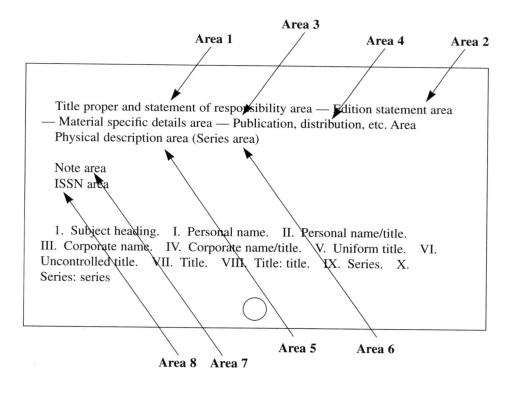

Area 3

Area 1   **Area 4**   **Area 2**

Title proper and statement of responsibility area — Edition statement area
— Material specific details area — Publication, distribution, etc. Area
Physical description area (Series area)

Note area
ISSN area

1. Subject heading.   I. Personal name.   II. Personal name/title.
III. Corporate name.   IV. Corporate name/title.   V. Uniform title.   VI.
Uncontrolled title.   VII. Title.   VIII. Title: title.   IX. Series.   X.
Series: series

Area 5   **Area 6**

Area 8   **Area 7**

Bibliography

SOURCES

Discussions in this handbook are based on rules and information contained in the following basic cataloging tools:

Anglo-American Cataloguing Rules. Edited by Michael Gorman and Paul W. Winkler. 2nd ed., 1988 Revision. Chicago: American Library Association, 1988.
Bibliographic Formats and Standards. 2nd ed. Dublin, Ohio: OCLC, 1996.
Cataloging Internet Resources: A Manual and Practical Guide. Edited by N. B. Olson. 2nd ed. Dublin, Ohio: OCLC, 1997.
Cataloging Service Bulletin, up to No. 71, winter 1996. Washington, D.C.: Library of Congress.
CONSER Cataloging Manual, with updates through winter 1995. Washington, D.C.: Library of Congress, June 1993.
Format Integration and Its Effect on the USMARC Bibliographic Format. 1995 ed. Washington, D.C.: Library of Congress, 1995.
Guidelines for Bibliographic Description of Reproductions. Chicago: American Library Association, 1995.
Library of Congress Rule Interpretations, with updates through December 1995. Washington, D.C.: Library of Congress, 1990.
Leong, Carol L. H. *Serials Cataloging Handbook.* Chicago: American Library Association, 1989.

RELATED READING ARTICLES

Hutto, D. H. "Cataloging electronic supplements to serials: Beyond the note field." *Serial librarian* 24, no. 3/4 (1994): 77–85.
Sha, V. T. "Cataloging internet resources: The library approach." *The Electronic Library* 13, no. 5 (October 1995): 467–476.

RELATED INTERNET SOURCES

http://lcweb.loc.gov/catdir/cpso/elec_res.html Announcement of Draft Interim Guidelines for Cataloging Electronic Resources. Cataloging Policy and Support Office, Library of Congress, 1998.

http://lcweb.loc.gov/marc/cfmap.html Guidelines for Distinguishing Cartographic Materials on Computer File Carriers from other Materials on Computer File Carriers, January 1998, prepared by the Library of Congress, Cataloging Policy and Support Office, Network Development and MARC Standards Office, Geography and Map Division, and Special Materials Cataloging Division.

http://lcweb.loc.gov/marc/ MARC Advisory Committee Proposals and Discussion Papers

Topical Index

This index covers topics included in the Discussion sections. References are to example numbers. Topics involving MARC tagging may be found in the Index to Variable Data Fields.

Abbreviated form of title, J7
Accompanying material
   booklet, Q14, R2
   CD-ROM, Q9
   diskette, Q10
   microfiche, Q11
   musical sound recording, Q5
   nonmusical sound recording, Q4
   sound cassette, Q12
Acronyms, *see* Initialisms
Added entry, analytical, *see* Analytical added entry
Added entry, corporate body
   for current issuing body, C9, D1, E1, H4, N6
   for new corporate name, I2, I6, N6
   for publisher, A1, A9, B2, C10, E3, E4, E12,
      F1, F2, M10, N6
   for sponsor of conference publication, B8, G2,
      M1, M2, M9
   for subordinate body, E10, M9
   in "published for …" note, E6
   in vernacular form, N16
   "official publication," J14, N18
   statement of responsibility, E1, E2, E4, E10
Added entry, personal, C1, O13
Added entry, series
   for microform reproduction series, P4, P5
   for parallel series, C13, G1
   for variant forms, G3
   uniform title heading, E7, G2, G9
   with section number and section title, C13, O14
Added entry, title
   for access to variant title, D1, N1, N2, N3
   for alternating section titles, J20
   for alternating title, B13
   for alternative title, B15
   for monograph, L28
   for name of conference as title, N7
   for other part of a joint title, B14
   for "other title:", H19, J12, N2
   for parent serial, H19, L13, N13, N20

   for portion of title proper, B6, D2, H1, N2, N3
   for related title, N8, N20
   for running title, N1
   for special issues, N12
   for spelled-out form, B2
   for sponsoring serial title, N14, N15
   for supplements not cataloged separately, N11
   for title cataloged separately, N19
   for title in another language, B12, C1, C2, C4,
      C7, C8, C11, C13, C17, C18, C19, C20,
      D2, H10, H20, N5
   for title on diskette label, N5
   for title on inverted page, C5, N17
   for title with separating punctuation, B5
   from "At head of title" note, H11, N4
Added title page title, C5
Analytical added entry
   controlled, N19
   name/title, N9
   uncontrolled, L18, L24, N9, N11, N12, N18,
      Q10
Analytical title page as chief source, A4
Alternating issues, B13, J20
Alternative title, B15
At head of title information
   added entry for, *see* Added entry, title
   as other title information, D10
   in a note, H11, N16

Changes
   between abbreviated form and full form of title,
      J7
   between alternating issues, J20
   between initialism and full form of title, J8,
      N19
   beyond first five words of title proper, J3, J4
   common title changes, J17
   corporate body qualifier in uniform title, I8
   fluctuating title proper, J15
   from "Annual report" to "Biennial report," J6

Changes *(cont.)*
  in conference name, *see* Conference name, changes in
  in corporate name, *see* Corporate bodies, changes in
  in designations, *see* Numbering designation, changes in
  in frequency, *see* Frequency, changes in
  in imprint, *see* Imprint, changes in
  in language of title proper, J16
  in order of title proper and parallel title, C14, J14
  in order of words of the title proper, J13
  in section title, J18
  in subordinate name, I3
  in title proper and parallel title, C15
  in title proper entered under corporate heading, J5
  parallel title dropped, C17, J19
  place of publication qualifier in uniform title, K14
  within first five words of title proper, J1, J2
Chief source
  colophon used as, A6
  for numbered series, A4
  for reprint, A8
  in a single source, A1
  masthead used as, A7
  more than one source, A2, A3
  stable title used as, A5, H3
Collections
  Organization and arrangement of materials, Q8
Colophon, A6
Common/Section title, H17, H18
  as added entry, A3, A7, B7, B10, F15
  in uniform title heading, O16, O17, O18
  with other title information, D7
  with subsection, B11
Companion volume, L26
Computer file serials, R Intro
  accompanied by booklet, Q14, R2
  CD-ROM, R1, R3, R4, R5, R6, R7
  continuing print version, R13, R14
  diskette version, R2, R8, R9
  electronic synopsis of videorecording, R20
  newspapers, R16
  of print version with a different title, R11
  of print version with the same title, R10
  original publication, R1, R2, R12, R13, R14
  single-record approach, R14, R17, R19, R20
  table of contents of a print serial, R17
  title same as that of an unrelated publication, R15
Conference name
  as main entry, B8, H6, I4, I7, M1, M4, M5
  as title proper, H6, M1, M5, N7
  changes in, I4
  generic term, M2

Conference publications
  named conference under title, M3
  with conference-like title proper, M6
  with thematic title, M4
Copyright date, F1
Corporate bodies
  as added entries, *see* Added entry, corporate body
  as conference name with a generic term, M2
  as issuing body, I2, J14, J17, M1, M9, N6, N16, N18
  as issuing body and publisher, A1, A8, B2, C10, E1, E3, E4, E12, F1, F2, H4, M10, N6
  as main entry, C4, E11, H12, H13, I1, I3, I7, J5, J6, M6, O20
  changes in, I1, I2, I5, I6, I7, J9
  in other title information, A2, D1, E8, I8
  in statement of responsibility, E1, E2
  name embedded in title proper, B5, H4, H5, I5
  used as title proper, B7, B8, O7
  with subordinate body, E10, H16, I3, I7, M9, M10
Corrected title, B16
Cumulations, K2, K3, K4

Description based on, combined with source of title, A4, A6, J4, R9, R16
Designation, *see* Numbering designation
Duration of publication, F17

Edition statement, K5, K11, L21, L22, O5, O9, R6, R7, R16
Electronic serials, *see* Computer file serials
Ellipses, *see* Mark of omission
Entry, *see* Main entry heading
Exhibition publication
  entered under corporate body, M7, M10
  entered under title, M8
Exhibitions
  named, B8, M7
  unnamed, M8

Festivals
  entry under own name, M9
  unnamed, M10
Fluctuating title, J15
Frequency, K7, K8
  as uniform title qualifier, O6
  changes in, K12
  in cumulations, K2, K3, K4

Imprint, E12, F3, N6, N16, N17
  changes in, B1, J19, K1, K13, K14
Index to one or more serials, L27
Indexes, J9, Q13
Initialisms, B3, D2, D3, D5, H7, H8, H9, J8
Issuing body note, *see* Notes

Language code, L11, N18
Language notes, C1, C2, C6, C17, C18, C20, E9,
    J16, N17, N18
Linking note
    "absorbed:", H2, L4
    "absorbed by:", L8
    "absorbed in part by:", L6, L7
    "companion to:", L26
    "continued by:", J3, J9, J12, K11, K15, L6,
        P2
    "continued in part:", J20, L7
    "continues in part:", C15, L2
    "has supplement:", L16, O17
    "indexes:", L27
    "merged with: ... to form:", L10
    "merger of: ... and: ...," H1, L3
    "other edition available:", L12, L19, L21, L22,
        O19, O20
    "other physical format:", K12, P3, P4, Q9
    "separated from:", L5
    "split into:", J11, L9
    "supplement to:", H19, N13, N20
    "translation of:", L11
Linking relationship
    absorbed by, L8
    absorbs, J16
    cumulation, K4
    continued in other format, P2, R14
    continues and updates a monograph, L28
    continues in other format, Q2, R13
    formed by the union of, H1, L3, R4
    language editions, L21, O9, O19, O20
    index, H18, L27
    indexed by diskette, Q13
    issued with, L23, L24, N19
    nonspecific relationship, L25-L28, Q3, Q13
    other editions, L22
    preceding entry, E10, E11, I1, I8, J1, J3, J5, J6,
        J8, J13, L Intro, L1-L5, R13, R17
    reprint, L19
    selection from, L25, N8
    separated from another serial, L5
    special issue, L17, L18
    succeeding entry, L Intro, L6-L10
    supplement, H19, L13-L15, N13, N20, Q5
    pre-AACR2 record, K10
    translations, L11, L12

Main entry heading
    corporate body
        conference, M1, M2, M4, M5
        emanating from, C4, E11, H12, H13, I3, J6,
            M6
        exhibitions, B8, M7
        festivals, M9, M10
        subordinate body, E11, H16, I3, J6
    personal name, E5, H15

title
    common title and section title, A7, B9, B11,
        C12, C13, G1, H17, J17, J18, L16,
        L17
    common title, section number and section
        title, B10, C11, D7, E12, H18, J20, L2
    exhibition, M8
    report-like title, H14
    section title, H19
    series designation and subseries, H20
    single word functioning also as a word in
        parallel title, B12, C18
    unnamed conference name, M3
Main series vs. subseries, G5, G7
Map/atlas/chart issued as a serial, Q7
Mark of omission, A5, B4
Masthead as chief source, A7
Microform
    cataloging guidelines, A8, P Intro
    continuing print copy, P2
    linking relationship, P2
    original microfiche, P1
    physical description, P1, P4
    reproduction
        in series, O14, P5
        note, O14, P3, P4, P5
        preservation master, P4
        service copy, P3, P4, P5
        uniform title heading of print version in,
            O14, P5
Mixed material as serial, Q8
Multiformat collection, Q8

Notes
    biographic or historical, Q8
    frequency, see Frequency
    "Includes:", L18, L24, M10, N9, N18, Q7c, Q9
    information about documentation note, Q14
    issuing body, E6, I2, I6, J14, N6, N14, N15,
        N18
    linking, see Linking note
    numbering peculiarity, see Numbering
        peculiarities note
    order of titles, C14, J14
    other title information varies, D9
    quoted, B1, D6, H7, H8, N9, R19
    type of file or data note, Q14
Numbering designation, F Intro
    added or dropped, F5, F6
    appearing in two or more languages, F2
    changes in, F5, F6, F9, F10, F11, F12, F14
    completed serials, F17, I6, K2, L10, N2, O15
    date as volume number, F3
    for cumulation, K3
    for individual parts, K6, K7, K8, K9
    in unformatted note, L6, L10
    more than one system, F4, F10

Numbering designation *(cont.)*
    "New series," F11, F12
    not appearing in single source, F1
    not sufficient to identify issues, F13
    preliminary issue, F8, F9, F10
    section volume numbered in overall system,
      F15
    successive designation, F9, F10, F11, F14
    vol. 0, no. 0, F7
Numbering peculiarities note, F5, F6, F8, F10, F12,
    F14, F15, F16, J4, K6, K9, K13, K15, N5,
    N11

Other title information
    alternative title used as, D12
    as added entry, N19
    as part of title proper, D11
    changes in, D9, I6
    full form vs. initialism, B3, D2, D3, D5, H7,
      H9, J7, J8
    in a note, D6
    includes statement of responsibility, D1
    more than one, D5
    phrase at head of title used as, D10
    supplied by cataloger, B8, D4, M5, M9, N7, O7
    with common title and section title, D7

Parallel common title
    in more than three languages, C13
    with no parallel supplement title, C12
    with parallel section number and section title,
      C11
Parallel conference name, C8
Parallel numeric designation, C9, F2
Parallel other title information, D8
Parallel publisher, C9, C10
Parallel series title, C13, G1
Parallel statement of responsibility, C1, C2, C3, C4,
    E10
Parallel title
    changes in, C14, C15, J14, C20
    in a note, H20
    in another language on later issues, C16, C20
    in more than one language, B12, C13, C19
    lacking in a later issue, C17, J19
    with no parallel statement of responsibility, C1,
      E9
    with other title information, C6, C7
    with parallel numeric designation and parallel
      publisher, C9
    with parallel statement of responsibility, C2,
      C4, E10
Parent record, H19, L13, L16
Personal name
    as added entry, C1
    as main entry, E5, H15
Personal statement of responsibility, E5

Physical description
    microform, P1, P4
    nonmusical sound recording, Q4
Pre-AACR2 records, K10, K11
Preliminary issues, F8, F9, F10
Prescribed sources of information for print serials,
    A Intro
Print serial indexed by diskette, Q13
Printed music serial, Q6

Qualifiers for uniform title headings
    by format
      CD-ROM, R4, R6
      compact disc, Q2
      computer file, R13
      diskette, R8, R9
      microfiche, O15, P2
      online, R10
    corporate name, E10, I8, M10, O3, O4, O14
    cumulations, K4
    date, H19, O16
    edition statement, K5, K11, L21, L22, O5, O9,
      R6, R7, R16
    frequency, O6
    name in vernacular form, O4
    place, K14, L12, O1, O10, O13, R15
    place and date, E4, O2, P3
    "(Series)," B7, D4, G2, O7, O8

Related Web site, R18
Reprints, A8, L19, L20, O13
Reproduction microforms, *see* Microform

Section title, *see* Common/Section title
Serial continuing monograph, L28
Series
    corporate body as series, G2
    designation and subseries as serial, G6,
      H20
    in reproduction microfilm, O14, P5
    main series and numbered subseries, G7
    series as serials, G5, G6, H20, O8, O8
    parallel series title, G1
    qualifiers
      corporate name, E7, G9
      (Series), G2
    span of issues in series statement, G9
    subseries as title, G5
    unnumbered series in series statement, G4
    variant form, G3
    with statement of responsibility, E7
Series added entry, *see* Added entry, series
Slides, serial on, Q3
Sound disc, serial on, Q2
Sound recording, nonmusical
    accompanied by kit, Q4
    physical description, Q4

Special issue
  added entry for, N12
  numbered in with regular issues, L18
  with its own numbering, L17
Statement of responsibility
  appearing at head of/after title, E1, E2
  as part of title proper, E4
  for title proper consisting of common title,
      section number, and section title, E12
  in a note, E6
  in more than one language, C1, C2, C3, C4,
      E11
  in other title information, E8
  in series statement, E7
  not transcribed, E3
  with parallel title, B12, C1, E9
Supplements
  cataloged separately, J10, L13, L16
  lacking parallel supplement title, C12
  notes, H1, J10, L14, L15, N11, Q10, Q11, Q12
  sound recording as, Q5
  to individual issue, L15
  updating main serial, L14

Title added entry, *see* Added entry, title
Title changes, J Intro, *see also* Changes
Title proper
  alternating with sections, B13
  choice according to language, H10
  conference name as, H6, M5
  corporate name as, B7, B8, D4, O1
  consisting of common title and section title, B9
  consisting of common title and section title with
      subsection, B11
  consisting of common title, section number, and
      section title, B10, L2
  consisting of initials, B3, D2, H8, J8, N19

  consisting of number, B2
  consisting of two titles, B14
  corporate body as integral part of, A6, B5, B6,
      H4, H5, Q9
  errors in, B16
  from ambiguous source, H11
  including a symbol, B1
  "incorporating," H1, H2
  initialism vs. full form, B3, D2, D3, D5, H7,
      H8, H9
  mark of omission, B4
  phrase as part of, H9
  single word used more than once, B12, C18
  stable title as, A5, H3

Uniform title
  in common title, O17
  in legal material, O12
  in linking field, N20, O19, O20
  under name heading, K5, O11, O12, O20
  with parallel title, O10
Uniform title heading
  as added entry, E7, G2, G9, H19, N20
  double qualifiers in, O8
  for original microform, O15, P2
  for other language edition, O9
  for reprint, A8, O13
  for reproduction microform, O14, P3
  in common title and section number, O16
  initial article in, L23, O18
  qualifiers, O Intro, *see also* Qualifiers for
      uniform title headings

Videocassette, serial on, Q1
Videorecordings, electronic synopsis of, R20

Whole numbering, F4, F10, F13

Index to AACR2R Rules and LCRIs

1.0E (LCRI)	B1
1.0F	B16
1.0H1c	A3, A7
1.1A1	C1, C2, C4, E10
1.1B1	A6, B1, B15, H9
1.1B2	B5, B6, E Intro, E4, H5
1.1B3	B7, B8, D4, H6, M5, N7, O7
1.1B5	B12, C18, H20
1.1B8	B12, C Intro, C4, C6, C7, C8, C11, C12, C13, C14, C17, C18, C19, C20, H10, J14, O10
1.1B9	B9, D7, H17, J17
1.1C (LCRI)	R4
1.1C2	P3, P4
1.1D1	C1, C13
1.1D2	B12, C Intro, C1, C13, H20
1.1D4	C5
1.1E (LCRI)	H8
1.1E4	D1, E8, H7, M4
1.1E5	C7, D8
1.1E5 (LCRI)	C6, D8
1.1E6	B8, D4, H6, H7, M5
1.1F1	E Intro, E6, E7, E11
1.1F2	C9, E6
1.1F3	B5, E2
1.1F10	C1, C2, C4, C8, E Intro, E9, E10, G1
1.1F11	C3, E Intro, E11
1.1F11 (LCRI)	C3, E11
1.1F13	E4
1.1F15	E3
1.2B1	R10
1.4D2	C9, C10, N17
1.4D2 (LCRI)	J19
1.4D3	E6
1.4D4	E1, E2, E12
1.4F6	F1
1.5E1	L13
1.5E1 (LCRI)	L14, Q Intro, Q9
1.6A2 (LCRI)	G Intro
1.6B (LCRI)	G1, G6, H20
1.6B1	E7, G3
1.6C1	G1
1.6E1 (LCRI)	E7
1.6H	G Intro
1.6H (LCRI)	G7
1.6H2	G7
1.6J (LCRI)	G8, G9

1.7A3	D6, L19
1.7B2	C6
1.9A1	L17
1.9B1b	L18
3.7B1	Q7
3.7B18	Q7
9.0B1	R Intro, R5
9.5B1 (LCRI)	R4
9.7B1	R Intro, R3
9.7B1b	R1
9.7B8	R8
9.7B16	R Intro, R5, R6, R7, R8, R9
11	P Intro, P1, P2
11 (LCRI)	P Intro, P3, P4, P5
11.0B1	P1
11.1C1	P1
11.4 -11.7	P3, P4
12.0 (LCRI)	B13, F15, K1, K2, K3, K4, K5, K6, K7, K8, K9, K15, L19, L20
12.0A (LCRI)	F13, M4
12.0A4e (LCRI)	L28, N11
12.0B1	A Intro, A2, A3, A4, A5, A6, B9, B10, B14, C4, E3, F Intro, F3, H3, R Intro
12.0B1 (LCRI)	A1, A4, A5, A7, A8, F7, F8, H3, K1, P3
12.0F (LCRI)	B16
12.1B1	H8
12.1B1 (LCRI)	B6, H1, H2
12.1B2	B3, D2, D3, D5, H7, H9, N1
12.1B3	B6, H4, H9, J12
12.1B3 (LCRI)	B6, D11, H1, H9
12.1B4	B9, B11, F12, G Intro, H17, J18, L16, L17
12.1B4 (LCRI)	A7, B9, G4, H17
12.1B4a (LCRI)	G4
12.1B4b (LCRI)	G4, G5
12.1B5	B10, C11, D7, G Intro, G7, H18
12.1B6	B9, G Intro, G6, H17, H19, H20
12.1B7	B4, H5, H6, M1
12.1B7 (LCRI)	B4, B13, H5, H6, H16
12.1D2	C11, C12
12.1E1	B3, D3, D5, E Intro, H7, H8, I6, N1
12.1E1 (LCRI)	A2, C7, D Intro, D1, D2, D5, D6, D7, D10, D11, D12, E8, H1, H7, H8
12.1F1	E1, E2, E5, I1
12.1F2	B5, E4, H4, H5, H13
12.1F3	E Intro
12.1F3 (LCRI)	E5
12.1F4	E12
12.2B1	L11, R7
12.2B2	E5, L20, L21, R5, R7
12.3 (LCRI)	F Intro, F1, F4, F13
12.3A1	F4
12.3B1 (LCRI)	F Intro
12.3B2	C9, F2
12.3C1 (LCRI)	F3
12.3C1	F Intro, F16
12.3C4 (LCRI)	F3, F6

12.3E (LCRI)	F Intro, F4
12.3D1	F Intro, F16
12.3E1	F10
12.3F1	F5, F17, L Intro, L6, L10
12.3G (LCRI)	F Intro, F5, F9, F10, F11, F12, F14, K13, L Intro
12.3G1	F9, F10, F11, F14
12.5B2	L Intro, L10
12.5B2 (LCRI)	F13, F17
12.5E1	Q Intro, Q9, Q14
12.6	P5
12.6B1	G3, G6, G7, G9
12.6B1 (LCRI)	G5, G8, G9
12.7A2 (LCRI)	L11
12.7B (LCRI)	F16
12.7B1	K3, K12
12.7B2	C5, E9, N18
12.7B3	A1, A4, A6, A8
12.7B4	J2, J4, J7
12.7B5	B1, C5, D6, D9, I6
12.7B5 (LCRI)	C12, C13, C14, C16, C17, C20, J14
12.7B6	E Intro, E6, I2, I3, K1, M1, N14
12.7B6 (LCRI)	E Intro, H10, H11
12.7B7	K2, K4, L Intro, L25, L26, L27, R2, R3
12.7B7a	L11, L12
12.7B7b	A1, C15, E11, I1, J1, J3, J5, J13, L1
12.7B7c	L6
12.7B7d	H1, L3, L10
12.7B7e	L2, L5, L7, L9
12.7B7f	L4, L8
12.7B7f (LCRI)	L4
12.7B7g	L21, L22, O9
12.7B7g (LCRI)	L22
12.7B7j	H19, L13, L14, L15, L16, L18, N11, N20
12.7B8	F intro, F5, F6, F7, F8, F10, F14, F15, F16, K6, K13
12.7B8 (LCRI)	F17, L6
12.7B9	J19, K1
12.7B9 (LCRI)	B1, K1, K13, K14
12.7B11	Q10, Q11, Q12
12.7B16	Q9
12.7B17	H18, J9, Q13
12.7B18	L24
12.7B21	L23
12.7B23	A8
12.7B23 (LCRI)	A4, A6
21.0B1	H11
21.1A1	E5, H15
21.1A1b	I5
21.1A2 (LCRI)	E5, H15
21.1B1	I4, M Intro
21.1B1 (LCRI)	M4
21.1B2	B7, C4, D4, E1, E2, H Intro, H14, I Intro, I1, M7, M9, M10, O3, O7
21.1B2 (LCRI)	H12, H13
21.1B2 (LCRI) (category a)	M10
21.1B2 (LCRI) (category d)	M Intro, M3, M9, N7

21.1B2a	C5, E11, H12, H13, I1, J5, J6, M6, M7, M8, M9, M10
21.1B2b	O12
21.1B2d	B8, C8, H6, I4, M Intro, M1, M3, M4, M5, M6, M8, N7, N10
21.1B3	H4, M8, O Intro
21.1B4	I3
21.1B4a	H16
21.1C1	E1, O Intro
21.1C1c	B7, M9, M10, O7
21.2	I Intro
21.2A (LCRI)	I5, J Intro, J4, J8, J9, J10, J17, K12, L Intro
21.2A1	C15, J Intro, J1, J2, J3, J4, J5, J6, J10, J13, J18, J20, L Intro, Q1
21.2A1a	J7, J8
21.2A1b	I5
21.2A1c	I7, J11, J12
21.2C (LCRI)	C13, C16, J14, J15, J16, J19, J20, K9, L Intro
21.2C1	J Intro, K1, L Intro
21.3	I Intro
21.3B (LCRI)	I Intro, I8, J Intro, L Intro, O15, P2, Q2
21.3Bc (LCRI)	I8
21.3B1	I Intro, I1, I3, J Intro, K1, L Intro
21.3B1a	I4
21.5A	M3
21.28A1	L10, L28
21.28B (LCRI)	H19, L13, L14, L15, L16, L17, L19, L27, N8, N11, N13, Q5
21.28B1	L28
21.29B	D1, I2
21.29C	B5, D1, H4, M1, N9, N17, N18
21.29F	I2
21.30A1	I6
21.30E (LCRI)	M9, N7, N16
21.30E1	A1, A2, B5, C10, E1, E3, E12, H4, M3, M8, N6
21.30G (LCRI)	K10, K11, R12
21.30G1	J10, L23, L25, N8, N13, N15, N20, R1
21.30H1	N14
21.30J (LCRI)	D1, M5, N2, N3
21.30J (LCRI) p.5	L14, L18, N11
21.30J (LCRI) p.7	I1, N7
21.30J (LCRI) p.8	C18, H12, I1
21.30J (LCRI) p. 9	B3, B5, N20
21.30J (LCRI) p. 11	B2
21.30J (LCRI) p. 12	B1, N3
21.30J (LCRI) p. 13	B6, B15, H17, N3
21.30J (LCRI) p. 14	N10
21.30J (LCRI) p. 18	B5
21.30J (LCRI) p. 20	B13, R1
21.30J (LCRI) p. 21	H10, H11, N4
21.30J (LCRI) p. 23	B3, B16, D2, D3, H7
21.30J (LCRI) p. 24	B12, C1, C4, C11, C13, C19, C20, D2, N5
21.30J (LCRI) p. 25	C16, C20, J11
21.30J1	A3, A4, A5, A7, B1, B2, B3, B9, B10, B12, B14, C1, C2, C4, C16, F15, J4, J10, J11, J15, L20, M5, N1, N2, N7
21.30J1b	H6
21.30L (LCRI)	G1, G2, G3, E7
21.30M	R1
21.30M (LCRI)	L14, L18, N Intro
21.30M1	N9, N12, N18, N19, R1

24.1A	O4
24.1B1	O4
24.1C1	I2
24.3A (LCRI)	C4
24.3A1	C10, J14, N16
24.4B1	B8
24.4C3	C10
24.7A1	I4, M1
24.13 (LCRI) type 3	M2
24.13 (LCRI) type 6	H16, M Intro, M2
24.13A type 6	H16
24.18 type 1	C4
25.3C2-25.3C3	O9, O19, O20
25.5B	R6, R7
25.5B (LCRI)	E4, F9, I8, K5, K14, L19, M9, M10, O Intro, O11, P2, P3, R4, R16
25.5B (LCRI) p. 1	I8, N20, O6, O10, R15
25.5B (LCRI) p. 2	E10, I8, M9, M10, O1, O3, O4, O8
25.5B (LCRI) p. 3	L21, O2, O5, O6, O15, P Intro
25.5B (LCRI) p. 4	O16, O18
25.5B (LCRI) p. 5	O11, O17
25.5B (LCRI) p. 6	A8, K14, L19, O13, O14, O15
25.5B (LCRI) p. 7	B7, D4, G2, O7, O8, P2
25.5B (LCRI) p.11-12	R Intro, R6, R7, R8, R9, R10, R13, R15
25.5B1	H14
25.5B4 (LCRI)	H14
25.5B7c	O Intro
25.5C (LCRI)	O19
25.5C1	L11, O9, O19
25.15A2	O12
25.15A2 (LCRI)	O12
A.4C1	B14, H1
A.23	H10, H11
Appendix B	O5
Appendix D	G Intro
Appendix D (p. 615)	B15, N Intro
Appendix D (p. 616)	A6
Appendix D (p. 619)	Q4
Appendix D (p. 620)	D Intro, H8, N Intro, N9
Appendix D (p. 622)	G Intro, J17

Index to CONSER (CCM and CEG)

CCM 3.2.1d	A4	CCM 7.2.2e	N17
CCM 3.2.2g	H3	CCM 7.2.3a	H12
CCM 3.3.2	H6	CCM 7.2.3e	N20
CCM 4.1.5	H12	CCM 7.2.4b	H6
CCM 4.3	H12, H13	CCM 7.5.1	N9, R1
CCM 4.4.1	H12, H13	CCM 7.5.2B	N15, R1, R12
CCM 4.5	H16	CCM 7.5.3	N10
CCM 4.6	H15	CCM 8.6.3	K13
CCM 4.8.3	N6, N9	CCM 9.2.4	K5
CCM 4.8.3c	N16	CCM 10.2.1	E3
CCM 5.2.4	P2	CCM 10.2.1c	N17
CCM 5.3.3	O11	CCM 11.4	Q Intro
CCM 5.3.4	O6	CCM 14.3.1	L11
CCM 5.3.5	R6, R8	CCM 14.3.2	L22
CCM 5.5.2	O7	CCM 14.4.2	L28
CCM 5.5.3	K14	CCM 16.2.1	J3
CCM 5.6.2	O19	CCM 16.2.2	J16
CCM 6.1.3d	H9	CCM 16.2.3	J8, J10
CCM 6.1.4c	H10	CCM 16.2.4	J15
CCM 6.1.4d	H7, H8	CCM 30.3.2a	R5
CCM 6.1.5	H5	CCM 30.5	R7, R9, R15
CCM 6.1.8	H6	CCM 30.10	R5
CCM 6.2.1	H17	CCM 30.11.1	R4
CCM 6.2.2	H18	CCM 30.12.4	Q14
CCM 6.2.3	H17, H19	CCM 30.14.1	R3
CCM 6.3.3a1	H1	CCM 30.14.5	R5, R7, R9
CCM 6.3.3a2	H8	CCM 30.14.7	Q14
CCM 6.3.3b	D Intro, D12	CCM 30.16.2	R5, R6, R7, R9
CCM 6.3.4	D4, E8, N19	CCM 30.16.3	R2, R3
CCM 6.3.4a	H8	CCM 31.3.4	R15
CCM 6.4	H10	CCM 31.6	R10, R13
CCM 6.5.5	H15	CCM 31.15.3	R15
CCM 6.17d	H2	CCM 32.3.2m	P3, P4
CCM 7.2.1c	H17		
CCM 7.2.1e	H10	CEG, Appendix M	P Intro
CCM 7.2.1f	H9		

Index to Variable Data Fields

034		Q7
041 0		C1, C2, C6, C19, E9, J14, N18
041 1		L11
043		C3
100		E5, H15
110 1		C4, E5, E11, I3, I7, J6, J11, M6, O12, O20
110 2		E2, H12, H13, H16, I1, J5, K10, M2, M7, M10, O11
111 2		B8, H6, I4, M1, M4, M5, M9
130 0		A8, B7, E4, E10, H14, I8, K4, K14, L11, L12, L21, L22, M8, M10, O1, O2, O3, O4, O5, O6, O7, O8, O9, O10, O13, O14, O15, O16, O17, O18, O19, P2, P3, R4, R6, R7, R8, R9, R10, R13, R15, R16
240		K5, O11, O12, O20
245	ab[ ]	B8, D4, M5, M9, N7, O7
245	abc	B12, C1, D3, E9
245	af	Q8
245	ahb	P3
245	anp	B10, H18, J20, L2, Q6
245	anpb	C11, D7
245	anpc	E12
245	ap	A7, B9, H17, L16, O16, O17, O18, Q7, Q13
245	apb	C12, C13
245	apc	G1, J17, L17
245	app	B11
246 0		B16
246 1	i	A8, B13, C13, C16, C20, F15, H2, H6, H11, I7, J2, J4, J7, J10, J11, J15, J20, K9, K13, L20, N4, N5, R8
246 13		A3, A7, H19, N2, N3
246 14		A4, A5
246 15		C5, H14, N17
246 16		A7
246 17		A7, B5, N1, N2
246 18		H6
246 2		N2
246 3		B1, B2, B5, C18, D1, F15, H12, N3, N10, N20
246 30		A3, A7, B3, B6, B9, B10, B14, B15, D2, D3, D5, D10, D11, D12, H1, H4, H7, H8, H9, H17, H18, H20, M1, N2, N3, N19
246 31		B12, C1, C2, C4, C7, C8, C11, C13, C17, C18, C19, C20, H10, H20, N5
250		K5, K11, L21, L22, O5, O9, R6, R7, R16
255		Q7
260		A1, A8, B1, C9, C10, E1, E3, E12, F1, F3, K1, K14, N6, N16, N17
300		K7, L10, O15, P1, Q4, Q9, R3, R4
310		K2, K3, K4, K7, K8, K12, O6
321		K3, K12
351		Q8

362 0	A8, C9, E5, F1, F2, F3, F4, F5, F6, F7, F8, F9, F10, F11, F13, H11, K4, K7, K8, K13, L6, L10, R3, R5, R10
362 1	F12, F17, L6
440 0	G4, G7, H3
490 1	C13, E7, G1, G2, G3, G5, G8, G9
500 (at head of)	N16
500 (description)	A4, A7, J4, R12, R16
500 (general)	C12, C17, H20, J14, R4, R12, R14, R18
500 (imprint)	B1, J19, K1, K13, K14
500 (includes)	L24, N12, Q7, Q9
500 (looseleaf)	K5
500 (order var.)	C14
500 (quoted)	D6, H7, H8, N9, R19
500 (scope)	M3, M10, N9, Q7, Q9
500 (spec. iss.)	L18, L24
500 (subtitle)	D9
500 (sup.)	Q2
515	F5, F6, F8, F10, F12, F14, F15, F16, J4, K3, K6, K9, K13, K15, N5, N11
516	Q14, R8, R12, R15
520	R1
520 (Include)	N9, N18
525	H1, J9, J10, L14, L15, N11, Q10, Q11, Q12
530	K12, Q9, R4, R5, R6, R7, R8, R9, R11, R17, R18
533	O14, P3, P4, P5
538	Q2, R1, R3, R4, R5, R10, R11, R12, R13, R16
545	Q8
546	C1, C2, C5, C6, C17, C19, C20, E9, J16, N17, N18
550	C9, E6, G2, I2, I6, J14, N6, N14, N15, N18
555	H18, J9, Q13
555 0	Q8
556 8	Q14, R1, R6, R8
580 (compan.)	L26, R2
580 (contained)	Q3
580 (continued)	P2, Q2
580 (continues)	C15, L28, O15, P2
580 (cumulat.)	K2, K4
580 (formed …)	H1, L3
580 (indexes)	L27
580 (iss. with)	L23
580 (other ed.)	K5, L21, L22, O9, O19, O20
580 (reprint)	A8, L19, O13
580 (selec. from)	L25, N8
580 (sep. from)	L5
580 (subseries)	G5
580 (suppl.)	H19, N13, N19, N20, Q5
580 (transl.)	L11, L12
630 00	L27
710 1	H4, J17, M10
710 2	A1, A2, C10, D1, E1, E3, E6, E12, H4, I2, I6, J14, M1, M3, M8, M9, N6, N9, N16, N18
710 22	N9
711 2	M3
730 0	H19, L13, L23, L28, N8, N13, N14, N15, N20, R1, R12
730 02	L23, N12, N19
740 02	L18, L24, N11, N18, Q9, Q10, R1
752	R16
760	G5

762	G5
765	L11
767	L12
770 0	L16, 017
770 1	J10
772 0	L13, L16
772 1	H19, L17, N13, N20, O17, Q5
775 0	R7
775 1	A8, L2, L18, L19, L21, L22, O13, O19, O20
776 1	K12, P3, P4, Q9, R4, R5, R6, R7, R8, R9, R11
777 1	L23, N19
780 00	A1, E10, E11, I5, I8, J1, J3, J5, J6, J8, J13, J16, J17, J18, K10, K11, L1, O2, O3, O11, O16, Q1, R13
780 01	L2
780 05	L4
780 10	R16, P2
780 14	L3
780 17	L5
785 00	J3, J9, J12, J18, K11, K15, L6, L7
785 01	L7
785 04	L8
785 05	L7
785 06	L6
785 11	J20
785 16	J11
785 17	L10
787 1	H18, L25, L26, L27, Q3, Q13, R2, R3, R19
830 0	C13, E7, G1, G2, G3, G8, G9, O14, P5
856	R9, R10, R11, R12, R13, R14, R15, R16, R17, R18, R19, R20
856 0	R13, R15
856 4	R17
856 40	R10, R11, R12, R15, R16
856 41	R9, R18
856 42	R13, R14

CAROL LIHENG (formerly Carol L. H. Leong) is Head of the Cataloging Department at the Hong Kong University of Science and Technology Library. She is associate professor emerita of Library Administration at the University of Illinois at Urbana-Champaign. Formerly she was the principal serials cataloger at the University Library. She is the author of *Dictionary of Library and Information Sciences: English-Chinese/Chinese-English* and the author of the first edition of this *Handbook*.

WINNIE S. CHAN is Head of Automated Systems Maintenance and Acting Head of Serials at the University of Illinois at Urbana-Champaign Library. Formerly she was serials cataloging coordinator for the Original Cataloging unit of the University Library. As a tenured faculty member, she is assistant professor of Library Administration of the University Library.

IRENE SHIEH is Assistant Law Librarian at the University of Hong Kong. Formerly she was cataloging librarian at the Hong Kong University of Science and Technology. She has extensive experience in serials cataloging and specialized in cataloging materials in special physical formats: visual materials, sound recordings, and computer files. She has been teaching extramural courses on cataloging for the University of Hong Kong and Chinese University of Hong Kong.